GOING TO HELL
TO GET THE DEVIL

MAKING THE MODERN SOUTH

David Goldfield, Series Editor

GOING TO HELL TO GET THE DEVIL

THE 1972 CHARLOTTE THREE CASE AND THE FREEDOM STRUGGLE IN A SUNBELT CITY

J. CHRISTOPHER SCHUTZ

Louisiana State University Press ▌▌ Baton Rouge

Published by Louisiana State University Press
lsupress.org

Designer: Michelle A. Neustrom
Typefaces: Minion Pro, text; Gotham, display

Cover photograph courtesy Adobe Stock/bilanol.

Portions of this text appeared previously, in somewhat different form, in the author's article
"The Burning of America: Race, Radicalism, and the Charlotte Three Trial in 1970s North
Carolina," *North Carolina Historical Review* 76, no. 1 (January 1999), 43–65.

Library of Congress Cataloging-in-Publication Data

Names: Schutz, J. Christopher, author.
Title: Going to hell to get the devil : the 1972 Charlotte Three case and the freedom
    struggle in a Sunbelt city / J. Christopher Schutz.
Other titles: 1972 Charlotte Three case and the freedom struggle in a Sunbelt city |
    Making the modern South.
Description: Baton Rouge : Louisiana State University Press, 2024. | Series: Making
    the modern South | Includes bibliographical references and index.
Identifiers: LCCN 2023045150 | ISBN 978-0-8071-8175-1 (cloth) | ISBN 978-0-8071-
    8215-4 (pdf) | ISBN 978-0-8071-8214-7 (epub)
Subjects: LCSH: Grant, James Earl—Trials, litigation, etc. | Parker, Charles, 1948–
    —Trials, litigation, etc. | Reddy, T. J., 1945- —Trials, litigation, etc. | North Carolina
    Political Prisoners Committee. | Civil rights movements—North Carolina—
    Charlotte. | Charlotte (N.C.)—Race relations—History—20th century.
Classification: LCC F264.C4 S38 2024 | DDC 323.0975676—dc23/eng/20231108
LC record available at https://lccn.loc.gov/2023045150

To Tommy and Joey:
May they come to inhabit an American future where
justice truly does roll down like waters.

And to the youth who populated the Alameda County, California,
Juvenile Hall in the late 1980s and early 1990s and the men of
Walker County State Prison of the 2000s. Their courageous struggle
against the still-unconquered demons of American racism and
poverty serves as an inspiration to my academic work.

The day I set up the card table
To give out the anti-draft news
Right next to the recruiting trailer

Some lady yelled down to me
From the apartment window.
She yelled at me, "Look out, son."

And she didn't know what I was doing
Down there when she called me.

"Look out, son."

—T. J. Reddy

CONTENTS

ACKNOWLEDGMENTS

I am greatly indebted to those who turned over their lives for my scrutiny in the form of oral interviews. It remains a difficult but necessary task to separate my roles as historian and witness to these people's stories. I have never left an interview without a greater appreciation—and, often, admiration—for the interview subject. And yet, I then am forced to make judgments as a historian that I would be entirely uncomfortable making on a personal level. Hence, I submit the words that follow with the understanding that this story tells of a tumultuous time in which personal decisions of the historical actors were often difficult and agonizing. While it may be necessary to criticize certain actions, I will not be so bold as to *personally* condemn any of the actors herein.

If the African aphorism that it takes a village to raise a child is correct, surely raising a historian requires only a little less. My debts are wide and many. At my two graduate institutions, the University of North Carolina at Charlotte and the University of Georgia, many thanks are due. My fellow graduate students created a rewarding intellectual and personal academic environment. Many thanks are due to Jon deKlerk, Rod Andrew, Karin Zipf, and Mark Huddle. Jonathan Sarris languished under the burden of being my closest student colleague and my frequently suffering chapter and paper reader with a keen eye and a welcome sense of humor. Numerous professors lent considerable expertise and compassion to my years in graduate school. Among them: Bud Bartley, Jim Cobb, Dan Dupre, Jean Friedman, Donna Gabaccia, Tom Ganschow, John Inscoe, Lyman Johnson, and Bob Pratt. My close colleagues at Tennessee Wesleyan University have continued that legacy, building an intellectual and supportive community in which I have been lucky to dwell.

I have also had the extreme good fortune of two extraordinary mentors: David Goldfield and Bill McFeely. David, as my master's director at UNC Charlotte, took me under his wing at the critical early stages of my graduate career and provided incalculably sage advice on the historical profession and my writing. My year as his assistant on the *Journal of Urban History* was one of the most rewarding in my time as a graduate student. After I moved on to the University of Georgia for my doctoral work and then into my academic career, he has continued to offer unfailing patience, compassion, and prudent advice. My doctoral advisor, Bill McFeely, lent a calming ear to the numerous crises that I confronted, whipped me into a much better writer, and aided me in locating research funding when it seemed impossible. Among his many kindnesses, I've reminded my younger son that few colicky infants can say they were comforted by a Pulitzer Prize winner.

This work could not have been completed without numerous helping hands. Among them: archivists at the University of North Carolina at Charlotte and the North Carolina State Archives, as well as the library staff at my home institution, Tennessee Wesleyan University. The wise and patient advice offered by the editor and readers at LSU Press deserves special commendation.

The deepest debt of gratitude, however, lies with my wife, Colleen, and our children, Tommy and Joey. Their love and support continue to sustain me well beyond measure.

Before I ever seriously considered entering graduate school, I worked for nonprofit agencies in California over a seven-year span in the mid-1980s to early 1990s—first running a county-wide food distribution program in Southern California, then working as a housing advocate at an AIDS Project in Oakland, and, for the final five years of that time, serving as a chaplain to incarcerated youth at the Alameda County Juvenile Hall near Oakland. Particularly during the latter work, the question began simmering that has served as the driving force behind my academic career. As I saw the disproportionate number of kids of color wedging their increasingly hopeless lives into the dead end of poverty and the drug trade, I became increasingly desperate to understand why they seemed so tragically left behind by the advancements of the prior decades, and thus appeared unable to channel their energies and anger against the economic and racial injustices they so obviously confronted. When Black Panther leader Huey Newton died on a front porch two blocks away from my former apartment and journalists took note of the lack of protest activity in the prior decade, I was shaken in a Sunday morning service into suggesting to the youth that—while everyone must pick up the mantle left behind by the 1960s civil rights movement—their community might especially welcome the leadership they could offer. I spent several short years trying to play my own small role in those solutions in California, and have for the past decade picked up the cudgel again on a volunteer basis in a prison in northern Georgia. Teaching a civil rights movement class inside that latter institution remains perhaps the most moving experience of my educational career. I hope that my academic work will play a small role in building a real system of justice in this country. This book, then, is dedicated to the inestimable courage with which so many of those young men have tried to persevere against the American burdens of poverty and racism.

KEY ACTORS AND ORGANIZATIONS

Afro American Unity Organization (AAUO)—a faction of the Black Culture Association (BCA), including activist Ben Chavis, that sought to become a local chapter of the Black Panther Party.

William Allison—attorney sent by the Southern Conference Educational Fund to defend Jim Grant in the 1972 Raleigh Two trial.

Black Culture Association (BCA)—an avowedly Black Power group that agitated for economic change through organized rent strikes, protests of the Housing Authority, and boycotts of alleged price-gouging white merchants, and for cultural change by demanding Black history classes Charlotte high schools. Among its members were Charlotte Three defendant Jim Grant and convict witnesses Al Hood and David Washington.

Black Political Organization (BPO)—formed in 1969, it sought to promote the election of Black political candidates in Charlotte.

Black Solidarity Committee (BSC)—founded in 1968, the group included attorney Julius Chambers, local Presbyterian minister Elo Henderson, and activists Reginald Hawkins and T. J. Reddy. Seeking a more moderate tenor to "work quietly to solve problems," the BSC addressed police brutality, advocated expanding the teaching of African American history in schools, and encouraged Black business growth.

Julius Chambers—the Charlotte attorney who led the victorious landmark 1969 school busing case, *Swann v. Charlotte-Mecklenburg Board of Education,* which was later affirmed by the U.S. Supreme Court in 1971. Chambers was part of the same law firm as James Ferguson.

Charlotte Area Fund (CAF)—the local agency of the War on Poverty's Community Action Programs. Its employees included Charlotte Three defendant Jim Grant for a brief period.

Benjamin Chavis—raised in the north-central North Carolina town of Oxford, Chavis came to Charlotte as a student at the University of North Carolina at Charlotte, where he helped form a campus Black Student Union. He became an energetic activist in Charlotte, and then across the state—which led him to be a defendant in the 1972 Raleigh Two and Wilmington Ten trials.

Mark Ethridge—*Charlotte Observer* investigative reporter.

Joseph Europa—Charlotte police intelligence officer who contributed to the prosecution of the Charlotte Three.

James Ferguson—civil rights attorney in Julius Chambers's Charlotte law firm who served as defense attorney in the Raleigh Two, Charlotte Three, and Wilmington Ten trials.

Frye Gaillard—*Charlotte Observer* journalist who befriended Charlotte Three defendant T. J. Reddy prior to the trial.

Joseph Goins—Jim Grant's roommate who was arrested in 1970 alongside Al Hood and Dave Washington. Goins was later revealed to be an FBI informant.

James Grant—activist who became a defendant in the Charlotte Three and Raleigh Two cases.

Clarence Harrison—original fourth defendant for the Lazy B Stables burning case, who pled guilty before the trial, leaving behind the Charlotte Three defendants.

Reginald Hawkins—local dentist and civil rights activist who led a number of protests and campaigns (most notably during the 1960s) to desegregate Charlotte and improve the standing of the city's Black poor. Hawkins made an unsuccessful 1968 run for governor of North Carolina.

Al Hood—Charlotte Three associate who agreed to cooperate with law enforcement to become a prosecution witness in the Raleigh Two and Charlotte Three trials, along with David Washington.

James McMillan—federal judge in Charlotte who issued the 1969 *Swann v. Charlotte-Mecklenburg Board of Education* decision that required busing students if necessary to achieve racial balance in public schools. His lower court decision was affirmed by the U.S. Supreme Court in 1971, setting off the subsequent busing controversy in many public school systems across the country.

Bill Medlin—owner of the Lazy B Stables, which burned in 1968, creating the crime pursued in the Charlotte Three trial.

Thomas Moore—Charlotte district attorney.

North Carolina Political Prisoners Committee (NCPPC)—organization of activists who raised bail funds and awareness to support the Charlotte Three and Wilmington Ten.

Charles Parker—local Charlotte poverty worker who became a Charlotte Three defendant.

Raleigh Two trial—a 1972 federal proceeding that occurred a few months before the Charlotte Three trial, it involved charges against Jim Grant and Ben Chavis stemming from violence that occurred in Oxford, North Carolina. Grant was convicted and Chavis acquitted.

T. J. Reddy—poet, artist, and activist who was one of the Charlotte Three.

Vicki Reddy—Charlotte activist and wife of T. J. Reddy.

Butch Rosen—Charlotte activist and a member of the North Carolina Political Prisoners Committee.

Michael Schwartz—*Charlotte Observer* investigative reporter.

Frank Snepp—presiding judge for the Charlotte Three trial.

Kathy Sparrow—New Left activist who came to Charlotte in the late 1960s to pursue activism. She befriended the Charlotte Three and later became active with the North Carolina Political Prisoners Committee, seeking to free the Three. She was the spouse of Marvin Sparrow.

Marvin Sparrow—New Left activist who came to Charlotte in the late 1960s to pursue activism. He befriended the Charlotte Three and later became active with the North Carolina Political Prisoners Committee, seeking to free the Three. He was the spouse of Kathy Sparrow.

William Walden—Alcohol, Tobacco, and Firearms (ATF) federal agent who pursued the Charlotte Three and helped organize the cooperation of and protective custody for Charlotte Three convict witnesses Al Hood and Dave Washington.

David Washington—Charlotte Three associate who agreed to cooperate with law enforcement to become a prosecution witness in the Raleigh Two and Charlotte Three trials, along with Al Hood.

Wilmington Ten Case—a 1972 trial charging local Wilmington activists with crimes of violence during 1971 rioting. Former Charlotte activist Ben Chavis was one of the defendants.

GOING TO HELL
TO GET THE DEVIL

INTRODUCTION

A s darkness began to fall on September 24, 1968, one account would later claim, seven men mixed paint thinner and wax flakes in Colt 45 malt liquor bottles in a bathroom sink. Loading them into cars, they drove to the woods that edged upon the Lazy B Stables. Having already cased the area, they knew how to avoid the floodlights surrounding the barn and the open grasses that lay in between. Two ran ahead, as four others readied their guns behind the cover of the trees closest to the open field. The leader waited behind to guard the getaway vehicles: a white Mercury convertible and a small, green Ford Falcon. The two assailants came quickly upon the structure carrying their homemade incendiary bombs and a gas can. So far, all had gone according to the plan they had mapped out in paramilitary fashion. Only crickets broke the expectant silence.

A barking dog suddenly shook the two men's nerves, but they carried out the precise instructions, pouring gasoline around the lower barn walls. It was then that the stillness broke further, as they began to hear the horses stirring inside to the smell of the fuel. The way now made ready, the first firebomb was thrown and burst against the wooden wall, beginning a slowly growing fire. The second bottle, however, bounced clumsily off the barn, unshattered. The hurler's comrade ran to the bottle and hurriedly tried again. The stubborn bottle left another dent in the barn wall but nothing more. By now, however, the first firebomb had done its intended work. The horses were beginning to kick and wail against the rising heat and smoke. As the two fled back to the safety of the woods' dark cover, the sharp stench of burning horse flesh stung one of the men's nostrils.

It was then that teenaged Judy Baldwin rushed to the door. When she had been previously aroused by the barking dog, she had seen nothing outside and had returned to her studies. She now saw the flames "way up there high," and heard the disturbing screams of the horses trapped in this furnace. She sped headlong toward the suffering animals—most especially to rescue her own horse inside. "I could hear them kicking and hollering," she would recall. "I wanted to save them." It took the intervention of a neighbor racing to the scene to prevent the recklessly determined Baldwin from suffering the same fate as her horse. The neighbor held her down as they watched the flames climb to two hundred feet.

The arriving firefighters could do little to alter events now. Fire Department deputy chief H. O. Hooper was stunned to "hear the horses squealing, kicking and trying to jump through the flames." Despite their best efforts, the entire structure and its fifteen equine inhabitants were a loss. Bill Medlin, the owner of the Lazy B Stables, did not arrive home until midnight. He was astonished to see his barn surrounded by a phalanx of fire trucks and television cameras. Medlin especially grieved over the loss of "Pee Wee," his favorite horse: "It's just like one of the family dying when you have a horse that long." It would take all night and into the next day before the smoldering wreckage was safely cold.

If the physical remains of the barn took a full twenty-four hours to cool, the figurative embers would not subside for another decade. The following morning, the firefighters found the unexploded bottle and little else in the ashes. Four years passed before the so-called Charlotte Three—an alleged team of Black Power militants—were tried for the crime. It would take far longer to sort through what really happened at the Lazy B that night, a story still shrouded in a mystery much deeper than the shadows of that September evening.

In four years' time, the controversy surrounding three Black activists charged with the crime would create a firestorm all its own. James Grant, T. J. Reddy, and Charles Parker—the so-called Charlotte Three—would be tried and convicted in a highly controversial case that drew so much scrutiny that Amnesty International would declare them political prisoners before their sentences were finally reduced by the governor in 1979. Grant, who had earned a Ph.D. in chemistry, had first come to Charlotte as an inspired participant in the War on Poverty, working for the Volunteers in Service to America (VISTA) program.

Reddy had come to attend college, became a published poet, and befriended Parker, a homegrown Charlottean, at an inner-city community center. The three young Black activists would join forces around the causes of African American poverty and civil rights in a city resistant to the full change they hungered for.

Their conviction and imprisonment became a lightning rod for the contentious tactics employed by local, state, and federal authorities against Black Power and New Left activism in the late 1960s and early 1970s. Did the American justice system properly convict the defendants for a clearly proven crime or merely seek to remove troublesome agitators from the streets on trumped-up charges? Even if the three men were guilty of the crime, many critics noted the unprecedentedly harsh sentences as an indication of the government's intent to punish activism in that era.

The Charlotte Three case was also part of a whirlwind of charges against North Carolina activists in 1972. Preceding the 1972 Charlotte Three trial by three short months was the Raleigh Two trial, which charged Ben Chavis and Jim Grant with aiding and abetting two convicts' flight from federal charges stemming from carrying dynamite and firearms into rural Oxford, North Carolina, amid rioting. The two fleeing convicts in question, Al Hood and Dave Washington, became paid prosecution witnesses against Chavis and Grant in that Raleigh Two trial—and, again later against the Charlotte Three. Chavis had been an activist while a college student in Charlotte alongside Grant and others before moving across the state to participate in a number of other civil rights campaigns. Two months after the Three were convicted, the Wilmington Ten case convicted ten activists of arson and conspiracy charges (including Ben Chavis) stemming from 1971 racial unrest in the coastal North Carolina city. The cases were all linked by federal involvement (including Alcohol, Tobacco, and Firearms agent Bill Walden) and paying convicts to testify against activists with considerably lesser criminal records.

If there were doubts about what really transpired the night of the Lazy B burning in 1968, far plainer was the shifting political and racial climate of the era. The once dramatic "Second Reconstruction" of the mainstream civil rights movement of the 1950s and early 1960s had likewise appeared to flame out by the late 1960s and early 1970s, leaving many to walk bewildered around the ashen wreckage of what was once perhaps the most dramatic social movement of the century. Now the high hopes of a generation of Blacks slowly resigned into the sad stasis that had characterized too much of America's lamentable racial history. It was a story all too familiar in the oral culture passed down from one hundred years ago.

Many racial progressives recognized that Richard Nixon had just won the presidency by writing off the Black vote in favor of resentful white southerners. This so-called Southern Strategy hauntingly echoed the dreadful aftermath of the "First Reconstruction" (freed Blacks' hopeful twelve years of short-lived progress following the Civil War). As Nixon's "law and order" administration prepared its retreat on civil rights gains, too many Blacks were reminded of the Compromise of 1877. In that nineteenth-century historical episode, the federal government withdrew its soldiers and its commitment to Black freedmen in return for southern congressmen's support for Republican candidate Rutherford Hayes's disputed 1876 presidential election. White southerners' violent and repressive retrenchment against emerging Black civil rights marked the years following that tragic federal retreat.

The losses were further cemented by the erosion of Black rights in the legal system, a critical factor in the losses to come in the late twentieth century as well. Politicians' late 1960s use of the phrase "law and order" was, in fact, sadly ironic for many African Americans. The late 1960s and 1970s would be marked by their weakening of a more racially impartial and fairly applied system of law. If Hayes had won the White House in a compromise that allowed whites their return to supremacy unmolested by federal authorities or the Constitution, Nixon's Southern Strategy had promised a similar compromise of far less federal intrusion into southern racial affairs.[1]

Fears that Nixon would begin the federal government's withdrawal on civil rights issues—and thus contribute to the further decline of the seemingly waning civil rights movement—were well founded. In 1970, President Nixon vetoed the congressional renewal of the 1965 Voting Rights Act. In direct opposition to the freshly minted 1968 U.S. Supreme Court ruling in *Green v. County School Board of New Kent County*, Nixon proposed "freedom of choice" plans that would have unconstitutionally circumvented school desegregation (by requiring Black parents to petition white schools to admit their children). His pleas for a busing moratorium bill bore fruit when one passed the House of Representatives (although the bill then stalled in the Senate).

When Nixon attempted to delay implementation of court-ordered Mississippi school desegregation, sixty-five of his own Department of Justice lawyers signed a letter of protest.[2] Just as in the late 1870s, the retreat on African American civil rights gains had begun.

There are, however, important distinctions to be made between the two Reconstructions' aftermaths. The federal government, an often reluctant promoter of racial progress (mostly catalyzed by the pressure created by activists), had indeed begun withdrawing its power from the support of civil rights by the late 1960s. But, while federal troops had left the 1870s South to its own devices, federal law officials remained in the South in the late 1960s and early 1970s, and their role was decidedly different from that of the soldiers in the previous century. If white southerners of 1877 had wanted the removal of federal forces so that the South could enforce its own regionally determined rule of law, state law officials now enjoyed the close and cooperative presence of federal law enforcement for years to come.

That federal collusion with southern state and local law enforcement was an especially new phenomenon to the recent South. In the ten to fifteen years following the 1954 *Brown v. Board of Education* decision, southern governors, mayors, and sheriffs had frequently conflicted with federal officials seeking to enforce the law—from law enforcement agents to judges, the U.S. attorney general, and the president himself. While federal judges in that period were particularly viewed as pariahs in the South, federal law enforcement agents were hardly welcomed either. As most southern peace officers struggled to maintain the Jim Crow order against civil rights protestors, they saw their federal counterparts as a worrisome intrusion in a region that knew how to take care of its own.[3] President Nixon's administration, however, ushered in a new era of active cooperation between federal and southern governmental forces, and thus exacerbated long-lingering Black grievances against a legal system too often used as a tool of racial repression.

The 1970s also brought full fruition to an enormously important shift of regional power in the United States. The once dominant industrial might of the urban midwestern and northeastern states began to give way to the "Sunbelt" of the South and Southwest. Charlotte sought to ride that profitable wave by attracting northern industry with the warmth of its weather, low taxes, and cheap labor. An important part of that sell would be municipal leaders promising a more placid business environment free from the confrontations of a unionized labor force and demanding urban bureaucracies.

Charlotte's civic leaders remained determined to steer any local change in manageable ways that would not disturb the careful, commerce-friendly public image they had worked so hard to build—one devoid of the more nakedly racist confrontations against civil rights change seen in other southern cities. Charlotte's powerful business community represented the new trend of Sunbelt cities poised to assure the nation that the civil rights movement had put an end to racial problems, and that now the South stood ready to move into a new era of economic prosperity.

For that reason, this is not the story of a visibly racially troubled southern city, like Birmingham, Montgomery, Little Rock, or Jackson; and, hence, it is a story of the future. The future of the Sunbelt South (and perhaps by extension, then, the story of the nation that would come to focus politically and economically on that region by the late twentieth century) was built not on those southern communities that would bear the burden of ugly racist media images from the early 1960s. The burnished iconography that made for the cruelest pictures of Jim Crow racism—fire hoses, police dogs, baseball-bat-wielding white hoodlums, and the dynamited bodies of young Black church girls—retarded the economies of those recalcitrant southern places for years to come. Charlotte, like its nearby cousins of Nashville and Atlanta, understood all too well the price of drawing a determined line in the southern sand by casting your lot with white supremacy. Emotionally satisfying as it might be to fight the Lost Cause of southern morays against Yankee interference one more desperate time, it was no path to the kind of economic success Charlotte's white leadership was determined to have. Charlotte built itself on the more moderate images of business growth and racial harmony—two commodities that came to reinforce themselves in the new normal of post-1965 Sunbelt racial and economic politics. As its economic might then grew dramatically, it carefully isolated and suppressed voices that advocated sharing the fruits of that growth with the Black poor on whose backs such southern metropolises had long been built, and the justice system became an important part of that strategy.

While the African American freedom struggle continued beyond the mid-1960s, it clearly labored to win the support and attention it had enjoyed in the prior decade. Many issues undeniably played significant roles in the downturn of the freedom struggle: the loss of public support as it shifted from issues of equal opportunity to those of economics, the 1968 assassination of Martin Luther King Jr. (the movement's great unifying figure), the erosion of whites' goodwill in the face of the more defiant Black Power movement, the proliferation of inner-city riots, and simple public exhaustion over dizzying 1960s social change. Just as vital was the impact of a federal law enforcement campaign to surveil, disrupt, and suppress activists across the country.

Further fueling this aggressive use of the justice system to curtail dissent was the well-documented polarization of late 1960s and early 1970s America. Historians have particularly shined a light on the excesses of the Federal Bureau of Investigation (FBI) during the era. Scholars have depicted the tactics of the FBI in that period—now widely viewed as excessively sweeping and extralegal—as clearly an extension of governmental officials at the time.[4]

This polarization would provide the vital backdrop for the prosecution of the 1972 Charlotte Three case. Local Charlotte authorities, with the assistance of state and federal law enforcement agents, successfully prosecuted three Black activists for the unsolved burning of a horse stable in 1968. The crime was allegedly a retaliatory act for the racist stable owner's refusal to allow two of the men to ride. They were given some of the stiffest sentences for unlawful burning in state history in a trial that was closely watched by both local residents and federal officials. Over the next few years, scrutiny of the case intensified as controversial government tactics in the case were exposed.

That this national trend of polarization visited Charlotte was surprising. The "Queen City" of North Carolina successfully rode the wave of Sunbelt business growth with its reputation for moderation and progressivism by heading off any burgeoning racial problems with ameliorating measures to the Black community.[5] There were flashes of racial militancy as the city struggled with its 1960s racial dilemmas, but white leaders carefully isolated African American leaders deemed too zealous. This civic strategy had been largely successful in pacing a comparably smooth transition to the desegregation of city schools and public accommodations. Part of that racial success story was the city's prominence as a test case for school busing through the 1969 federal court ruling of *Swann v. Charlotte-Mecklenburg Board of Education.* Unlike many other court-ordered busing communities, Charlotte appeared admirably to avoid disturbing and violent unrest. According to journalist and author Frye Gaillard, the community resolution of the case produced a "Golden Decade" of racial accommodation and cooperation beginning in the mid-1970s.[6]

Beneath this patina, though, the city remained racially unsettled in the late 1960s and early 1970s. Charlotte's pride as a city of moderation was tested by the emergence of a cadre of Black Power and New Left activists that sought to challenge municipal business leaders to share the fruits of the city's skyrocketing Sunbelt economic expansion more widely with the African American poor. The local War on Poverty agency—the Charlotte Area Fund—became a consistent irritant to many more traditional civic leaders, a potential affiliate of the Black Panther Party emerged, as did other Black Power groups, antiwar organizing was on the rise, and federal judge James McMillan eventually issued a restraining order on the police department to stop harassment of New Left activists. It was an unusual time indeed for this city so accustomed to the image of placid progress.

By the mid-1960s, most Americans had presumed that the successes of the civil rights movement and the landmark civil rights bills of 1964 and 1965 ensured that the national dilemma finally had been put to rest. Adherents of the Black Power and New Left movements, together with some progressive liberals, however, felt that if equal opportunity (in public accommodations and the voting booth) had been addressed, equal justice still lay beyond the reach of far too many Black brethren. That latter issue clearly emerged in a torrent of grievances in the late 1960s and 1970s: from police brutality to domestic intelligence excesses, selective law enforcement, and sentencing disparities. These matters, along with that of economic justice, became the central concerns of Black Power and the New Left. That those issues have never fully disappeared—indeed have repeatedly been raised in the years that followed—from the 1992 South Central Los Angeles riots to the 2012 Trayvon Martin shooting to the 2020 slayings of George Floyd and Breonna Taylor on the one hand to the regrettable American distinction of having the largest income gap between rich and poor in the industrialized world—reminds us all the more that ignoring them has surely only made them fester in the decades thereafter.

1

BUSINESS LEADERSHIP AND DESEGREGATION IN 1960s CHARLOTTE

All of the usual trappings were there: white businessmen, an assortment of local politicians, a scattering of media, and the ceremonial shovels. After a few local luminaries ritually planted a dogwood tree in front of the new General Tire and Rubber Company plant outside Charlotte, North Carolina, the participants warmed themselves from the November cold at a luncheon. It was here that Governor Dan Moore treated the 1967 crowd to an ample helping of southern boosterism. Moore's claim that the American South held nationally unrivaled "assets for growth and development for improving the standards of living for all our people" may have been the standard spin one expects from a governor championing his state. What was more surprising was his invocation of the ideas of one of Dixie's harshest critics: W. J. Cash.[1]

Noting a new biography on the former *Charlotte News* editorial writer and author of the famed *The Mind of the South*, Moore celebrated a vision that contradicted Cash's 1941 recriminating assessment of the South as a region stubbornly resistant to any criticism or progressive change. "This is the day of the New South," asserted Moore, "with greater and more numerous opportunities for all people. The mind of the South is no longer continuous with the past. . . . The mind of the South today is attuned to the present and it constantly looks ahead to assure a better tomorrow." He claimed that these qualities "were emphasized in the decision of General Tire and Rubber Company to come to North Carolina." Recognizing that "many difficult situations [still] demand our attention" in this New South, Moore asserted that "these are no longer problems peculiar to the South." Moore went on to ponder what Cash's "reaction would have been to the changes of the last 25 years. Time has proved him something of a prophet. As he concluded a generation ago, in the coming days and probably soon, 'the South is likely to have to prove its capacity for adjustment far beyond what has been true in the past. And in that time I shall hope its virtues will tower over and conquer its faults.' This has happened in the South. Our virtues do tower over our faults."[2]

Cash had focused his concerns primarily on the need for progress in the region's race relations and intellectual climate. Moore was chief executive of a state that had spent much of the century trumpeting a "progressive" image, built chiefly on a superior state university in the University of North Carolina at Chapel Hill, comparatively moderate southern race relations, and the eager recruitment of industry.[3] Charlotte in particular had nurtured a vision of local progress as integrally entwined with business improvements. *Charlotte News* editors shared equally in Moore's sanguine assessment of the city and of Cash's twenty-six-year-old book. Cash, they claimed, "would surely have been pleased to see the kind of industrial diversification typified by plants such as Charlotte's $18-million new General Tire and Rubber plant. He would have been pleased, if not astounded, to hear Morgan J. Morgan, the president of the company's tire division, allude to the Charlotte of 1980 as the hub of a vast area containing over 14 million people."[4]

Whether the creation of tire and rubber plants would have been Cash's solution to the region's problems is quite questionable. What is unquestionable is that Charlotte enjoyed a long and fruitful relationship with business interests. Local civic and political leadership had had great success building the city into a regional hub for railroad—and later highway—travel, textile mills (made possible by the abundant electrical power from dams and plants along the nearby Catawba River), and finance.[5]

The frequent participation of business leaders in municipal political leadership ensured that the symbiosis of industry and city politics would continue. From 1935 to 1975, eight different men held the office of mayor. All but one was the president or owner of his own business. Two consecutive mayors left the city's Chamber of Commerce presidency to take the mayor's chair.[6] A 1960 *Charlotte Observer* editorial proudly heralded this harmonious relationship:

"Some towns are run by one, some by a handful of men. Not Charlotte. Ask ten people who's boss of the local bailiwick, or who exerts more power, and you're likely to get as many answers, all of them different. But if that seems to imply a vacuum of leadership, it's time to guess again. Charlotte is run, primarily and well, by its Chamber of Commerce. . . . We are pleased to acknowledge its bossism and to wish it continued health."[7]

With those close ties to the business community, Charlotte seemed particularly poised to ride the wave of an important national shift occurring in the 1960s and 1970s. World War II had proven the watershed for regional change, as the federal government invested massive sums below the Mason-Dixon, particularly building military bases and defense plants. Military recruits further infused cash into a South still lagging economically behind the country. The astonishing result in the 1940s South was the tripling of per capita income and a 30 percent increase in urban growth.[8] By the mid-1970s, a name had been given to this important phenomenon: the Sunbelt. Meant to describe the South and the American Southwest, that portion of the country experienced a remarkable infusion of investment and growth as many northern-based firms searched for answers to the new discouraging international economy and the suddenly vibrant competitors in Asia and Europe. The South's answers, in particular, were a high percentage of nonunion, low-wage employees and a low tax rate. Those advantages enticed a number of northern corporations to move operations into a South whose leaders were eagerly and actively rolling out red carpets furthered cushioned by additional corporate tax breaks. Charlotte certainly wanted its piece of this considerable pie, and fervently billed itself as a rising Sunbelt metropolis.[9]

An important piece of city leaders' promotion of Charlotte as a Sunbelt city was steering clear of unsavory racial conflagrations. Atlanta was an unmistakable model for Charlotte's civic plan. The Georgian metropolis, which deliberately billed itself as the "City Too Busy to Hate," featured a business community equally involved in the city's development as its North Carolina neighbor—including a determination to avoid public racial unrest. Charlotte likewise sought to avoid the reputation of ugly racism that prevented so many other southern communities from attracting industry—particularly industry from outside the South. Hence, Charlotte's commercial and political leaders eagerly wished to achieve racial progress in moderation and avoid the distasteful publicity that comes with noisy and militant protests. With an eye aggressively directed to presenting a positive image for potential businesses, Atlanta also had a Chamber of Commerce heavily involved in steering the progress and process of racial change. Atlanta Chamber members, related one of its own in the early 1960s, "weren't do-gooders. They were hard-headed businessmen who realized that you can't sell peanuts at a funeral."[10] Atlantan Ivan Allen, by rising from prominent businessman to Chamber president to mayor, exemplified a model copied by Charlotte as well. Allen won his first mayoral election in 1961 against segregationist Lester Maddox by reminding crowds of the fate of Little Rock, Arkansas, after it drew national attention through its troubled and violent school desegregation in 1957. "Little Rock," he intoned, "hasn't had the job expansion, the opportunity, or the admiration of the rest of America that Atlanta has had."[11]

* * *

Despite business leaders' best efforts, however, Charlotte was not without its own civil rights agitation. Just eight days after four young men famously launched the sit-in movement at Greensboro, North Carolina's whites-only Woolworth lunch counter in February 1960, approximately one hundred African American students performed sit-ins at eight different Charlotte lunch counters. The broader phenomenon of student sit-ins arrived like a thunderbolt in the urban South, and that thunder cascaded through the South for several years to come. While sit-ins had been used sporadically in other southern cities before, the Greensboro action suddenly drew widespread support across Greensboro's Black youth. More importantly, publicity and word-of-mouth enthusiasm spread like wildfire. Within weeks, college students were carrying out sit-ins in cities all over the South. Hence, one prominent historian of the recent South has dated the true beginning of the civil rights movement's "revolt against segregation" as the Greensboro Woolworth sit-in, instead of the more popularly understood 1955 Montgomery bus boycott led by Martin Luther King Jr.[12]

Charlotte's foot soldiers in the burgeoning sit-in movement came from the local Black college, Johnson C. Smith University (JCSU), which would remain an early 1960s recruiting ground for young civil rights adjutants. The sit-ins quickly won wide support among JCSU's Black students—and more slowly among Black ministers and then a few white ministers. Demonstrations continued for five months. After urging the students to cease their activities, Mayor James Smith finally established a special study group on race named the Mayor's Committee on Friendly Relations. When student protests continued unabated, the Mayor's Committee secured the downtown store lunch counters' desegregation commitment in July 1960.[13]

By November of 1961, JCSU students returned to the streets to picket the continuing segregation of several restaurants and hotels. The Mayor's Committee quickly stepped into the breach with an offer of mediation. While the affected merchants still refused to meet with student activists, the businessmen did agree to talk to the committee and new mayor, Stanford Brookshire. Brookshire brokered a deal in which Belk's and Ivey's department stores would end restaurant segregation as long as the student activists ended their pickets "immediately" and agreed "now and in the future, to bring their grievances through this committee before resorting to public demonstrations."[14]

Mayor Stan Brookshire was a snug fit for the commerce-oriented city. As a clear sign of his business-friendly administration, Brookshire won the 1961 mayoral election as standing president of the Charlotte Chamber of Commerce. Having described his Chamber administration with the slogan "Beauty and Betterment with Growth and Greatness," he pushed a similar agenda as mayor. In his new office, he stressed industrial growth, the need for urban renewal, extending services to the city's rapidly growing outlying areas, and better jobs and housing for African American residents. Brookshire also reorganized the lame duck Friendly Relations Committee, changing its name to the Community Relations Committee (CRC).[15]

Brookshire remodeled the CRC carefully, intending it as an outlet for Black grievances. As such, he hoped African Americans would embrace it as an alternative to disruptive street protests. He deliberately included African American leader Fred Alexander and several other moderate African American community leaders among the CRC members. Brookshire excluded others just as deliberately. Chief among the more militant Black leaders left out was the often rhetorically combative Dr. Reginald Hawkins, a local dentist. As Brookshire would explain to U.S. Attorney General Robert Kennedy two years later, "[W]e studiously avoided any who held extremist views. For this reason, we did not include any of the protest leaders in our community."[16]

The new mayor was a racial moderate cast in the tradition of Charlotte's civic leadership who believed that aggressive civil rights tactics would only slow inevitable civic progress and create public controversies, undermining the city's progressive reputation.

* * *

Reginald Hawkins had aroused the ire of many white leaders in Charlotte with his repeated attacks on city segregation from the late 1950s through the 1960s. A South Carolina native, he came to the Queen City's historically Black Johnson C. Smith University at the age of fifteen. He moved on to the storied Howard University for dental school, where he further sharpened his leadership and civil rights training. After a stint in the military, Hawkins returned to Charlotte to begin his dental practice—and renew his civil rights agitation. During his college years as Johnson C. Smith's blocking back, it had once been this tenacious, longtime activist's job to clear a path for the running back on the football field. In 1957, Hawkins brought the same intense determination to clear the way through a far more hostile crowd for a frailer teammate—young Dorothy Counts, who sought to be part of the token number of African American children launching the slow desegregation of Charlotte's public schools. Hawkins also led the drive to desegregate the city's hospitals in the early 1960s.[17]

In the coming years, Hawkins particularly irritated Brookshire's stubborn insistence on a *carefully controlled* program of racial progress. "Charlotte is a funny town. It's typical North Carolina," claimed Hawkins, that the state projects a progressive image but is "very sophisticated in its denial." City leaders, he noted, "would pick and determine who would be the leaders. . . . So when Blacks make protest, there's always a stir among the power structure who did not want to yield."[18]

In 1963, Brookshire publicly and angrily responded to Hawkins's threat that the all-Black Good Samaritan Hospital's staff would strike if the white Memorial Hospital did not merge with it: "I shall hold you and the organizations you represent responsible for any exhibition of bad faith that might destroy racial accord and progress in Charlotte. We all have citizenship and responsibility in preserving the peace and good image of our city." Nine days later, however, Brookshire and Memorial Hospital acquiesced to Hawkins's demands. A year earlier, the mayor had verbally attacked Hawkins's pickets and protests of Memorial Hospital as "belligerent acts of pressure [that] will result in building resentments and antagonisms. Such acts tend to destroy the good will, so necessary to any progress, which this community has been working to establish. I believe that [the student picketers] are unwisely following a minority leadership." Through public pressure and court suits, Hawkins would also force the all-white North Carolina Dental Society and the YMCA to desegregate.[19]

In the first two years under Brookshire's administration, the CRC would work unsuccessfully to convince local operators of hotels, motels, restaurants, and theaters to open their businesses to African Americans. Fully aware of the disorder and negative publicity mounting against Jim Crow in other southern cities, Brookshire sought action in 1963. There was a compelling financial reason for Brookshire's move against the city's public accommodations segregation. In March of that year, Charlotte had placed thirty-fourth in *New Yorker* magazine's survey of the nation's best trade areas, had won Standard and Poor's "AA" credit rating, allowing the city to borrow at cheaper rates than before, and claimed $5 million in income from conventions and trade shows during 1962. Local businessmen clearly wanted to keep the city's well-oiled economic machine running smoothly.

Charlotte was now bidding for the Southern Conference Basketball Tournament, and Conference officials scheduled a late March 1963 visit to "take a look" not only at the city's basketball arena but—more importantly for the city's concerns—at hotel and motel accommodations. Clearly, no conference—athletic or otherwise—that garnered national attention relished the bad publicity associated with publicly displayed racism. Brookshire sought to avoid the predicament that would befall New Orleans in May when that city lost $10 million in tourist income after the American Legion relocated its scheduled convention because the group's African American delegates could not find hotel rooms there.[20]

Reginald Hawkins also continued his pressure on the mayor. As the scheduled date of another major convention approached—the International Trade Fair—for late April and early May, Hawkins threatened to hold demonstrations protesting continued hotel discrimination. For municipal business leaders who had long anticipated the convention and its resulting publicity, the

Hawkins-led assault on racial discrimination would be an embarrassing attack on Charlotte's progressive image before a wide array of media outlets attending the convention. The Community Relations Committee thus announced that several unnamed local hotels had agreed to accept African American customers during the week-long convention. Calling it a "tremendous breakthrough," Hawkins called off protests, especially as rumors spread that this would be a permanent change.[21]

Hawkins's quiescence was brief, however, and further action would be needed to maintain the city's positive image. After he honored his half of the bargain by allowing placid streets to prevail during the convention, Hawkins tested the city's half by arriving at the Manger Inn Restaurant for dinner. He was turned away. When the state attorney general refused to enforce a state law requiring "every inkeeper . . . [to] provide suitable food, rooms, [and] beds" for all, Hawkins returned to the streets of the Queen City. As Charlotte celebrated "Mecklenburg Independence Day" on May 20, 1963 (honoring a document allegedly written before, and serving as a model for, the subsequent Declaration of Independence), Hawkins led marching Johnson C. Smith University students to the county courthouse. He called on the city to honor the pledges in its cherished "Mecklenburg Declaration" by giving African Americans their entitled freedom.[22]

Under this mounting pressure, civic and business leaders finally took action against public accommodations segregation, and thus built one of the legends of Charlotte's racial progressivism. After the CRC had negotiated intermittently behind the scenes for two years, Brookshire phoned Chamber of Commerce president Ed Burnside. The two men agreed that it was time for the Chamber to act on the problem, and four days later its board of directors met and voted unanimously to "recommend that all businesses in this community catering to the general public be opened immediately to all customers without regard to race, creed or color."[23]

On the same day, nine representatives of hotels, theaters, and restaurants met with the Chamber's board to discuss the implementation of the resolution. Burnside told the representatives that desegregation was "the right thing to do." Furthermore, he highlighted the cost of inaction. Board members noted the once high hopes of Birmingham's business community for its own Sunbelt success—which were dashed by the publicity surrounding the unsavory, violence-soaked 1963 civil rights protests. Little Rock, they were reminded, waited a long time before new industry arrived after its 1957 school desegregation fiasco. If the moral arguments had not moved the business representatives, the economic arguments certainly did in the view of one board member: "Two or three years without a single new industry in Little Rock. They just couldn't take that." One week later, Chamber members began going to lunch with African American leaders in a coordinated campaign with restaurant owners to desegregate their establishments. In the next several weeks, a similar process was used in movie theaters, until both had been largely desegregated by July 1963.[24]

The action was especially significant in the wake of the reproachful national media attention on Birmingham's ugly resistance to Black civil rights. In this context, the desegregation drive spearheaded by the city's political and economic leadership became another vital brick in the construction of Charlotte's progressive image. The *Charlotte Observer* would laud the mayor's and the Chamber's efforts, calling Charlotte "a most un-Southern Southern city." Stealing a page from W. J. Cash, the paper claimed, "Resistance to change is a trademark of the South, yet in the chemistry of Charlotte, change is the basic element."[25]

Charlotte's reputation for being a racial success story spread. The *Washington Daily News* would run an article on "How Charlotte, N.C., Desegregated Quietly," noting an anonymous "Negro leader's" praise for the Chamber's action. "This could have been another Birmingham," he contended. "It wasn't . . . this, to me, is just good, sound leadership." The *New York Herald Tribune* invited an editorial letter from the mayor on the city's accomplishment. Brookshire wrote that the "choice [to proactively confront racial strife] should not be too difficult if we admit in all honesty that discrimination based on the color of a man's skin is legally and morally wrong and economically unsound." Not doing so would place "the community's pocketbook . . . in jeopardy, as Birmingham and other cities have learned from experience."[26] In further national recognition of the city's accomplishment, Stan Brookshire was offered the directorship of the new national Human Relations Committee by President Lyndon Johnson and a post as assistant secretary of the federal Department of Housing and Urban Development by Secretary Robert Weaver. He declined both, citing his obligation to the city and his business.[27]

The Chamber of Commerce desegregation effort—while laudable for taking action many other southern cities failed to do, and surely involving chivalrous intentions—is also critical to understand in its context. Besides the important economic motivations that promoted it, local student activists and Black leaders like Hawkins provided the vital pressure to ensure the issue of civil rights simply would not go away. Without Hawkins and others' constant agitation, the sudden movement of city fathers seems highly improbable. "The only things that we got," asserts Hawkins, "we got through protestation."[28] And, under that unrelenting irritation, white civic leaders no doubt further understood that they were far better off launching racial reform in their always preferred way—carefully controlled and managed by the business community itself. The lack of such control over reform in the years to come would clearly disturb those white power brokers and bring a wave of measures to reassert that mastery.

* * *

November 1965, however, brought a stiff challenge to Charlotte and its cherished reputation. Dynamite exploded at the homes of Reginald Hawkins, newly elected city councilman Fred Alexander (the first African American to be elected to the office in the twentieth century), local NAACP chapter president Kelly Alexander, and the recently arrived civil rights lawyer Julius Chambers (who, in 1965, had already begun to push the landmark 1969 school busing case, *Swann v. Charlotte-Mecklenburg Board of Education*). No one was injured. The bombs shattered not only the homes' windows and bricks but Kelly Alexander's faith in Charlotte as well. "It will only mean my activities will be intensified, as long as this type of thing goes on," he maintained. "But it's a discouraging feeling. We thought we were making better progress than that. We thought Charlotte was an oasis."[29]

The bombs also threatened to shatter the long-built image of the Queen City. Charlotte's business and civic leaders went quickly into action. Brookshire maintained his city was "ashamed and horrified," and called on residents to help rebuild the homes themselves, or offer the funds to do so in his so-called Operation Rebuild. Over 150 white carpenters, masons, bricklayers, and other construction workers arrived at the damaged homes to carry out the

mission. The *Charlotte Observer* offered a $400 reward for information lead-
ing to the bombers' conviction.[30]

Six days after the bombings, an interracial crowd of three thousand Charlotteans gathered in the municipal auditorium to rally to the cause of racial
harmony and civic pride. Brookshire, one of the twenty-two speakers there,
claimed that Charlotte's response to the crisis "has shown that [the city] can
withstand the assaults of prejudice, hate and crime, without falling victim to
panic, and that I think is an omen of strength, character and will-to-progress."
As invited guest NAACP executive director Roy Wilkins spoke to the crowd,
it became clear that the city had created another success out of the jaws of ugly
publicity: "I have no desire . . . to rub Charlotte's nose in the dirt. . . . Charlotte
is to be commended for its actions, thus far, in its reaction to the bombings."
A few days later, the *Boston Globe* would meet the charge to celebrate Charlotte's progress in a newspaper editorial reprinted in the *Charlotte Observer*.
Noting the "affirmative action . . . taken this week by the white people of Charlotte" in reaction to the bombings, the influential northern paper concluded
by contending that "Charlotte, N.C. has set an example of race relations for all
Americans."[31]

Despite the very positive publicity in the wake of these bombings, no one
would be charged—let alone convicted—for the crime. City police, county
police, State Bureau of Investigation agents, state troopers, and Federal Bureau
of Investigation agents all reportedly looked into the case. Bomb debris was
examined at the FBI laboratory in Washington, D.C. Still, the case remains
unsolved.[32]

If the lack of a conviction remained a troubling remnant of the incident,
psychological scars remained as well. Despite his pleas to local Blacks not to
retaliate, Hawkins revealed his own rising frustration with city officials in the
bombing's immediate aftermath. The activist held state officials—including
Governor Dan Moore—responsible for allowing a state climate where such
violently inclined racists "feel they have open season on us. . . . They believe
they have the tacit approval of high officials across the state." He further complained of police indifference to earlier attacks. After reporting gunfire leveled
on his home a few months before the bombings, for instance, he claimed that
police had done little.[33]

* * *

For Hawkins, the incident had tapped an ugly reservoir of injustice. African American suspicions about police indifference, or even hostility to Black concerns, had roots firmly grounded in the soil of the southern past—a past going back to slavery and the lost hopes of Reconstruction. Antebellum southern law enforcement clearly attached itself to the maintenance of white supremacy—primarily because of white fears of slave insurrection, and the considerable economic interests of the region's powerful planters. The Civil War and Reconstruction, however, caused African American hopes to soar that a newly interventionist federal government might begin to challenge southern brutality and suppression of civil rights.

Sadly, after a few promising Reconstruction years, those high hopes quickly scattered amid the darkness of a reemergent white supremacist regime in the postbellum South. As historian Eric Foner has put it, "the wave of counterrevolutionary terror that swept over large parts of the South between 1868 and 1871 lacks a counterpart either in the American experience or in that of the Western Hemisphere societies that abolished slavery in the nineteenth century."[34] A vital component of that postbellum white southern rule was lynching, which was widely understood—by both Blacks and whites—as simply an extension of the formal southern justice system. Local and state law authorities typically ignored these extralegal executions or endorsed them. The federal government remained likewise on the sidelines with rare exception. All 248 federal anti-lynching laws introduced to Congress between 1881 and 1951, for example, failed to pass.[35]

Alongside that tragic indifference lay another cruel irony. Southern law enforcement agents combined their willful inaction against the violent repression of Black citizenship rights with a newly active and eager pursuit of Blacks as criminals. In antebellum Dixie, the standard tool for suppressing African Americans had been the slavemaster's dominion. With the "peculiar institution" now gone, responsibility for controlling African Americans under a vigorous regime of white supremacy now fell on the southern sheriff. Emancipation hence became the watershed for a sharp escalation in Black incarceration rates.[36] Once arrested, those Black inmates were often then sold by the justice system to years of involuntary servitude in southern mines, mills, and plantations—in a condition that hovered tragically close to the allegedly abolished system of slavery.[37] In short, southern justice for the African American was all too frequently an oxymoron.

* * *

A little over two years after the bombing of his home, Dr. Reginald Hawkins would take his crusade for racial and economic justice to the ballot box as a candidate for governor. During the 1968 campaign, Hawkins proposed a "massive expenditure" of state funds for low-rent housing construction, job training, public school education, public teacher salary raises, and inner-city employment. This would be a program, he claimed, to "attack . . . the ghetto's dehumanization and exclusion from the prevailing political, economic and social concerns of the state." Hawkins's disturbing national backdrop was the frightening escalation of urban riots—which announced its alarming arrival with the 1965 Watts uprising and continued with little abatement through the summer of 1968. Without a concerted effort to address the "root causes of riots," Hawkins feared "an explosion whose effects we might not be able to control."[38]

For Hawkins, one important riot prevention measure would be attacking poverty in the state. Going beyond the more traditional, less radical solutions of Charlotte's civic leaders, he addressed the issue of income distribution. Hawkins noted that regional business recruitment was too often grounded in selling North Carolina workers as cheap labor. "We should make industry pay its way," he stated publicly, "and stop going after marginal industries which are interested only in slave labor. The big people problem in North Carolina isn't unemployment, but underemployment. People are working day in and day out and still making less than $3,000 a year. North Carolina ranks fiftieth in average manufacturing wages paid. The type of industry we have been getting hasn't brought us assets interested in raising the per capita income."[39] On the nationally emerging issue of "open housing" to eliminate residential racial segregation, Hawkins assured voters that the state had "open housing all right. We've got plenty of it. You go out in the country or down in the ghetto and you'll find it. You'll see the houses are wide open. So wide the wind blows right through. The doors are off their hinges, there are holes in the roof. I ask you, 'That's open housing isn't it?'"[40]

Unfortunately for Hawkins, his campaign and its themes were clearly swimming against the southern political stream. In the 1960s, Charlotte was just beginning to rise on the vital Sunbelt tide that swept the city into prominence by the 1980s. That tide rolled over a low-paying, nonunion workforce offered by the South and Southwest to American companies hungry for new cost-cutting measures.[41]

Hawkins's campaign received a tremendous morale boost when Martin Luther King Jr. announced his plans to tour the state to support Hawkins's candidacy in early April. An excited Hawkins asserted that "Dr. King and I are interested in the same things—poor people and voter registration. I have geared my campaign to help upgrade the little man as well as the other people and Dr. King and I will visit with the little man and talk to him about his problems." Clearly the Hawkins campaign evoked the themes of King's late 1960s shift into the issue of economic justice. In this time of substantive transition for the African American freedom movement, King had grown disturbed by the rising Black rage reflected in the urban riots. It led him to launch a campaign in Chicago in 1966 to ambitiously attack the poverty and despair that still lingered among inner-city Blacks, whose problems lay largely unaddressed by the gains of the movement of the 1950s and early 1960s. "The problems that we are dealing with," King warned, "are not going to be solved until there is a radical redistribution of economic and political power." In private he even confided to staff doubts that "capitalism as it was constructed could meet the needs of poor people, and that what we might need to look at was a kind of socialism, but a democratic form of socialism." Hawkins's political campaign also mirrored the end of King's long-running deliberate avoidance of an explicit political stance (best expressed—in King's case—by his controversial public opposition to the nation's Vietnam War policy). For King, this foray into policy, politics, and economics culminated in the "Poor People's Campaign" he did not live to see. It brought thousands of impoverished Americans of all ethnic backgrounds to Washington, D.C., to push for economic reforms in the summer of 1968.[42]

King's persistent drive to help "the little man" brought him to Memphis in the waning months of a life cut short by his April 1968 assassination. Asked to bolster a Black sanitation workers' strike there, King had seized the opportunity to dramatize the fusion of economic and racial issues reflected in both the

Memphis struggle and his upcoming Poor People's Campaign. The Memphis events, however, forced King to postpone his planned appearances for Hawkins's political campaign in the neighboring state. As fate would have it, King was scheduled to touch down in Charlotte on the very day that he died on the balcony of Memphis's Lorraine Motel. One month later, so too would the gubernatorial campaign of Hawkins.[43]

And, only a few days after King's death, Hawkins befittingly struck a somber tone in a King memorial march through Charlotte. "Our young people, many of them, were living on hope," he told the crowd. "Now their hope, Dr. King, is dead. I am fearful for the morality of this country. Something evil must be tearing at our moral fiber."[44] While the city congratulated itself on avoiding the post-assassination rioting that bedeviled other cities across the country, Hawkins's concern was not misplaced. The last great prophet of nonviolent civil rights protest was gone, and with him the most hopeful chapter in the postwar African American freedom struggle. The unresolved anguish of America's young Black working class would be particularly evidenced by the growth of more radical tactics to address the city's lingering racial problems in the late 1960s and early 1970s.

It was in this tumultuous, desperate time that such rage may have found a voice in the flames that engulfed a building across town. Just a few months after Dr. King's demise, Charlotte's Lazy B Stables burned to the ground, killing the fifteen horses who inhabited it as well. The September 1968 arson resulted in $20,000 in property damage. While much smaller than the tragic conflagrations of the large urban riots of the late 1960s, the Lazy B burning would have yet unforeseen consequences for race relations in the Queen City. The fire remained an early mystery to investigators. Gradually, though, authorities carefully constructed a case around the image of angry Black militants who committed a symbolic, desperate act against white racism. The stables owner, it seemed, had denied Blacks the right to ride.[45]

It took three years before authorities would bring indictments in this Charlotte Three case. By then, Charlotte was fully in the throes of one of the most serious challenges to its progressive image—the 1969 *Swann* school busing case. Despite the civic turmoil that ensued over the city's schools, white civic leaders managed to steer Charlotte back to its progressive, business-friendly image by the mid-1970s. Once again, the city would successfully portray itself as a model of economic and racial progress. Once again, it would do so through the cultivation of moderate African American leaders, the use of ameliorating measures from the halls of white civic and economic power, and the exclusion of Charlotte's more assertive and militant Black leadership. The latter strategy, however, would take on a far more aggressive form in the late 1960s and early 1970s. It would call into question who was a larger threat to the "moral fiber" of the community that so concerned Hawkins—the increasingly radical Black militants or the law enforcement agents who sought to suppress them.

2

"OUTSIDE AGITATORS" AND THE STRUGGLE FOR POWER

On May 14, 1968, an estimated 450 men, women, and children walked into Charlotte and some local controversy. The marchers, who came to the city without proper bedding supplies, did bring with them their dreams for national economic change as part of the now-deceased Southern Christian Leadership Conference president Martin Luther King Jr.'s planned Poor People's Campaign (PPC). Mayor Stan Brookshire, however, had publicly questioned "the wisdom of the march," calling it "likely to build more ill will than good will." Seeing the demonstrators' arrival as an unwarranted distraction by outsiders, he asserted that a "priority on my time and energies should be given to efforts in improving the environment and lives of Charlotte citizens.... [The city] has neither the authority nor money that can be used to feed, house, provide medical attention, provide clothing, or provide transportation for the marchers."[1]

By choosing to see PPC marchers as an irrelevant intrusion into his harmonious city—as "outside agitators"—Mayor Brookshire was in good southern company. Stretching back to the early days of Dixie, "outside agitators" had largely meant newcomers—most especially northerners—who lacked the proper respect for any southern community's careful control of its color line. Such "outsiders," both Black and white, were deemed hopelessly naive about "how we do things down here" with "our Negroes"; the tumultuous civil rights movement years were only the most recent reminders of that. Chicagoan Emmett Till's 1955 murder and mutilation and the charred station wagon once containing the eager young activists Andrew Goodman, Michael Schwerner, and James Chaney in 1964 Mississippi were only two of the most famous ex-amples.[2] In the civil rights years, recalcitrant white southerners came to apply the "outsider" label to anyone—northerner or southerner—who came from outside the community to rock the boat of Jim Crow. In some cases, even federal law enforcement bore that ignominy (which, as we will see in the next chapter, surprisingly reversed in the late 1960s). Martin Luther King especially bore the brunt of a resentment that asserted things were "just fine between the races" before such "agitators" came from outside the community. In his renowned 1963 "Letter from a Birmingham Jail," King addressed white Bir-mingham's "outsider" criticism as his first order of business.[3]

In Charlotte, no doubt, the "outside agitator" explanation for any uncom-fortable social unrest had an unmistakable appeal. The city, so its white lead-ership believed, had long ago resolved how to steer clear of such problems—through racial moderation and business growth. If Charlotte was expected to be immune from the disturbances to which other southern communities fell prey, then the reason for discord was clearly "outsiders" bringing in their un-Charlottean poisons and ignorance of how the city handled its own. Hence, like so many other southern locales, "outsider" was a critique not of activists' place of origin, but of their insistence on operating outside traditional white elite-controlled civic modes of operation and power.

The irony of that objection, however, was that the Queen City had always eagerly sought and welcomed outsiders who were white businessmen. From its earliest days as a business-oriented town, Charlotte had accepted arriving corporate executives with open arms. Furthermore, as will become painfully clear in the chapter to come, the city's power brokers may have always be-lieved that anyone "outside" of traditional white commercial leadership was likewise unwelcome to the halls of municipal power.[4]

Thus facing city leaders' deaf ears, the "outsider" PPC marchers were forced to rent the city's coliseum with local donations after a last-minute appeal to use public school facilities turned fruitless. The rain-soaked participants ar-rived at the facility greeted by approximately two thousand Charlotte sup-porters, some of whom treated them to musical entertainment and dinner. The marchers left the next morning in search of the economic equality still denied much of Black America despite the gains of the civil rights movement. A sixty-five-year-old woman from Jackson, Mississippi, put it succinctly: she was going to the nation's seat of power "to find somebody who'll give me just what's mine, if not anything more."[5]

At 11:40 A.M. that morning, the PPC bus caravan was gone, but the issues were not. If Mayor Brookshire hoped remaining in his office throughout the marchers' visit would mean the controversial issue of how power was distributed in his city *would not visit,* he was sorely mistaken.[6] Despite its best efforts, Charlotte would not be immune to the trials and tribulations of virtually every other American city in the late 1960s. In the next few years, the Queen City would struggle mightily with turmoil over residential racial segregation, inadequate housing for the poor, income distribution, school busing, and the specter of rioting and radicals.

* * *

The national emergence of Black Power was a critical backdrop to the city's struggle with these problems. A broad movement incorporating many strains, Black Power advocated African American unity and consciousness of Blacks' history of oppression. Since African Americans had been so long denied power over their own lives, they were to unite as a people and strive for the acquisition of their own community institutions—for some of its followers, through violent means if necessary. Black Power devotees' acquisition of Black educational institutions was to pave the way for the promotion of a more realistic view of the African American legacy: a better appreciation of African American cultural and social contributions and a new awareness of the history of white supremacist oppression through the teaching of Black history. For some, that celebration of African American unity became a separatist urge. The acquisition of political institutions would enable Blacks to exercise power in elective governmental positions and bodies of decision-making power. Historically, economic power had been one of the most powerful ways to oppress the African American, and the acquisition of economic institutions such as community businesses and loaning institutions would thus be an important goal for Black liberation.[7]

In those years, Charlotte featured its own New Left activists (a national movement dominated by white college students who loosely espoused democratic socialist ideals) and certainly some explicit adherents of Black Power ideology.[8] Many other local Black leaders, however, chafed at wearing the

Black Power label. To be sure, wide debate raged over defining the phrase "Black Power." Richard Nixon tried to use the term in his 1968 presidential campaign to mean the fostering of small Black businesses in the capitalist marketplace. Stokely Carmichael implied a Marxist analysis imbued with racial separatism and a rejection of the adherence to nonviolence.[9]

While important recent works have begun to shape our understanding, historians have long debated the meaning, boundaries, and contours of what came to be called Black Power. For this study, the critical issue regarding its importance remains the rising awareness of power relationships in America that animated much of the debate and activism in Charlotte in the late 1960s and 1970s. Like other southern cities that participated in the earlier period of the civil rights movement reform of the late 1950s and early 1960s, activity in Charlotte had centered on opening up accommodations and opportunities to all. At the heart of the city's most bedeviling dilemmas in the late 1960s and early 1970s lay the fundamental issue of how power would be distributed between the city's Black and white citizens. Charlotte's Black community—and its New Left allies—was no different: it sought to sit at the city's table equally and share in its fruits in all the ways that power is exercised in America. It sought the same thing that sent the sixty-five-year-old Poor People's Campaign marcher from Jackson to Washington: "to find somebody who'll give me just what's mine, if not anything more."

In terms of the power to control their own educational messages, African Americans made significant headway in late 1960s Charlotte. In the summer of 1968, the Black Culture Association formed in the Queen City to espouse Black pride and agitate for Black history programs. Black student unions found a stormy but successful path at the local state colleges, Central Piedmont Community College and University of North Carolina at Charlotte. At the high school level, the county school district reluctantly agreed to offer Black history supplementary materials in the curriculum, and a number of protests surrounded the closing of historically Black public schools due to urban renewal or the school desegregation process.[10]

In terms of political power, the number of African American candidates would significantly increase in the late 1960s. But it would not be until the mid-1970s that Blacks would begin exerting their political force more fully and winning electoral victories more widely. In 1965, Fred Alexander became

Charlotte's first Black city councilman of the twentieth century. The Reverend Coleman Kerry, the well-respected pastor of the influential Friendship Baptist Church, became the first African American to sit on the Charlotte-Mecklenburg School Board in April 1968. A year after Dr. Reginald Hawkins's groundbreaking 1968 run for state governor, the Black Political Organization (BPO) formed to push the election of African Americans in Charlotte. The group carried the banner for five City Council candidates. Two other Blacks ran independently for a council seat. Only Fred Alexander won, as an incumbent. Another BPO candidate, the Reverend George Leake, ran unsuccessfully for the mayor's chair.[11]

In terms of economic power, Charlotte grappled with issues of income distribution by participation in the nationwide War on Poverty. First, it did so through its own branches of two prominent federal antipoverty programs: the Office of Economic Opportunity (locally housed in the Charlotte Area Fund) and the Model Cities program. Second, activists and community leaders sought to remedy another nationwide dilemma: the lack of housing for the city's poor and residential racial discrimination. Agitating for economic power would become the most contentious of these Black Power issues in Charlotte.

Lastly, African Americans —especially poor African Americans and their advocates—sought to break through the traditional matrix of white business and civic leadership. That established power base, of course, saw no ready reason to abandon its past formula for economic advancement. Hence, city leaders approached this period of reform just as they had the civil rights revolution of the late 1950s and 1960s. First, they pursued recognition as a community in the forefront of the progress shared by other prominent American cities. Second, they sought to control this change through its regular channels of business, civic, and political leadership. Just as it could be economically injurious to earn the reputation of being backward, it would be likewise pernicious to earn the reputation of a city under leftist turmoil. In the coming years of the late 1960s and early 1970s, however, Charlotte would face some of its stiffest challenges as a contingent of New Left and Black Power advocates emerged, and the schools bred community turmoil after the 1969 *Swann v. Charlotte-Mecklenburg Board of Education* decision, a federal ruling that ordered busing to achieve school desegregation.

* * *

When the Queen City made the federal Housing and Urban Development Department's (HUD) list of the first sixty-three awards for Model Cities grants in November 1967, local officials saw it as another sign of Charlotte's ability to stay on top of every trend—as well as another opportunity to infuse further financial resources into the city's rising economic might. In its bid for this War on Poverty program designed to revitalize America's inner cities, Charlotte targeted a section of Black neighborhoods near the crucial downtown financial business hub. The city's accepted proposal included plans for constructing more low-cost housing, refurbishing schools, parks, and public buses, and addressing the job outlook for the area's working-class Black residents.[12]

While city leaders enthusiastically saw the large federal grant as further confirmation of Charlotte's favored national status as a progressive city on the right road, an unwanted controversy lay in the weeds. Residents of the program's target area questioned their limited role in the project's decision making. Thirteen separate community groups from the Model Cities program's designated neighborhoods promptly organized themselves. Gathering over seven hundred signatures to a petition protesting the lack of residents' "equal representation" on the decision-making bodies, they elected the Reverend J. A. Frieson as president of a united group to press their case with city officials—all within three weeks of HUD's funding decision. Frieson urged Mayor Brookshire to reconsider the board's makeup of members from the City Council, Board of County Commissioners, and school board. Frieson vividly described target area residents' strong desire to exercise power over their own destinies: "[we] want to be a part of this program. We want to be able to tell our children that we were instrumental in bringing about better living conditions, better jobs and better education for our communities. We are organized. We are ready to go to work. We recognize the problems unique to our communities."[13]

Even the moderate Kelly Alexander stepped into the fray. Warning the mayor that time was running out on his previous pledge to change the board's makeup, Alexander suggested the possibility of a legal suit to block federal funds disbursement. In keeping with city leaders' track record of controlling municipal progress, Brookshire sought to keep the lid on the simmering controversy. Such measures, he contended, would only "throw roadblocks, delay and in many cases destroy conscientious efforts being carried out." Clearly resistant to sharing power outside of the traditional business power brokers, he lectured his critics that it was "the responsibility of every good citizen to see that this does not happen in Charlotte."[14]

Unfazed, Kelly Alexander and other African American leaders turned white city leaders' own narrative against them, warning that the city's uncommon good fortune in avoiding major urban riots could be threatened by the increasing presence of "outside agitators" in the city. Giving the local poor an active role in decision-making power, they maintained, was the best antidote to this danger. In a reminder that could raise fears for any city mayor in the late 1960s, Frieson counseled: "We don't want a long, hot summer in Charlotte. But the way to answer any outside agitators who come in here stirring up trouble is to tell them this is our baby. We're feeding it and we love it—get out and leave us alone."[15]

Under this powerful political pressure, Charlotte's Mayor Brookshire began seeking a compromise on Model Cities board seats. He first suggested reducing the residents' request for six board members to two. After heated objections, he acquiesced to demands for six target area community representatives. Once again, however, Brookshire turned to the business community as a stabilizing force, adding three seats representing business concerns to offset his concession of six new community member seats.[16]

Despite this temporary settlement in January 1968, the debate over power distribution rose again four months later. Many Black Charlotteans had long seen the city's system of at-large city councilmen as a method to block Black political power, since it undermined their population strength in some potential neighborhood voting districts (i.e., if council members were elected exclusively by neighborhood voting districts, then heavily Black neighborhoods could elect one of their own). At issue now was the proposed merger of the city of Charlotte and the surrounding county of Mecklenburg. African Americans' suspicions arose over the timing of the proposal. Recent white flight to city suburbs had led to an increasing African American population in the incorporated city left behind, and white leaders sought—in the words of Black school board member Colemon Kerry—"a way to get around" predominantly Black voting districts. Whites now sought to revise the system of having a specific population choose a representative to report directly to that district. Maintaining the old electoral system would mean that some now overwhelmingly Black city districts could command important voting power over that representative. A city-county merger would restore a safe white majority to the voting constituency, and—many Black leaders feared—ensure its continued domination of city government. Clem Baines, director of the Charlotte Area Fund's Eastside Community Center, was blunt: "It's a master plan, a blueprint to colonize Black people in a two by four area, but insuring the decision-making powers remain where they are."[17]

The protests over the merger, however, would be to no avail. As for a "long hot summer in Charlotte," it never arrived. The "outside agitators," determined to shake up power in Charlotte, however, did.

* * *

When Marvin Sparrow and his wife, Kathy, brought their Volkswagen Beetle to Charlotte in early 1969, they were "well into the [New Left] movement." Having worked in antipoverty agencies in inner-city Durham, North Carolina, Marvin Sparrow had come under the harsh microscope of federal officials for his antiwar activities in the eastern part of the state while serving as a Volunteers in Service to America (VISTA) volunteer. He and his wife had considered remaining in Durham, which "was a hotbed of activism," or moving to the nearby towns of Raleigh or Chapel Hill, where activist movements flourished in the late 1960s. Instead, they chose Charlotte, which regional New Left activists "considered untapped territory where nothing was happening. . . . So, we sort of had an idea that we were going to go there and promote these things that we were interested in."[18]

The Sparrows were part of the broader New Left movement inspiring so many young people in the mid- to late 1960s. Employing some of the techniques of the renowned community organizer Saul Alinsky, New Left adjutants launched myriad projects in American inner cities. Students for a Democratic Society (SDS), the best-known organization of the movement, sent hundreds of their members into nine different troubled urban areas to agitate the impoverished into demanding change as early as 1964. When SDS members moved on, many of these student activists, like Sparrow, continued this work as employees of the rising programs of Lyndon Johnson's War on Poverty.[19]

Friends of the Sparrows sent them looking for Charlotte's "hippie house," which had been subject to extensive police scrutiny, including nine different raids, culminating in its closure after building inspectors declared it "unfit for human habitation." Inspired to carry the mission forward, the Sparrows soon rented a home to serve as "a little commune" and sanctuary for New Left and counterculture adherents on Charlotte's Central Avenue.

Eager to inspire others into New Left activism, the Sparrows' open door policy at their new commune quickly created domestic chaos, however: "All of the sudden we had 25 people living there. . . . So, there was a lot of activity there—and, you know, the generational gap stuff—people getting into fights with their parents, wandering people going from city to city and so on." As a drop-in center for local counterculture, the Central Avenue house began to develop a cult following. "It got to be *such* a big thing," recalls Marvin Sparrow, "that we actually had people come and park across the street in a parking lot and watch our house. You know, like instead of going to the movies: 'We'll watch the hippie house and we'll see what's going to happen.'"[20]

Others were less amused. "The police got very interested in it," recalls Sparrow, "and started raiding the place—mainly looking for runaways." The rising tension between police and the Central Avenue commune reached its apex, according to Sparrow, in "a big bust" that apprehended a teen runaway and evicted all residents.[21]

Out on bail for their arrest (the Sparrows would later be convicted and then have that conviction overturned), the couple faced the task of finding a new home in a community that had little interest in welcoming them. On that frustrating mission, a scenario would repeatedly play out. "We must have had six or seven apartments that [the owners] told us, 'Yeah, you can do it,' and in some cases we even gave them a down payment, and then we showed up the next day and they said, 'No, we can't rent it to you.' They had checked with someone or something." The baffling experience would later be explained by a common acquaintance's discovery of a Charlotte Board of Realtors' rental "blacklist" bearing the Sparrows' name. This informal but effective handout apparently had been distributed to members of the Board of Realtors to discourage rentals to the hippie couple. After several months spent on friends' couches and the Quaker Meeting House "crash-bed place" set aside for draft resisters, the Sparrows finally gave up and bought their own house. The un-friendly business and realty interests "couldn't do much with that one," Sparrow muses.[22]

Butch Rosen, a Connecticut native and Vanderbilt University graduate, also found locating a home to be a difficult proposition. After moving to Charlotte, Rosen quickly "became active in the community and involved in an [interracial dialogue] group called 'Change,'" which met informally to discuss race and politics as "a way for those committed to progressive issues to support one another, get to know one another." "Change" also took occasional public stands in the community on those concerns. In January 1969, the group joined several other organizations to represent local youth concerns in upcoming municipal elections. In coalition with these other liberal groups, it proposed a slate of local political candidates to address issues of progressive change, such as low-cost housing and a less regressive tax system. Through the group and other settings, the young, white college graduate befriended local African American community activists.[23]

Rosen's widening circle of African American companions, however, did not sit well with everyone. After an interracial gathering of five or six friends at his apartment to watch the 1968 Republican National Convention on television, Rosen was chided by his white building manager for having "a loud party." During the small get-together the night before, Rosen had rebuffed a Black friend's suggestion that they not stand together in his open doorway. "'Why? We're not doing anything,'" Rosen had replied. But Rosen's companion again implored him: "'Just listen to me. We better get inside.' So, not really understanding, I did. A few minutes later, the building manager (who was a white policeman) came to the door and said he had had complaints about a loud party. I told him to take a look and see that nothing was going on. 'You can see for yourself.' The next day I was evicted for having a loud party."[24]

In the search for a new place to accommodate himself and his visitors of color, Butch Rosen experienced nothing like the drama of the Sparrows' blacklisting. Instead, he endured the far more mundane, everyday barriers of American residential segregation. Locating an old house he wished to rent, the realtor "started giving me the runaround." The agent assured Rosen that he didn't want to move into "the Black part of town. I demanded that I be allowed to take it." Rosen, outraged by the insanity of not having anywhere to live in the racially divided community, told him, "'Look, I've been thrown out of the white part of town, now you're trying to tell me that I can't live here either?' So, it was that kind of a time. It was very racially charged."[25]

Charlotte was not alone, of course, among American cities saddled with deeply divided residential racial segregation. Martin Luther King's 1966 Chicago campaign had attacked the issue with limited success, but open housing remained a troubling dilemma for the nation's liberals. The 1968 Civil Rights Act, while well-intentioned, provided little teeth to attack the problem.[26]

* * *

The already problematic residential segregation of Charlotte was exacerbated by the city's participation in the nationwide "urban renewal" campaign. Begun in the 1950s, urban renewal extended into the 1960s as a national response to the white middle-class flight to the suburbs after World War II, which left behind a decaying sector of impoverished residents in many municipal cores. Civic leaders, who wanted to reassure their suburban commuters and downtown office workers that the inner cities were still safe and open for business, began to tear down working-class minority neighborhoods in favor of shiny new buildings, highways, and stadiums. Mayors often did so with assurances to the newly displaced poor residents that better housing would be built elsewhere to accommodate them. Those promises were rarely fulfilled, particularly since the working-class minorities were commonly left with little or no voice in the process. Hence, urban renewal—while done in the name of economic growth—clearly privileged middle-class white residents and shunted poor minorities. The phenomenon often played out in an especially harsh and racially tinged manner in southern cities.[27]

Charlotte's campaign proved to be much the same. The city's Redevelopment Commission formed in 1959, launching its costly and ambitious work by looking immediately to the local Brooklyn neighborhood as "the obvious target of the city's [first] urban renewal efforts." The commission called the neighborhood "an environment of filth, rats, flies, disease, periodic flooding and perpetual violence," and—perhaps more importantly to the image-obsessed Queen City—"only a few hundred yards from the center of downtown Charlotte, and right across the street from City Hall."[28] The city garnered over $40 million in federal funds from 1959 to the early 1970s to bulldoze several inner-city neighborhoods and replace them with pristine business, governmental, and upscale residential developments—including the Charlotte Governmental Plaza, a downtown city park, the Charlotte Convention Center, a luxurious Radisson Hotel, and the high-rise headquarters of North Carolina National Bank (which later merged to become Bank of America). All but a seven-city-block section of the bulldozed neighborhoods were exclusively Black.[29]

So extensive was Brookshire's commitment to urban renewal and the city's image that, in a 1966 speech, he enlisted all municipal residents to take part. While boasting about the demolition of the "creeping menace" of the slums near downtown, he happily noted the "new modern structures" of the Law Enforcement Center and jail "rising on this reclaimed land." Brookshire designated March 21 to April 9, 1966, as "a period of citywide improvement." "Take a good look at your home, business or neighborhood," he challenged Charlotteans. "Does it need improvement? Can it be made beautiful with grass, trees and flowers? You can start by removing eye-sores, trash, rubbish, obsolete objects and structures."[30] The Charlotte City Council followed the mayor's zealous lead when it enacted two laws on April 4 of that year making it illegal for residents to leave in their yard papers, rags, boxes, wood, rubber, leather, yard trimmings, dust, and ashes.[31]

Despite the usual eager support of prominent white leaders for city policy, some African American leaders feared that urban renewal meant regarding indigent Black Charlotteans as just another kind of "eye-sore," like the yard trimmings, dust, and ashes, or another brand of unfortunately "obsolete objects" for a city promoting its Sunbelt modernity. Particularly disturbing was the campaign's trend to further segregate the city in the name of aiding the Black poor. The Brooklyn neighborhood renewal project's refusal to replace razed housing with new affordable housing sent an early notice of what was in store for the city's poor inner-city Black community. The massive "renewal" of Brooklyn demolished 1,480 buildings and displaced 1,007 families, but built not a single new housing unit. Instead, former residents were referred to the Urban Redevelopment Commission's "Relocation Officer," who compiled a list of available housing primarily supplied by the Charlotte Board of Realtors. Families moving under this system found themselves in already heavily segregated northern and western sections of the city, or, in a few cases, moving into working-class white neighborhoods adjacent to the African American section of the city. Even such borderline city neighborhoods quickly converted into African American neighborhoods as remaining working-class whites promptly fled their new Black neighbors.[32]

As early as 1960, the local NAACP branch questioned the Redevelopment Commission's refusal to build public housing to shelter Brooklyn's newly displaced. Kelly Alexander and other local African American leaders' concerns grew gradually more serious, and Alexander began to call on the City Council to intercede. Reginald Hawkins then called for a federal investigation and—in the meantime—for Washington to withhold the Redevelopment Commission's federal funds until an African American was appointed to the commission. After the federal Urban Renewal Commission finally threatened to halt funding if Charlotte did not build some public housing for the displaced, the city agreed to build six hundred new units.[33]

This seeming victory for critics of the intensifying residential segregation ended in a muted success, however. The city created two hundred of the six hundred new units by razing a working-class white neighborhood and building what would then become a virtually all-white senior citizens' complex on the site. City urban renewal officials created the other four hundred by demolishing another historic Black neighborhood and erecting a public housing complex in its place. Not only had the city destroyed an additional Black neighborhood in the name of assisting those displaced by a previous neighborhood demolition, but the Earle Village complex erected there had fewer units than the neighborhood it had leveled.[34] As this trend of residential segregation only intensified in the mid-1960s, the politically moderate African American city councilman Fred Alexander warned the city, "We're building our future Watts right now."[35]

The 1965 riot in the African American Watts district of Los Angeles had alerted the nation to the potential of inner-city violence, and any reference to it was a disconcerting reminder for American white communities. Sadly, Watts was just the beginning. Officials documented forty-three "racial disorders" (the broad term employed by government authorities for urban riots) in 1966, and 164 more in the first nine months of 1967 alone. The nature and intent of these urban uprisings became contested ground among public figures, both white and Black. Some Black Power activists characterized them as an attempt to express and resist the white supremacist superstructure under which so many African Americans continued to suffer. Others, including some civil rights leaders—fearful of alienating whites increasingly resistant to racial protest (nonviolent or otherwise)—discouraged the notion of conflating them with more traditional nonviolent protest methods.[36]

Still, local liberal white optimism remained high as ground broke for Earle Village. The complex was to be the pride of Charlotte's urban renewal and public housing campaign. Completed in October 1967, the Charlotte Housing Authority-designed neighborhood had 409 units. Earle Village also had its own "community center" boasting a basketball court, five hundred-square-foot stage, a kitchen, meeting rooms, and a playground with tennis courts, a jungle gym, and a wading pool. Mindful of increasingly vocal critics who complained that the city was gradually converting its historic Black neighborhoods into distastefully uniform ghettoes, Housing Authority director Harold Dillehay assured the citizenry that he and his staff would rigorously enforce tenant contracts. Those contracts stipulated that Village residents bear full responsibility for the upkeep of their apartments and surrounding yards. To ensure contract fulfillment, the Housing Authority would periodically make inspections of units and their environs. "Time and use" could conceivably make Earle Village and its bright new community center "just another slum," *Charlotte News* editors conceded, but it confidently assured readers that "it will take some doing."[37]

* * *

Butch Rosen needed no such massive government intervention. He only wanted a home to share with his multiracial companions. He and his wife, Shirley, finally found one together with their friends Vicki and T. J. Reddy. Vicki Reddy, a white Chicago native, had come to Charlotte as a VISTA worker in 1967. She joined the antipoverty campaign in Charlotte by starting a community center in the neighborhood behind Johnson C. Smith University. The center ran daycare services for the poor during school hours, after-school activities for neighborhood teens, and evening educational programs and activities for adults. In this context, she met her future husband, young Black poverty worker T. J. Reddy. After quitting a library job over a supervisor's objection to her marriage to a Black man, she later worked for the first integrated law firm in the state—which notably included Julius Chambers and Jim Ferguson. (Both would become noted civil rights attorneys in the state. Chambers pursued the *Swann* busing case among other civil rights causes, and Ferguson's cases would include the Charlotte Three.)[38]

T. J., like the Rosens, the Sparrows, and his future wife, Vicki, was a Queen City transplant. He had come to Charlotte in 1964 from New York City as a Johnson C. Smith University student. An emerging young writing talent, he transferred to the University of North Carolina at Charlotte in 1969 (where he became vice president of the newly formed Black Student Union) and became a *Charlotte Observer* intern correspondent. In the next few years, his poetry would appear in a number of local and regional periodicals and in a compilation of local artists entitled *Eleven Charlotte Poets*. It was his antipoverty work—as project director for the Tenth Street Community Center for poor Black youth (a local church-funded initiative)—that brought him into contact with Vicki.[39] But it was his antiwar work that brought him into contact with local law enforcement.

Besides the newly displaced Black poor, Earle Village saw the arrival of military recruiters for the Vietnam War in August 1968. Touting the military's training opportunities for school dropouts and the unemployed, the recruiters stationed themselves at the Village's community center two days a week. Antiwar leaflets followed the army personnel one week later. Slipped under Earle Village doors one night, the literature noted that a "black man has three times as many chances of ending up on [Vietnam's] front lines as a white soldier . . . three times as many chances of getting killed."[40] While the leaflets were left anonymously, it was only three days later that T. J. Reddy and his cohort, Jim Grant, another young African American, leafleted in broad daylight in front of the Earle Village community center. An unsympathetic community center employee greeted the two men with two equally unsympathetic police officers. The latter took Grant and Reddy—whom police admitted had broken no laws—downtown to discuss their day with Charlotte police intelligence officer Joseph Europa. Europa held the two young African Americans for thirty minutes in pursuit, he said, of "trying to understand each other."[41]

New to Charlotte, Jim Grant had grown up in the Black middle-class home of a Hartford, Connecticut, postman. His family was well-known in the Hartford community, and young Jim had left for a college education at the University of Connecticut, then a master's degree in chemistry, which he gained in 1960. For the next eight years, Grant vacillated between his pursuit of a chemistry Ph.D. and teaching jobs, until finally gaining his doctorate at Pennsylvania State University in 1968. Hungry to participate in the growing movements for social change swirling around him, though, he enlisted in VISTA. After completing his training in Maryland, Grant had hoped for a return to Philadelphia, where he could continue working for a tutoring program he had started in the Black community there, but his superiors sent him south instead to work for the Charlotte Area Fund (CAF).[42]

Grant soon joined the local Black Power group, the Black Culture Association (BCA). As a showcase for Black consciousness, the BCA headquartered itself in a house, painted it black, and created a mural on its walls that included Malcolm X, Frederick Douglass, and W.E.B. Du Bois. Even the house's furniture was black. The BCA did not limit itself to cultural reform, however. It also agitated for economic change through organized rent strikes, protests of the Housing Authority, and boycotts of allegedly price gouging white merchants.[43] The BCA's Youth Council of approximately forty high schoolers gave the organization a more visible footprint in the community, including a student boycott to demand Black history classes at the city's high schools. The group was even solicited by a Black high school principal to function as "marshals," enforcing order at high school football games, in response to a prior violent incident.[44] The BCA also pressed the issue of better recreational centers at City Council meetings, challenging the inequitably limited municipal funds in inner-city neighborhoods and administrators' refusal to allow BCA functions at local centers because the group was too "controversial."[45]

Not surprisingly, the BCA drew few admirers among city authorities. Reginald Hawkins, a regular irritant to city leadership, appeared at rallies, noting his son was a member and telling the crowd that Black police had told him the group was regarded as a "bad organization" at headquarters. BCA rallies were closely monitored by police, with the Charlotte police chief issuing some reports directly to the mayor. The group complained of harassment and surveillance. At one point, a member caught a policeman recording license plates at their events. At another, members charged that they were "bodily thrown out" of the police station while trying to file a complaint.[46]

* * *

Whether Europa had learned anything from his August 1968 conversation with Grant and Reddy was unclear, but depending on one's view, Grant proved slow to comprehend the police perspective or slow to submit. And four months later his next publicized antiwar action drew even wider attention. Grant, his colleague Charles Parker, and four other members of the Black Culture Association were renewing the campaign to alert Charlotte's Black youth of the "plot" by the "universal military syndicate that runs this country." Parker, along with T. J. Reddy, had been an officer in the Black Student Union at UNC Charlotte and an employee of the Tenth Street Community Center.[47] They represented an unsettling trend for city leaders of increased agitation and trouble.

According to leaflets that Grant and his associates were distributing to the city's Black poor, the "universal military syndicate" had a two-pronged agenda to exterminate young African American males. First, "Get the Black men off the street by drafting them and sending them to Vietnam," where they would be disproportionately sent "to the front lines to make sure they don't get back." "White racist cops" would then execute the second part of the "plot," "kill[ing] off . . . in the line of duty" the African American males left behind. The leaflets also listed Grant and Parker as contacts.[48]

When the news media contacted the CAF for comment, new director Robert Person was apparently caught off guard by Grant's activities and called an immediate meeting with his employee. Grant had entered a politically volatile situation. Like many other local branches of the federal War on Poverty's Community Action Programs (CAPs), the CAF had become a lightning rod for municipal controversies by trying to walk the increasingly difficult tightrope of agitating for social and economic change without running afoul of local political leadership. By attracting Black Power advocates who eagerly tied economic progress to the continuing African American freedom struggle, the CAF paralleled many other CAPs across the tumultuous late 1960s America.

In January 1968, the three-year-old Charlotte agency drew criticism for inviting the outspoken Black Durham activist Howard Fuller. Just a few months prior, a local TV station had aired an incendiary piece on Fuller's work in the Appalachians, claiming he was "organizing a rebellion" against those regional "politicians, health departments, and even the Welfare Department itself."[49] As the date of Fuller's three-day community organizing training for CAF staff had neared, local U.S. Representative Charles R. Jonas phoned to ask CAF board chairman Charles Lowe whether he knew that Fuller was "a Black Power advocate."[50] In short, the CAF and its organizers had begun to challenge the traditionally firm hold by moderate business leaders on the direction of the city. Civic leaders had the crucial lever of money to drive the CAF to the political middle, and they would use it to force the removal one by one of the group's more controversial members and programs.

As antagonism between the CAF and Charlotte's civic leadership grew, the supervising federal Office of Economic Opportunity (OEO) criticized the problematic "communication gap" in a January 1968 report.[51] In July 1968, the local City Council and County Commission withheld promised fund disbursements to the CAF until it rid itself of "agitators."[52] County Commission chairman Gus Campbell, one of four Republicans swept into office in 1966 on the five-seat commission, called white CAF director John Zuidema a "disruptive influence." Campbell even objected to the Black CAF Summer Youth Program coordinator Stan Alexander's private participation in a BCA-supported demonstration advocating public school Black history classes. Calling Alexander's participation "community agitation," CAF board member Gus Campbell charged that it would "force the [Charlotte Area] Fund to decide whether it wants to go the activism route or cooperate with the community and local government."[53] Under heavy criticism, Zuidema resigned in September 1968.[54]

With its director now gone, the CAF voted to renew funding to two of the Fund's most controversial programs—the Charlotte Youth Board and the Welfare Rights Organization (WRO). The disgusted Campbell now asserted that he could no longer "in good conscience remain on a board which not only condones, but actively supports [such] activities." "Knowing the past histories of the leaders of these two programs," Campbell went on, "I am firmly convinced that these two programs spell serious trouble for our community." The "dangerous tactics" of "confrontation and community agitation," contended Campbell, could "easily culminate in community uprisings or riots." Commissioner Pete Peterson joined Campbell's pledge to once again deny funding to the CAF. As Peterson put it, "We are not at all interested in supplying money to them to fuel the fire with."[55]

Fueling "the fire" in this case were the controversial CAF programs advocating for economic change. The CAF, like many other CAPs across America during the War on Poverty, had veered at times from the more broadly appeal-

ing self-help programs to the more unsettling issue of redistributing financial and political power. Many local civic and business leaders believed CAF
employees had been behind the late 1967 outcry over the Model Cities board
representation. County commissioner Gus Campbell in particular charged
CAF employees with "trying to dictate" the direction of city initiatives by organizing Model Cities residents around their grievances. The CAF's neighborhood centers, for example, had become the locus of community organizing around long-held concerns—including the lack of participatory power on
city boards.[56]

Under the threat of funding cuts, the CAF finally capitulated to local
government complaints and submitted a penitent "Reorganization Plan" that
insisted the CAF staff would no longer "use political confrontation as an instrument of social progress," nor "become involved in controversy with local
government." In the plan, the CAF reassured authorities that this revamped
CAF would better control its more militant staff and "the influence of extremist elements," avoid "power confrontation and disruptive tactics," and more
closely adhere agency actions and policy to board directives.[57]

It was Noble Coleman and his Welfare Rights Organization (WRO) that
Campbell and his conservative allies on the County Commission had especially in mind as "agitators." Coleman was another "outside" disturber of the
city's status quo. An African American from the Oakland, California, area, he
spent three years in the Air Force before coming to Charlotte as a community
organizer for the CAF. Observing a need for organizing the welfare recipients
with whom he worked, he started the WRO to address their grievances. He
and his newly formed organization quickly earned the ire of the county's Welfare Department director, Wallace Kuralt. Instructing the poor on their rights
as welfare recipients and how to more fully avail themselves of welfare funding began to test Kuralt's patience as he wondered how far his welfare budget
would stretch.[58] On new CAF director Robert Person's first day on the job, he
fired the controversial Coleman and the CAF Youth Board director, Stan Alexander. Alexander, like Coleman, had courted the disfavor of reluctant purse
string-holding county commissioners through his "agitation."[59]

With these controversies still fresh on his mind in December 1968, Robert Person requested that the federal VISTA program transfer Grant out of
Charlotte. Surely Grant's having joined other militants in their vocal oppo-

sition to the hiring of Person as CAF director two months prior did nothing to strengthen his bargaining position. Washington officials responded by removing Grant from VISTA altogether. A disgusted Grant gave up "all hope for the poverty program as it now stands," and called Person's action an "unjust" firing. Grant claimed that the director "knew about everything I was doing . . . [but] didn't care as long as it didn't make the newspapers." Person admitted that CAF supervision of some workers was "lagging . . . due to problem areas in the Fund, but this is being worked on." Mindful of previous scraps with city officials, Person sought to walk a delicate middle ground by saying, "We try to permit [CAF employees] a degree of flexibility, but require that they work within the framework of our program and that they certainly discuss all of their activities with us."[60]

Clearly the unwelcome arrival of Black Power, New Left, and counterculture activists had set Charlotte's city fathers on edge. For now, the white business leaders had once again won the day, carefully controlling the direction of power distribution in their rising Sunbelt city. While this ended Grant's employment with the CAF, it certainly did not end his activism—nor that of his companions and colleagues. In the coming months, activists pushed to the municipal margins as unwelcome "extremists" and "agitators" would become further marginalized and vulnerable when law authorities became activists themselves. The increasing polarization had done its work. The city's more strident activists would become targets of a nexus of criminal charges that would forever derail their search for local Black power in Charlotte.

3

LET JUSTICE ROLL DOWN LIKE WATERS

From a War on Poverty to a War on Crime

C harlotte police chief John Ingersoll was teed off in September 1967. While the usual target of his anger would have been criminals, this time it was a presumed partner in the prosecution of crime: U.S. Attorney General Ramsey Clark. At issue were Clark's remarks on Charlotte and the state of North Carolina before a Senate judiciary subcommittee. Clark had appeared before the subcommittee advocating for legislation that would make it a federal crime to harm or threaten civil rights workers. As Senator Sam Ervin of North Carolina challenged Clark on the need for and the constitutionality of such a law, the attorney general responded by listing thirteen unresolved and unprosecuted North Carolina racial incidents. Clark included the unsolved November 1965 bombings of Charlotte's prominent African American leaders (Reginald Hawkins, Julius Chambers, Kelly Alexander, and Fred Alexander), a 1966 Charlotte car bombing against a man refusing to support neighborhood initiatives against school integration, and several cross burnings at the homes of Mayor Stan Brookshire and Mayor Pro Tem James Whittington. "If law enforcement in the South would meet its responsibility for solving all of these crimes," explained Clark, "we would not need federal intervention. And we would prefer it that way."[1]

An angry Ervin bristled at this presumed attack, contending that Clark and the Lyndon Johnson administration sought to make the South their "whipping boy." Chief John Ingersoll called Clark's remarks "grossly unfair," and remained "appalled that a cabinet-level officer of this great nation would stoop to such a low level for political advantage." Ingersoll asserted that none of the unsolved crimes indicated any lack of effort on the part of Charlotte police. Charlotte's Mayor Stan Brookshire, City Manager William Veeder, and Mayor Pro Tem James Whittington quickly queued up to decry Clark's comments. Whittington expressed his desire to see Charlotte "left alone. We are attempting to do a good job in this city among all our people. I agree with Senator Ervin that we have one of the best police departments in the country." Brookshire contended that Clark's implication that the city's police are "either lax or inefficient in their efforts . . . is to be regretted." Defending Charlotte's progressive public image, Whittington called it "unfortunate and unnecessary that the Attorney General selected Charlotte to lower the boom on, when Charlotte's record in community relations has been most excellent."[2]

Perhaps the most astonishing thing about the entire episode was how notably out of step Ramsey Clark would be in the coming months, not only with Charlotteans' portrayal of their beloved city, but with the general trend of federal authorities in the late 1960s. Rather than criticizing their southern peers, federal law enforcement would be working in close and cooperative tandem with those agents in the coming years of the late 1960s and early 1970s. Clark's frustration with southern officials' sluggish pursuit of justice for African Americans and activists made him hopelessly anachronistic as Richard Nixon neared his presidential victory the next year under the prominent banner of "law and order." As the expensive Vietnam War dragged on and positive results from the Great Society seemed—at least to many white Americans— maddeningly elusive, Lyndon Johnson's War on Poverty was in rapid decline, to be supplanted by a new battle: the War on Crime.

The 1968 Omnibus Crime Control and Safe Streets Act visibly represented this shift away from an emphasis on civil rights and civil liberties to addressing a society seemingly spinning out of control with rampant crime and radicalism. Ramsey Clark and President Lyndon Johnson had both reluctantly supported the bill as it neared passage (with only four senators and seventeen House members voting against). Johnson finally signed the bill into law in June 1968 because it contained "more good than bad." The "good" for Johnson was the $400 million in block grants targeted for state and local law enforcement improvements. That portion of the new law had been introduced by the president in 1967, and then became the shell of this later statute, as congressmen added their own addenda to the bill. But there was also the "bad." Johnson and Clark particularly lamented the section that widened electronic surveillance by law enforcement on the federal, state, and local levels. Terming that provision "unwise and potentially dangerous," Johnson called on Congress to consider repealing it "immediately"—a plea that went unheeded. Clark warned that "public safety will not be found in wiretapping.... Nothing so mocks privacy as the wiretap and electronic surveillance. They are incompatible with a free society."[3] Views such as these only heightened the sense that the men were swimming against the rising conservative tide. Johnson, of course, had already declared he would not stand for his party's renomination that year. Attorney General Clark had become so politically toxic for his more liberal law enforcement views that even Vice President Hubert Humphrey, who carried the Democratic Party's nomination for the presidency, made a campaign pledge to remove Clark if elected.[4]

Before the 1967 Senate subcommittee, Attorney General Clark had observed, "The difficulty in the South has been that local law enforcement has not equally protected the rights of all citizens."[5] For Charlotte's activists, that assessment sharply resonated in the last year and a half of the 1960s. 1968 and 1969 would bring a consistent rain of criminal charges and prosecution on those activists who had proven themselves so troublesome on racial and economic matters in the Queen City. Just as the courageous and determined campaigns of grassroots civil rights demonstrators had opened a window of federal government sympathy for civil rights protestors, so the equally determined hand of "law and order" again slammed it shut amid the turbulence of rioting and rising crime rates across the country.

In early 1968, U.S. congressional representatives carried strong messages from their home districts to Capitol Hill on "law and order." Gallup pollsters, in fact, querying nationwide respondents in January about the "most important problem facing this community today," found "crime and lawlessness" cited twice as often as any other problem.[6] Asked in a May 1968 Gallup poll whether police shooting store looters on sight during a race riot was "the best way to deal" with them, 47 percent responded in the affirmative.[7] This thinking troubled a great many observers. "We're headed right toward lynch law if the people can't get protection from public officials," warned Representative W. R. Poage of Texas. Supporters of civil rights and antipoverty programs such as Representative F. Bradford Morse of Massachusetts lamented, "The liberal community feels impotent about the race crisis. They don't know what to do."[8] Their opponents did. The determined FBI director, J. Edgar Hoover, warned Congress that Black "militant" organizations such as the Student Nonviolent Coordinating Committee (SNCC), the Nation of Islam, and the Revolutionary Action Movement (RAM) were "a distinct threat to the internal security of the nation."[9]

The rising tide of constituent concern in 1967 and 1968 only intensified federal lawmakers' determination to push "law and order" legislation early and often. On October 21, 1967, President Lyndon Johnson signed a law just a few hours before a scheduled anti-Vietnam War protest in the nation's capitol. The law made it illegal to picket, demonstrate, or use loud, threatening, or abusive language in the Capitol Hill area. It would later be overturned on appeal, but not before police arrested demonstrators that day for reading lists of Vietnam War dead on the Capitol steps (1,200 more demonstrators were later arrested under the statute for listening to a congressman's speech at the Capitol during May 1971 antiwar protests).[10] In the Federal Appropriation Act of 1968, the national legislature codified excluding anyone from welfare payments who had been convicted for participation in a riot.[11] Later that year, the U.S. House Un-American Activities Committee (HUAC) issued a report recommending the implementation of the Internal Security Act's provision for concentration camps, to be used for the "temporary imprisonment of warring guerillas," such as members of the New Left's Students for a Democratic Society.[12] In the same year, Congress passed a statute making it illegal to travel or communicate across state lines with the intent to incite or promote a riot, another to outlaw defacement of the American flag, and one law to deny federal financial aid for two years following a conviction for riot participation (which revealed white perceptions of the link between the urban poor's dangerous street agitation and the power and resources that aided it—particularly War on Poverty programs).[13]

* * *

North Carolina proved no exception to this nationwide concern about radicalism. For many Tar Heel politicians, the preferred solution for the problem became its criminalization. The 1967 North Carolina General Assembly created the Governor's Committee on Law and Order to address the issue and to better coordinate state and local law enforcement attacking it.[14] But it was the race for the state governor's chair that confirmed the state's adherence to the national obsession over militants and crime.

The 1968 North Carolina gubernatorial campaign featured its first Black candidate since Reconstruction: Charlotte's Reginald Hawkins. Hawkins spoke emphatically about the need for increased attention to the state's poor and minorities on the stump, but the contest also brought fervent practitioners of "law and order" rhetoric. Democratic candidate Mel Broughton called for a special session of the North Carolina legislature in mid-April on the issue (sitting governor Dan Moore declined). Broughton also called for a law authorizing a statewide curfew, and another allowing a court to use the presence of defendants at a riot as evidence of their participation—a bill that potentially would lead to imprisoning innocents with the misfortune of living in the inner cities where the racial uprisings commonly occurred. The national alarm over these inner-city riots began in the Watts district of Los Angeles in 1965, continued the next summer, and exploded in the summer heat of 1967. Detroit and Newark had the worst human and material casualties that year.[15]

Republican John Stickley, a U.S. representative from Charlotte running for governor, urged President Johnson to "announce that this nation will not tolerate looting, burning and rioting any longer," and that government aims to "meet force with force wherever and whenever necessary." Instead, just days after the smoke was still clearing from America's April 1968 post-King assassination riots, the U.S. Congress passed the 1968 Civil Rights Act—a largely toothless and ineffectual attempt to legislatively support nondiscriminatory open housing. With the bill's passage, Stickley "saw the flag of glory not lowered to half-mast, but lowered to the ground when a cowardly Congress yielded to [the] blackmail" of giving the rioters what they wanted.[16] U.S. Representative Jim Gardner (another Republican gubernatorial candidate) had already made his name as a vocal opponent of the federal War on Poverty. During the state campaign for governor, he would assert in racially tinged rhetoric that the epidemic of American inner-city rioting had "made a jungle of so many of the nation's great cities." He charged rioters as "men whose hatred and prejudice has grown to a serious sickness." Gardner called it "an outrage that this country has to deal with a second front at home [beyond Vietnam] against rioters and beatniks."[17]

Lieutenant Governor Bob Scott, gearing up for his successful bid for the governor's chair as the Democratic nominee, joined the chorus, railing against "a growing and tragic disrespect for law and order in America. The courts in the land show more concern for the depraved criminal than for his innocent victim." Later in the November 1967 speech, Scott decried the erosion of respect for authority being nourished on college campuses. He spoke for the suspicions of a growing number of Americans that Black Power was breeding violence. He called it a breach of academic responsibility when a university—such as UNC Chapel Hill had recently done—"employs a faculty member—full time or part time—who is widely believed to be an advocate of 'Black Power.' I believe it wrong for a college or university campus to be used as a forum of Black Power advocates—where they make such statements as 'No Black person should be fighting in Vietnam,' and 'We can start our own Vietnam in this country to keep them busy.'"[18]

Law and order, according to Scott, was under attack well beyond the college campus. When Black high school students in Hillsborough, North Carolina, boycotted classes and marched to protest the sluggish desegregation of county schools, Scott urged "local school officials to take firm steps to end this challenge of authority by suspending or expelling the leadership of such movements in the schools."[19] In an August 1968 speech, he evoked campaign themes of Republican presidential nominee Richard Nixon. Like Nixon, Scott played on white America's growing exhaustion with civil rights pressures and poverty programs that appeared to bring nothing but exasperating unrest and a futile drain of tax dollars. "On every hand we see violent storms of protest," he told the Raleigh Jaycees. He was quick to distinguish himself from "some politicians on the national scene [who] lean over backwards to favor those marching the streets while drawing welfare checks." In images strikingly similar to Nixon's powerfully effective "silent majority" campaign theme (which contrasted the supposed majority who refrained from the protests and unrest that had rocked 1960s America), Scott assured the audience that his mission was to carry the banner of

the "forgotten Americans." . . . They are the Americans who do not march—
who carry no placards—who evade no laws. They are the men and women
who go to work in the morning and return to their families at night. They are
the men and women who pay their taxes. The forgotten Americans are the
men and women who carry the heavy burden of self-government, without
complaint—and with infinite patience. . . . These "Forgotten Americans"—
young and old—are . . . the real strength of North Carolina—but they are
growing frustrated and irritated at the current trends. . . . These forgotten
Americans do not believe we have attained utopia—but neither do they feel
the prospect of a better life should be—or can be—purchased with a fire
bomb. These forgotten Americans do not believe in a government of men—a
government whose benefits go to those who scream loudest. But, they do
believe in a government of laws. They do believe in trying to make a better
world for all people—so long as it is done within a legal framework. These
forgotten Americans do not believe our society should be operated on the
basis of threats—or riots—or intimidation.

Scott went on to outline a "12-point program" to "improve respect for the law
in North Carolina," including the increase of law enforcement officers and
"programs . . . in our public schools to instill more respect for law and order,
and to teach moral values to our young people."[20]

Hitting on another popular campaign theme, Scott assured his August
1968 audience that civil rights activists' shift into Black Power and economic
issues was misguided. "We cannot guarantee every jobless man an income
by taxing men who work for a living and have no such guarantee," he told
them. "We cannot legislate equality—only equality of opportunity." Scott put
that concern into practice by targeting a state antipoverty program for alleged
abuses of the public trust. As the gubernatorial campaign entered its final few
months, Scott approached the press with his contention that a Wake County
branch of the War on Poverty had pressured youth employees to kick back
some of their salary to purchase weapons. Black culture classes at the program, he claimed, had attempted to incite Black youths to violence. In what
he deemed further questionable conduct by the local office, Scott produced
documents for the press demonstrating that a youth employee had received
office funds to travel to New York and purchase African history books, "Mal-

colm X scrolls, African costumes and jewelry, incense, and incense holders." Scott's allegations found no home in a courtroom, however, after an internal investigation by the national OEO office and a state investigation by the North Carolina State Bureau of Investigation (SBI) turned up no evidence.[21] Scott's successful campaign rhetoric did find him a home in the governor's mansion after winning the November election.[22]

The race for state attorney general brought out another champion for law and order: state senator Robert Morgan. Morgan had proven his commitment to the cause back in 1963 as a prime backer of the state's "Speaker Ban" law. (The statute had prohibited state university branches from inviting "known" Communist Party members, those "known" to advocate the state or federal constitution's overthrow, or those who pleaded the Fifth Amendment to questions on communist subversion.) On the heels of a virtual explosion of civil rights protests across the state in the spring of 1963, Morgan and other state legislators had seen the University of North Carolina at Chapel Hill as a locus of controversial protest activity—particularly demonstrations in the nearby state capital of Raleigh. Notably, Morgan's mentor was ardent segregationist and 1960 Democratic Party gubernatorial candidate I. Beverly Lake. In the wake of the 1954 *Brown* school desegregation decision, Lake had announced his determination to "fight the NAACP county by county, city by city" as the organization was "trying to condition" North Carolina children before they were "old enough to be conscious of sex, to accept integration, not only in the classroom, but in the living room and the bedroom." Having learned his lessons well, Lake's apprentice Morgan condemned 1960 appearances at UNC by Martin Luther King and African American poet Langston Hughes. Morgan also contended that African American leaders had used the UNC-based educational television station to promote a civil rights agenda that year. In June 1963, Morgan and other concerned state legislators promptly passed the Speaker Ban law on the same day it was introduced.[23] Two days after the Speaker Ban law was declared unconstitutional by a panel of three federal judges in February 1968, Morgan stood by the law's "useful and worthwhile purpose" in a speech to a Charlotte Lions Club. Morgan's campaign defeated incumbent Wade Bruton that fall.[24]

* * *

In Charlotte, the Chamber of Commerce selected author and educator Dr. Kenneth McFarland as their keynote speaker at the December 1967 annual meeting. Reflecting the views of many civic leaders, McFarland called crime the "number-one problem in this country," and suggested that continued rioting in city streets would eventually pave the way for an American dictator. "This is exactly what brought Hitler and Mussolini to power. The man on the white horse says I will give you order in exchange for your freedoms." The solution, he suggested, was tougher law enforcement measures. Leery of the controversial 1966 *Miranda* case and other recent liberal U.S. Supreme Court rulings limiting law enforcement powers, he insisted, "We must take the handcuffs off our police and put them back on the criminal."[25]

To be sure, Charlotte did experience the same increase in crime that many other American cities saw in the late 1960s. In 1967, the year prior to a gubernatorial and presidential election year, the Queen City saw a 15.6 percent rise in criminal activity. Most alarming was a murder rate that jumped 45 percent in a twelve-month span.[26] Early 1968 only continued the trend, showing a 36.6 percent crime increase in February 1964 from the previous year.[27]

The calls for removing "the handcuffs off our police," however, faced a much harsher reception among Black leaders. A few months after his mayoral campaign defeat, the liberal Black minister Reverend George Leake spoke angrily about the popular political catch phrase—"law and order." "Law and order [are] relative terms" that "camouflage" a desire to return to days when the KKK enforced the "law" with "orderly" beatings and lynchings.[28]

While Leake and other Black leaders may have faced deaf ears on the issue of crime among their white counterparts, some African American leaders faced the unwelcome prospect of criminal charges themselves in this period. In the same election year, Dr. Reginald Hawkins found himself embroiled in the "law and order" debate in a very tangible way. On May 24, 1968, he emerged from Mecklenburg County Superior Court with an acquittal on charges of voter registration fraud. Thrown out by the judge for lack of evidence, the damage to Hawkins had nevertheless been done. Beyond the disputed evidence, Hawkins was alleged to have circumvented the use of a literacy test on a Black voter. When the 1965 Voting Rights Act had outlawed such tests as a discriminatory bar on Black voting, the entire basis of the case against Hawkins—which had dragged on well past the new federal law—

would appear to have been moot. "It is a sad thing," he lamented, "that I have been put to great expense, using my money as a taxpayer, to defend myself against charges brought against me as a means for intimidation." The case, according to Hawkins, had been "an attempt on the part of the county and state to assassinate me politically . . . in order to deny poor people their place in the scheme of things in North Carolina."[29]

These were not the only legal charges that had bedeviled Hawkins on the eve of the gubernatorial primary. The North Carolina Dental Society had charged him with malpractice for allegedly filing false claims on unperformed dental services under a 1966 government-funded program for impoverished youth dental care. Hawkins clearly felt his successful 1966 lawsuit to desegregate the state Dental Society inspired the allegations, and called the proceedings a "case based on bigotry." Racial tension filled the Dental Society hearings into the matter, and sparked several angry exchanges between Hawkins and Dental Society prosecutors. On one occasion, Hawkins's defense attorney, LeVonne Chambers, rose to object to white prosecutor Thomas Starnes's softened pronunciation of "Negro," which slid too easily into the sound of "nigger." Murmured "Amens" rumbled across the pockets of Black spectators before Starnes denied that "[i]t was . . . my intention to insult or degrade . . . anyone with my pronunciation."[30] After a lengthy delay due to scheduling conflicts of the principals, the Dental Society released its verdict in the fall of 1968. Hawkins was found guilty of "malpractice and willful neglect," and his dentistry license was suspended.[31]

Hawkins was not the only outspoken activist in Charlotte to suffer criminal prosecution in the late 1960s. The year 1968 brought a remarkable harvest of criminal indictments against troublesome activists. Noble Coleman, the director of the controversial Welfare Rights Organization, ran afoul of Charlotte prosecutors himself in October. Charlotte police officer G. W. Shore had arrested Coleman outside the Charlotte bus station in September for breach of the peace. Called into the bus station just after midnight by a restaurant employee, Shore had found Coleman and another man arguing. Coleman proved reluctant to comply with the officer's request to leave. As the officer grew anxious when Coleman "started mouthing off" and a crowd began to gather in that Black area of town, Shore made his arrest.[32]

After the judge threw the case out for lack of evidence, Charlotte police stood ready immediately outside the courtroom with another summons: failure to support his daughter financially.[33] Coleman pled guilty to those charges, and was back in court ten weeks later on a warrant for a worthless check and nonpayment of $50 for his rent. He turned himself in to police, and received a fine and a thirty-day suspended jail sentence.[34]

* * *

In May 1968, the first city chapter of the American Civil Liberties Union (ACLU) in North Carolina was established.[35] It was not a moment too soon. The new office and its exceptionally busy white lawyer, George Daly, quickly went to work defending a plethora of cases against Charlotte activists. Daly made quite a favorable impression in his first meeting with one of those activists, Marvin Sparrow. "I was being booked [at a Charlotte police station]," recalls Sparrow, "and this guy walks in on the other side of the counter and says, 'You let that man out right now. You've got no right to hold him. You're violating his constitutional rights.' And I said, 'I like that fellow.'" Marvin's wife, Kathy, had picked up Daly's name from a mutual friend and called him in desperation.[36]

The child of a well-to-do white family from Columbia, Mississippi, Daly seemed an unlikely figure to rock the boat in a prominent city of the New South. At an early age, however, he had developed liberal views by going away to a Tennessee prep school. "And when I was home," he contended, "nobody asked me my opinions about anything, so I didn't have to stake myself out. They just assume down there, you know, that you're thinking right. So the attitudes there just never affected me." An English major at Princeton University, he went on to Harvard Law School and graduated in 1961. Eight months of practicing law in Mississippi and six in the Army, though, were not what he had in mind. Daly left on a cattle boat for Europe with two pair of blue jeans, two work shirts, and fifteen pounds of luggage. There he "read books that I hadn't had time to read in school and studied French."[37]

One year later, Daly was living in San Francisco with several friends in "kind of a commune. . . . I guess it would be called a hippie house now." He slept in a sleeping bag, held an occasional odd job, and studied Asian philosophy. After a stunted six-week stay in the Peace Corps, Daly switched directions again, marrying and embarking on a year-long honeymoon around the world in 1965. The couple spent six of the twelve months "in the Orient, [visiting] religious shrines and making pilgrimages here and there to see what interested us." In 1966, the restless lawyer finally settled down in a Charlotte law practice, and then volunteered for service in the ACLU. The organization paid nothing but expenses, but it did give him "a chance to express my convictions about personal freedom. And better yet, I can do something about them in court."[38]

The new ACLU office and its self-described "ex-beatnik" lawyer George Daly first drew citywide attention in the February 1969 hippie house case. Daly had taken up the cause of the eighteen counterculture residents arrested on a 1905 vagrancy statute at their Kingston Avenue home the previous month. The case was widely seen in activist circles as proof positive of the police department's determination to give no safe harbor to "hippies" in the Queen City. Daly believed the vagrancy law to be unconstitutional, and began a series of appeals on the case.[39]

The challenge of the vagrancy law culminated before a three-judge federal court panel beginning in August 1969. The brief defending the law was submitted by the state's attorney general, Robert Morgan. Morgan claimed that the law was necessary for "the elimination of a standard of conduct conducive to crime."[40]

Daly's ninety-two-page formal appeal took quite a different slant than Morgan's rigorous legalistic document. While Morgan cited the standard legal precedents, Daly's appeal cited Mark Twain, John Steinbeck, David Gascoyne, George Orwell, Allen Ginsberg, Arthur Compton-Rickett, Errol Flynn, Edwin Zeydel, Jake Mills, Hugh d'Orleans, Norman Mailer, and Walt Whitman. Under the state vagrancy law, contended Daly, those famous figures or their fictional creations would have been locked away just as had the eighteen young "hippies" of the Kingston Avenue house. "'Other places do seem so cramped up and smothery, but a raft don't,'" Daly quoted Huck Finn as musing to his slave companion Jim in Twain's classic *Adventures of Huckleberry Finn*. Both beloved American fictional characters would have been North Carolina criminal vagrants as they floated the Mississippi in flight for Jim's freedom. Likewise, the lawyer claimed, Steinbeck's Joad family in *The Grapes of Wrath* would have been jailed, and Walt Whitman would have been afraid to write "Song of the Open Road."[41]

Daly's court battle finally succeeded in a November 1969 U.S. Circuit Court decision. A three-judge panel ruled that the vagrancy statute violated a citizen's constitutional right to "due process of law" under the Fourteenth Amendment. The judges criticized police behavior as "outrageous." Officers had "on their own initiative decided that the [young hippies] were undesirable," asserted the judges, "and harassed them systematically to discourage them from visiting and occupying" the Kingston Avenue house. "Seemingly the plaintiffs never committed a crime," the ruling continued, "nor was there any probable cause to suppose they did." Their "real offense consisted of being hippies." In addition to declaring the law unconstitutional, the panel ordered the city to refund the plaintiffs' court costs and expunge the record of the arrests.[42]

Daly now continued his legal activism in the courtroom of federal judge James McMillan. McMillan would later rattle Charlotte with his 1969 *Swann v. Charlotte-Mecklenburg Board of Education* ruling mandating school busing (the ruling would later rock the nation as well when his decision was affirmed by the U.S. Supreme Court in 1971). Like Daly, McMillan's background provided scant evidence for the social tremors he created on the racial status quo. Raised in rural North Carolina, James McMillan called himself "a traditional Southerner with a pride in the South" whose years earning a Harvard law degree did nothing to "disturb my acceptance of apartheid as a way of life." When World War II duty called, the navy assigned this quiet but stubbornly deliberate man who would later set off local whites' explosive reactions a highly ironic job: defusing bombs. But duty called again in 1968, when he was appointed to the federal court in Charlotte. In a further sign of the surprise awaiting the southern gentlemen who appointed him, McMillan was chosen over his close friend Joe Grier. McMillan would always wonder if Grier's very public early 1960s stand against public park segregation while serving as Charlotte's Local Parks and Recreation Commission chairman ensured his own selection for the judgeship.[43]

But the momentous 1969 *Swann* ruling was still a few weeks away from McMillan's courtroom when George Daly managed to elicit the judge's injunction against the Charlotte Police Department. McMillan contended that the department's series of "searches, seizures, visits, arrests and threats and 'advice' . . . ultimately accomplished the apparent purpose of disbanding the 'hippies,'" while accomplishing "no results in the realm of law enforcement or prevention or detection of drug usage or other crime." He found that the activists' "rights in their private dwelling, free from unreasonable search and seizure, have been violated and threatened and suppressed by the actions of the police." In a topsy turvy turn, the judge enjoined police from further action against the hippies "without legal probable cause or with any purpose to harass, intimidate or frighten" them in violation of their rights.[44] McMillan also ordered police to return the five-foot metal policeman that had once hung from the Kingston Avenue house front porch. The metal dummy with an eager smile and uplifted hand had been taken down a few months prior by officers who insisted that the hippies' sarcastic gesture was "making other police officers angry."[45]

In May 1969, Marvin and Kathy Sparrow were not as lucky in court as their hippie counterparts at the Kingston Avenue hippie house. The couple lost their court battle over the police raid of their Central Avenue hippie house. Each had already received a six-month suspended sentence for contributing to the delinquency of a minor and interfering with a police officer. The charges stemmed from the police raid in search of a fifteen-year-old runaway hiding there.

The Sparrows' first appeal on the Central Avenue hippie house convictions brought even stiffer sentences in Mecklenburg County Superior Court: fifteen to eighteen months for Marvin Sparrow and nine months for his wife, Kathy. While the Kingston Avenue hippie house residents had faced a more sympathetic federal judge, County Superior Court judge Rudolph Mintz chastised the Sparrows at sentencing. "This has been a tedious case for me," Mintz complained. Reflecting the day's concerns over apparent moral decay and rising youth crime, he told the courtroom that it "distresses me that we can't offer more protection for youngsters of tender age than we do. This case is a good example of the problems and challenges that we have." The runaway's reluctance to testify in the case also brought Mintz's consternation: "I am concerned that she was so infatuated with this life [with the Central Avenue commune residents] that she almost refused to testify."[46]

For Marvin Sparrow, courtroom proceedings had also raised fears. "The channels for peaceful change are closing," he contended. He and Kathy left the court with clenched fist salutes and appeal papers. The latter were filed and successful, eliminating the conviction and sentence before they were served.[47]

In another case four months hence, he was arrested for allegedly stealing milk and orange juice—$2 total in value—from a neighbor's porch. A judge later dismissed the case at trial.[48]

The issue did not end there, however. Less than two weeks after the Sparrows' first appeal over the hippie house case, state senator Martha Evans picked up Judge Mintz's cause. Pointing to several such Charlotte hippie house cases, Evans proposed a new law in the state legislature. The bill would have raised the age of parental supervision of children from sixteen to eighteen. "Hundreds of young people are going into these places," she warned. "One will open and within 24 hours, 24 or 25 other young people will be there." Her intention was to further empower purportedly hampered law officers: "Police have no authority if the child is over 16 and the Welfare Department doesn't have enough caseworkers to handle this problem."[49]

The Sparrow prosecutions had followed years of close surveillance by law enforcement. Marvin Sparrow's FBI surveillance had begun with a simple act: the exercise of his right to free speech in a 1967 letter to the newspaper editor against the Vietnam War.[50] Sparrow would continue to appear in FBI files for everything from his activities while a college student with the Students for a Democratic Society and Southern Student Organizing Committee, participation in a planned demonstration during a visit to the city by President Nixon, similar protests against visiting General William Westmoreland, distributing anti-Vietnam War leaflets at military induction centers, desecrating an American flag, and hanging a Viet Cong flag from his second-story window.[51] The FBI also placed Marvin Sparrow on its secret "Administrative Index," which denoted dangerous individuals who should be watched closely, and possibly rounded up in the event of national emergency.[52] Sparrow remained under FBI scrutiny until as late as November 1975, when he was also removed from the Bureau's index.[53]

* * *

Amid the arrest of Charlotte activists and the public outcry for "law and order" came increasing African American community concerns over police brutality. As early as March 1968, poor Black residents voiced their police treatment concerns at a community center public forum. The Black Solidarity Committee (BSC) in particular took up the cause. Founded in July 1968, the BSC included the civil rights attorney Julius Chambers, Dr. Reginald Hawkins, activist T. J. Reddy, and founder Reverend Elo Henderson—all African Americans. Seeking a more moderate profile, Henderson said the group's intention was to "work quietly to solve problems." Besides confronting alleged police brutality, the BSC aimed to encourage the teachers and principals at Black schools to teach Black history and raise the quality of African American education, to encourage the proliferation of Black-owned businesses, and to provide a more concerted forum for the airing of African American grievances.[54]

In June 1969, the BSC's Reverend Henderson and other African American leaders called for the resignation of Charlotte police chief J. C. Goodman due to the department's alleged "brutal" treatment of Blacks. Henderson told an open meeting of the Mayor's Community Relations Committee, "The trouble with Charlotte is that the Police Department is ready for a riot. [Goodman] is doing everything in this world to precipitate one. There are policemen on the force who all their lives have longed for the opportunity to hit a Black man. The Police Department is trying to control the Black community with fear."[55] Following an internal Charlotte Police Department review validating only two of fifteen alleged cases of police brutality, Henderson labeled the report "a whitewash of the real issues," and again called for "a competent and unbiased police chief." The BSC's other demands included more African American police, promotion of Black officers (the twenty-two Black policeman in the 395-officer department all held entry-level positions), and a civilian review board to oversee disciplinary cases. Another minister, the Reverend C. E. Quick, delivered a petition of approximately three hundred signatures demanding an investigation into "police brutality and harassment."[56]

Six weeks later, a BSC spokesman claimed that police brutality had only increased. When asked if the BSC had taken their complaints to the police department, Henderson replied, "We have been everywhere, and we have gotten no satisfaction of any kind. All we have gotten is empty promises."[57] The BSC next took its case before the Charlotte-Mecklenburg Christian Ministers Association, calling on member clergy to "join us in doing something about this barbaric situation."[58]

Tension between Charlotte's African American community and the boys in blue only rose over the coming months, as the arrests of activists likewise seemed to increase. Charlotte's Black activists were especially frequent targets of criminal prosecution. Besides Reginald Hawkins and Noble Coleman, many other more militant Black activists would find themselves the targets of criminal prosecution in the late 1960s and early 1970s. The Black Culture Association (BCA) would be especially hard hit.

One factor in the rise of police attention to the BCA had to do with its inclusion of some members already well-acquainted with police booking stations. Like many other Black Power organizations of the late 1960s and early 1970s, the group's avowed commitment to the African American poor and leftist ideals brought it into closer contact with the Black working class. Black Power's active recruitment of that sector of the Black community and its espousal of "self defense" also drew in criminals. Martin Luther King's 1966 Southern Christian Leadership Conference (SCLC) campaign in Chicago had actively recruited the Black poor—some of whom had criminal backgrounds, including some of the city's youth gangs. The SCLC, of course, would continue to link civil rights with poverty issues in its involvement in the 1968 Memphis sanitation workers' strike and the multiracial "Poor People's Campaign." Malcolm X, an important early figure in the rise of Black Power, rose through the ranks of the likewise influential Nation of Islam, as did many of his peers as a convicted felon. The Black Panther Party, which had emerged out of the hardened California ghetto of West Oakland, continued that legacy by including a number of convicts in its membership rolls—including its onetime minister of information, Eldridge Cleaver, and minister of defense, George Jackson.[59]

The inclusion of working-class African Americans in an organization did not, of course, mean that violence would follow simply because statistically poor Black males from the American inner city had greater rates of arrest and incarceration than their middle- and upper-class counterparts. (The same may be said for whites of similar socioeconomic categories, of course.) Impoverished Black males also had less investment in playing by the rules of exercising their right to vote and doggedly pursuing their still limited economic opportunities. Indeed, a principal reason for the rise of Black Power had been the belief that removing legal barriers to traditional opportunities would not be enough to catapult the masses of poor Blacks into the mainstream of American life. Hence, many young male residents of American ghettoes lived out grim lives with little hope that hard work and traditional middle-class values would produce the same results their wealthier counter-parts received. Such a population, then, was more prepared to employ more desperate or extreme methods to achieve a measure of success for themselves. Certainly many Black Power advocates had seen these embittered youth as a fertile recruiting ground for their message of "self-defense" and outspoken "self-determination."

The BCA's Black Power ideals had won converts in several members of Charlotte's African American working class—including Alfred Hood and David Washington (both later to become prosecution witnesses against the Charlotte Three). No stranger to a patrol car, Dave Washington had been con-victed for larceny and breaking and entering by his twelfth birthday. Before he turned twenty he had been convicted of multiple further charges, including assault with a deadly weapon. He entered the Marine Corps in 1964 at the age of twenty-two, but was diagnosed a schizophrenic and given a medical dis-charge in 1967 after only five and a half months of Vietnam service.[60] Military documents referred to his "homicidal tendencies," evidenced by massacring Vietnamese civilians and shooting at his own sergeant.[61]

Al Hood may have lacked Washington's psychiatric record, but he did share a number of significant similarities. Hood, like his friend Washington, was a Vietnam veteran, and had attended Central Piedmont Community Col-lege in Charlotte, where he was active in forming its Black Student Union.[62] Like Washington, he was familiar with the streets of working-class Black Char-lotte, and—like Washington—he was familiar with the backseat of a Char-lotte police patrol car. His string of criminal charges included auto theft, as-sault with a deadly weapon with intent to kill, and assault on a police officer.[63]

* * *

Hood and Washington's welcome by local young Black Power advocates wid-ened their traditional circle beyond Charlotte's gritty inner city. When Wash-ington faced an August 1969 trial for his alleged participation in a January 1969 armed robbery of a Charlotte convenience store, the young Charlotte poet and activist T. J. Reddy served as his alibi witness. Reddy testified that Washington had spent the night at his home on the night the robbery oc-curred.[64] Two days into the trial, however, Washington changed his plea to guilty and earned what even the judge admitted was a lenient sentence. John

Cutter, Washington's attorney, later told reporters when questioned about the plea change, "That is what we have wanted all along—to get psychiatric treatment for him." He told the judge prior to sentencing, "Let's treat him as a sick man." Washington's mother, Edna Cooper, had testified on the adverse psychological effects of her son's Vietnam military service, which she described as "battle fatigue." She had told the court that Washington had been treated in several Veterans Administration hospitals and now received 100 percent medical disability for his mental illness.[65]

Judge T. D. Bryson, apparently heeding Cutter's advice, sentenced Washington to five years on probation with a twenty- to twenty-five-year suspended sentence. Washington's mental illness was not the only persuasive factor, however. Referring to Washington's military service, Bryson said, "It is the only reason I'd think about giving you that sentence. . . . You went over there to look after me and everybody in this country." Bryson coupled this light sentence with an authoritative speech on the strict conditions for the first three years of probation, which included: an 8:00 P.M. to 5 A.M. curfew, regular psychiatric treatment until cured, and abstention from alcohol and narcotics. (A Veterans Administration hospital psychiatrist's report had called Washington a heavy drinker and regular marijuana user.) Bryson concluded emphatically, "You disobey these conditions in the slightest and you've got 20 to 25 years."[66]

In March 1969, police arrested Al Hood for leading an abortive rally on the grounds of Second Ward High School. Demanding that the city build a larger high school to house the increasingly displaced African American high school students, Hood was arrested as a nonstudent attempting to lead a demonstration during school hours. The arrest brought further demonstrations at the booking police station, and arrests for Hood's activist cohorts Ben Chavis and Jerome Johnson.[67] (Chavis and Johnson would later form a potential local affiliate of the Black Panther Party). Eight months later, Hood received a thirty-day jail sentence for assault on a police officer. Officer M. S. Gaines claimed that Hood not only kicked him but had lunged for the officer's gun.[68]

Frye Gaillard, an author and investigative journalist for the *Charlotte Observer*, would later do extensive investigative reporting on the Charlotte Three case. His reporting brought an increasingly harsh view of what inspired the two men. "They didn't give a shit about that kind of stuff [civil rights or Black

Power issues]," he concluded. They were *just criminals,* that's all. . . . I mean, these were street people. These were thugs."[69]

Whatever Hood's and Washington's primary motivations, certainly most of Charlotte's liberal and leftist activists—Black or white—took no part in such violent criminal activities, but it was a sign of the period's polarization that such activists sometimes found it palatable to travel with those who did run afoul of the law. The extreme measures and alleged police brutality being perpetrated against activists made extreme and otherwise questionable actions of your allies seem more reasonable and justifiable.[70]

As criminal charges—and narcotics charges, in particular—continued to mount against members of the BCA, the group began to splinter. One member who left—Jim Grant—would embark on his long career of shifting between a number of different social and racial justice groups. His penchant for short stays with the different organizations might appear like a contradiction; to Grant, it was not. What was important was his work—not under whose auspices the work was done. As Butch Rosen, Grant's friend and former activist colleague, explains, "Jim [Grant] never particularly cared who paid his check or which group he was under. His beliefs remained the same, and so did his work, regardless of his organizational affiliation: he was a community organizer, plain and simple."[71] On the national level, the late 1960s and early 1970s was a period rife with the splintering, merging, and disintegration of civil rights groups: from the merging of the Student Nonviolent Coordinating Committee and the Black Panther Party (BPP) to the more frequent infighting between groups like the Los Angeles-based "US" organization and the BPP (who appeared to have every reason to unite in the common cause of Black nationalism). William Chafe has called the phenomenon a "civil war on the left."[72] As will be discussed later, the questionable actions and pressure tactics employed by law enforcement certainly exacerbated the phenomenon.

The arresting of Black militants often followed mounting surveillance. Jim Grant's interests particularly generated law enforcement intelligence activity in the late 1960s and early 1970s. His anti-Vietnam activities attracted the attention of not only local Charlotte police and his VISTA employers but the FBI as well.[73] The North Carolina State Bureau of Investigation kept a close eye on the February 1970 sanitation worker strike that Grant and Ben Chavis helped organize for the American Federation of State, County and Municipal Employees local. The strike's impetus (the workplace death of two Black employees amid unsafe conditions) tragically mirrored the impetus for the Memphis 1968 sanitation worker strike that drew Dr. King for his final campaign. Taking an aggressive stand, Charlotte authorities stamped out the calls for change by simply firing the striking workers.[74] Prior to that, Grant and Chavis, as Southern Christian Leadership Conference (SCLC) coordinators for western North Carolina, helped plan SCLC's April 1969 "Mountain Top to Valley March" to protest Hyde County's sluggish school desegregation plan. The march garnered not only SBI surveillance, but was included in U.S. military intelligence reports.[75] (Such reports were routinely shared with the State Bureau of Investigation.) Grant also assisted North Carolina SCLC coordinator Golden Frinks in eastern North Carolina, as Hyde County Black activists fought to save two historically Black public schools from closing during the county's desegregation process.[76]

Grant continued his work for the SCLC by focusing his attention on nearby Shelby's segregated school system, and aroused SBI concern that the small city would be drawn "into the Charlotte school situation," which suffered unrest over its attempts to desegregate. A September 1970 report noted that Grant "has been in and out of Shelby" and advised that state authorities "discreetly check the situation out" and issue a report. Approximately a year later, the SBI twice highlighted that Grant "had been observed around" the town of Kings Mountain's high school. By February 1971, Grant was receiving enough attention to warrant mentioning that a "Subject fitting the description of James Earl Grant was seen in [the] area" of a Charlotte high school before sporadic interracial fighting broke out in the halls and restrooms.[77]

* * *

One former faction of the BCA, led by Ben Chavis and his cohort Jerome Johnson, a Johnson C. Smith University student, left to form the Afro American Unity Organization (AAUO)—a group seeking to become a chapter of the national Black Panther Party. Chavis had come to Charlotte from the north-central tobacco town of Oxford, North Carolina, in 1966. By 1969, he had participated in a number of protests and demonstrations, brought controversial Black Power advocate Stokely Carmichael to the UNCC campus, been a driving force behind the creation of the UNCC Black Student Union (BSU), and run for City Council under the banner of the progressive-minded Black Political Organization (BPO).[78] The BSU had stirred enough controversy on the UNCC campus that one of its members was questioned by the FBI.[79]

Inspired by Stokely Carmichael's late 1968 speech at a UNCC Black Student Union event, Chavis became "minister of information" for the AAUO.[80] While the organization awaited formal affiliation with Black Panter headquarters, it took on the trappings of the party. Members were noted by the FBI as "wearing the garb of the BPP," including berets and Black clothing, carrying rifles, and extensively discussing the party's foundational "Ten Point Plan" at evening meetings. The AAUO also attempted to recruit members in the African American community through local presentations, rallies, and selling the BPP newspaper. One June 1969 rally in which the AAUO took part called attention to African American community concerns ranging from police brutality and housing segregation to the racially discriminatory placement of city parks, roads, and highways. AAUO rallies also promoted the gubernatorial candidacy of Dr. Reginald Hawkins, raised bail funds for members who had been arrested on a variety of charges, and demonstrated against the Vietnam War and a visit by Vice President Spiro Agnew.[81]

As community—and particularly police—concern mounted against the AAUO, so did the tension. In one July 1969 incident, AAUO members demanded sheriff's deputies not carry out an eviction order in a poor Black neighborhood. Cradling rifles as they shouted obscenities, one member warned the deputies not to return: "We're going to be waiting on you." When one deputy turned his back after a verbal confrontation, an AAUO member audibly began working the bolt on a rifle. No violence erupted that day, however.[82]

Through its rhetoric and incidents such as these, the AAUO quickly captured the attention of law enforcement authorities. It was not the first time a Black Power organization became the immediate and frequent target of FBI surveillance. Besides FBI surveillance, though, the North Carolina State Bureau of Investigation and the Charlotte Police Department had kept close tabs on the local situation, and the BCA in particular had been an early target of local police attention. In September 1968, Mayor Stan Brookshire received two separate surveillance reports on BCA rallies. The reporting officer noted that a "speaker's terminology was typical of the Black power movement in the usage of terms such as 'hunkies' [sic] with reference to the white race." BCA members complained that local police kept close tabs on activities at the BCA meeting house.[83]

As a potential affiliate of the national Black Panther Party, AAUO members were certainly subject to careful and consistent law enforcement scrutiny—by federal, state, and local officials.[84] AAUO members complained of frequent police surveillance on their organizational headquarters, and the FBI often took clandestine photographs of attendees at AAUO functions.[85] Minister of Information Ben Chavis was a chief target of this attention. FBI reports noted his chairing various organizational meetings, running a Charlotte public park rally for the group, and serving as the AAUO head during Jerome Johnson's stint in jail for an armed robbery indictment. Chavis, in fact, was deemed sufficiently dangerous to merit a report that an FBI agent had simply observed him "milling around the Administration building at [nearby] Belmont Abbey College."[86]

This pattern of surveillance and frequent arrests of Black Power and New Left militants was not unusual in the late 1960s and early 1970s United States. During appeals for Mississippi's 1973 Republic of New Afrika Eleven trial, a FBI document emerged revealing the Bureau's strategy with the RNA's leader, Imari Obadele: "If Obadele can be kept off the streets, it may prevent further problems involving the RNA inasmuch as he completely dominates this organization."[87] In a 1968 FBI memo to its field offices, headquarters recommended the successful campaign in Philadelphia against the Black Communist Revolutionary Action Movement (RAM). In that instance, the cooperative FBI field office alerted Philadelphia police to the group, and city lawmen "put RAM leaders under close scrutiny. They were arrested on every possible charge until they could no longer make bail. As a result, RAM leaders spent most of the summer in jail and no violence traceable to RAM took place." As the FBI special agent in charge had previously communicated to his director in 1967, "Any excuse for arrest was promptly implemented by arrest. Any possibility of neutralizing a RAM activist was exercised."[88]

Besides removing allegedly dangerous radicals from America's streets, the practice of law enforcement surveillance and repeated arrests served another purpose: the draining of energy and resources into legal appeals and bail money fundraising. In the case of the Philadelphia RAM organization, the campaign of successive and frequent arrests—sometimes on charges later found to lack evidence for prosecution—began to take its toll on the organization: "RAM people were arrested and released on bail," the FBI report noted, "but they were re-arrested several times until they could no longer make bail." After interrogation for distributing controversial leaflets, one member was arrested as a suspected narcotics user when an officer observed "alleged needle marks" on his arm. When another member "was advised that he was again under arrest and that his wife and sister were also under arrest, he lay down on the floor of his residence, beat the floor with his fists and cried."[89]

* * *

Law enforcement scrutiny was not the only vexing issue confronting the AAUO. It repeatedly and unsuccessfully sought affiliation with the national Black Panther Party based in Oakland, California, beginning—according to FBI files—in December 1968. The BPP, however, refused Charlotte a charter because of its own disarray. The national office had its principal leaders jailed and was engaged in an internal purge to rid itself of "informants and undesirables."[90] The BPP later apparently refused because the AAUO presumptively began calling itself an arm of the BPP without Oakland's authorization. The Oakland central office also took offense at an alleged August 1969 shootout between AAUO members and two Black men. In a speech at Chapel Hill, the BPP's Illinois field secretary, Bobby Lee, worried that the latter incident "will cause Panthers to be killed nationwide" if the public confused the Charlotte group for Black Panthers. Lee unfavorably compared the Charlotte organization to the Ku Klux Klan: "At least KKK don't be shooting at their own people." Chavis in particular earned Lee's designation as a "simple mother fucker."[91] Finally seeing the writing on the wall in the form of a BPP newspaper article that warned the AAUO of the possibility of "extreme bodily harm" if it continued, the Charlotte group agreed to disband at an October 1969 meeting.[92]

In addition to the antagonism with and subsequent threats from the Black Panther Party national office, another factor brought the demise of the AAUO. Like RAM in Philadelphia and other Black militant groups across the country, the AAUO weakened under the heavy burden of the constant diversion of members' arrests and jailings. Clearly some members of the BCA and AAUO hurt their own cause by apparently drifting into criminal activity on occasion. But while BCA members had been mostly ensnared by narcotics convictions,

AAUO members more frequently fell under charges of violence or conspiracy to commit violence.

In May 1969, a team of at least one dozen law enforcement agents (AAUO members contended that thirty to forty participated) raided the AAUO head-quarters. Members of the Charlotte police force (including a member of the Intelligence Unit), the county police force, and federal Alcohol, Tobacco, and Firearms (ATF) agents kicked in the back door and seized three 7 mm German Mauser rifles, three .22-caliber rifles, one Japanese-made 6.5 mm rifle, one 12 gauge Remington shotgun, and sixteen boxes of food intended for distribution to the poor. Federal, state, and local agents had put the new wave in federal crime control legislation to good use. The raid was officially sanctioned to capture organizational member James Covington on federal charges of falsifying documents and obtaining a firearm, in violation of the 1968 Gun Control Act. Local police also had a warrant for another AAUO member for an attempted robbery of a cab driver. While Covington was ensnared, Jerome Johnson's absence from the house left him free on his state charges of conspiracy to commit armed robbery. AAUO member Michael Laney was also arrested for interfering with Covington's arrest. Just a few days before, police had arrested Jose Banks at the house on auto theft charges.[93]

AAUO member Cordell Kennedy told journalists the raid demonstrated that "this community needs a Black Panther Party. If this could happen to this group of people it could happen to anybody in the city of Charlotte. We intend to follow this through in the courts to its fullest extent." The AAUO did just that with the assistance of local ACLU attorney George Daly in a $170,000 lawsuit charging "a policy, pattern and practice" by forty-one different law officers "directed against plaintiffs and members of their class on grounds of their race and political views." Daly claimed that these practices reflected law enforcement's determination "to harass and intimidate [the defendants] . . . particularly [to thwart exercise of] their rights to peaceable assembly and freedom of ideas."[94]

The AAUO's grievances against law enforcement officials, however, would be hampered by the group's continuing apparent criminal activity. In the early morning hours of August 16, 1969, Otis Blackmon spotted AAUO members James Black and James Prather lurking in the shadows of his Chicken 'n Ribs restaurant—an establishment that had been the site of previous AAUO rallies.[95] Blackmon's son, Otis Jr., even noticed some of them inside the restaurant's truck. Apparently concerned about potential auto theft, Otis Blackmon Jr. demanded they leave. An argument ensued, and Prather contended that the owner's son cut his arm with a knife. An hour later, approximately ten AAUO members returned clad in Black clothing and black berets, and this time gunfire broke out. The five-minute gun battle wrought four injuries—three of them to AAUO members. Two of the latter were arrested.[96]

Also damaging to their public cause was an incident two weeks prior to the restaurant shoot-out. In a curious but disturbing encounter in early August 1969, ten AAUO members in a rental truck chased down and opened fire on a car with two white teenage couples. After an angry verbal exchange at a stoplight, the would-be Panthers pursued the two couples in a fifty-miles-per-hour car chase through the streets of Charlotte until the whites' car stalled. Terrified, the teens jumped out of the car and ran to the refuge of the nearest stranger's house as the AAUO members fired gunshots from behind. The latter then tumbled their truck on its side as they attempted to swing it around and continue their pursuit. All ten AAUO members were picked up by police.[97]

The AAUO agitants were charged in the car chase and the restaurant shoot-out with a law never intended for use against African Americans. The crime was "going armed to the terror of the people"—a statute pushed by its racially enlightened authors through the North Carolina state legislature during Reconstruction. Supporters hoped to allow wider prosecution of white "night riders" terrorizing newly freed African Americans.[98] It was tragic irony that Blacks supposedly fighting for justice would bring that law down on themselves. Just four years after the celebratory climax of the civil rights movement in the 1965 Voting Rights Act, the times had clearly changed.

Certainly the sponsors of that law during the First Reconstruction could not have foreseen their bill being used to protect whites from Blacks. During the First Reconstruction, owning a better team of horses or hogs than your white neighbor could become an explosive symbol of Black empowerment that could lead to tragic white-on-Black violence. Black Power in the waning years of the Second Reconstruction (the civil rights movement) had come to mean something decidedly different. The propensity for some Black Power advocates to resort to violence—and the reluctance of many others to clearly dissociate themselves from the former—contributed to the beleaguered American public turning against further racial reform. In a sign of the still escalating violence surrounding the AAUO, one member who was indicted under that Reconstruction era law was spared potential conviction by his own murder one week prior to his trial in November 1969.[99]

These heightening concerns in the late 1960s caused many Americans, then, to begin to conflate social and economic reform movements with simple street crime. Such a conceptual association would not only be disastrous for fundraising activities by reform organizations, it would also bolster a public outcry for indiscriminate law enforcement action against anyone connected with those groups. Guilt by association followed. In those years, tremendous time and resources were placed into the surveillance, intelligence gathering, arrest, and trials of those identified with threatening reform. This careful pursuit by law enforcement only nurtured the widening fear among their targets of a conservative witch hunt. Such concerns would only multiply into growing polarization—and, at times, even paranoia—on both sides.

If BCA members were in fact guilty of narcotics charges and AAUO members of gun battles and unprovoked attacks on unarmed white civilians, the steady parade of criminal prosecution against a local nonviolent civil rights leader and dentist, Reginald Hawkins, and a low-paid antipoverty worker, Noble Coleman, seemed less explainable. Many local Blacks and their white liberal allies wondered if police would have invested so much into those prosecutions if they had been quiet community librarians. Likewise, local police spent a great deal of time and energy pursuing New Left activists for, among other things, stealing a neighbor's carton of orange juice. Even a judge agreed that some of the police's tactics constituted actual harassment.

Nevertheless, the dragnet of local and federal law enforcement pursuit had already closed in significantly. By now, the AAUO had virtually disappeared, and only a shell of the BCA remained. The organizations had lost much of their efficacy in attacking what they saw as the problems of the Queen City. The city's antipoverty programs were also in decline, and one of their leaders— Noble Coleman—had suffered his own series of criminal proceedings.

Not all the city's troublesome agitators had been removed from stirring up unnecessary turmoil, however. As the decade of the 1970s began, several of these militants would continue to undermine the determination for social stability in Charlotte and in North Carolina. Ben Chavis had returned to his hometown across the state, Oxford, by 1970. As trouble brewed in that tobacco town of the north-central part of North Carolina, he would draw in some of his old Charlotte cohorts, and there they would provoke yet another confrontation with the forces of law and order.

4

BLOOD REVOLUTION IN A TOBACCO TOWN

Racial Turmoil in Oxford, North Carolina

As law enforcement's crackdown on Black Power in Charlotte mounted, one affected activist left the Queen City to continue the cause across the state in the rural community of Oxford: Ben Chavis. No stranger to Oxford, Chavis was not only born and raised there, but came from one of the town's best-known African American families. Ben Chavis Jr.'s mother, Elisabeth Chavis, was a Granville county teacher for thirty-five years. His father, another longtime teacher in the county, also ran a restaurant, the Ridley Drive-In, which provided an important gathering place for the local Black community. He received his nickname "Major Chavis" in recognition of his status as a revered community leader, which largely extended to the white community as well. Oxford mayor Hugh Currin calls the couple "the nicest [people] that ever walked the face of this earth."[1] Their son, Ben Chavis Jr., now graduated from UNC Charlotte, followed his recently deceased father's calling to become a teacher in his hometown's predominantly Black high school.[2] He reopened his late father's restaurant as well, naming it Soul Kitchen. The restaurant quickly developed a clientele of young Blacks, as it was one of the few locations that welcomed them in the still largely segregated Oxford. The Soul Kitchen thus became a hangout for young Blacks hungry not just for the food but for racial progress. George Wright, a local African American activist with the NAACP, was not a frequent customer, but he did go occasionally to see his old friend Ben Chavis. "That was kind of a meeting place. I went down a couple of times and met some of his friends. Sometimes

I would go by and they were having meetings [to strategize for local racial change], and that's when I met [Jim] Grant," who stopped by occasionally to catch up with his fellow former Charlotte activist.[3]

Oxford was the seat for Granville County, an agricultural region in the north-central part of the state whose people had long made their living on tobacco. Due in part to the intense labor required for the crop's cultivation, the county had had the highest slave population in antebellum North Carolina. Long after the Civil War, Oxford continued to rely on tobacco production, boasting the oldest tobacco research facility in the world. The location of several warehouses in the downtown area curing local farmers' crops spoke to the leaf's central place in the county economy. By 1970, Oxford had a population of 7,600 and an emerging success at attracting small industries to the area as well. At least for the city's white population, the dawn of the 1970s was a hopeful time.[4]

Little, then, did white Oxfordians expect their town to fall prey to the racial conflicts sweeping through much of the nation in the late 1960s and early 1970s. The coming race riot in Oxford would pay dividends for state and federal law enforcement, by ensnaring one of the Charlotte Three (Jim Grant) in a precursor trial to the Charlotte Three case (the Raleigh Two trial), and set in motion the cooperation of two convict witnesses who became key factors in the Charlotte Three convictions two years later.

Black Oxfordians began 1970 hoping that they might turn the tide on the town's racial legacy. A campaign for racial change had begun there by the late 1950s, using the growing civil rights movement's nonviolent resistance tactics against local stores and restaurants and the town's movie theater.[5] The rising tension spilled over in the early 1960s in Grab-all, Oxford's main African American section. "[P]eople divided on very violent lines," local Black activist Ralph Hunt maintains. Because the main street through town, state Highway 15, ran directly through Grab-all, whites' cars gradually became targets of the long-festering resentment bred by Jim Crow. "Some [Black residents] went to their outhouses, filling jars with defecate and throwing it into people's cars as they were passing by. They were throwing it right into the windshield, and in the summertime back then lots of cars didn't have air conditioning, and they were throwing it inside the car."[6]

Another factor exacerbated Oxford's racial tensions. The longtime tobacco town in rural North Carolina was not isolated enough to avoid the on-set of Black Power. For George Wright, hardly an extremist, it had an im-portant influence on the town's African American community still struggling for their constitutional rights. Despite the gains made in the early 1960s in Oxford, segregation remained not just in the school system, but in many busi-nesses as well. To counteract the lingering segregation, Oxford's Black activ-ists resorted to economic boycotts. "When we withdrew our money it made a difference," contends Wright.[7]

For Wright, the use of these economic tactics went hand in hand with the advent of the Black Power movement. After the long and often torturous road to racial progress in Oxford, Black Power "started giving Blacks some personal pride," contends Wright. "Maybe we are something. Maybe together there's strength. And, it became customary to give the Black Power sign [as a greeting to other African Americans]. It did a lot to unite us as a people." Specifically, Wright maintains, Black Power "woke us up that we did have power and that it was economic." Hence, the use of that power through boycotting did finally shake the foundation of racial supremacy in Oxford.[8]

Assistant Police Chief Nathan White remembers that period in Oxford well. As anger among the town's Black poor escalated in the late 1960s, it spilled over into the streets. Sporadic small-scale violence sometimes gave way to Molotov cocktails among the township's disillusioned African Ameri-can youth. "It started in 1968 and went on into 1971," recounts the white police officer. "It was just kind of a [community racial] flareup. . . . You and your girl-friend might be coming on by in a car [through the working class Black neigh-borhood of Grab-all] and you stopped at a light. And, all at once a brick come out of the crowd [of Black youths] and hit the side of the car. You come over and report it, then [the perpetrators] go and scatter all about. . . . I didn't un-derstand" such acts of random violence. "I thought if something was wrong, you take it to a big meeting and discuss it—not the Molotov cocktails."[9]

White particularly cites one person as a principal instigator of the ran-dom racial violence of the late 1960s:

We had a fellow here named Ben Chavis. . . . He would go back in these alleys. . . . [H]e would go all in there and he'd be standing there [and whispering in a huddle with other young Black companions], and, then, when a police car would come by, then they'd stop [and talk casually to one another]. Then, a few minutes later, you'd get a call that someone had driven by and thrown a Molotov cocktail at a house. Then it would quiet down a little bit. It got so that all along there, it was thick [with young Blacks] on both sides of the street, and one car right after another [would be hit]—sometimes a brick hit the windshield, and it frightened a lot of people. And, it got [to be] a lot of disturbance of the Black against the white.

While White provides no direct evidence of any criminal wrongdoing on Chavis's part, certainly Chavis—and, later, his visiting friend Jim Grant—did continue to be associated in the minds of police with violence and conspiracy.[10]

Those rising tensions, however, were merely a prelude to a series of incidents in 1970 that would change this tobacco town forever. For activist Ralph Hunt, it began with a phone call in his Durham home. Having left Oxford in the mid-1960s for wider opportunities for a Black man in that much larger city nearby, Hunt would later become a successful businessman, a city councilman, Durham's mayor pro tem, a state senator, and a state utilities commissioner.[11]

On May 11, 1970, those individual achievements since leaving Oxford behind mattered little to him, as the racial limitations of white Oxford justice came flooding back. Willie Mae Marrow had called to say her husband—and Hunt's nephew—was on his way to a hospital in Durham. Hunt hurriedly made his way to meet the ambulance, but Willie Mae's husband, Henry, would be dead. Marrow's gunshot wounds to the back and head reportedly had been inflicted by white Oxford businessman Robert Teel for alleged suggestive comments made by Marrow to Teel's daughter-in-law. Marrow apparently had learned his Jim Crow lessons poorly: it was a cardinal rule that a Black man was never to intimate anything remotely sexual to a white woman.[12]

Ben Chavis was at his Oxford restaurant, Soul Kitchen, when word came. His cousin William Chavis had been wounded at the same shooting that killed Henry Marrow. Robert Teel and his eighteen-year-old son, Larry, were the suspects. Rumor had it that the local sheriff had initially refused to arrest the Teels until authorities became concerned about angry Blacks gathering on downtown Oxford street corners.[13] After the Teels' arrest at 6:00 A.M. Tuesday, a stormy crowd of Blacks began to congregate at the local jail.[14] It was a reversal of the long heritage of bristling white mobs menacing jails for Black suspects who might become lynching victims. In this case, the Teels were whisked away from the Granville County Jail to Raleigh under the heavy guard of the State Bureau of Investigation.[15] A racial uprising was soon to follow.

* * *

May 1970 was an ugly month for America. It had begun just after a presidential announcement: U.S. soldiers were crossing the Vietnamese border and invading Cambodia.[16] Americans embittered over a war in Vietnam now feared they would also have a war in Cambodia—and maybe someday in Laos as well. Tension only escalated when the president termed antiwar protestors "bums [who are] . . . blowing up the campuses."[17]

College students defiantly responded in the first few days of May. An Ohio State University protest of two thousand students for increased Black enrollment and abolition of the campus ROTC program took a tumultuous turn when one hundred of the demonstrators barricaded a campus entrance gate. As arriving police sought to reopen it, students greeted them with rocks and bottles, and then began a nine-hour rampage, drawing in an estimated four thousand students who smashed windows and stoned police. Four hundred police and twelve hundred National Guardsmen began taking occasional sniper fire from the crowd. Ninety-five injuries resulted (thirty-five police and sixty civilians—including eighteen students with police buckshot wounds). At the University of Maryland, some five hundred students demolished the ROTC building's windows and furnishings, and then set fire to the architecture building. Stanford University endured three gunshots at the university's ROTC commander's home, and a hail of rocks thrown at police. Two Molotov cocktails were thrown into Princeton University's ROTC building amid protests there.[18]

But the worst was yet to come. On May 4, four students' deaths from the rifles of National Guardsmen would come to be infamously associated with just two words: Kent State. "My God! They're killing us," freshman Ron Steele had exclaimed. Two of the dead had simply been on their way to class. Ohio governor James Rhodes, pursuing a U.S. Senate seat largely on the issue of his determination to end campus disorders, had already set a discordant tone a few days before the shootings. Coming to the campus amid protests over the Cambodian invasion that similarly inflamed campuses across the nation that first week of May, Rhodes had declared martial law, ordered in the National Guard, and called students engaged in window smashing and attempted fire-bombing of the ROTC building "worse than the 'brownshirt' and the Communist element and also the night-riders and the vigilantes . . . the worst type of people that we harbor in America. We are going to eradicate the problem," he warned the students. "It's over with in Ohio."[19]

He was wrong. It would be far from over there, or across the nation. The campus protest explosion that had begun in the days after Nixon's invasion announcement only blew higher and wider in the days after Kent State. Seventy-five thousand students descended on Washington, D.C. The National Guard was called out in Illinois, Maryland, New Mexico, Wisconsin, and Kentucky. Over twenty colleges reported riots, 536 shut down for at least one day over unrest related to Cambodia and Kent State, and fifty-one of those closed for the rest of the semester. When the month was over, more than thirty college ROTC buildings had been damaged by students, and 169 bombings and arsons had occurred—ninety-five of them on college campuses. In Buffalo, New York, students had thrown rocks at police and taunted, "Shoot me! Shoot me!"[20]

It was not just leftists, however, who were generating violence that month. As New York City's college students marched in the city's financial district, two hundred construction workers met them with anger, fists, crowbars, and metal wrenches. The "Hard Hat Riot" produced seventy injured students and a brief new historical phenomenon. The blue-collar ethnic whites had grown tired of the continuing protests of students raised in an era of prosperity and apparent contempt for traditional patriotism. The "hard hats" held a few more marches in New York City, and even ceremonially issued Richard Nixon an honorary hard hat. Violent street protest in May 1970, it seemed, had spread to conservatives as well.[21]

Behind the furor over the continuing Vietnam War that month lurked another lingering American specter: race. Ten days after four lay dead at Kent State University, the two issues made for an explosive mix on the grounds of Mississippi's historically African American college, Jackson State. Protests by students there ended in a macabre replay of the Kent State tragedy when police, apparently believing that they had been fired upon from a women's dormitory, let loose their considerable firepower. They sprayed approximately four hundred bullets and buckshot—including armor-piercing ammunition—

for thirty-five terrifying seconds into the women's dormitory building and the bodies of fourteen students, two of whom were killed. While the Jackson city police and state troopers had brought with them rifles, shotguns, carbines, and a submachine gun, they had left behind less lethal instruments. Notably, they had no tear gas. They had appeared to unleash their weaponry rather indiscriminately, as the five-story building was full of bullet holes, top to bottom; every window was shattered. There had been no warnings to the crowd, not even warning shots. When a presidential investigative commission reported a few months later, it criticized law enforcement behavior there as "an unreasonable, unjustified overreaction." Vice President Spiro Agnew saw it differently, terming the commission's report "pablum for permissivists."[22]

In a sober signal to activists reeling from these multiple law enforcement shootings, one day before the Jackson State incident a federal grand jury returned its findings on the December 1969 Chicago police shooting of Black Panther Fred Hampton. (Police had raided Hampton's apartment with a search warrant for a suspected cache of arms and ammunition and killed Hampton and fellow Panther Mark Clark—purportedly in self-defense.) The report criticized the Chicago Police Department for the raid itself (which it claimed was "not professionally planned or properly executed"), implied that officers were less than truthful after the raid (citing "irreconcilable disparity between the accounts given by the officers and the physical evidence"), and chastised the departmental investigation that followed the incident (which it contended "was conducted not to obtain all the available evidence but to try to establish the authenticity of the account given by the raiding officers"). The commission deemed the raid itself grounded in a fear of the Black Panthers "totally out of proportion to the minuscule number of members." On the other hand, the grand jury failed to return any indictments against any of the officers who had carried it out.[23] If the report seemed to confirm liberal suspicions that an open season on leftists remained in effect, the failure of the grand jury to issue any indictments against Chicago police suggested yet another case of miscarriage of justice when Black activists were involved.

One day before the Chicago report was issued, rioting in Augusta, Georgia, erupted. That proved disturbing for two reasons. First, it demonstrated that the violence that month was far from over. Second, the riots in Augusta defied southerners' reassuring stereotype that racial disturbances had finally traveled out of the South to the North and West by the mid-1960s. This was no Watts or Detroit or Newark—it was a relatively small city of seventy thousand, a symbol of southern gentility.

The Augusta unrest had begun with the death of a jailed sixteen-year-old mentally disabled African American youth, Charles Oatman. Outrage began over rumors that jailers had slain Oatman. While Oatman's killers proved to be fellow inmates, Black community outrage did not subside as facts of his death became public. Oatman had been burned and relentlessly beaten by his inmate attackers, resulting in his death by brain hemorrhage and fluid in the lungs. If his brutal death had not happened directly at the hands of his jailers, the mentally disabled boy had at least died while in their custody. A long-nurtured bitterness spilled into Augusta streets that night, as rioting and looting ensued.

At just the time a calming influence was desperately needed, Governor Lester Maddox stepped into the chaotic void instead. In his radio address that announced the mobilization of twelve hundred National Guardsmen and 150 state troopers, he decried "the Communist conspiracy" that was "trying to bring this country to its knees." As for the Guardsmen and troopers, "They're going in with live ammunition," he warned. "We're not going to tolerate anarchy in this state." "We're in a war at home," he later told law officers in Fort Valley, Georgia. "So when you're on the field of battle and someone shoots you down, on the way down—if you get a chance—you kill him, don't you?" When it was over, Augusta's casualties were tragically predictable: fifteen buildings burned, sixty injured, and six dead (all were Black). All six of the latter died of double-aught buckshot fire in the back—apparently fired by law enforcement.[24]

* * *

Details of events leading up to Henry Marrow's death at the hands of agitated white Oxfordians, which occurred the day before the Augusta riots, remain sketchy. The Reverend Vernon Tyson, a local pastor and member of Oxford's Human Relations Council, told the *Raleigh News and Observer* of a witness who informed him that Marrow and four other Blacks had taunted the Teels as they walked by their businesses in the shopping center, and then "made a remark to one of the girls in Teel's establishment." According to this account, the Teels then came out with guns.[25]

The son of a impoverished tenant farmer, Robert Teel had first come to Oxford from eastern North Carolina as a barber. After cutting the hair of many of the townspeople for fifteen years, Teel had made enough money to build a small shopping center in 1969 with a barber shop, a convenience store, a small motorcycle dealership, a car wash, and a laundromat on a corner adjacent to Grab-all. Teel's reputation for racism and a quick temper, when combined with his stores' location, spelled trouble; but Teel recognized that there was a lot of money to be made in Grab-all—particularly with his laundromat in a community where few residents had their own washing machines.[26]

If Teel had not garnered the admiration of Oxford's Black community, neither had he earned many friends in the police department. In less than a year before the Marrow shooting, he had gone to court on two separate cases of assaulting a police officer. Assistant Police Chief Nathan White remembers Robert Teel as a man who "just kind of drank and cut up all the time. He'd come up the street and talk with you, stomp down and get mad in just a matter of a few minutes." One month before the Marrow shooting, a local Black schoolteacher argued with Teel over poor treatment at the Teel car wash. Teel decided to settle the altercation with his pistol pointed at the man's head, and either slapped him or pistol-whipped him—depending on whose version is to be believed.[27]

Five days before Marrow's blood spilled, Teel appeared in court on charges of assault by pointing a gun and assault and battery on the teacher. The judge found Teel not guilty on the first charge and suspended judgement on the second, with an order to pay the teacher's $100 medical bill. The judge's decision continued Teel's remarkably good legal fortune. In February, a judge declined to activate two suspended sentences when he was convicted on a new criminal assault conviction (i.e, the judge could have easily forced Teel to begin serving those suspended sentences due to his new conviction). In April, Teel escaped that fate once again, walking out of court a free man. City Manager Tom Ragland claims that "he assaulted the same [white] police officer on two or three different occasions, and every time the judge would give him a lighter punishment. I remember that *distinctly*. It kind of got to be a bad joke: if he hit him one more time, they were liable to give him some kind of an award." To many African American residents, though, this was merely business as usual in a prejudicial system of justice. As one Black businessman later told reporters about the Black community's perception, if Teel had been Black he would have been "in jail after his first assault. There would have been no suspended sentences. Many of us feel that there is a dual standard of justice in Oxford."[28]

William Chavis, also wounded on the scene, was one of the four African Americans accompanying Marrow that day. He described the younger Teel, Larry, attacking Marrow with a stick. Then Chavis heard a shotgun blast and saw Marrow fall, hit in the legs and buttocks with shotgun pellets. Chavis himself was then hit in the forehead, neck, and shoulders with a second shotgun blast as the Teels stood over the prone Marrow. William Chavis recounted that Larry Teel began to kick Marrow, who told the assailants, "Okay, so you got me. Let's forget it." Chavis then recalled the elder Teel telling his son, "Shoot the son-of-a-bitch." Larry Teel allegedly did just that, firing into Marrow's forehead with a .22 rifle. "They were right on top of him," claimed William Chavis. "The barrel was down on his head, touching it."[29]

* * *

If the Oxford authorities had hoped that the arrest of a white citizen for the murder of the Black man would calm the unrest, they were sorely disappointed.[30] On the night of the murder (Monday, May 11), rumors abounded that carloads of Klansmen from surrounding areas, southern Virginia, South Carolina, and as far away as Tennessee had begun arriving to protect Teel's property.[31]

The rumors that Teel himself was a member of the Klan have never been confirmed. Tom Ragland, city manager at the time, and Mayor Currin insist that they've never seen any sign of KKK activity in the county. At the time of these riots and racial tension, contends Ragland, "Blacks, I think, sort of fantasized that all these people who acted like or looked like or were suspected of being anti-Black were members of the KKK." George Wright remembered the history of Granville County a little differently. "We have plenty of them here still, in the 1990s," he claimed. "In fact, I remember back in those days [the 1960s] a retired local court judge was hard of hearing and he went into the local Oxford bank. That story was that J. P. Harris—old man Harris—the president of the bank was there, and that this hard-of-hearing judge yelled across the bank, 'J. P., you going to the KKK meeting tonight?'"[32]

There were other indications of KKK activity in Granville County. In the 1960s and early 1970s, a billboard on Interstate 85 welcomed motorists to "Granville County. Ku Klux Country. Fight Integration and Communism." The sign caused Oxford officials dismay, including Ragland. He urged the state's Department of Transportation to have it removed. "It was right on the I-85. Shortly after that it disappeared—which it should have." Ragland was not the only one who noticed the sign. Certainly it was a cause of consternation for Oxford's Black citizens, but enough tourists were disturbed by the sign that several wrote the governor.[33]

George Wright was hardly alone in following KKK activity in the county. The State Highway Patrol, in fact, reported two Klan rallies in Granville County in 1967. Patrolmen estimated 500 people were at one that occurred just seven miles south of Oxford on private property, and 250 people were at the other. Each featured a cross burning.[34] Moreover, Assistant Police Chief Nathan White remembers such rallies off Highway 96, leading out of Oxford. "They gathered on a big field out there. . . . on Sunday afternoon when I'd be working. . . . Women and men stood up there and listened to [speakers]. . . . It was a nice gathering, just like you have been down the road with your wife or family or whatnot. Only most of them had on their white hoods, and they didn't make any bones about it." While there is nothing to suggest that fully robed Klansmen ever paraded through Oxford, White does recall such an event in Henderson, North Carolina—just eleven miles east of Oxford in neighboring Vance County.[35] More broadly, a 1965 congressional study revealed North Carolina to be "the most active Klan state in the nation."[36]

The night after the murder brought both a rally outside of Ben Chavis's Soul Kitchen restaurant and more rioting downtown. Groups of Black youths (police estimated the total to be seventy-five to one hundred) roamed the city, smashing seventeen storefront windows and starting several fires. Fires struck several sporadic locations, one of which was the car wash and shopping center owned by Teel. At least two firebombs were hurled into stores. "A large amount of car damage" also occurred, according to Oxford police chief D. E. White. Police reported thirty-five to forty Black youths throwing rocks at police cars, and a bullet fired from their direction hit one police car.[37]

The rioters operated with little police resistance. "We had a good police force," contends Hugh Currin, Oxford's mayor in 1970. "But, it was such a large number, it was just foolish to try to go down there and try to subdue it. So, we didn't do it. We stood and just watched, because if we had sent the police in to try and break up the riot, somebody would've gotten hurt. And, as it happened, nobody got hurt." Currin did patrol the town with the police chief, however. "If you want a good feeling [for what the riots were like], I'll tell you right now. I was in the South Pacific [in World War II] and I would've just about as soon have been back there as been in Oxford once those riots started." Currin had good reason to make the comparison. He was sitting in the front of that patrol car when a gunshot hit its rear passenger door. But Currin takes a forgiving view of the incident. "I think this," he insists. "If anybody wanted to shoot me, as close as they were—they were behind the wall—even though they were using a pistol and they were poor shots, they wouldn't have had a bit of trouble, because I wasn't more than ten feet away from them. I just think somebody shot to scare me."[38]

The damage could have been much worse. Responding to reports of the violence, George Wright rushed downtown to persuade the angry Black youths to go home. "I was one of the few who went downtown and tried to quiet [the rioters] down," he recalls. Due to Wright's civil rights background and his role as a youth adviser to the local NAACP, "They had a little respect for me. . . . And, believe me, that took some doing to go out there among those folks and try to stop them. . . . You had to go in [amidst the crowd] and talk and walk and keep talking and walking through all of them, so that all of them could hear what you were saying."[39]

On Wednesday, May 13, the governor's office declared a state of emergency for Oxford. At the request of Mayor Hugh Currin, he ordered thirty-eight riot-trained state highway patrolmen to supplement the sixteen-member local police force, with more on standby alert. Currin ordered a dusk-to-dawn curfew and enlisted the State Highway Patrol to service checkpoints entering and exiting the town, as well as to enforce the curfew.[40]

State Bureau of Investigation (SBI) agents also arrived in Oxford, and notified their superiors that the "Situation [in Oxford] is considered extremely tense." They noted that "several sources . . . feel there is a 50–50 chance that the curfew will work," but also surmised that "young Blacks are likely to be out looking for trouble anyway." During a rally the next day, SBI agents took note of several speakers' presence in Oxford: Ben Chavis, Jim Grant, Joe Goins of Charlotte, and Arch Foster of Durham. Chavis, Grant, and Goins would all later be connected to the 1972 trials of the Raleigh Two (the April 1972 federal trial of Chavis and Grant), the Charlotte Three, and the Wilmington Ten. (Foster was listed by the SBI as being "connected with the Black Panthers.") On the following day, SBI agents notified the SBI director that "it is . . . worthy of note that it is apparent that there is some outside agitation pursuant to the Oxford disruptions as two of the principal leaders in Black demonstrations and rallies held there yesterday were Arch Kenneth Foster, Black militant of Durham, and Black militant Benjamin Franklin Chavis of Charlotte. Both of these subjects are known Black Panther sympathizers in their respective cities." To describe Chavis's presence in his hometown, where he was also an employee of the public schools, as "outside agitation" is, of course, a rather loose interpretation of the phrase to say the least. However, SBI agents' association of him with Charlotte was a clear reflection of their documentation of his extensive activism in the Queen City.[41]

After the meeting, local white authorities sought out moderate Black leadership to denounce the violence. Several went on television and radio to do so. Sam Cox, a Black Oxford high school teacher and businessman, was among them. Acknowledging that "some people are going to be mad, but I'm going to say it anyway," he contended, "the court system here in Oxford has not been fair. But we can't solve this with violence, with this burning. We must be nonviolent."[42]

* * *

At 11:40 P.M. on Thursday, May 15, three young African Americans from Charlotte attempted to enter Oxford in their Budget rental car. Authorities at a South Oxford road checkpoint pulled them over in violation of the curfew and found seven sticks of dynamite, a .30-30 rifle with a power scope, a .22 red rifle, and a .25-caliber Spanish import pistol.[43] Walter David Washington, Theodore Alfred Hood, and Joseph Preston Goins were all charged with violating the curfew and the 1968 Federal Gun Control Act. Hood and Washington, of course, were cohorts of Grant and Chavis from Charlotte, and Goins was Grant's roommate. The three told authorities that Grant, who had already come to Oxford to join Chavis, had called and asked them to make the drive. Grant and Chavis would later disavow any knowledge or connection to the explosives that the three men carried.[44]

As Mayor Hugh Currin remembered it, the state troopers "had a checkpoint and these people [Hood, Washington, and Goins] were coming into town and took the wrong road, and they drove right up to where the checkpoint was." City Manager Tom Ragland remembers when the men were brought into the police station, where Ragland remained during the riots to monitor the crisis: "They were stopped and they brought all three of them down to the police station. I remember that. The deal was that they had high-powered weapons and some dynamite in their car." News of the arrest quickly spread. "It alarmed people," contends Dan Finch, chair of the town's Human Relations Council. "It was very much the talk of the town—parlor talk, coffee talk."[45]

It turned out to be more than parlor talk. It had law enforcement agents taking note as well. North Carolina's SBI agents wrote the SBI director the next day of the event: "It should be noted for your consideration that three subjects (all black) were apprehended" who "were all three from Charlotte and are known to have Black Panther leanings in that city." The report then explicitly named Goins, Hood, and Washington and added that "known Charlotte Black Panther Jim Grant has been observed in the Oxford area."[46]

Twenty-eight years later, both Mayor Currin and City Manager Ragland remembered Grant's name. "Grant was the man who had a degree in chemical engineering. He was an expert in starting fires. . . . He could start a fire in a rainstorm," recounted Ragland. "Word was around that he and Ben Chavis were mighty close." Among the law officials who had gathered to assist Oxford's police—including the State Highway Patrol, the FBI, federal Alcohol, Tobacco, and Firearms agents, and the SBI—Grant's reputation for "starting fires" "got to be a pretty well known fact," according to Ragland. It "was common knowledge among the police organizations of just about everybody around here." As such, contends Ragland, he was closely watched. "It was a well-known fact that the way they [Grant and militants like him] operated was—you see, adults did not do the burning. They trained these little kids to do it on the theory that if they got caught, there wouldn't be much punishment because they're minors. They were the ones that were out doing the real stuff, and the other people were behind the scenes instructing them." Like Chavis, though, these rumors on Grant remained unsubstantiated, at least until his controversial 1972 conviction in the Charlotte Three case.[47]

Ultimately, however, what Grant, Chavis, and civil rights militants of the late 1960s and early 1970s had in mind was far more extensive than starting a few fires, according to Ragland.

> What this was all about from day one was organized on the part of the Black Panthers to bring about an improved situation for the Black race. It has been referred to as a conspiracy—you can go with a 'plan' or a 'conspiracy' or whatever you want to call it. But, from my point of view, what happened here in Oxford was that the fire got a little hotter and a little more serious . . . than anybody anticipated it would. I am of the opinion that the guy that got killed [Marrow] was sent there to begin with to provoke some kind of confrontation. Nobody, I don't think, really ever thought it would turn into a murder. In 1974—four years later—I was at a meeting in Atlanta, Georgia. . . . We had people from all over the southeastern United States, and . . . I got to talking to some of these folks. And they really opened up my eyes. I come to find out that the same thing that was going on here in Oxford in 1970 was going on in a lot of towns in the southeastern United States, and probably in towns outside of the southeastern United States. In other words, what I'm saying is that I believe it was all planned with goals and objectives, and, to accomplish certain goals and objectives over a period of time. If you go back into your civil rights efforts and all the things that occurred, sooner or later it will point to another thing which I believe to be a fact of life. In the history of human beings—you can go back and you can read history for centuries and centuries and centuries—and here's what you'll find: nothing significant ever happened in the tradition of the human race short of a blood revolution. Now, you may think that's strange, but if you go back and read, all the significant points and changes have occurred and only occurred after a blood revolution. Changes don't happen when people sit down and talk. And I'm not advocating revolution, you know, but looking at it from the perspective of centuries of history—that's what you'll find. . . . And this ought to fall into that category. It wasn't quite as bloody as some of the others. But, nevertheless, underneath it all, it was a revolution that was going on step by step.[48]

Hood, twenty-three at the time, and Goins, twenty-four, were each held on a $20,000 bond. Washington, then twenty-three, was also charged with violation of the 1968 Omnibus Crime Control and Safe Streets Act—one of the signature acts of the late 1960s federal campaign against crime. He was given a $25,000 bond. Their bonds were reduced to $15,000 each two days later, which they later met, and they were released.[49] Their federal trial was set for September 14, 1970.[50]

* * *

It would take several months for civic calm to return to Oxford. Boycotts and demonstrations would continue throughout the summer and into the fall. The riots were not over, either. What the *Oxford Public Ledger* termed "the most devastating fire in Oxford history" took place one week after Marrow's death. Two large downtown warehouses of tobacco—the economic lifeblood of Oxford—went up in a firebombed blaze that lit the town's night sky, doing an estimated $1 million in damage. The day before, an office building and several local businesses also were firebombed.[51]

The escalating attack on Oxford's white community sobered many civic leaders. John Nelms, chair of the Oxford City Planning Commission, contended, "Feelings are very bad in the white community. Many whites feel as though they've been betrayed. Either that, or they're afraid they might be burned next." Mayor Currin again called on assistance from the State Highway Patrol. In addition to the worries of further rioting, concerns escalated that the continuing racial unrest was attracting white racists into Oxford. The night after the warehouse firebombing, Currin told the State Highway Patrol of a rumor that "KKK members were coming into town in an attempt to burn a Negro establishment in retaliation of attempted burnings by Negroes in Oxford." Oxford, it seemed, had become a racial powder keg.[52] Further stirring white angst was the arrival of Charlotte civil rights leader Reginald Hawkins and Golden Frinks, a field secretary with the Southern Christian Leadership Conference civil rights organization. Among other things, they helped lead a march to the state capitol.[53]

What followed was a remarkable series of changes to the town's racial structure. In the week following the riots, several members of the local Human Relations Committee called a special, unprecedented open meeting of the citizenry simply to listen to the Black community's concerns. The meeting was intended to be—in the words of its chairman, Dan Finch—"a sounding board, an open forum for discussion in an atmosphere of mutual respect."[54] Local Black leader Sam Cox told the racially mixed group of approximately 120 that "there is no justice in the judicial system of Granville County. That is the crux. Something needs to be done about it." Reflecting the white community's concern about continued unrest, City Manager Tom Ragland told the assembled Blacks, "You've got our attention. We're not going to sit dumb as we have in the past. I think that now something will be done. The judicial system must serve the people and not the system."[55] Outside, approximately two hundred African American high school-age students marched; a leader shouted, "We're going back to our community and we ain't going to let no white folks in."[56]

The Oxford Board of Commissioners called a special meeting to deal with the grievances submitted by Black leaders. Reforms followed in quick succession. The commissioners quickly authorized the promotion of an African American police officer.[57] Mayor Currin agreed to present federal guidelines on hiring discrimination to the Chamber of Commerce and pressure it for better enforcement.[58]

Much remained to be done, but now the cause of racial change snowballed. In the coming months, a series of boycotts and picketing campaigns were used against white-owned stores that practiced discriminatory hiring and segregation. Hence, the economic power exercised by the Black community in the months after the riots became an extension of the threat to whites' homes and businesses posed by the rioting. "A lot got done" in those months, contends Wright. "To save your town and to save your pocketbook and to save your property, you'll do things, you know. But we had to *make* them do it. It was not voluntary. We had to threaten their livelihood. That was the only way we got anything done."[59]

By the end of that tumultuous year, the white businesses had capitulated, and a sea change had occurred in Oxford's racial practices, if not in its psychological attitudes. The gradual hiring of Blacks as store employees was the particular victory that African American activists had won. The fact that rioting was the beginning of that long-sought racial progress is bittersweet for George Wright. No admirer of violence, Wright begrudgingly now admits that the violent uprising "in a strange way" may have finally been the cause of the white community's mobilization to respond to Black concerns. "[B]ut my thing is that, like most Blacks, I believe 'Let's get along. Let's live together.' And my only reason for going down there [on the first night of the riots] was just for that reason: 'We still got to live with white folks.' You know, 'Let's not burn our town down. Let's not get our young people in jail.' Because I know eventually that we don't want to have to pay the price. But there comes a time when people have just had all they can take, and you never know which straw's going to break the camel's back."[60]

* * *

Despite the civil rights gains achieved, there was another, less hopeful end to the drama. For Henry Marrow, there was the matter of justice. And for Oxford's Black community as well, making progress at lunch counters would not necessarily mean progress in the judicial system.

In Marrow's death, Robert Teel was charged with "murder by aiding and abetting." Teel's eighteen-year-old son Larry was charged with outright murder. As their July 1970 trial began, the courthouse took no chances. Seven highway patrolmen stationed inside the courtroom searched those entering. Rumors had flown that Black Panthers had come to the proceedings. Defense attorneys stationed armed guards at their offices, and lead defense attorney Billy Watkins had another armed guard watch over his home.[61]

Joining the prosecution was NAACP attorney James Ferguson. "We called the NAACP down in Charlotte," Ralph Hunt recalls, "and, of course, they sent him up here because . . . it appeared as though this was a good case for them to be a part of." A native of Asheville, North Carolina, Ferguson had joined the civil rights movement in the late 1950s by founding the Asheville Student Committee on Racial Equality. He then left for college at North Carolina Central University. Never forgetting the two African American lawyers who had helped him and his student activist cohorts in Asheville, he took his undergraduate degree to Columbia University Law School to make his professional career a continuation of his passion for racial and social change. "You don't ever put your idealism aside. You keep it in front of you," he would later insist to a journalist. Ferguson had first come to Charlotte in 1967 to join noted civil rights attorney Julius Chambers. Together with new white colleague Adam

Stein, Ferguson and Chambers formed the state's first integrated law firm. In subsequent years, Ferguson also served as Reginald Hawkins's gubernatorial campaign manager.[62]

The evidence against Robert and Larry Teel was considerable. The defendants had already admitted to being the ones at the scene of the crime. Numerous eyewitnesses corroborated William Chavis's account of Marrow's death at the hand of the Teels.[63]

On the third day of testimony, the Teel trial took an unexpected turn. Several eyewitness accounts of the shooting included the memory of a third white man with the two Teels, but the "third man" remained a mystery to the police and the prosecution until Teel's stepson, Roger Oakley, took the stand. Oakley claimed to not only have been at the scene, but that he held the murder weapon when the fatal shot was fired. Oakley contended, however, that he did not intentionally shoot at Marrow. Instead, he asserted, "somebody pushed my shoulder . . . and, the gun went off" after Larry Teel had removed a knife brandished by Marrow. When District Attorney W. H. Burgwyn cross-examined Oakley about that testimony, Oakley declined to answer any questions about firing any other shots than the fatal one by citing his Fifth Amendment right against self-incrimination. Exasperated with the logic of refusing questioning on the grounds of self-incrimination after confessing to holding the murder weapon, Burgwyn asked Oakley, "Don't you think you've already incriminated yourself?" The testimony, if true, meant not only that this had been an accidental shooting, but also that prosecutors did not even have the man who held the gun on trial.[64]

It took less than twenty-four hours for the all-white jury to reach its not guilty verdicts. As Ralph Hunt sat next to the newly widowed, pregnant wife of his deceased nephew, he could not shake his resentment of the sheriff's behavior toward Teel's mother earlier in the trial. Hunt had observed Teel's mother "sobbing and carrying on—I don't know whether it was genuine or not and whether it influenced the jury. But while she was doing that, the sheriff during the course of the trial came over and patted her on the shoulder with his hand. You know what I mean? It was just that blatant. And the Ku Klux Klan was over there standing along the wall to sort of protect against anything which might happen. And, you know, we had more reason to sob and carry on. One of our family members had been murdered." Laughing in disbelief,

Hunt muses, "And, I'm sure he got reelected—the sheriff—by the element that you would associate with that type of support."[65]

Despite the acquittals, Judge Robert Martin issued bench warrants (a preliminary move authorizing police to question someone suspected of a crime) for Roger Oakley, Robert Teel, and Larry Teel over the courtroom revelations of their involvement in Marrow's death. (Oakley and Robert Teel were given bench warrants for first degree murder, and Larry Teel for assault inflicting serious injury). The judge's intercession would come to nothing, however. A grand jury refused to follow through with formal indictments, and no one was ever convicted of anything for Marrow's death.[66] Several months later, Robert Teel's three businesses burned down in what authorities concluded was arson. His dreams of wealth had run aground years later with a much smaller home and a single small barbershop outside of town; nevertheless, the Marrow family could not mistake that Teel left the Granville County Courthouse with both his life and his freedom on that late summer day in 1970.[67] No matter whatever positive changes may have arrived in the streets outside, the narrative of the justice system for Black Oxfordians seemed all too tragically familiar.

As Robert Teel continued his judicial good fortune, the events in Oxford would lead to still unforeseen prosecutions in the coming few years. Armed with the new federal crime legislation, federal law enforcement agents would use the Oxford events to begin building their case against Jim Grant and his fellow Charlotte activists. They would do so with the strangest of allies: Al Hood and Dave Washington, the very men who had been identified with a lengthy list of violent crimes, including the most recent attempt to smuggle dynamite and several firearms into a riot area. These were strange times indeed.

5

STRANGE BEDFELLOWS

Al Hood, Dave Washington, and the War on Crime

Like so many of the militants it would become his job to pursue, Bill Walden was an outsider to North Carolina. "I was born in a deep holler in East Kentucky," he recalls. "I had to look up to see the sun. It was an area of the world some people call the armpit of the universe." It was a hard life that Walden largely shrugs off. When he was two years old, his mother died "and my father just wasn't able to care for me by himself." Walden's childhood became chaotic, shifting between "aunts, uncles, friends and relatives. I traveled all over—Texas, Florida, North Carolina." After this nomadic existence at such a young age, the young white man finally found a resting place for a few years with a North Carolina couple who were not blood-related. "When I was 14, I hopped a freight from Texas to Asheville and hooked up with a family I had met before that had three other children, and they became my substitute parents."[1]

Walden earned a bachelor's degree at North Carolina State University in Raleigh and then settled into a life as an insurance company claims adjuster and investigator in the early 1960s. With his wife and three kids, and a tobacco farm on the side, he might have built the kind of quiet stability he had never known before. But Bill Walden still had a restlessness about him. "I was looking for something better, something more interesting and better paying." So, he applied for a job with the U.S. Treasury Department's Bureau of Alcohol, Tobacco, and Firearms (ATF). "The ATF turned out to be very interesting and kept your adrenaline flowing. I liked that."[2]

Walden started his career with the ATF in 1964, during the thick of the southern civil rights movement. He was stationed in Birmingham. Certainly he is not alone in his assessment of the city in the mid-1960s: "Birmingham was touchy then. There was a lot of violence." Nevertheless, Walden began his career with the ATF during an era when the agents had a limited jurisdiction. It was the FBI's role to investigate the murders and injuries that came to be associated with Alabama's racial violence. Walden, instead, spent most of his time pursuing moonshine cases.[3]

All that suddenly changed in 1968. Congress's passage of the Gun Control Act in the War on Crime quickly widened the ATF's responsibilities. Without the expanded power to pursue federal cases involving firebombs and guns under the new law, Walden might never have been involved in the three 1972 cases involving North Carolina civil rights activists: the Raleigh Two, the Charlotte Three, and the Wilmington Ten.

It was still a volatile time, with many racial disturbances and with activists eagerly pursuing social change. Ben Chavis and Jim Grant had left the trouble in Oxford for other North Carolina locales. Grant kept up his frantic pace of traveling around the state to racial trouble spots. He remained an enigmatic figure to many. "The character of Jim Grant," contends fellow activist Marvin Sparrow, "is that he goes here and he goes there and you never get any sense of where he is. So he would just show up every once in a while, and say, 'Hey, what's going on?' and sit down and talk to you for a while. But he put just thousands and thousands of miles on his car because he drove all over the state doing organizing stuff."[4] As for Chavis, the Reverend Leon White (the African American director for the North Carolina and Virginia division of the United Church of Christ's Commission for Racial Justice) had noticed the young man through publicity on the Oxford disturbances and had hired him. During the next few years, Chavis traveled throughout North Carolina, and Virginia, aiding and assisting local movements. Chavis would become a veteran community organizing troubleshooter for the commission, earning his stripes in 1970 and 1971 in such North Carolina communities as Henderson, Warrenton, Elizabethtown, and Wilmington.[5]

Grant's and Chavis's days of agitation were running short. The arrest of Black Charlotteans Al Hood and Dave Washington for possession of dynamite, which had shaken the town of Oxford, would prove to have even more far-reaching implications than could have been foreseen. Their ensnarement by federal authorities would eventually provide investigators with the leverage necessary to force the two convicts to testify in two important cases: the federal April 1972 Raleigh Two case, and the state's July 1972 Charlotte Three case. For the former trial, Hood and Washington implicated longtime agitators Jim Grant and Ben Chavis for aiding and abetting the witnesses' flight from federal charges stemming from carrying dynamite and firearms into Oxford. In the Charlotte Three case, Hood and Washington would allege that Grant and his cohorts, antipoverty workers T. J. Reddy and Charles Parker, were responsible for an unsolved 1968 horse stables burning. The national obsession over crime would pave the way for the extensive outlay of interest and resources in these cases.

* * *

Urban rioting was one clear cause of the public outcry over crime in the late 1960s and early 1970s. Examining the ways in which many of the larger riots had begun reveals one notable similarity: police action. The uprisings in 1964 Harlem and 1966 San Francisco and Atlanta had all exploded with the shooting of an African American teenager by a white police officer. Likewise, the 1964 Philadelphia riot, the 1965 Watts riot in Los Angeles, and the 1967 Newark riot all began with routine traffic stops that went awry. The 1967 Detroit riot began with a police raid on a ghetto tavern. President Lyndon Johnson's National Advisory Commission on Civil Disorders (better known as the Kerner Commission) examined these uprisings, and in its 1968 report it contended that the prime catalyst was lingering racism. The Kerner Commission, chaired by Illinois governor Otto Kerner, saw a nation disturbingly "moving toward two societies, one black, one white—separate and unequal."[6]

The intense difficulties of battling this widening social crisis began to show. In response to the March 1968 release of the Kerner Commission report, an exasperated spokesman for the New Jersey State Patrolmen's Benevolent Association asked of the commissioners and public:

> When a law enforcement officer, faced with the extremely dangerous task of quelling what is in fact an armed rebellion, is the target of snipers' bullets, rocks and bottles, just exactly what constitutes "undue force"? Were any of the commissioners who accuse police of using undue force on the firing line? Do they really know what they are talking about? Use of the term "undue force"

is an exercise in tortured semantics that police refuse to accept. Not only is the charge without merit, it is an insult to brave men who risked their lives for the public and equally unacceptable to reasonable people.[7]

These difficult times also bred an increase in police brutality claims as inner-city citizens of color grew increasingly alienated from law officers. The New Jersey governor's Select Commission on Civil Disorder contended that "there was virtually a complete breakdown in the relations between police and the Negro community prior to the disorders. . . . Distrust, resentment and bitterness were at a high level on both sides."[8]

A series of U.S. Supreme Court decisions that bolstered defendant rights in the 1960s, often called the "due process revolution," drove a further wedge into the growing polarization. In *Mapp v. Ohio* (1961), the Supreme Court ruled that any evidence obtained through an unreasonable search should be excluded in both federal and state courts. In the 1963 decision *Gideon v. Wainwright*, the court ruled that an impoverished defendant had the right to a state-paid attorney. The most controversial Supreme Court decisions, however, protected a defendant's right against self-incrimination: *Escobedo v. Illinois* (1964) ensured a suspect's right to consult with an attorney as soon as police were targeting that suspect for the crime, and *Miranda v. Arizona* (1966) guaranteed a suspect's right to be warned of his rights at the time of his arrest.[9]

Senate hearings on crime before the Subcommittee on Criminal Laws and Procedures in 1967 and 1968 became an important forum for the "law and order" reaction to these Supreme Court reforms. Quinn Tamm, executive director of the International Association of Chiefs of Police, indicated his "firm opinion that the majority of the decent people of this country had had about enough of a judicial system which allows criminals to roam the streets and commit vicious, depraved acts time after time." Tamm pointed to the lack of "more realistic Supreme Court decisions" as the cause. Likewise, Pennsylvania Supreme Court justice Michael Musmanno told the subcommittee that the recent Supreme Court decisions had created an environment wherein "many cancerous criminals and pestilential psychopaths are stalking the streets of the nation, polluting the communities through which they move" simply because police had "failed to administer the paregoric [recitation of rights] prescribed in *Miranda*."[10]

Senate subcommittee chair John McClellan had opened the hearings in 1967 during Law Enforcement Week with the immodest prediction that it was "quite probable that these hearings and the bills we will be considering will mark the turning point in the struggle against lawlessness in this nation."[11] An important law did, in fact, originate from the subcommittee: the 1968 Omnibus Crime Control and Safe Streets Act. The 1968 statute made possible the widened use of electronic surveillance by law enforcement, sought to circumvent three recent U.S. Supreme Court decisions (*Mallory v. U.S.*, *Miranda v. Arizona*, and *U.S. v. Wade*) that would have restricted the admissibility of certain confessions and line-up identifications, and established the Law Enforcement Assistance Administration (LEAA) to disburse large-scale law enforcement funds to the states. North Carolina, in fact, would receive its own large block grants from the LEAA.[12]

But this was by no means the only federal governmental action on the "law and order" issue. Four years before Richard Nixon rode the tidal wave of public fears over the issue to the White House, Republican presidential candidate Barry Goldwater had already sounded the alarm. In a September 1964 campaign stop, he decried the recent series of Supreme Court decisions on defendants' rights. If elected president, Goldwater promised to appoint the federal judges necessary to "redress constitutional interpretations in favor of the public." Criminals, he charged, were being overly indulged "just to give [them] a sporting chance to go free." It was time for a president, he asserted, who would "use [his] power and influence to see that law enforcement officers, on the state and local level, get back the power to carry out their job."[13]

Goldwater's determination to make "the abuse of law and order in this country . . . [an] issue" in the 1964 presidential campaign signaled an important political shift. The federal government had concerned itself with special crime-related issues in the past, such as the Communist-targeted Red Scares (which followed each of the world wars of the twentieth century) and the rise of prohibition-related organized crime. Now, however, it focused on ordinary crime as well—the rise in assaults, robberies, and other violent crimes that seemed to undermine the very everyday quality of American life. During the following six years, the U.S. Congress enacted some sixteen different national crime control bills, including the Law Assistance Act of 1965, the Bail Reform Act, the D.C. Crime Control Act, the Anti-Riot Act, and the Organized Crime

Control Act. The horrifying wave of assassinations in the 1960s made these bills' path to adoption especially smooth. The Omnibus Crime Control and Safe Streets Act passed two days after Sirhan Sirhan felled presidential candidate Robert Kennedy.[14]

Lyndon Johnson had not been immune to the public outcry over crime. Noting the political danger of not addressing the issue, President Johnson established the President's Crime Commission in 1965 to study the matter, called for a War on Crime, and pushed parts of the Omnibus Crime Control and Safe Streets Act through Congress (even though he felt the final product included some elements that went too far). It was not the presidency of Johnson that would carry the banner for the cause of "law and order" fully, however. Johnson showed signs of tentativeness on the issue of crime during his tenure even as he bowed to political and public pressure. His attorney general, Ramsey Clark, in fact, had come to fear the increasingly extremist rhetoric among conservatives. Clark worried that should he continue to reject conservatives' rising demands to increase sharply federal troop presence in local racial disorders, "It is quite possible that the commanding generals would get together and take over. Of course, like putting the troops there in the first place, it would all be done in the name of saving the country."[15] Such reluctance to fully embrace the new War on Crime caused Clark's detractors to dub him "Ramsey the marshmallow."[16]

But a new wind was blowing as Richard Nixon steadied himself for his ascent to the Oval Office. Not only would the wiretapping expansion provision of the 1968 Omnibus Crime Control and Safe Streets Act not be repealed by Congress (as Attorney General Clark had hoped), but the new Nixon administration lacked the qualms over surveillance that had come to characterize the Johnson administration. Nixon's attorney general, John Mitchell, sought to clearly differentiate himself from his liberal predecessor: "There's a difference between my philosophy and Ramsey Clark's. I think this is an institution for law enforcement, not social improvement." On college campus demonstrators, Mitchell was equally unswerving. "When you get nihilists on campus," he reasoned, "the thing to do is to get them into court."[17] While Richard Nixon had declared on election night that "bring us together" would be the theme of his presidency, his vice president later provided further clarification. "It is time to rip away the rhetoric and to divide on authentic lines," contended

Sprio Agnew. "When the President said 'bring us together,' he meant the functioning, contributing portions of the American citizenry."[18]

Early on, Nixon and Mitchell set about demonstrating their distaste for Johnson's more liberal approach to national crime and unrest. A new environment clearly reigned in the White House. The president's legal counsel, John Dean, would oversee an "enemies list" that fulfilled the purpose—as he bluntly characterized it—of using "the available federal machinery to screw our political enemies."[19] Twenty-nine-year-old White House staffer Tom Huston was charged with devising a proposal for expanding domestic surveillance in June 1970. The resulting Huston Plan was a wide-ranging proposal to improve the administration's domestic intelligence on leftist organizations, including electronic surveillance, mail openings, "surreptitious entry" (law enforcement agent break-ins without a warrant), and an increase in campus informants and military undercover agents. Huston himself, in a secret memo, conceded that at least two of the recommendations in the report—which would be approved by President Nixon—were illegal. Use of the "surreptitious entry" recommendations, he informed the president, would be "clearly illegal: it amounts to burglary."[20] Nixon contended that he later rescinded his approval of the Huston Plan when FBI Director J. Edgar Hoover voiced objections. True or not, some of its recommendations clearly went into effect.[21]

Chief among the recommendations was the Intelligence Evaluation Committee (IEC), formed in December 1970. The committee included representatives from the White House, FBI, the Justice Department, the CIA, the Defense Department, the National Security Agency, the Secret Service, and the Treasury Department. Its charge was to share domestic intelligence information and thus provide the president with a better source of intelligence on leftists' activities.[22] Outside of the IEC meetings, the participating federal agencies were hard at work expanding their domestic intelligence activities—from the CIA's MERRIMAC program and Operation CHAOS to the FBI's COINTELPRO, the military's CONUS program, the National Security Agency's MINARET program, and the IRS's Special Service staff.[23]

Chosen to head the IEC was Assistant Attorney General Robert Mardian.[24] Mardian, a muscular, opinionated, and sometimes combative man, had earned the reputation of a stalwart conservative with what John Dean called "very far right" political views. His nickname among detractors was "Crazy Bob." An

Arizona native, he had managed the western states for Barry Goldwater's unsuccessful 1964 presidential bid, then performed the same function for Richard Nixon in 1968. Nixon rewarded him with the post of general counsel to the Department of Health, Education, and Welfare. There he worked doggedly to soften school desegregation guidelines, alienating many of the remaining liberals in the department. He then took over the Justice Department's Internal Security Division (ISD), rejuvenating a division that had grown lifeless since the Second Red Scare of the 1940s and 1950s. Under Mardian's watch, the ISD pursued a number of federal conspiracy cases against leftists, including the Harrisburg Seven, the Seattle Seven, the VVAW Eight (of the Vietnam Veterans Against the War), and the Camden Twenty-Eight. Impressed by Tom Huston's work, Mardian tried to hire him as his own deputy, but even the crafter of the controversial Huston Plan deemed Mardian overly zealous. "Mardian didn't know the difference between a kid with a beard and a kid with a bomb," said Huston. Mardian would come to play his own direct role in the Charlotte Three case.[25]

* * *

For Bill Walden and his ATF colleagues, the 1968 Gun Control Act opened up whole new areas for their criminal investigation. "Title 2 of the Gun Control Act regulated destructive devices—bombs," recounts Walden, which gave the ATF responsibility for overseeing their lawful enforcement. The historically territorial FBI and its headline-seeking director, J. Edgar Hoover, were not enthusiastic. "The Gun Control Act caused some resentment on the part of the FBI. It expanded ATF jurisdiction [into traditionally exclusive FBI territory on the federal level]." It is interesting to note that, in Walden's view, the new law may have saved the ATF from becoming a largely obsolete agency. "The truth was that the moonshine industry was disappearing," maintains Walden. "There were reasons for this. Some people claimed that it was because we had done such a good job. Certainly that was part of it, but also the price of sugar had gone up, making it more expensive, and difficult to compete with legitimate producers." Despite the law ensuring his continued ATF paycheck, even Walden contends that "[a] lot of the Gun Control Act was written in haste, after the [Robert] Kennedy assassination. Some of it bordered on unconstitutional and hard as hell to enforce."[26]

Bill Walden was reassigned to North Carolina in 1969, where he was stationed principally in the Raleigh area. But Walden also enjoyed a certain "latitude to investigate what was necessary. Eventually I started working more complicated investigations—conspiracy, for example. They gave me a hell of a lot of latitude to follow up on stuff. Some of these investigations were to take months. . . . If I felt some lead needed to be chased, I would pretty much go ahead and do it." Now that ATF agents' responsibilities expanded, Walden and his colleagues "went to 'bomb schools,' and we also traveled around North Carolina educating local law enforcement agencies about bombs and explosives. I must have traveled from one end of the state to the other doing that."[27]

Not all of Walden's time, of course, was spent as a traveling educator. His job often took him right into the heart of some of North Carolina's most explosive situations. So it was that "the State Highway Patrol called me at 2:00 A.M. from Oxford [during the May 1970 racial unrest] to come in. I got out of bed and drove up there with another agent. They had Al Hood, Dave Washington, and Joe Goins in custody" for carrying guns and dynamite into the riot-restricted Oxford. "I didn't know what I was getting into at the time. These guys were under my jurisdiction under federal law [for violating the Gun Control Act], and I remember photographing them. I would tell them to turn to the left and turn to the right, but when Goins came in he did that automatically without me having to tell him. And I said, 'Oh boy, what have we got here,' because I knew right away that he was a guy used to being arrested."[28]

The three men met their bonds and awaited their September 14, 1970, federal trial. Hood and Washington failed to appear, and warrants were issued for bond default. Goins did show, but prosecutors dropped the charges, saying officially that the case against him was weak.[29] That determination was no doubt driven by the clandestine fact that Goins—Jim Grant's roommate—was an FBI informant, although Walden noted in a June 1971 memo that "during the time of this disturbance, his presence or whereabouts were unknown to them [FBI personnel]."[30]

Hood and Washington had gone to Canada. After a week's stay at the Toronto YMCA, they tired of their exile and returned to Charlotte. There they now faced further charges on bond jumping.[31] Washington began negotiating through his attorney to turn himself in to authorities. He finally did so two days after Christmas.[32]

Washington attended a pretrial hearing on the bond-jumping charges on February 1, 1971. His attorney informed the court of his history of psychiatric difficulty and his placement on 100 percent mental disability, and the judge released him to the psychiatric observation of the Springfield, Missouri, Veterans Administration hospital (his sixth trip in five years to a mental institution).[33] The hospital released Washington to federal authorities approximately two months later. His medical reports pronouncing him to have "schizophrenic tendencies" added, "but at this time is confident and rational."[34] Washington returned to Raleigh in April under federal custody to hear that Hood had been held in Charlotte for armed robbery since February 19, 1971. Federal agents also told Washington that Hood was beginning to talk to them about the same alleged crimes Washington had previously discussed.[35]

Hood and Washington had not always talked so readily to authorities. Early on in their imprisonment for the bail-jumping charges, Walden remembers, the two men "thought they were the last of the tough guys. They told me, 'We've had a lot of Black Panther training. We can stay in here as long as possible, as long as it takes.' So I left them alone in jail for a few months and came back, and their feelings had started to change. I told them, 'Who's driving around in a Cadillac while you're stuck in here? You say you're making a sacrifice for your cause, but what are your leaders doing out there while you're paying the price in here?' They came around, and started talking about their leaders."[36]

On March 15, 1971, Hood signed a sworn statement to Walden implicating Grant and Chavis for conspiracy in his and Washington's 1970 bail jumping. Hood contended that Grant contacted them in Charlotte after their bond release on the Oxford arrest and encouraged them to leave the country "because he did not think it wise for them to go to court in this case."[37] Hood claimed that Grant gave them contacts' names in Toronto and a check for $150 drawn on a "Black People's Society" account in Shelby, North Carolina, for which Grant was the treasurer. He then put them on a bus for Durham, North Carolina, with instructions to meet Chavis in Oxford and cash the check. Hood stated that Chavis gave them extra money and deposited them on Oxford's outskirts, where they were to hitchhike to Canada to conceal their whereabouts. Once in Canada, Hood asserted, Grant and Chavis planned to get the two fugitives to Hanoi or Algeria. When this assistance failed to materialize, the men simply returned to Charlotte.[38]

Federal Alcohol, Tobacco, and Firearms investigators determined that a check meeting Hood's description had indeed been written and cleared at approximately that time. At that point, Walden turned over the accumulated evidence to a Charlotte FBI agent. In a June 1971 memo, he recalled his expectation that "they would proceed towards an indictment on the aiding and abetting" case against Grant and Chavis. The move to indict, however, was slowed by a Charlotte FBI agent, who became "interested in making an informer out of Grant"—a move that apparently went nowhere.[39]

Taking matters into his own hands, Walden then traveled to Raleigh for a June 23, 1971, interview with Washington in the presence of John Cutter (Washington's attorney), FBI agent Jim Roach, and Assistant U.S. Attorney David Long.[40] Justice Department agents and Long's representatives had already been questioning and negotiating with Washington after his psychiatric release "with regard to possibly implicating others, namely Ben Chavis and Jim Grant in this case."[41]

What made Justice Department officials so eager to make a deal with two men who had such extensive criminal records? In addition to both men's thick file of criminal offenses, federal agents had to overlook the fact that Charlotte police at the time considered Washington a "prime suspect in five murders in the Charlotte area" in order to gain testimony against two men with no criminal records at all. The polarized times had made the otherwise unreasonable seem reasonable. Amid the rising violent crime rate, Rap Brown's call to "Burn, baby, burn!," philosophy professor Angela Davis's well-publicized flight from the FBI, George Jackson's meteoric rise to militant fame as a state prison inmate and simultaneous Black Panther Party minister of defense, the 1970 University of Wisconsin math building bombing, and Weatherman's "Days of Rage" in 1969 Chicago, Hood and Washington's non-politically oriented crimes seemed like small pickings to law enforcement. Weapons charges and armed robberies—and possibly even murder itself—were not nearly so dangerous as the potential overthrow of the government. As Mecklenburg County (in which Charlotte sits) district attorney Tom Moore would later explain to defend the subsequently publicized questionable investigative tactics, "Sometimes you have to go to hell to get the devil. The crimes were committed and we had to go with the testimony we could get."[42]

The Charlotte Three and Raleigh Two defendants were not just *any* "devils." Federal agents aggressively interrogated Washington and Hood to surface not simply anyone who may have been involved in possible crimes. The two witnesses had, in the words of ATF agent Stan Noel, "given statements implicating James Earl Grant and Ben Chavis. These are two of the top militant leaders in the State of North Carolina. The statements implicate Grant and Chavis in the Oxford, N.C. riot [which became the Raleigh Two indictments] and Grant and other militants in the Charlotte, N.C. area [which became the Charlotte Three indictments]."[43]

* * *

After a long period of incarceration and then negotiations for Hood and Washington, ATF agent Bill Walden had cultivated two witnesses substantiating criminal activities by Jim Grant and Ben Chavis. In the succeeding months of 1971, Washington supplied federal, state, and local investigators with detailed accounts of the alleged activities of Grant, Chavis, and T. J. Reddy.[44]

Washington claimed to have first met Grant in September 1968 at a meeting attended by Charlotte activists Jim Grant, T. J. Reddy, Charles Parker, and a Charlotte Area Fund (CAF) youth organizer named Stan Alexander.[45] Later that month, Washington professed planning and executing the 1968 burning of the Lazy B Stables along with Grant, Parker, Reddy, and Hood. (He alleged that the firebombing was retaliation for the owner's refusal to allow Reddy and his integrated group to ride some nine months earlier). That allegation later surfaced as the Charlotte Three trial.[46]

According to Washington's testimony, he and Hood received a message from their cohort Grant on May 14, 1970, to join him at the civil rights protest underway in Oxford, North Carolina. They met Grant and his friend Chavis at the Soul Kitchen restaurant in Oxford later that day. Grant and Chavis, according to Washington, offered him and Hood $5,000 to kill Robert Teel and his son, the two suspects in the slaying of the young Henry Marrow. Grant then allegedly placed a .22 magnum rifle and a bag containing "three dynamite bombs complete with caps" in Hood and Washington's rental car. Together with Joe Goins, they drove from the restaurant into downtown Oxford with some women. At approximately 11:00 P.M., they left the women and decided to return to the restaurant, but were stopped and apprehended at the State Highway Patrol roadblock. Washington testified to Walden that he and Hood had decided not to follow through on the Teel murder, and, instead, were "returning to the Soul Kitchen to get further instructions."[47]

Before hearing Washington's allegations, Walden had already made a connection between Hood and Washington's trip to Oxford and Jim Grant. After their arrest, he had traced their rental car to a professor at the University of North Carolina at Charlotte. "That professor was tied into Grant somehow," Walden had discovered, "and had apparently helped out Hood and Washington by putting their car rental on his credit card. I called him about it and he was terrified." For the university teacher, it was a case of good intentions gone awry, claims Walden, and the man feared violent repercussions should he be seen with a federal agent. That fear took him to extraordinary lengths. "He was very scared something would happen to him if he cooperated with me, so I agreed to meet him [about forty miles] out of town in Statesville one night in a motel room and interview him. I knew he had nothing to do with all of this, but had gotten himself stuck in a bad situation."[48]

Concerned that Washington's psychiatric record would render his testimony "probably of little or no value except as corroboration," Walden now met again with Hood. The latter convict "related some of the bombing incidents as Washington [had], but refused at this time to give enough evidence to implicate Grant until he was granted certain conditions." Washington, however, informed Walden that "if he could have a few minutes with Alfred Hood that he believed that Hood would testify to the same facts."[49] Thus, Walden called the Charlotte Police Department to arrange for Hood's transfer from Charlotte's Mecklenburg County jail to Raleigh so that, in Walden's words, "Washington and Hood can be allowed to discuss this matter."[50]

After federal authorities gave Hood and Washington the chance to meet privately, they emerged willing to give statements and testimony, which would be virtually identical.[51] At that time, Washington demanded termination of his Mecklenburg County Superior Court-ordered probation, which the Oxford charges had violated—and would, thus, activate his twenty-five-year suspended sentence without court relief. Charlotte district attorney Thomas Moore sent Joseph Europa, of the Charlotte Police Intelligence Division (who

had already targeted Jim Grant and T. J. Reddy for their 1968 antiwar activities), to participate in Hood's and Washington's questioning in Raleigh. The
result was a deal in which state authorities terminated Washington's probation
in return for his and Hood's testimony in the state's Charlotte Three case, as
well as the federal Raleigh Two case against Grant and Chavis for aiding the
new federal witnesses' bond jumping.[52]

The existence of a separate Intelligence Division within the local Charlotte Police Department is representative of what author Frank Donner calls
the local "police intelligence surge" of the late 1960s and early 1970s.[53] Europa was notorious among local community activists at the time for being—
according to Kathy Sparrow—"absolutely out to get Jim Grant" and militant activists like him. Sparrow compared Europa's Intelligence Division to
the U.S. House Un-American Activities Committee. "Back then, [Europa]
was in charge of subversives, and Jim Grant was definitely considered a subversive."[54] Butch and Shirley Rosen remember Europa showing up at Grant's
home unexpectedly at strange hours and warning Grant that "he was going to
get him."[55]

Grant himself did nothing to lessen law enforcement agents' determination. According to Grant's white activist colleague Marvin Sparrow, Grant
"had offended enough people and done enough things, and eluded [law enforcement agents] in enough ways that they were coming after him." On one
occasion, according to a story Grant had told Sparrow, ATF agents had shown
up at his door wanting to search his rental home. Grant's domicile was, by
choice, the lone residence at the end of a gravel road that led across a bridge
to his front door. There, says Sparrow, Grant "confronted Alcohol, Tobacco,
and Firearms people at his front door armed. . . . And he said, 'Have you got
a warrant?' And they didn't have a warrant, and he had his gun, and they had
their guns." After a long standoff, the federal agents were forced to drive away.

> You know, he was the Black Panther-like person who just wasn't going to put
> up with their stuff. And Jim had decided years ago that if he got killed, that
> was okay. . . . Jim did a lot of stuff, and he was usually so clever about it. You
> know, the whole thing with Alcohol, Tobacco, and Firearms—he was abso-
> lutely correct, and they were just as pissed as they could be. They couldn't do
> anything about it. And he was also very active. He just was all over the state,

mostly [pursuing] the kind of issues that [concerned] Black communities—
issues about someone having been killed by the police or beat up by the police.
. . . But he just went all over the state keeping up his contacts with the Black
communities. And I think they were quite aware that he was involved in a lot
of this stuff. And taking him off the street for five years—well, he had longer than that [after he was convicted in both the Raleigh Two and Charlotte
Three trials]—was a great accomplishment from their side of it.[56]

The cooperative work with local and state officials to facilitate Hood's and
Washington's testimony was not the first time that Walden had worked closely
with local authorities. Whereas the relationship between southern state and
local law enforcement and that of federal law officers had been marked by
isolation or animosity in the Kennedy and Johnson administrations, the late
1960s and 1970s became a new era of cooperation. The fears of "law and order"
had convinced federal law enforcement that the new brand of activists—in
the form of Black Power and leftist militants—were a brimming conspiracy
needing to be checked. No longer did federal law agents approach southern
state and local law officers with caution or suspicion. Against the new threat
of anarchy, violence, and leftist revolution, they were now all on the same side.
    So it was that Walden had developed warmer ties with local authorities.
"In Charlotte, we had a real good working relationship with the police department. They could get me anything I needed. I remember once in the middle
of the night they got me a fire truck so I could climb on top of a school and get
down an unexploded Molotov cocktail." Walden especially remembers working "quite a bit" with the Charlotte police's Sergeant Joe Europa. For Walden,
the police intelligence officer, who had earned the approbation of so many of
the city's activists, was "a good source of information and an above average
investigator."[57]

* * *

Following a series of meetings with ATF agents and Charlotte district attorney representatives in Assistant U.S. Attorney David Long's office in Raleigh,
Hood and Washington told virtually identical accounts of Grant's and Chavis's actions in Oxford. They described the $5,000 offer to kill Teel; Grant and
Chavis, they claimed, then urged and assisted their jumping bond. Hood and

Washington also discussed the 1968 firebombing of Charlotte's Lazy B Stables along with Grant and three Black Charlotte students—T. J. Reddy, Charles Parker, and Clarence Harrison. The firebombing was planned and executed, they claimed, by a group led by Grant named "United Soul"—of which they were members.[58] In return for their sworn statements on July 21, 1971, Hood and Washington received immunity from prosecution stemming from their testimony, the termination of Washington's probation, and federal protective custody (which included housing, food, clothing, and subsistence money for them and their families).[59] Federal agents justified the protective custody by arguing that Hood's and Washington's lives were endangered by their cooperation and testimony.[60]

Long concluded that the state crimes Hood and Washington described were more alarming and worthy of prosecution than their own federal charges. On this basis, he lent his full support to state prosecution of Grant, Reddy, Parker, and Harrison. Hood's attorney and ATF agent Stanley Noel later testified that the package offered to Hood and Washington for their testimony was intended to cover their participation in both the federal and state trials. Because the state had no resources for providing witness protection, Bill Walden got approval to continue the protective custody until the witnesses testified in a state trial scheduled three months after the federal proceedings. That arrangement apparently was in violation of the federal Organized Crime Control Act, which stipulated that authorized "relocation payments" and protective custody should be provided only for witnesses participating in a federal trial involving organized crime.[61] Federal agents continued to show an active interest in the state's case after the federal trial's conclusion, and during the course of the state trial, federal agents even provided some investigative services at District Attorney Moore's request.[62]

Hood and Washington had plans to set a high price for their sought-after testimony. Washington's attorney, John Cutter, told federal agents and U.S. Attorney Warren Coolidge that his client would require "in excess of $25,000," which he ambitiously planned to use to relocate to Barbados to begin a political career. Hood planned to join him in Barbados, and his attorney, Arnold Smith, told authorities that his client would cooperate with "some clear and direct guarantee of $50,000 . . . [to] be deposited in some foreign account [Hood] can get to." The astounded federal agents mockingly suggested that

Smith try for $500,000. The two witnesses would settle for what ATF agents told them would be an unspecified "maximum amount" they could get (which turned out to be—to Hood's and Washington's chagrin—$4,000 each). "Apparently Washington had already been to Barbados," recalls Walden, "and wanted to go back. I just about dared them to never come back. We wanted to get them out of the country, because we figured they would get killed. It may have been no great loss," he concedes, "but we felt an obligation to protect them from harm."[63]

Despite settling for less than the original asking price, Hood and Washington could take pride in the results of their efforts. The two men who began with a thick file of criminal offenses, who had carried several guns and even dynamite into a town in the midst of an official state of emergency, and who had subsequently fled the country to escape apprehension by agents of the U.S. government were released on their own recognizance within two months of signing their sworn statements.[64] They remained under the protective custody of federal agents for approximately nine months. During that time they received "subsistence" payments for rent, food, and clothing. The Justice Department also financed three months at Atlantic Beach, North Carolina. Supporting the two cost the government $10,800, not including the salaries and expenses of the protective personnel.[65]

It also cost the federal law enforcement personnel—ATF agents and later U.S. marshals—some considerable headaches. The two men continued to haggle for more money and argued with agents over the insufficient luxuries of their beachfront motel rooms and restrictions of movement. Dave Washington fought when ATF agent Stan Noel blocked him from going "deep sea fishing" off the Atlantic coast. Early on in their stay at Atlantic Beach, Hood complained that Washington's children were grating on his nerves. He then demanded and got a room further removed from the young nuisances. Later, after the men had provided their April 1972 testimony in the Raleigh Two federal trial against Grant and Chavis—and less than a month before they were due to testify in the July 1972 Charlotte Three case—they slipped out from under the nose of federal marshals stationed next door and drove to Guadalajara, Mexico. Noel was only able to locate them through Washington's mother and ensure their return in time for the Charlotte Three trial using the lure of the still unpaid cash payments for their testimony.[66]

Despite their eventual disappointment over the size of the Justice Department's cash payout, Hood and Washington had clearly enjoyed the ride. For two young, inner-city Black men in the early 1970s who had served grueling time in Vietnam, this kind of attention from their government was something long in coming. "To them, it was like 'The Life of Reilly,'" recalls former *Charlotte Observer* journalist Mark Ethridge, who later did much of the newspaper's Charlotte Three trial coverage. "The government forgave all their crimes and took them to the beach."[67]

* * *

After federal agents provided Hood and Washington with protective custody resources and prosecutors with further evidentiary investigations, the federal Raleigh Two trial against Jim Grant and Ben Chavis began on April 18, 1972.[68] Facing charges on "aiding and abetting" Hood and Washington's flight from U.S. agents and on possession of dynamite, the Raleigh Two trial began a five-month stretch of three separate trials including either or both of the two activists long well-known to the North Carolina intelligence community: Jim Grant and Ben Chavis—the April 1972 Raleigh Two trial, the July 1972 Charlotte Three trial, and the September 1972 Wilmington Ten trial.[69]

Given the intensity of manpower and resources already invested in prosecuting Chavis and Grant, the U.S. attorney's office was taking no chances. Federal agents exercised extremely tight security at the Raleigh Two trial, including placing federal marshals with two-way radios at every door and searching spectators' purses and coats. The federal marshals accompanying Grant and Chavis also tried to sit at the defense table. This was blocked only by a successful defense complaint that their presence would exacerbate the prosecution's claim of the defendants being dangerous elements.[70]

In the Raleigh Two trial, Hood and Washington recounted their previous testimony to state and federal agents. They discussed "United Soul," the supposed African American militant organization they claimed masterminded activities like the manufacture of explosives and the planned demolition of white racist targets.[71] Washington also testified that Grant had commanded him to "take money from white storekeepers" selling in the Black neighborhoods of Charlotte. Washington dubiously claimed for the first time that his 1969 armed robbery conviction stemmed from this plan.[72]

Defense attorney William Allison, who had been sent by the Southern Conference Educational Fund to defend its employee Jim Grant, confronted Washington with his January 3, 1971, statement to FBI agents that claimed the seized dynamite "belonged to [his companion Joseph] Goins." This conflicted with later testimony that he had seen Goins and Grant go together to place the explosives in the car. Shown a copy of the statement during testimony, Washington claimed, "That's nothing. I refused to sign it." Prodded further by Allison, Washington mysteriously maintained that "I didn't think I had to tell the FBI the truth." "So you told a lie?" Allison queried. "Yes I did," Washington replied. He went on to say that he had *assumed* Grant had placed the dynamite in his car trunk when it was found later at the roadblock.[73] Washington maintained that he lied because he feared Grant might harm his wife and three children, and because he was not under oath.[74]

During his testimony on the bond-jumping arrangements, Washington made additional allegations against Grant. Going beyond Hood's testimony, he claimed Grant had told them that it "wouldn't be wise [to meet their September 1970 court date,] and the best thing to do would be to leave the country."[75] Grant had become alarmed when he realized Washington and Hood were prepared to "tell the truth" about the dynamite belonging to him. Washington contended that Grant had stashed three sticks of dynamite in Washington's home in 1969, and now warned that "just like he left the dynamite in my house, he could leave a bomb there."[76] Whether true or not, these new charges must have served the interests of federal prosecutors in two ways. They shifted more responsibility for the bond-jumping away from the actual fugitives (Hood and Washington)—who would never be tried—and toward Grant. These new unsubstantiated allegations also justified Hood's and Washington's protective custody.

Under cross-examination, Washington dramatically turned on defense attorney James Ferguson, implicating the lawyer in illegal activities. Questioned about his admitted use of heroin, LSD, and "large quantities" of marijuana and alcohol, Washington claimed that he only began drug use to drown his guilt for his Vietnam War transgressions, including "being responsible for civilians being killed."[77] Under continuing scrutiny, he snapped at Ferguson, claiming that he had acquired LSD from Ferguson's secretary and her husband—who were Vicki and T. J. Reddy.[78] Under later examination by Fer-

GOING TO HELL TO GET THE DEVIL

guson, Washington explained his motivation for testifying by claiming, "I was tired of running from Jim Grant and you and your organization." Asked what organization that was, Washington refused to name it, saying only, "That organization you and Grant are in right now. . . . The same organization that pays for everything Grant does." Cryptically, this was the only occasion that Washington implicated Ferguson as a member of "United Soul" or any other alleged subversive organization. Ferguson professed to have "no idea" to what organization Washington was alluding.[79]

Al Hood likewise proved a less-than-ideal prosecution witness. During cross-examination, Ferguson questioned him about the alleged $5,000 offer for killing the Teels. When Ferguson asked if he would kill anyone for $5,000, Hood paused, then told the court, "I would seriously consider it."[80] On the following day, Hood evaded Ferguson's questions about where he got the cars and money to sustain himself between his September 1970 flight to Canada and his February 1971 arrest. "I'm not going to tell you," he said. Pushed further, he replied, "I don't remember." When Ferguson demanded to know why he didn't "remember what anybody did but James Earl Grant and Ben Chavis," Hood countered, "I remember what's necessary for this case."[81]

Jim Grant created his own commotion in the courtroom and earned no ally in Judge John Larkins during the trial. On the day proceedings got underway, Larkins reprimanded him for being ten minutes late. Later in the trial, Larkins chastised Grant for "chewing gum" and "writing letters and licking stamps" during proceedings.[82] In contrast, Benjamin Chavis (by then founder and pastor of the Wilmington, North Carolina, First Church of the Black Messiah) came to court with a black jacket, clerical collar, and a Bible.[83]

In a surprise move, defense attorneys declined to call their thirteen potential witnesses after the prosecution rested. As Ferguson and Allison told the press during a recess, he and Allison had reached the decision because the prosecution had not "presented any believable witnesses."[84] Judge Larkins denied their motion for acquittal on the grounds of insufficient evidence.[85]

In concluding remarks, the defense portrayed the government's case as built around the testimony of "two thugs" who were "so desperate for freedom they'd lie about anyone."[86] In producing these witnesses, they had "scraped the bottom of the barrel of our society, consorted with them and agreed with them to present a pack of lies."[87] Ferguson claimed that federal authorities had dropped Hood's and Washington's charges so that they would "come in here and convict someone the government wanted worse."[88] Allison called the conspiracy statute a "questionable law" traditionally used by the government to convict people when it doesn't "like their ideas."[89]

The prosecution concluded its case with a rhetorical flourish that relied heavily on "law and order" fears of a dangerous radical underground. In themes that would be reiterated in the upcoming Charlotte Three trial, prosecution attorneys painted Hood and Washington as only "the henchmen" of the "big men" Grant and Chavis. They painted the "mastermind" Grant as especially dangerous. Together, Grant and Chavis used Hood and Washington to "carry out their dirty work."[90]

The jury went to work swiftly, reaching verdicts in four and a half hours. It declared Chavis not guilty, and Grant guilty on both counts of conspiracy and of aiding and abetting fugitives. Following defense pleas for leniency because of Grant's VISTA and community work and clean criminal record, Judge John Larkins sentenced Grant to the maximum sentence of five years on both counts, and ordered them to run consecutively.[91]

That such different verdicts could be based on the same testimony became a source of consternation, but prosecutor U.S. Attorney Warren H. Coolidge would only tell the press that he "learned a long time ago never to argue with a jury verdict. We presented the best case we had." Coolidge, a recent Republican nominee for state attorney general, claimed to have "no feeling one way or the other" over the Chavis verdict.[92] For the jury, Chavis's religious connection no doubt evoked a more traditional, less threatening brand of southern civil rights activism from the late 1950s and early 1960s, where religious imagery had played a key role. Grant, by contrast, symbolized the more defiant, dangerous, anti-authority stance of the newer, more unsettling style of the Black Power movement. Thus, the trial outcome may have become a twelve-person referendum on the rising apprehension over the direction of the Black freedom struggle.

*　*　*

Clearly now under heavy government scrutiny, both men went into immediate law enforcement custody after the trial to await other state trials. Grant was led away by federal marshals to begin serving the newly minted Raleigh

Two conviction and await the Charlotte Three trial (on state charges of fire-bombing the Lazy B Stables in 1968).[93] On the day before the Raleigh Two verdict was returned, Wilmington, North Carolina, authorities also indicted Chavis on arson and conspiracy charges stemming from a February 1971 riot in Wilmington, North Carolina. (The case, which was tried in September 1972, included nine other defendants and became known as the Wilmington Ten. Like the Charlotte Three case, it involved ATF agent Bill Walden and the payment of convict witnesses.)[94] Before state officials escorted Chavis to jail on those new charges, the judge allowed him a few minutes to speak with his three-year-old daughter, his mother, and his sister.[95]

Defense counsel immediately posted an appeal to Grant's conviction.[96] Judge John Larkins set bail at $50,000 and declined to allow Grant supporters to follow the usual practice of submitting 10 percent of the bail for release. The Reverend W. W. Finlator, chairman of the North Carolina Advisory Committee to the U.S. Commission on Civil Rights, issued a report holding that "the conclusion is inescapable that bail of this amount has the effect of retention in custody and raises serious questions in light of the constitutional protection against excessive bail." Finlator added that the course of this case illustrated how "political structures often operate not in the administration of justice, but for the purpose of controlling and impeding those who seek for greater justice and opportunity within the social order."[97]

Speaking for many who were angered by the tightening noose of "law and order," the Reverend Leon White (an African American minister who worked with Chavis for the Commission for Racial Justice) held a press conference on the day following the trial. He called the case a "smoke screen to help the efforts of the U.S. government eliminate anyone that speaks out against the oppression of Blacks and other minorities." Asserting that charges should never even have been brought against the two, he lamented that "for too long we [Blacks] have respected the courts of this nation. But this day is over."[98]

While that day may have been over for White, there was a long, anxious way to go before the sun set on law enforcement's efforts. Federal, state, and local government involved in the prosecution of Chavis, Grant, and the eleven others targeted in their state trials had already paid a high price in terms of financial compensation to witnesses, staffing hours, and surveillance budgets. What was perhaps unforeseen in June 1972 was the price North Carolina's progressive image would pay for ensuring the suppression of these supposed revolutionaries. By 1980, when the last of the Wilmington Ten and Charlotte Three were paroled, the cases had become the subject of national columnists, *60 Minutes* television coverage, U.S. Department of Justice pressure, international scrutiny, and an Amnesty International investigation that declared the defendants "political prisoners." In the polarizing climate of the times, however, this price was simply seen as the cost of holding together a fragile republic.

6

CONVICTING THE WIZARD, THE POET, AND LITTLE CHARLIE

The Charlotte Three Trial

I n February 1971, two and a half years after the Lazy B Stables had burned to the ground (which would not lead to the Charlotte Three trial until 1972), another blaze started across town in a law office. Unlike in the Lazy B case, the source of the fire seemed far more explainable. One of its resident attorneys, Julius Chambers, had been the legal mind behind the lawsuit against the city's segregated school system, *Swann v. Charlotte-Mecklenburg Board of Education.* Pushing that case through the court system, the African American attorney had finally won a federal court ruling in 1969 from Judge James Mc-Millan that ordered busing to achieve a proper racial balance in the schools. Not all of Charlotte's citizens, of course, took a liking to the ruling, nor especially to the attorney who had shepherded the case through the legal system. The city was still four years away from reaching a final agreement on a busing plan that Judge McMillan deemed fair to all the city's residents. In the intervening years, the city would be home to more than its share of turmoil, a crucial context for the 1972 Charlotte Three prosecution yet to come.[1]

This was not the first time that Chambers had been the victim of white racist violence. The still unsolved 1965 bombing of his home (simultaneous with explosions at the homes of Reginald Hawkins, city councilman Fred Alexander, and local NAACP chapter president Kelly Alexander) cast a shadow over the new ashes of his law office. The jeopardy to himself and his family

had only intensified after his success in the *Swann* case. He received numerous anonymous threats, including one that contended his fate would be the
same as the violent conclusions to John and Robert Kennedy and Martin Luther King Jr. Even Chambers's father in nearby Mt. Gilead, North Carolina,
had been dragged into the violence when his repair garage was torched twice
within five months.[2]

Since Chambers's partner at the office was Jim Ferguson, of course, so
much the better for the white racist who no doubt set the building ablaze. The
firm as a whole, including attorneys Adam Stein and Jim Lanning, had been
taking civil rights cases from all over North Carolina. "We were the only law
firm [in the state] that had that as its principal goal," recalls Ferguson. Ferguson left his mark on the 1972 Raleigh Two case against Grant and Chavis as he
had the 1970 Oxford case against the Teels.[3] (Ferguson later served as defense
attorney on the Charlotte Three and Wilmington Ten trials as well.)

The violence that grew in the early years of the 1970s in Charlotte, however, was not so exclusive as to include only four lawyers. The nationwide violence in 1970 became an inflammatory backdrop to the 1970 Oxford rioting,
and Charlotte too fell prey to the disease. The celebratory atmosphere that
came to characterize Charlotte's busing success story by the mid-1970s lay in
the all-too-distant future. The white federal judge James McMillan, whose job
it became to oversee a just implementation of a school busing plan, received
his own share of threats. So much so, federal marshals eventually were assigned to him for around-the-clock protection.[4]

More than that, though, the city's school children also fell prey to violence
on public school campuses. Bomb scares were a frequent occurrence, but violence was not just threatened. In October 1970, six Blacks robbed a white
boy at knifepoint at West Mecklenburg High School. At West Charlotte High
School in December 1970, a white boy drew a pistol on several Black students.
In March 1973, full-scale riot conditions prevailed between Black and white
students at Independence High. And Independence was not alone. Between
1970 and the early spring of 1973, nine of the ten high schools in the Charlotte
school system would close at some point due to racial rioting.[5]

Exacerbating matters was the unusual silence of the city's business elites
in the late 1960s and early 1970s. The implementation of *Swann*'s school busing order had become a troubling exception to the city's business leaders'

strong hand in solving civic problems. Many of the city's middle and working classes complained plaintively about southeast Charlotte's obvious exclusion from the early school busing plans. The business elites, many of whom resided in those wealthy white southeast Charlotte neighborhoods (including some of the recalcitrant school board members), were noticeably slow to respond to the public outcry. Only the perseverance of Judge McMillan, who was determined to create a fair and equitable busing plan, ensured the final acceptance by all quarters of the city. By the mid-1970s, city business leaders would join others in the city to embrace once again Charlotte's long-cultivated progressive image. But, as 1972 opened on Charlotte, this city used to social tranquility seemed to be straining at the seams.[6]

* * *

Three months before Grant and Chavis faced the Raleigh Two trial, a Charlotte grand jury served indictments on Jim Grant, T. J. Reddy, and Charles Parker for the largely forgotten and unsolved 1968 burning of the Lazy B Stables on the city's outskirts. Their alleged crime was a supposed retaliation for the racist owner's refusal to rent his stable horses out to Reddy one Sunday afternoon in October 1967. Before the summer of 1972 was over, however, the three men would own some of the stiffest sentences for unlawful burning in state history. Their convictions would come to be questioned by national columnists, U.S. congressmen, international media sources, and Amnesty International.

The grand jury had, in fact, also indicted a fourth man, Clarence Harrison. Harrison appeared at the trial but quickly pled guilty and made a concerted effort to differentiate himself from the other three defendants—a prudent move, given their impending fate at the trial. Harrison would become an exception to the other three defendants both in his plea and his sentence, which was extremely light compared to the three others. Harrison would never be imprisoned for his conviction, removed himself from the actual trial proceedings by his plea, and made a clear effort to isolate himself from the other defendants. Hence, the case would become known as the Charlotte Three. For some observers, Harrison's guilty plea would leave lingering questions about the Three's claims of innocence, as Harrison simply slipped away without disputing the convict witnesses' account or delivering his own testimony, never to be heard from again.

The indictment process itself had sent up warning flags among the Three's supporters. One noted that defense attorney Jim Ferguson "felt like from day one, that there was something very suspicious about it, just because of the way they charged them. It was very rare to go to the grand jury and get an indictment. You don't know what's being told to a Grand Jury. It's secret. There are no transcripts of what's being said. It's just a different way of charging someone. Normally, the D.A. decides he's going to prosecute the case."[7]

Indeed, liberals had begun to raise a series of issues by the early 1970s about the misuse of grand juries. The bodies were originally intended by the constitutional framers as a way to limit government overreach (since their average citizen members could investigate officials' conduct, and grand jurors' approval was required for prosecutors to proceed with indictments). In practice, however, the legal laypersons who comprised them frequently deferred to prosecutors—especially as the legal system became increasingly professionalized and complex.[8]

On the federal level, grand juries during the Nixon administration became a virtual arm of the Justice Department Internal Security Division's (ISD) intelligence gathering operations, and another indication of the expanding and aggressive War on Crime, according to author and civil liberties attorney Frank Donner. As a result, the grand jury was converted "from its traditional and recognized function, deciding whether the prosecutor has presented sufficient evidence to justify an accusation of law violation, into a cover for a variety of intelligence-related pursuits." The grand jury is a particularly effective vehicle for that function because of its subpoena power and authority to compel testimony at the risk of contempt. From 1970 to 1973, grand juries on the federal level returned approximately four hundred indictments, many of which were against young leftists, Black militants, and antiwar activists. The rate of convictions or pleas produced from the indictments fell below 15 percent, compared to 65.2 percent in ordinary criminal cases—a testimony to those grand juries' aggression and the resulting lack of credible evidence supporting their criminal indictments. In 1973, Senator Edward Kennedy called this grand jury phenomenon "unprecedented" and "a throw-back to the worst excesses of the legislative investigative committees of the 1950s." An appeal circuit court judge, alarmed by the high number of cases "arising out of grand jury proceedings concerned with the possible punishment of political dissidents," warned that "it would be a cruel twist of history to allow the institution of the grand jury that was designed at least partially to protect political dissent to become an instrument of political suppression."[9]

Despite Ferguson's suspicion about the origin of the charges, many of the activists close to the Charlotte Three remained unruffled over the indictments. Like many of those who had been indicted by those aforementioned grand juries and not been convicted, many Charlotte Three supporters saw the indictments as groundless intimidation likely to wither under courtroom scrutiny. "One of the things about it was that I didn't take [the indictments] all that seriously at the time," recalls activist Marvin Sparrow. "I remember seeing Jim Grant on the UNCC campus when the charges had first been brought and I said, 'Jim I saw all this in the paper. What's that all about?' And, he said, 'Oh, it's a bunch of bullshit. Nothing to it.' And, I said, 'Well, okay.'"[10] That perception would prevail among many surrounding the Three all the way up to the latter stages of the trial.

* * *

In an inauspicious sign for the defense, Frank Snepp was named the Charlotte Three trial judge. As a state representative from Charlotte, Snepp had earned a reputation as unfriendly to African American concerns. In the late 1950s' wake of the *Brown v. Board of Education* decision, Snepp had been a staunch but wily defender of the state's resistance to court-ordered school desegregation. When the North Carolina General Assembly considered a 1957 bill to require the National Association for the Advancement of Colored People (NAACP) to disclose its membership lists (a tactic used in other southern states to target members for recrimination) and to refrain from paying civil rights litigation costs, Representative Snepp successfully urged the Assembly to drop the bill for fear that "All we are doing is putting the State to a court test.... [I]f the federal court knocks this down it will set a pattern. Our school laws on the subject [resisting school desegregation] would be in danger." Snepp's dogged resistance to racial progress was not without its detractors. His own son, a decorated CIA officer, later called his father "an old Dixiecrat" who "was a man of an earlier time. Though a brilliant jurist, he had grown up in a deeply divided South, in a household that still viewed Blacks as somehow intrinsically inferior. He also suffered from a kind of emotional schizophrenia, widely shared by many of his peers, that could support compassion in personal inter-racial affairs and rank prejudice in the abstract."[11]

In 1959, Snepp successfully represented the Charlotte-Mecklenburg County School Board against an NAACP desegregation suit. In February 1970, Judge Frank Snepp entered the Charlotte busing controversy on the side of the conservative, anti-busing Concerned Parents Association (CPA). By granting the CPA's request for a restraining order against the school board's purchase of buses, Snepp temporarily thwarted federal judge James McMillan's momentous busing order in the *Swann v. Charlotte-Mecklenburg Board of Education* case.[12] Fortuitously, McMillan would come to play his own role in Snepp's Charlotte Three case.

Like two of the defendants before him, Snepp was an outsider to North Carolina. A Tennessee native who had graduated from the Duke University School of Law in 1948 after a stint as a Marine Corps captain in World War II, Snepp took up a Charlotte law practice until his 1967 appointment to a Superior Court judgeship. It was in those intervening years that he was elected to the North Carolina Assembly in 1957. After concluding his second term in 1961, Snepp decided not to run again. "I watched politics corrupt people," he would later say. "Politics is a heady wine. But it gets to the point where you have to compromise your principles."[13]

After donning judicial robes in the late 1960s, Snepp quickly became known as a brash, outspoken judge for the local Superior Court. "When you come into his courtroom, it's 'Yes, sir. No, sir. I'm a good little Marine, sir,'" Mecklenburg assistant district attorney Stephen Ward contended years after the Charlotte Three trial. "He's in control at all times." Snepp's strict control of his courtroom would become an issue during the Charlotte Three trial, as would media controversy. In a 1968 speech, the judge had insisted that "Blame for a criminal trial being turned into a circus . . . must be placed . . . upon the shoulders of the judge presiding."[14]

Judge Snepp had also become known as a staunch conservative. After the U.S. Supreme Court's *Miranda* ruling became a popular whipping boy of "law and order" politicians across the country, Judge Snepp added his own voice to the crescendo. Decrying the recent series of 1960s Supreme Court decisions bolstering defendants' rights, Snepp warned that "the thrust" of many of the Court's recent rulings was

not toward the ascertainment of truth in criminal cases, but toward a proliferation of technical rules in an area where there is already a plethora of
technical rules. . . . Many [criminals] have "beaten the rap" because of [those
decisions] and so have increased their contempt for the law. With many of
these persons, it is a game in which ability to take advantage of the rules is the
only real consideration. They give no thought to the conduct in which they
engaged. In their own minds they are imprisoned not because of what they
did, but because their talismanic "rights" somehow failed to protect them.

The judge who, during sentencing, sometimes cited childhood fairy tales to
underscore his old-fashioned conservative ideas, predicted a more conservative court in the future, less interventionist in state courts, and "much less
activist than it is at present." "It will not be surprising if in the next few years"
the Supreme Court "even modifies some of the doctrines which have been laid
down by the Warren Court," he contended.[15]

An avid reader, Snepp had also developed an early fondness for history.
That devotion became an inspiration for his years of public service and his
determination to leave his own historical mark on the legacy of his state—
something he would no doubt do in the case he was about to begin. "I suppose
really that Frank's political service is an outgrowth of his interest in history,"
his wife maintained, "and his desire to do his part. . . . Sort of the back door
to entering politics," she claimed.[16] His role in the history of regional race relations through the Charlotte Three case, however, would not be without its
detractors. Snepp's own son later recounted that "my family and I had many
heated discussions with him about his ruling. Leaving aside the consequential issue of guilt or innocence, the harshness of the sentence [that he was to
deliver in the case] seemed far out of proportion to what had happened, especially in the heated atmosphere of the civil rights struggles of the time when
compassion, not vindictiveness, seemed the only answer to the great schisms
dividing us. It took many years for my father to have second thoughts. But I
know he did."[17]

* * *

Proceedings for the Charlotte Three trial got underway approximately ten
weeks after the Raleigh Two federal trial against Chavis and Grant. On July 6,

1972, defense attorney James Ferguson argued in pretrial proceedings that the state was obligated to disclose to defense counsel its evidence against the defendants. He noted that no preliminary hearing had been held, that the prosecution had waited over three years to issue an indictment on the case, and that "we are completely in the dark about what the charges are." Assistant District Attorney William Austin resisted Snepp's suggestion to provide prosecutory witnesses' written statements to the defense, claiming that releasing witnesses' names would "subject them to harassment, threats and violence."[18] Snepp ruled the following day for the defense, saying, "I don't have any evidence that witnesses have been harassed or are likely to be." He also turned to the defendants, T. J. Reddy, James Grant, Charles Parker, and Clarence Harrison, and said, "I recognize that there are some things about this case that are inflammatory. I intend to do my best to give you four men a fair trial on the charges against you and nothing else."[19]

After a brief recess at noon, the four defendants entered their pleas. Many of the courtroom spectators and reporters had left already, deeming this portion of the trial proceedings merely a formality. These presuppositions proved true for only three of the four accused—all pleading not guilty. The fourth, Clarence Harrison, pled guilty—to the surprise of the other defendants. Behind the scenes and unbeknown to the other three, Harrison had been offered—but refused—a prosecution deal to become a state witness and join the ranks of Hood and Washington. Judge Snepp questioned Harrison to ensure he understood his possible sentence of up to thirty years. Assuring the judge that he did, he then left the court under his original bond, to return later for sentencing. Snepp then revoked the bonds on the remaining three defendants over defense objections and placed them in the sheriff's custody for the trial's duration.[20]

With the final preliminary defense objection cleared and the pleas entered, jury selection began. So did the trial drama, which included tight government security and controversial public protesters outside. Among them were University of North Carolina at Charlotte professors (many of whom knew Reddy as a former student) and friends of the defendants.[21] Over the weekend, supporters had collected $900 for defense costs and three hundred signatures on a petition protesting the case coming to trial. Using language common to the era's leftist activism, they called the case "clearly designed as a political maneuver to silence three critics of the power structure of the State." Just after the proceedings began, the group presented the petitions to the press and read a statement in which it accused "the Government [of] . . . attempting to establish an effective method of legally lynching Black people now that outright lynching has become unpopular."[22] *Charlotte News* reporter Ellison Clary (a UNCC student during Reddy's student days) noted protestor Pamela Owens's claim that the defendants were under indictment for being "Black men active in the struggle for liberation." Ben Chavis was present in the courtroom, but "only as a spectator," he claimed.[23]

Hearing about the small demonstration, Snepp issued an order that any further protests in or around the courthouse building would result in contempt of court citations.[24] The order, he maintained, sprung from the need to prevent picketing and leafletting, which he felt "would tend to influence or intimidate" jurors and witnesses.[25] Snepp also tightened security in the courtroom, doubling the usual number of deputy sheriffs guarding the court. He ordered them to search any spectator's umbrella, coat, bag, sack, or parcel. Among the items seized were a teacher's rounded-edge child safety scissors.[26] The trial's heightened security resembled the earlier precautions at 1972 Raleigh Two trial (which had emerged from Grant and Ben Chavis's presence amid the 1970 Oxford unrest). Again it reflected law enforcement's conspiracy concerns, and encouraged public perception of the defendants and their colleagues as dangerous elements.

Protestor Richard Rosen (and brother of activist Butch Rosen) contacted ACLU attorney George Daly about Snepp's ban on demonstrations. Daly agreed that the decree violated the First Amendment right to free speech. Mindful of federal courts as a traditional place in the South to get liberal justice, the ACLU attorney brought a complaint to U.S. District Court under Rosen's name on the same day that testimony began in the Lazy B Stables trial.[27] The presiding judge was James B. McMillan, the same jurist who presided over the *Swann* busing decision. McMillan declined to make an immediate decision on the matter until he had time to "put more thought into it." While McMillan did express concern over the plaintiff's complaints, he also felt that Snepp had a legitimate right to concern himself with the "tranquility of the court."[28] In a conciliatory move, McMillan encouraged Daly and the state attorneys to meet with Snepp on the issue. This strategy paid off when Snepp withdrew the demonstration ban later that afternoon, saying that jury selection was over and that he would make sure that jurors had no contact with demonstrators. Rich Rosen stated his intention to resume demonstrations the next morning "to show support for people on trial and show it's not just a criminal trial, but a political trial as well."[29] The small protests on the courthouse sidewalk and Snepp's reaction to them would remain an issue throughout the trial, however.

* * *

On July 10, the first day of trial testimony, the prosecution called twenty-three-year-old Judy Baldwin. She had lived with the Medlins, the stable owners, in 1968, and was the only person in their home the night of the burning. The blaring sirens of a fire engine were her first warning of the fire, she told the court. "I could hear [the horses] kicking and hollering," she sobbed. "I wanted to try and save them," but she was restrained by a neighbor from rushing into the blazing barn.[30] Prosecution witness Charlotte Fire Department captain William G. Stuart then described his discovery of a homemade firebomb that had failed to ignite beside the barn's remains. Fire Department district chief K. D. Helms testified that this evidence was later lost when the Fire Department moved its headquarters.[31]

The informants Al Hood and Dave Washington later offered the prosecution's central testimony. Hood took the stand, curiously wearing sunglasses, and detailed the exploits of "United Soul" (duplicating his account of the group in the recent Raleigh Two trial), which had allegedly executed the Lazy B burning. He described a group consisting of himself, Washington, Harrison, and the other three defendants.[32] Hood claimed he first met Grant, Reddy, and Parker in early September 1968 at the Tenth Street Recreation Center, a church-funded community center for poor Black youth directed by Reddy and Parker.[33] He had talked with them for several hours about racism and Charlotte. Reddy read poems to them and played Malcolm X records.[34]

After this initial meeting, Hood testified, they set up regular Tuesday and Thursday meetings that included the defendants, Washington (a mutual friend), and Harrison, whom Hood had known from his studies at the local Central Piedmont Community College.[35] A week later, they discussed techniques of firebomb construction and possible targets, according to Hood. Among them was the Mecklenburg County Courthouse and a bank in the heart of downtown.[36] The group then began holding regular Saturday target practice with a number of different weapons at an abandoned house. During one of these target practices, he maintained, they practiced making and throwing firebombs. Grant boasted that his doctorate in chemistry meant he "could make any kind of bomb." Hood recalled Reddy teaching the group the best way to make and throw a firebomb.[37]

In continuing testimony, Al Hood claimed that the group's next Tuesday meeting was devoted to "T.J. [Reddy] and C.P. [Charles Parker] . . . talking about something which had happened to them." This was a reference to Lazy B Stables owner Bill Medlin's refusal to allow Reddy a horse ride in 1967. That incident had been followed the next day by a small civil rights protest featuring Reddy and Parker, which resulted in Medlin's capitulation to allow the young Black men to ride.

According to Hood, though, the protest did not end in 1967. On that night in September 1968, Hood contended that either Parker, Grant, or Reddy suggested that they all go that night to "paint the barn." While Hood and Washington interpreted this to mean "burn the barn," they felt Harrison—who had not attended the meeting where firebomb construction was discussed—might have misunderstood that. (Members used the code word "paint" out of fear that the house might be bugged and government informants might be present.) Grant then took paint thinner and Ivory soap into the bathroom to build firebombs, asserted Hood. He distributed guns and rifles to Washington and Harrison, and Hood carried his own rifle equipped with a telescopic sight. According to Hood, Reddy drew a diagram of the area and designated positions to everyone. Parker and Reddy would be the ones to do the burning, while the others would act as lookouts and possible cover.[38]

Hood told the court that the group divided into two cars, drove to an apartment house parking lot near the stables, and took their assigned places. (Grant remained behind, guarding the getaway cars.) Hood stood guard by a tree, shrouding his view of what happened near the barn. Reddy and Parker went to the barn and doused it in gasoline. Then, Hood heard a bottle burst. As the flames and horses' screams filled the darkness, Hood saw Reddy and Parker running from the tinderbox. The winded troupe of conspirators met again at the cars, Hood testified, where Grant told them, "It's been taken care of. That's the only way to deal with them."[39]

Before stepping down, Hood answered the inevitable question (and a future cause for considerable scrutiny) served up by the prosecution: why he was testifying in the case. He did admit being motivated by his immunity from prosecution on the Lazy B Stables case, but went on to say, "I have found out that it wasn't a race issue that brought off the burning of the Lazy B Stables. It was a personal grudge, and . . . they used us . . . to have us burn down this place . . . when the only thing it was was a personal grudge on the world."[40]

Dave Washington followed Hood to the stand and told a similar version of events. Unlike Hood, Washington claimed his view as a lookout was "pretty clear in all directions." "The front door to the barn was directly to my left [, and] . . . it was pretty light." He saw Reddy pouring gasoline and both of them throwing firebombs. Then, "they all ran out [away from the barn] and said, 'let's go,' and I joined them. We all ran back out."[41] When asked his motivations for testifying, Washington also mentioned his immunity from charges on the Lazy B burning. His first response to the question, however, evoked personal repentance: "I gave the statements to the people because I realized for some time I had been involved in activities that were wrong and I had a chance to justify . . . as well as find out about James Grant and T.J. Reddy, about some of the things they had been involved in, because they have a large following of people, and they have been tricking them for quite some time, and then they would be exposed."[42]

The defense began its case with a number of alibi and character witnesses for Jim Grant. Four claimed that Grant had visited them in Pennsylvania on or near the time of the burning. One of these witnesses was Pennsylvania State University economics professor Wells Keddie. He recalled an appointment with Grant on the afternoon of the burning and brought his appointment calendar as evidence.[43]

The prosecution's repetitive cross-examination of defense witnesses' membership in various organizations drew attention to the case's political underpinning. When Joseph Hahm, one of Grant's alibi witnesses in Pennsylvania, came to the stand, prosecuting attorneys asked him to list the organizations to which he belonged. When done, the prosecutor received Hahm's permission to look at his wallet. He then asked Hahm dramatically, "Mr. Hahm, did you not forget to mention that you are a card-carrying member of the American Civil Liberties Union?" When asked again if there were any other "organizations" that the court should know about, he replied, "the Republican Party," to laughter in the courtroom.[44] The second defense witness, Andrew Brown (who was African American), was asked if he belonged to any "Black-oriented or other militant organizations." The prosecution asked all the Pennsylvania witnesses if they belonged to a prepared list of organizations, including "The Marxist Study Club" and "The Pennsylvania Socialist Society." Dr. Robert Miller, a character witness for T. J. Reddy, was asked if he had attended a Chicago conference that opposed the Vietnam War and supported Black Power ideology. "Yes, that was a conference of the Lutheran Church," he retorted.[45]

On the last day of testimony, T. J. Reddy testified on his own behalf. He denied any participation in or knowledge of the Lazy B burning. He disavowed belonging to "United Soul" or any other organization with Hood and Washington. He also claimed that the meetings discussed by the two men never happened. Several character witnesses for Reddy followed his testimony and closed the defense's case.[46] Given the lack of hard evidence, one of the Three's supporters remembers feeling "confident about their [the defendants'] hopes for acquittal up to that point."[47]

Her confidence was not misguided. During lunch recess, Judge Snepp called District Attorney Moore into chambers alone. Grant's alibi witness, Wells Keddie, had "screwed me up nicely," remembers ATF agent Bill Walden, who was present for the trial. "The judge even called in the prosecutor and balled him out for shoddy investigating. He didn't mean me, but someone else. And he threatened to dismiss the case unless we came up with something." Snepp's warning sent prosecutors frantically scrambling. Walden skipped his lunch that day and scurried out of the courtroom. "I went to a bank where Jim Grant had set up an account, and talked to the teller who he'd set up the account with. A real nice little old lady. She said [to the idea that he was out of state on the day of the burning], 'Hell no, he was in here setting up an account and talking about how he'd just come back from Russia.'"[48]

The busy lunch hour left the prosecution tardy in returning, but by no means empty-handed. The "nice little old lady," Laura Booton, became a prosecutorial bombshell. Booton, an administrative assistant at the Mechanics and Farmers Bank, took the stand and claimed to remember Grant submitting a signature card for the Southern Student Organizing Committee account on the day of the burning—thus countering Hahm's testimony placing Grant in

Pennsylvania at the same time.[49] Although the bank document was dated, Booton's testimony was crucial since it could have been signed on the date written, but submitted to the bank later. "That was a big blow," recounts Grant and Reddy's close friend Butch Rosen.[50] Indeed, one of the jurors later confided that he could not have agreed to the guilty verdict if prosecutors had not been able to refute Grant's Pennsylvania witnesses.[51]

The credibility of Booton's story to Walden led him back to Keddie's testimony. It would be too late, though. "That professor who was an alibi for Grant with his appointment book was smart," contends Walden. "He got in his car after testifying and drove off that day. We wanted his ass for perjury. It may have been hard to get him, though. He was careful. He never said that Grant came to his office on that day. He simply said he had an appointment with him."[52]

Most ardent Charlotte Three supporters link that bank signature card to a break-in at Grant's apartment in May 1972.[53] The incident was suspicious because Grant lost nothing of value, although his apartment was thoroughly ransacked. Virtually every piece of paper had been handled. It appeared that the intruders were looking for something among Grant's personal documents.[54] Grant had called the Reddy's that evening, and one activist supporter remembers the chaotic appearance: "Everything was just destroyed. It was mainly papers. They were just thrown *everywhere.*"[55] Butch Rosen notably queries, "Ask yourself what would lead the cops to a bank or a bank teller after four years. What sends you to that branch? How did they get to that person?"[56] The answer to this question among Charlotte Three supporters is that federal or state law enforcement agents broke into Grant's apartment themselves looking for evidence. Grant later claimed that his bank records mysteriously disappeared in the incident.[57]

The trial's concluding arguments reflected the deep division between sides of the courtroom aisle. Defense attorney James Ferguson attacked Hood's and Washington's credibility. He called the prosecution's effort surrounding the trial "one of the biggest deals made with criminals in our time. . . . [in which] agents of our government have conspired with criminals, thugs, and liars because they want to get T.J. Reddy . . . [and] James Earl Grant . . . I hope you are as ashamed of our government as I am," he told the jury. He called on the jury to "see the racial and political overtones in this trial. The defendants ask that you reject racial and political oppression."[58]

District Attorney Thomas Moore then emphasized his rebuttal witness as proof of the defendants' guilt. Denying Ferguson's accusations of the trial's "political overtones," he predictably referred to the defendants as "Black militants" and called Grant "the Wizard, the Chemist, the Professor," and Reddy "the Poet, the Psychological Man." Moore saw Parker, on the other hand, as "little Charlie Parker who went along with it all."[59]

Two hours were sufficient for the Charlotte Three jury: all three defendants guilty as charged. It was now Judge Snepp's turn. He called the stable burning "one of the most inhuman crimes I have ever heard of. You burned 15 horses in that stable. What you would do to human beings, God only knows." Judging them "dangerous to society," he proceeded to size them up individually before passing sentence.[60] Butch Rosen especially remembers Snepp "leaning over the bench at them and saying that he didn't think they were capable of being rehabilitated because they were educated."[61] Snepp assessed Grant as "the most culpable. You are the organizer and leader. That was your brainchild." He referred disappointedly to Reddy as "a man of promise, of talent" gone wrong. Snepp saw Parker as young and easily led astray by Grant and Reddy. Implying that the defendants shared responsibility for the protests that had so angered him outside the courtroom, he told them that "if you did not instigate the picketing, I know you could have stopped it with a word." He then passed sentences. Grant received twenty-five years, Reddy received twenty, and Parker received ten. (The maximum possible was thirty.)[62]

Charlotte Observer reporter Nancy Brachey claimed that "a low murmur swept the courtroom" of spectators (who were mostly supporters of the defendants). Both newspaper accounts and interviews describe the spectators as simply "stunned." Many cried and held one another in disbelief.[63]

* * *

Two days after the verdict brought the official conclusion to the Charlotte Three trial. Clarence Harrison, the lone guilty plea among the four defendants, stood before Judge Snepp—who had doled out fifty-five years among three others less than forty-eight hours before. Harrison brought with him his wife and two young children and H. B. Starnes, his employer and character witness. Starnes testified that Harrison had been working seven years for him, moving up from a warehouseman to an assistant supervisor, and he sought the defendant's continued employment.[64]

Michael Shulimson, Harrison's attorney, claimed that his client had no prior convictions and that this crime reflected a period when Harrison had been much "younger and wilder" before he had "changed his ways." Shulimson tried to distance Harrison from the other defendants and the controversial protests by calling it "ironic that there was a group demonstrating and calling Harrison a political prisoner. Not even Harrison would agree with that." After noting Hood's and Washington's testimony that Harrison had not understood that the group would burn the barn as they left that night, he requested that the court be lenient. The prosecution seconded the motion.[65]

Judge Snepp then asked Harrison if Hood's and Washington's accounts had been true. Harrison responded affirmatively. He did likewise when Snepp asked if he had "gotten over this" and was now able to "live and work things out with people in a peaceful way." Apparently pleased with what he heard, Snepp issued five years probation under a seven-year suspended sentence since "you were not one of the instigators of this and didn't understand what was to be done and how you were being used."[66]

Snepp's sentencing comments undergird the perception that the state and federal authorities perceived Grant and Reddy as leaders and masterminds inciting the Black masses to conspiratorial anarchy. If Harrison was not an "instigator," surely Grant and Reddy were. Snepp's characterization of Harrison as someone who "didn't understand" invoked the same leniency shown toward Hood and Washington. Hood had told the court that he was motivated to testify since Grant and Reddy "used us" to avenge "a personal grudge on the world."[67] Washington had emphasized that testifying afforded him the opportunity to speak out about Grant and Reddy's "large following of people, [how] they have been tricking them for quite some time, and then they would be exposed."[68] The prosecution had painted the two as psychologically manipulative and controlling figures: Grant as "the Wizard, the Chemist, the Professor" and Reddy as "the Poet, the Psychological Man."[69]

Charles Parker, the only defendant to bring to the court a previous criminal record (a narcotics possession conviction for which he served five months in early 1972), paradoxically received the most lenient sentence by far among the not guilty pleas. Like Harrison, Hood, and Washington, the judge and prosecution saw Parker as manipulated by the two ringleaders. District Attorney Thomas Moore, the lead prosecuting attorney, had contrasted Grant and Reddy with "little Charlie Parker who went along with it all," and Snepp revealed his feeling that Parker had been young and easily led astray.[70] According to Butch Rosen, the state tried to make a deal with Parker similar to the one offered Hood and Washington, but he had refused. Presumably, the state tried to use the same leverage of leniency or immunity on his drug conviction prior to the trial.[71]

Many of Grant's and Reddy's close associates felt that Parker and Harrison were simply peripheral to the state's real interests. No one close to the defendants remembers any personal connections between the Charlotte Three and Harrison before the trial. Butch Rosen believes that "the state wanted him out. . . . He simply got caught in the net of this, and the state didn't care about him. They were after Grant and Reddy." Charlotte Three supporters also saw the state as only marginally interested in Parker, despite his ten-year sentence. Activist Kathy Sparrow's impression is that Parker simply "paid the price for being in the wrong place at the wrong time. He . . . just got involved somehow."[72]

Despite the state's apparent limited interest in prosecuting Harrison and Parker, however, they still may have played an important role in the case. By including two men who were not outspoken leaders, the prosecution could head off the appearance of a witch hunt aimed at activists with clean records. According to Butch Rosen, "Having Charles Parker as a defendant gave the government the appearance of being more objective, since he really wasn't much of an activist. It said, 'Look, we're not just after activists here.'"[73] Another possible scenario is that the authorities were always after only Grant and Reddy. Their only plans for Parker and Harrison were using them to testify against the ringleaders.

The designation of a "mastermind" behind the crime fits snugly into a traditional white southern perception of African Americans as inherently childlike, stemming back to their days of bondage. Its corollary is that any Black defiance must necessarily be led by a few misguided, antisocial provocateurs unnecessarily stirring up trouble in a system that already adequately serves African American interests. Judge Snepp's sentencing comments evoke such a view. He called the burning the "brainchild" of the "instigator" Grant, lamented Reddy as a "man of talent" gone bad, and Parker as sadly led astray by the psychologically powerful Grant and Reddy.[74]

Prosecutors made a clear effort to separate the burning participants into two groups: the masterminds and the misled. Most of the "misled" (Washington, Hood, Harrison, and Parker) had criminal records and would ordinarily be considered more culpable. In this trial, however, it was the criminally clean "masterminds" (Grant and Reddy) who were most culpable—for having corrupted the minds of the other Black innocents. Part of the prosecution's pursuit of these "masterminds" was its emphasis on the alleged underground organization "United Soul." "There was a clear effort to portray these guys [the Charlotte Three] as some kind of mafia syndicate," relates *Charlotte Observer* journalist Mark Ethridge. "They [federal and state authorities] wanted them to be perceived as an organized crime group that was a threat to America." This portrayal also made the invocation of the 1970 Organized Crime Control Act (which authorized the protective custody expenditures spent on Hood and Washington) for this case much more credible.[75]

After the shock of the guilty verdicts and severe sentences for the Charlotte Three, what awaited their supporters immediately outside caused yet more disbelief. Deputy sheriffs quickly cleared the courtroom.[76] Snepp had more than doubled the usual number of sheriff deputies again, stationing nine deputies inside the courtroom for the day of sentencing. This, according to the *Charlotte News* reporter Ellison Clary, was intended to "quell any possible outbreaks from the audience [which was largely defendants' supporters]."[77] When the Three's supporters walked out onto the courthouse steps, "all you saw was cops," recalls Butch Rosen: "It was crawling with cops. There were police cars all over the place with their lights going. There were police on all the street corners in the surrounding area. There was a row of police across the street in riot gear. There were police with guns on all the rooftops. Here we were just crying and not knowing what to do next, and they were all expecting World War III," contends Rosen. "This told us what the trial was all about. It told us a lot about their perceptions. To them, we were a dangerous group of people."[78]

Dangerous indeed. It was not just *the people* who were dangerous, though. The issues raised by the trial were dangerous. Despite the best efforts of many involved in the government to muffle these militant Black voices, discussion over the trial and the government's role in it proved more difficult to silence in the years that followed.

* * *

The polarization of the period played out tragically for Jim Grant, T. J. Reddy, and Charles Parker. If several talented young Black men *did* burn the Lazy B barn in 1968, they might have thought such a course overzealous in 1978. Similarly, the Oxford murder of Marrow might not have caused violent racial uprisings in another era. Grant's and Chavis's association with violent criminals like Hood and Washington might have seemed foolhardy. In another time, law enforcement officers would not have released two violent convicts to ensnare several others—most of whom were criminally clean. Three men would not have received some of the stiffest sentencing for unlawful burning in state history. In the late 1960s and early 1970s, though, the drama played out as if to some macabre script.

But, perhaps, a more fitting end to the Charlotte Three trial came five days after the Three's conviction, when Al Hood and Dave Washington met ATF agent Stan Noel. Keeping good on his promise, Noel had checks from the U.S. government for the two men. Noel issued them each $3,000, but he felt it was not enough and beseeched his superior for more. Noel also disbursed plane tickets to Mexico to the men, their revised choice for relocation. Hood and Washington's new plan was to open a motel there.[79]

On August 8, 1972, however, Judge Frank Snepp heeded the recommendation of Dave Washington's exasperated probation officer. Washington had been under a five-year probation for his 1969 armed robbery conviction. Violating that probation should have activated a suspended twenty-five-year sentence. Washington had clearly done so on the occasion of his May 1970 arrest in Oxford. Judge Snepp acted over the protest of District Attorney Thomas Moore, who had promised Washington that his testimony would mean terminating his probation without penalty.[80]

Noel disbursed the last of the U.S. government's bounty to Hood and Washington on August 21 and 22, two weeks after a warrant went out for Washington's arrest. Noel later conceded to reporters that it "could be" that he knew of the warrant at that time, but could not say for sure. "It was more or less secondhand (information) and I didn't go down and verify there was a state charge and I had no jurisdiction" to arrest Washington. This meant that the federal agents issued government money for "relocation" to a wanted man. The payments to the two witnesses had always been justified as money for them to leave the country and flee potential retaliation. Whether Hood and Washington ever temporarily relocated in Mexico in the days after the trial remains unclear, but it is clear that they were back permanently in Charlotte by late August 1972. But, had Washington used the federal law enforcement payments for its designated purpose, he would have "relocated" himself from official criminal charges.

As for the warrant for Washington's arrest, it would not be served for another eight months. When it was, the resulting May 1973 hearing continued Washington's remarkable good fortune. Jimmy Craig, his former probation officer, told presiding judge Robert Martin that Washington had quite simply "violated the terms of probation since it was issued." Craig was outmanned and outgunned, though, by a remarkable array of officials. At the pleading of District Attorney Thomas Moore, Assistant U.S. Attorney David Long, and a letter from the Criminal Section chief of the U.S. Justice Department, Martin terminated Washington's probation and absolved the twenty-five-year sentence hanging over his head. Dave Washington once again walked out of the courtroom a free man.[81]

Perhaps Al Hood delivered the clearest assessment of the justice done in the case a few years later when he unexpectedly ran into defense attorney James Ferguson in a nightclub. Speaking cryptically from behind his signature dark glasses, he whispered to Ferguson through the smoke, "It's all a game, man. Don't you understand? It's just a game."[82]

7

THE NORTH CAROLINA
POLITICAL PRISONERS
COMMITTEE

I n the wake of the bewildering Charlotte Three convictions, supporters of
Jim Grant, T. J. Reddy, and Charles Parker did what they had always done.
They rallied around one another and took action. At a meeting a week after
the sentencing, they formed the North Carolina Political Prisoners Committee (NCPPC). Over the next seven years, some seventy-five people took part,
with at least twenty-five remaining active throughout the group's campaign,
providing a consistent presence to ensure that the Charlotte Three case would
never completely disappear from the media and government radar screen.[1]

Awaiting the new group's attention was an extremely difficult issue. Charlotte Three trial judge Frank Snepp, who had taken an increasingly combative
stance toward the Three's supporters' courthouse demonstrations, had set un-
usually high bonds on the defendants awaiting appeal ($50,000 each on Grant
and Reddy, $25,000 on Parker). It was one more unfriendly facet of a justice
system they had found consistently hostile. To compound matters, the clerk
of court refused to accept anything less than the full cash amount. This defied
the customary practice of accepting 10 percent through a bail bondsman. "We
were dumbfounded" upon discovering this from the clerk of court, says Butch
Rosen. "We thought, 'We'll never raise that much money.' We were poverty
workers, community organizers, and we simply didn't have access to that kind
of cash."[2]

It would take some time before all could fully grasp their friends' imprisonment. Butch Rosen remembers those days well. "At first [after the trial] we

were just afraid. They might now come and get *us.*" Given the dizzying mystery of these convictions, Rosen felt unclear as to what fate lay for himself and the other activists—and who was really behind such a conspiracy: "maybe not so much the police, but the KKK or somebody, and if *they* came, the police sure as hell weren't going to do much to protect us." For Rosen, the full force of his mounting anxiety arrived at a definable place and time, as if it were an evangelical conversion experience devoid of warmth or reassurance. A few months after the trial, as Rosen was sitting in an easy chair, the full emotional impact of the trial suddenly "just swept over me like a wave. The hair on the back of my neck and arms stood on end and I broke out into a cold sweat. I can remember clutching the arms of the chair as the realization came over me: 'No one is safe. If they want to get you, they'll get you.' Before that I had had a feeling of security that there was oppression, but that the system could still work with some vigilance. But that moment just changed my life. I've never looked at things the same way again."[3]

While such moments do not arrive rationally, from the very beginning of the group's post-trial life there was reason for some paranoia. At the NCPPC's formation meeting, as members gathered to plan, comfort, and console, they were being watched. In their midst sat yet another unwelcome component of the justice system they had so come to fear: an informant. The Charlotte Police Department's Intelligence Division had sent one of their own as an undercover agent. That informant, of course, would only make the going rougher for the NCPPC. At a subsequent, unsuccessful bail appeal hearing on the case, the Intelligence Division's Sergeant Joseph Europa revealed the placement of his man at the meeting, and claimed the subject had advised that the group planned on raising bail to allow the Charlotte Three to flee the country. That an informant had been at the meeting "did not surprise" Butch Rosen, but he calls Europa's alleged information from the contact "a blatant lie. We certainly discussed gathering the bail money, but never anything about them skipping it."[4]

The use of secret informants was a common tactic by law enforcement units who targeted Black Power and New Left agitators of the time, and was one more indication of the seriousness with which the Three and their activist colleagues were viewed. Like many other aggressive law enforcement trends of the time, FBI Director J. Edgar Hoover had led the way in making such informants a high priority. So great and constant was Hoover's pressure on this matter that some FBI field offices actually invented fictitious informants on paperwork forwarded to headquarters to avoid superiors' displeasure. Charlotte, then, like so many other local units, developed so-called "ghetto informants" to penetrate Black Power and New Left organizations that mingled among the inner-city poor (as opposed to the long-used informants who provided leads on more common crimes).[5]

Approximately a week after the Charlotte Three sentencing, the newly founded NCPPC issued a press release. The statement excoriated "the corrupt and malign misuse of the criminal justice system, as exemplified in the harsh treatment of brothers Reddy, Parker, and Grant." The group sought "first to raise bail funds for the Charlotte Three . . . ; [and] secondly to speak to the issue of political repression as it occurs around the state." It encouraged letter-writing to the governor and press, and financial contributions to the bail fund. It also distanced itself from "destructive measures such as the recent bomb threat" against the courthouse a few days before, saying the committee "can see no positive results from such tactics." To further its goals, the NCPPC began producing and mailing newsletters to sympathizers.[6]

Besides the pressure applied by the NCPPC, another unforeseen event would aid the cause of the Charlotte Three. When five men broke into the Democratic National Committee headquarters on June 17, 1972, no one could have predicted that it would become a national firestorm that would shake the White House. Neither could Charlotteans have known that a burglary hundreds of miles away could impact a stable-burning case. On the national scene, long-held liberal suspicions of Nixon's "dirty tricks" turned to documented evidence of wrongdoing. The conservative campaign of "law and order" had already done much to undermine public support for the polarizing fringe of militant leftists in the late 1960s and early 1970s. The Watergate scandal would force conservatives to reconsider the politics of extremism on the right side of the political spectrum. In the Queen City, Watergate also created an important moment for Charlotte Three supporters. Suddenly their claims of government conspiracy in the case seemed reasonable. This would be particularly true in the halls of the local newspaper, the *Charlotte Observer*, which would begin to pursue its own story of apparent government power run amok.

One month before the U.S. House of Representatives Judiciary Committee initiated a full-scale presidential impeachment inquiry, the *Charlotte*

Observer published its March 1974 series on the Charlotte Three case. The NCPPC had been the driving force behind the newspaper's reluctance to forget a two-year-old court trial, and the articles were a tremendous boost to the pardon hopes of the Charlotte Three. The series revealed questionable government tactics in its prosecution of the defendants, including secret cash payments to their star witnesses Hood and Washington. Perhaps even more dramatic was the case's tangible connection to the Watergate scandal. The *Observer* disclosed U.S. Assistant Attorney General Robert Mardian's involvement in the case. The series sent shockwaves through Charlotte, but it also drew attention all over the country—from politicians to major newspapers to human rights groups.

* * *

On the morning after Harrison's sentencing, the *Charlotte Observer* already showed itself friendly to the Charlotte Three. An editorial criticized Snepp's sentencing of the Charlotte Three as "out of line with sentences imposed in other unlawful burning cases in North Carolina in recent years." It highlighted all other unlawful burning convictions in the previous ten years—fifteen in all—and revealed that all carried lesser sentences than the Charlotte Three trial. These previous convictions included an April 1970 five-year punishment levied on a man who burned his estranged wife's occupied home, and fifteen years given to a seventeen-year-old who burned three occupied houses. Acknowledging that the Lazy B blaze was a "considerable loss in property and a blow to horse-lovers' sentiment," the *Observer* questioned whether "the offense [was] greater than the others cited here? Are those 15 horses worth 25, 20, and ten years of three men's lives?"[7]

Class became an important factor in public reaction to the case, as evidenced by the notice taken of the Charlotte Three's education level. During sentencing, Butch Rosen recalls that Snepp justified Grant and Reddy's higher sentences *because* of their education—seeing it as reducing the probability of their rehabilitation. If the usual goal of rehabilitation was to educate a convict of his own self-destructiveness, then a fully educated man appeared to Snepp to be a less promising subject for social redemption. On the other hand, the Charlotte Three supporters suggested that the defendants' talent and education made it less credible that they would commit this common crime, and concluded that the lengthy removal of the men from their communities was even more of a tragedy because of their talent.

The issue of the defendants' education played out most explicitly in the case of the artist and poet T. J. Reddy. His art became an important touchstone with which sympathetic middle- to upper-class whites could identify. One man wrote the *Observer* editor of the "spectacle" of convicting "a poet and dramatist of uncommon, God-given talent" such as Reddy. "That so fine, so promisingly talented a man could be crucified on the evidence of 'star' witnesses who [had] . . . serious criminal records . . . seems an outrage of unspeakable horror."[8] Charlotte Three trial juror B. L. Bradshaw wrote that because Reddy was "very impressive on the witness stand," he "could not have returned a guilty verdict" had the state not "so convincingly disproved the testimony of the Pennsylvania witnesses."[9]

Reddy's talent brought not only admirers but important allies in powerful circles. The Reverend Carlyle Marney, former pastor of the wealthy and influential Myers Park Baptist Church, donated $2,500 to the NCPPC bail fund. Marney wrote Bill Pinson, chair of the Church Board of Deacons in early 1973, and recruited him to donate the same amount. Pinson forthrightly admits being "very reluctant, but I put up the money anyway. I stuck my neck out on it, but I believed in Marney so much, that I did it." He recalls his lawyer advising, "You can kiss that money goodbye. He'll leave the country probably. You ought to go talk to the judge."[10] Reddy also later attracted Nobel Prize-winning biology professor George Wald as a pen pal and a spectator at his December 1973 appeal hearing. A March 1973 cocktail party and legal fee fundraiser in the elite Charlotte neighborhood of Myers Park featured Reddy entertaining questions from accountants, lawyers, city councilmen, and local university professors.[11] According to Julie Wheeler, a friend of Reddy's who was active on civil rights issues and whose husband, Raymond, served as the president of the Southern Regional Council in the late 1960s and early 1970s, "Many people sided with T. J. because of the fact that he was the kind of person he was. They regarded him as a comer, an attractive, bright, talented young man—not some uneducated bum."[12] The *Charlotte Observer* newsroom still remembered the talent of Reddy as a young intern, and the paper ran two political cartoons featuring the defendants' talent as a rationale for their release.[13]

The NCPPC had also been hard at work. Members gathered together to compose and mail their newsletters on the cause, and they began to connect themselves with the broader "political prisoners" movement in the early 1970s, seeking to draw attention to the growing phenomenon of jailed activists. The list was lengthy, amid numerous antiwar activist cases: the 1968 Catonsville Nine, the media-frenzied Chicago Eight stemming from the 1968 Democratic convention, myriad Black militant trials like the Angela Davis fugitive drama and the Panther Twenty-One, and—not to be left out—cases against other ethnic militants, such as the Wounded Knee trials (involving Native American activists) and the East L.A. Thirteen (targeting Chicano activists).[14]

One natural ally for the NCPPC was the Wilmington Ten Defense Committee. That group sought to free the ten activists (including former Charlotte agitator and Raleigh Two defendant Ben Chavis) who had been convicted in Wilmington, North Carolina, on arson and conspiracy charges in September 1972 stemming from a February 1971 riot. Like the Charlotte case across the state, the Wilmington Ten story also included ATF agent Bill Walden (and other federal agents) and paid convict witnesses.[15] Together, the two defense groups shared information and, occasionally, resources.[16]

Besides the newsletter and letter-writing and petition campaigns targeted at the governor, the NCPPC designed a slide show that dramatized its support for the Charlotte Three. "God knows I traveled all over North Carolina with that slide show," contends Marvin Sparrow. Members showed it and fielded questions primarily at church and civic groups to generate interest. The nature of the NCPPC's work, then, took members far afield of their usual battlegrounds. As Marvin Sparrow recalls, "The whole political prisoners committee movement was trying to get into the solid middle class of America and try to get them to see that there was something wrong—primarily because I think there was a need to have people with some kind of clout and power to do something about it."[17]

That focus on the middle class and those with "clout and power" is likely one of the myriad reasons that the NCPPC remained largely white in membership over the years. In later years, as the NCPPC struggled to keep its cause afloat, that issue became increasingly troubling to many members. Kathy Sparrow remembers consistent involvement in the committee's work by several African Americans, but they always remained in the minority.[18]

Several other factors may have lent to the low numbers in Black membership. Notably, Charlotte activists had already had some degree of racial separation before the trial. That separation was by no means a strict one. There had always been crossover between Blacks and whites on issues, and some Black activists—Jim Grant and T. J. Reddy among them—had moved fluidly between the two racial groups. Marvin Sparrow claims that many of Charlotte's Black activists "just weren't interested in antiwar stuff," a central concern for many of the city's white militants. (Grant, Reddy, and Parker were all exceptions to that rule—one reason why they were better connected to white activists than many of their racial counterparts.) That racial division reflected the city in which the activists operated. "Charlotte itself was a very [racially] divided city," maintains Marvin Sparrow, and this constrained greater interracial contact among activists as well.[19]

The fate of many of the more militant Black leaders of Charlotte in the late 1960s only compounded the problem. As the Charlotte Area Fund had fallen under attack by civic leaders for its alleged troublemaking, the agency had been forced to curb or fire some of its more outspoken and strident community organizers. Reginald Hawkins had been undermined by a succession of criminal indictments, and the Black Culture Association and Afro American Unity Organization (AAUO) had disappeared under a rain of charges. Granting that the latter two groups may have partly hastened their own demise through actions that allowed law enforcement to ensnare their members, the loss of Black militants was nonetheless unmistakable. The AAUO was "basically . . . in disarray soon after it was born. I mean, it just *crumbled* under the police pressure," contends Marvin Sparrow. The removal of Black militants made the potential of white militants' sizable like-minded coalitions with African Americans all the more difficult.[20]

Particularly during the era of heightened Black consciousness, T. J. Reddy's white wife, Vicki, may have distanced some Black Charlotteans from rallying to the Three. Furthermore, since Vicki Reddy (as the closest relative to any of the defendants) became the natural focal point of defense activity, many of her white activist friends rose to her support, and the Charlotte Three defense appeared to some as a "white" cause to be handled by that white activist community.[21] "Part of it was that T. J. had so many white friends," recalls Frye Gaillard, who was another white friend of Reddy's as well as a local journalist. "Now, he had Black friends. He was certainly not ashamed of being Black, but for whatever reason, he had lots of white friends." Thus, according to Gaillard, the Charlotte Three defense issue "sort of hooked in that whole white liberal/radical network in Charlotte."[22]

The Charlotte Three case also suffered by comparison to the media attention granted the more renowned North Carolina "political prisoners" trial, the Wilmington Ten. The case stemmed from the 1971 burning of a white-owned grocery in the midst of African American community school desegregation protests in Wilmington, North Carolina. (The city first desegregated its high schools in the 1970–1971 school year under a court order.) Ten of the community activists were charged, and later sentenced to a combined 242 years on arson and conspiracy charges in 1972. They included former Charlotte activist and Oxfordian Ben Chavis, who became a magnet during the 1970s for his cause. It also drew the notable attention of firebrand Angela Davis, who fought her own court battle in the early 1970s as an alleged "political prisoner" before her 1972 release. Activist Kathy Sparrow maintains that Davis "had a lot to do with making the Wilmington Ten a national issue."[23]

The attention of Charlotte's African American community to other pressing concerns also hurt the NCPPC's cause. The busing controversy that raged in the late 1960s to mid-1970s certainly sapped significant energies that might have gone to other causes. Charlotte's Black population was also no different from those of the vast majority of southern—and even some northern—cities in celebrating their 1960s civil and voting rights victories by moving en masse into electoral politics in the 1970s. In 1974 alone, longtime Black city councilman Fred Alexander would win the race for state senator, and African American architect Harvey Gantt would take his seat on the City Council (from which, in 1983, he would later ascend to the mayor's chair).[24]

Lastly, there is little doubt that the taint of a felony conviction and imprisonment (including animal cruelty) did much to mute support of already controversial activists. While Black Charlotteans would be expected to have a greater sensitivity to injustice in the court system, that sensitivity was unlikely to triumph over many middle-class Blacks' hesitancy to rally to the cause of three convicts (who were not imprisoned for more traditional civil rights era crimes like disturbing the peace during a nonviolent march)—particularly when the avenue of expressing their concerns through electoral politics was now open.

* * *

Despite those concerns, NCPPC members continued to press ahead. They felt one of the most effective tactics would be to draw attention outside the state. Many saw it as a productive opportunity to pressure the governor and state and municipal agencies in a state that prided itself on its progressive reputation. Former *Charlotte Observer* reporter Mark Ethridge called it "a natural point of leverage, and the NCPPC used it. It was particularly important to involving people outside North Carolina. They hammered it, and outside journalists hammered it."[25] Years earlier, *Observer* editor Pete McKnight had been a participant in the Charlotte Chamber of Commerce meetings leading to the 1963 public accommodations desegregation. Local *Observer* journalist and author Frye Gaillard recounts him telling the group at the time, "'It all depends on whether you want to act on this [public accommodations] or read about it yourself in *The New York Times*.' So, that impulse in wanting to be perceived as a progressive state [has always existed]—image has always been important in this state. Not that we've always behaved in a rational way if that's the case, but I think that there's no doubt that that was important to politicians at the time."[26]

The strategy of attacking the city's reputation appeared to first pay off with a November 1972 three-article series in Jim Grant's hometown newspaper, the *Hartford Courant*. In sectionalist overtones, the Connecticut daily began the series with a front-page story bearing its title in large print over the masthead reading, "Dixie Fire Frameup, Says Ex-City Man."[27] The articles were quite sympathetic to Grant (the last featured a photo of Grant's parents peering mournfully at Grant's graduation picture), and included financial appeals to their readers. Discussing their inability to raise more than $5,000 of the $150,000 bond, NCPPC member Richard Rosen (brother of Butch Rosen and former housemate of Reddy) told the *Courant*, "We didn't have the class of wealthy liberals here that you have in the North."[28] The nationally known Charlotte author and syndicated columnist Harry Golden told the paper that "racism was not the concrete phase of the trial, but the attitude was always there to put the Negroes in their place." *Hartford Courant* correspondent William Cockerham's interview with the jailed Jim Grant included Grant's assessment that "North Carolina is one of the most reactionary, fascist, backward states in the South. It uses the University of North Carolina as public relations material to peddle to the rest of the country that it is progressive." Grant claimed that the state had more Ku Klux Klan members than any other, and that their "influence . . . extends into the highest reaches of state government and the courts."[29] No doubt considered hyperbole by some, North Carolina actually laid claim to more chapters of the United Klans of America than all other southern states combined at its mid-1960s peak.[30]

In January of 1973, Don Noel, editor of the African American paper the *Hartford Times,* ran an editorial calling the case "symptomatic of one of the most backward elements of the 'New South.'" (Local Charlotteans got their own chance to hear his comments when the *Charlotte Observer* reprinted them.) The New England newspaper editor claimed, "Justice seems to rest mostly in federal courts, and not in the state judiciary," and concluded, "Grant is 'guilty' of four years' Black activism in a community that was unprepared, as recently as 1968, for even so commonplace a brand of activism as appeals for Black pride."[31]

Hartford, Connecticut, interest was not limited to newspaper ink. Hartford residents received continued exposure to the case through television coverage as well, peaking in a locally produced documentary in December 1973.[32] To channel Hartford community concern, Jim Grant's parents set up the James E. Grant, Jr. Defense Fund, which later successfully collected the $50,000 state bond from local citizens.[33] In January 1974, Connecticut governor John Meskill wrote North Carolina governor James Holshouser to highlight "the many comments from citizens of Connecticut concerning Dr. Grant," particularly the clemency requests by "Dr. Grant's parents [who] have been to my office . . . and the Hartford City Council [which] recently passed a resolution [to that effect]." Meskill, aware that Grant was now eligible for parole on the federal conviction if he should be freed of the state sentence, conveyed his "hope that you consider these requests as you review this case."[34]

The NCPPC also tried to attract more widespread attention by recruiting a speaker who already enjoyed a national reputation: militant civil rights spokeswoman and avowed communist Angela Davis. By staging a rally with her in December 1972, the committee hoped to broaden the base of local Black support as well. In doing so, however, the organization was forced to deal with the social division of the era. While featuring Angela Davis could draw Black community enthusiasm to their white-dominated committee, some NCPPC members also worried that the controversial Davis might alienate moderate supporters. In the end, they "decided that the benefits far outweighed the risks."[35]

Unfortunately, Davis "appeared" at the rally only through the telephone wire. Fogbound at the Atlanta airport, her voice, emanating from a public phone, was broadcast to a disappointed capacity crowd of two thousand in Charlotte. Her comments furthered the committee's attack on North Carolina's progressive reputation. Davis maintained that the state employed the currently popular tactic of using the judicial system as "a key weapon in the arsenal of reaction." She concluded that "North Carolina now represents the worst kind of racist tradition in this country."[36]

In June of 1973, the NCPPC wrote U.S. congressional members, enclosing literature, to encourage them to investigate as well as pressure the governor. Noted African American representative John Conyers of Michigan wrote the NCPPC back for further information on the case, "interested in the possibility of testimony concerning this affair coming before the appropriate subcommittee" at a later date.[37] The committee also contacted Senator Lowell Weicker of Connecticut in June 1973, hoping to capitalize on the burgeoning Watergate concern and the senator's representation of Grant's home state. Weicker sat on the Senate Select Committee on Presidential Campaign Activities investigating the Watergate scandal just then getting underway. He claimed that the NCPPC letter—because of the tie-in to federal involvement—"is most helpful to me in connection with my Watergate investigation and I very much appreciate" the factual enclosures on the case, which would "greatly facilitate my investigation." Neither of these possible investigations ever materialized, however.[38]

* * *

While the Charlotte Three and their supporters continued their long road for judicial redemption, Al Hood seemed utterly unredeemed by his association with the right side of the law. On August 30, 1972—one week after his final federal government payoff and one month after the Charlotte Three trial—the Charlotte Police Department issued a warrant for Al Hood's involvement in a housing project gunfight that killed convicted heroin pusher Earl Mackey. Authorities claimed that Hood and two others had ambushed Mackey in a execution-style shooting between the eyes. Police believed the murder was part of a gang war over the local heroin trade, and stated that they had information that the three assailants had sought Mackey for three months. This would have meant Hood stalked Mackey even before the Charlotte Three trial, and Mackey was no ordinary drug pusher. A gang member by age twelve, his twelve arrests ranged from store-breaking to murder to numerous drug charges, and police posthumously identified him as "the number one man" in the very dangerous Oaklawn area drug trade that had already produced two such murders in the first half of that year. Hood turned himself in to authorities nine days later, and was then released on a mere $4,000 bond on first-degree murder charges (12.5 percent of what Grant and Reddy each received for their unlawful burning conviction appeal).[39]

In late November 1972, while still awaiting trial on murder charges, Hood was arrested for possession of marijuana and again released pending trial on that charge. Hood failed to appear for the preliminary hearing on the marijuana possession. The day after the court issued a warrant on his failure to appear, he was again arrested for marijuana possession, compounding his mounting charges. He also faced charges for violating his probation.[40]

As for Dave Washington, he too had been busy following the May 1973 hearing terminating his probation (over the advice of his exasperated probation officer). Washington—who had returned to the United States in 1967 without penalty for shooting at his army sergeant and reportedly massacring Vietnamese villagers—would elude innumerable criminal charges and two near fatal shootouts. In one early 1974 incident that evoked almost Rasputin-like abilities to dodge his own downfall, Washington remarkably drove himself to the hospital after being shot twice in the stomach.[41]

* * *

In March 1973, T. J. Reddy and Charles Parker greeted a small group of two dozen family and friends outside the walls of the Mecklenburg County jail. The North Carolina Political Prisoners Committee had succeeded in posting the $75,000 bond for the two men awaiting appeal. The NCPPC's bond-raising efforts had finally prevailed when UNC Charlotte history professor John Hall offered his home as collateral. The liberal professor had taken a particular liking to Reddy during his years as a student there.[42]

Although Jim Grant's parents had raised his state bond in Connecticut, it was not submitted since he was still obligated to serve his federal sentence. Three days before Reddy's and Parker's release, the U.S. Fourth Circuit Court of Appeals denied Grant's stay of judgement request on his federal conviction. This cleared the way for his transfer to an Atlanta federal prison shortly thereafter. Putting up bond on the Three's state conviction would not have released him from federal imprisonment.[43]

Understanding that his venture into freedom might only be temporary, T. J. Reddy attempted to capitalize on the opportunity to build support for the North Carolina Political Prisoners Committee. (The shy Parker made far fewer appearances.) Reddy gave interviews and spoke to fundraising parties and innumerable civic and religious groups. He prepared his poems—many of which were written in confinement—for publication by the major national publisher Random House. He rallied further support in Grant's home state of Connecticut, speaking at the University of Connecticut and Yale University, at several churches, and with local media. All the while he told of the cause and of "the big ordeal of having to spend eight months inside of a cage."[44]

While the activists pursued their cause with the public, Jim Ferguson continued to press forward on the legal front. At the August 1973 conviction hearing before the North Carolina Court of Appeals, Ferguson asserted that the Charlotte Three were "tried for political activity" amid "an attitude of hostility on the part of the trial court." To back up the point, Ferguson introduced a dramatic guest: Joel Carlson, representing the internationally recognized human rights watchdog organization Amnesty International. Carlson exhorted the court to overturn Grant's conviction, saying, "We believe Grant is a prisoner of conscience. He is being prosecuted for his beliefs, not his actions."[45] Apparently unmoved, the North Carolina Court of Appeals upheld the convictions of the Charlotte Three a month later, concluding that trial judge Snepp's "careful and systematic approach to sentencing deserves to be encouraged, not hindered."[46]

* * *

"It's a nightmare. I guess I'll be waking from it sometime," said T. J. Reddy, joining Charles Parker to again surrender themselves to imprisonment. They did so on January 29, 1974, after the denial of their appeal and Governor Jim

Holshouser's failure to move on a pardon by that time. Fifty others, many weeping, went as far as allowed with them. Reporters noted that, amid the unusual public attention, Clerk of Court Max Blackburn's "hand [was] visibly shaking" as he signed papers committing the two at last to state prison. "I was surprised by the sudden influx of all those people," Blackburn claimed. Attorney James Ferguson told reporters he would not appeal to the U.S. Supreme Court, choosing instead to put his hopes in a possible pardon from Governor Jim Holshouser.[47]

Despite the decidedly dark day that January, the Three's cause appeared to be gaining momentum in the early months of 1974, culminating in a startling *Observer* series on the case in March. Letters to the governor and to newspaper editors had sprinkled in fits and starts from September 1972 to early 1974, but a late January 1974 *Observer* editorial catalyzed a period of much greater scrutiny on the case. Entitled simply "An Injustice? Lazy B Case Needs Inquiry," the piece stressed the lack of physical evidence linking the defendants to the crime and the marginal credibility of the witnesses who delivered the bulk of the evidence. It urged the governor and his parole board—who had informed the public of their official inquiry into the case—to "inquire carefully" into the "convictions and the circumstances of the trial."[48] After an upsurge of letters to the editor on the case, the *Observer* ran another editorial four weeks later urging Governor Holshouser to commute the sentences.[49]

The backdrop of national public scrutiny on the alleged abuses of the so-called "imperial presidency" of Richard Nixon only made these local concerns more credible. After months of stonewalling, Nixon yielded to a wave of public outrage and released seven subpoenaed White House audiotapes in the Watergate scandal. Charges would soon be filed against seven high-level administration officials, including Assistant Attorney General Robert Mardian, whose role in the Charlotte Three trial was yet to be revealed.[50]

Reflecting the increasing concern in the Charlotte Three case from outside North Carolina, Charlottean Micki Esselstyn wrote the *Charlotte Observer* editorial page that the "shocking" Charlotte Three sentences had "drawn deserved and infamous nationwide attention to North Carolina—a lynching 1973-style." Kathryn Houlihan of Minneapolis, Minnesota, had read a recent Charlotte Three story that circulated the national UPI wire, and she wrote the *Observer* to question such convictions in "the land of the free and the home of the brave."[51] Ralph Grosswald, "a member of the Charlotte business community," wrote of his fear that the case would mean "our state judicial system will be tainted in the eyes of others."[52]

Meanwhile, other outsiders continued to act on behalf of the Charlotte Three. Connecticut's Governor Meskill sent his personal appeal for leniency in the case to Governor Holshouser. In early March 1974, *Washington Post* editorialist Colman McCarthy called the case another example of "the crudeness and arrogance that characterized John Mitchell's regime as Attorney General ... [in which] the law can be used against citizens judged to be a threat to 'law-and-order.'" McCarthy contended that "the governor of North Carolina has an obligation to act, either to remove all doubts about the case so that the guilt is factually based, or to drop the sentences so that justice in North Carolina is no longer mocked."[53]

It is no mystery where this upsurge of interest came from. While the *Observer* played a pivotal role in generating interest, the paper was spurred on by the indefatigable work of the North Carolina Political Prisoners Committee. Members remember the persistence of the committee as being pivotal in generating the daily's stories and editorials on the case. NCPPC members doggedly raised the issues of the case in the community and especially among the *Observer*'s reporters.[54] Indeed, reporter Michael Schwartz remembers the NCPPC members as keeping the case "in the public eye not only here but Connecticut and all over the world actually. They just kept hammering and hammering away at wherever they could and the newspaper was a place where they were kind of relentless."[55] His colleague Mark Ethridge remembers newsrooms at that time as "very open places. There was really no security. They encouraged any citizen to come in and ask to spend time with reporters. [NCPPC members] would come into the newsroom and collar a reporter or city editor and say, 'These guys were all framed.' And people would listen. We were one of their avenues of hope. The lawyers were handling one end of it, and we were handling another."[56]

Besides the NCPPC's perseverance, the burgeoning Watergate investigation also clearly heightened interest in the case. "After Watergate," Butch Rosen asserts, "the *Observer* finally started listening to us. It then became credible that the government could have a conspiracy." Earlier, NCPPC allegations of governmental conspiracy against Black activists could be dismissed as wild-eyed "paranoid" delusions of young activists grieving over their jailed friends. Now, the Watergate investigation documented the "dirty tricks squad's obsession with getting radicals off the street. It gave an official name to what we had thought was going on all the time," maintains Rosen. Perhaps more importantly, "it gave a trail by which reporters and investigators could trace it. It gave an official opening to go through."[57] Reporter Michael Schwartz remembers those activists insisting that "the government was out to get [the Charlotte Three], and this is around the time where you did have the counter-intelligence program [the FBI's newly revealed controversial COINTELPRO program, which heavily targeted Black activists using sometimes illegal surveillance]. People were becoming aware of what the government had been doing. So, it was an environment where you couldn't just be as dismissive as you might have been before all that happened."[58]

During this period of increasing attention to the case in late January 1974, the *Observer* dispatched two of its best investigative reporters (Mark Ethridge and Michael Schwartz) to examine the issue. In addition to Ethridge's memory of the NCPPC "creating a lot of noise" about the case, the *Observer* newsroom had an interest in the story because of its fondness for its former young intern T. J. Reddy. Ethridge and Schwartz began by looking at the trial transcript, and discovered what Ethridge called a "shocking piece of evidence. The witnesses [Hood and Washington] had been paid a lot of money for their testimony—they were basically bribed by the government to put away these activists."[59]

While Hood's and Washington's protective custody expenses had been revealed, Ethridge maintains that defense attorneys had "never bothered to fully add everything up [all the separate government expenses of paying and supporting these witnesses] and push its relevance in the trial." By doing that themselves, Ethridge and Schwartz discovered minimum total expenditures—not including payroll costs for their "bodyguards"—at over $18,000. They also constructed a paper trail of federal involvement that led them to the witness "relocation" payments of $4,000 each, never revealed in the trial.[60] While an anonymous Justice Department source told the *Observer* that such "reward" payments were not unusual, their existence remained secret during the trial. Furthermore, during courtroom cross-examination, Hood denied that he had been paid any money in exchange for testimony.[61]

Ethridge and Schwartz also uncovered several conflicts in Hood's and Washington's accounts of the Lazy B burning. By comparing trial testimony with earlier sworn statements on the crime, the reporters noted contradictions over who manufactured the firebombs used and whether the witnesses had a clear view of the firebombs being thrown. Hood, for example, recounted the stable doors as closed, while Washington claimed to be only a few feet away from him with a clear view inside of an open barn. Another major discrepancy was the role of Clarence Harrison. Harrison received a suspended sentence on the basis of a guilty plea and Hood and Washington trial testimony that he had no prior knowledge of the burning before arriving at the stables. In a separate statement, however, Hood claimed that Harrison had actually helped Reddy make the firebombs for use at the Lazy B.[62]

The involvement of Robert Mardian, a U.S. assistant attorney general, further riveted attention to the case. As head of the Internal Security Division, Mardian was second only to Attorney General John Mitchell in the federal Justice Department. He had rejuvenated the division after its languishing since the 1950s McCarthy era, pursuing a series of cases against leftists and radicals with a well-earned reputation for his take-no-prisoners brand of prosecutorial activism.[63]

Mardian himself, the *Observer* reporters had discovered, had personally approved the Hood and Washington expenditures. Just three weeks before the *Observer* series ran, this Nixon administration true believer became one of seven Nixon aides indicted for the Watergate conspiracy. He and Mitchell stood accused of suggesting to White House counsel John Dean that the Watergate burglars be paid through CIA covert funds.[64]

This link to a primary Watergate conspirator fueled suspicions of a local conspiracy. The real catalyst for the prosecution's efforts, however, continued to be its own sense of urgency as defenders of a country besieged by dangerous radicals. Assistant Attorney General James Magner reflected those concerns at the August 1973 appeal hearing when he described the stables burning as "sounding like an attack in Vietnam."[65]

ATF agent Bill Walden contends that Grant had bragged of a visit to Russia, and queries, "Now, what's he doing going to Russia? And where's he getting the money to go to Russia? I think there's a connection there." Noting Grant's extensive travels in pursuit of racial trouble spots in North Carolina, while working for social change groups with few financial resources, Walden recalls, "I always wondered where he got the money to keep doing all that." "What's the goal of Marxism and communism?" he asks. "What do the history books tell us about Lenin's ideas? It's to destroy from within. Go into a country and destroy it from within. Attack it from the schools and government and communities."[66]

In interviews for the explosive upcoming March 1974 *Observer* investigative series, federal and state agents revealed their fears of letting such dangerous elements slip through their anxious fingers. Former assistant district attorney William Austin, who helped prosecute the case, admitted that the government conceded so much to Hood and Washington because they were eager to get the Charlotte Three, and the two men provided the only evidence to do so: "This is not burning a barn on a lark. They did it as an act of political terrorism." Former assistant U.S. attorney David Long, who prosecuted the April 1972 Raleigh Two federal trial, indicated that the government was willing to deal with the two convicts because "the government did believe that Grant and Chavis were the leaders and therefore more important to the government than Hood and Washington."[67]

Hood and Washington told authorities that they used the $4,000 in "relocation" payments to take their endangered lives to Mexico and start a motel business. "I understand it failed," William Behen, the agent-in-charge of the ATF's North Carolina division, later drily told newspaper sources. In fact, the federally funded witnesses, who had justified the relocation disbursements by claiming fear for their personal safety after testifying, returned to the streets of Charlotte within two months.[68] Behen felt it "very foolish of them to return to Charlotte. You understand, we can't control them. Their actions are their own."[69]

The insider's view afforded *Observer* journalists tarnished their impression of the government's behavior surrounding the Charlotte Three, and the national story over the Watergate scandal lent further credence to the possibility of government wrongdoing. As Butch Rosen had told them when trying to generate an investigative story, the Nixon administration's "'dirty tricks squad' was obsessed with getting radicals off the street," and would stop at nothing to do so.[70] Reporter Frye Gaillard felt the series had convinced the *Observer* newsroom that "the prosecution was motivated by politics more than criminal justice—if, in nothing else, in who it decided to put in jail, and who it was willing to let go." Returning again to the question of who was "dangerous," Gaillard considers the long criminal record of the prosecution witnesses and asserts that "if you had a choice today, I think you'd put Hood and Washington in jail and let T. J. Reddy go in exchange for testimony against them. They seemed to me pretty dangerous people."[71]

Mark Ethridge's work on the case also convinced him of the excesses of the federal government. He discovered "a general mindset in the Nixon administration that your Black protestor was a bad guy. They were the same people who thought it was okay to shoot protesting college students. It was an article of faith to stop these guys."[72] Ethridge now understands that the trial was not so much about what the Charlotte Three had done, but what they might do: "There was a belief that if even if a protestor had not been violent before, they probably would be eventually." He takes Gaillard's reinterpretation a step further, declaring Nixon administration officials "bad people. They were far more a threat to the republic than the Charlotte Three. They didn't decide to gang up on the Charlotte Three in particular. There was no *specific* conspiracy. They were doing it to activists all over the country."[73]

The March series produced a flurry of subsequent *Observer* articles on the case, many of them on the front page. The stories further detailed the case and its mysterious inner workings.[74] On the day following the initial two-part series, the *Observer* featured a political cartoon and editorial on the Lazy B trial. The latter highlighted the judge, jury, and defense counsel's ignorance of the $4,000 payments to Hood and Washington. The newspaper now claimed "that this was not a fair trial" and suggested that "the best way to resolve the matter" would be a new trial since "commutation would not settle the question of guilt or innocence."[75]

In short, the very heralds of "law and order" had undermined the law and increasingly the sense of order that proper jurisprudence and impartial law enforcement is meant to provide the public.

* * *

The March 1974 *Observer* series played a crucial role in changing community sentiment on the trial. Ethridge feels that it "clearly showed for the first time that there was good evidence that the Charlotte Three had been screwed. It got a lot of momentum going, and it did change a lot of minds," since it "outlined to what lengths the government had gone to get these guys." The Three's supporters regarded the articles as *"extremely* favorable," partly for swaying public opinion and partly for providing new evidence with which to challenge the convictions. Butch Rosen assesses the stories' role more modestly. Dividing the community roughly between liberals, "law and order" conservatives, and those in between, he asserts that the series did not change the first two factions' view of the case, but "for those more in the middle, it moved them a little to support the defendants."[76]

The two-part *Observer* series also stimulated reaction outside the newspaper. The *New York Times* featured an early April story on the North Carolina Board of Paroles' deliberations over the case. The Black newspaper the *Hartford Times* ran another editorial on the case later in June 1974.[77] More importantly, defense attorney James Ferguson noted the new evidence. He told the press after the stories broke, however, that he would continue to await the outcome of the governor's deliberations over the case. If Governor Holshouser took no action, Ferguson claimed he would then decide whether to move for a new trial on the basis of the witnesses' nondisclosure of the payments. Within days after Holshouser declined to pardon or commute the Charlotte Three in July 1974, Ferguson moved to overturn the convictions. In a sign of the NCPPC's effectiveness, Holshouser admitted to receiving over ten thousand letters on the defendants' behalf.[78]

Inside the Cleveland County Prison, T. J. Reddy had not spent his time idly either. Improvising ashes from cigarette butts and burnt matches to render charcoal drawings, he added some accent of color to his art by processing the few small flowers and dandelions to be found in the bereft prison yard. More notably, Reddy published a book of poetry entitled *Less Than a Score, But a Point.* From the hundreds of poems he wrote inside the walls, one referenced Judge Snepp's sentencing characterization of Reddy as a twisted "man of talent" now beyond rehabilitation:

Judge said he thinks I am intelligent, creative
Said I had a future
But since those voodoo dolls
Keep looming in his mind
And his fears mounting

Judge Snepp snips snaps at my heart
Labels me tactician, conspirator, overeducated revolutionary
Beyond rehabilitation.

Another described his prison experience:

One shower stall for 16 of us
Puddles of dirty water
always on the floor . . .
Bible stuck between the bars
Flies and roaches in the cell . . .
Food pushed through holes.

He spoke too of the dashed hopes for the cause that had been his devotion
before the legal onslaught:

Like days of old days into years ago
We had every shackled hope broken
by rejections, denials
Just to keep us quietly
hoping, praying, wishing, longing for a yes
But it seems all we got and get is no
Like days of old days fading into years
the hate and senseless hurt against us
To keep us quiet, corralled, waiting
for what turns out to be slaughter
hasn't changed that much
Break the nigger's spirit,
keep him quiet and still
Break the nigger's spirit,
and break his will to live
Break the nigger's spirit,
keep him caged and hated
Make him give in to despair and take his suffering
Break the nigger's tongue

blind his eyes from the sun
Break his neck–
that will do it
Like days of old days into years today
Break the nigger's spirit
oppressors say.

Reddy and the NCPPC hoped the volume would serve both as a professional achievement for him and as a magnet drawing others into their cause.[79] After a number of successful delay requests by the state, Mecklenburg County Superior Court judge Sam Ervin III presided over a mid-December 1974 hearing on defense motions to overturn the Charlotte Three convictions. Defense attorney James Ferguson argued that the state failed to obey Judge Snepp's pretrial order to produce any evidence beneficial to the defense. He further cited prosecutors' omission of witness payments and certain Hood and Washington statements (some of which conflicted with later statements). District Attorney Thomas Moore testified before Ervin that he submitted to Ferguson all such documents available to him at the time. He claimed to have been out of town when Snepp's order occurred, and thus did not ask federal authorities for other possible statements. Ervin closed the hearing suggesting that he would rule on the defense motion sometime after final prosecutory arguments were submitted on January 25, 1975.[80]

Coinciding with Reddy's poetry publication, national attention continued to focus on the Charlotte Three case in late 1974 and early 1975. Just days before the December hearing, Colman McCarthy wondered on the *Washington Post*'s editorial page "why the March [1974 *Observer* series] revelations were not enough to free the men on bond. What purpose has been served by keeping them in prison when such strong doubts have been raised?"[81] *New York Times* columnist and native North Carolinian Tom Wicker wrote two editorials on the subject at the turn of the year. A noted journalist, Wicker brought an especially salient perspective—not only because of his North Carolina heritage but because of his recent sobering experience during the momentous Attica Prison event. When the inmates took over a portion of the upstate New York facility for four days in 1971, Wicker had been one of the few they welcomed in as an observer and negotiator. He was badly shaken first by the substandard conditions in the institution and then far more by the brutality of law enforcement's treatment of the prisoners during the retaking of Attica (in which thirty-nine died) and the days thereafter. He wrote somberly in a book published later that "even in the suspicion and distrust of their hard experience, many of these despised inmates finally had not believed that the state—society, The Man—would shoot them down. The hard truth was that the Attica brothers had had more faith in the state than the state had had in them." Now reflecting the more introspective national mood of the mid-1970s, which eschewed the dichotomized nation of the late 1960s and early 1970s, Wicker called the Charlotte Three case "one more of those vengeful miscarriages of justice by which comfortable society attempted to label urban unrest, racial disorders, campus disturbances, and antiwar activity as the work of agitators and terrorists, rather than the result of economic and political injustices."[82] The *New York Times* also ran an article on the December Superior Court appeal hearing in Charlotte.[83]

Nobel Prize–winning Harvard biology professor George Wald became another symbol of artist T. J. Reddy's appeal to a liberal white constituency. Wald, who first encountered Reddy during the latter's fundraising tour of New England just before his return to prison in January 1974, began regular correspondence with the defendant thereafter. Wald sent an open letter to the *Charlotte Observer* as he traveled South to attend the December 1974 Charlotte Three appeal hearing. Mindful of how the long-perceived exclusively southern problem of racism had come North in his own city's violent rioting over school busing, Wald acknowledged that "this is hardly the time for anyone from the Boston area to preach race relations in Charlotte." With that aside, Wald made clear his admiration of Reddy, who was "one of the most gifted and creative persons I have ever met. I think it an intolerable violence to imprison such a person, sensitive and decent as I know him to be." He cited Watergate indictee Robert Mardian's involvement and asserted, "It would be comforting to think that Watergate stayed in Washington; but no, the sickness is national and needs to be treated nationally." He concluded by reflecting on the Boston racial crisis, saying he had come to Charlotte "in the spirit of those high school students" being bused across town in both cities. "My generation made the mess that young people everywhere now have to try to live with. Let us older persons do what we can to help them."[84]

Wald's humility over the Boston busing crisis illuminates another important force in Charlotte in the middle 1970s: the reconciliation of Charlotte's busing controversy. The previously stormy local school system of the early 1970s had given way to acceptance and determination to make the 1971 U.S. Supreme Court affirmation of the 1969 *Swann* ruling work for the community and its children. By the mid-1970s, this New South city had become a surprising success story for busing.[85]

A January 1975 *New York Times* editorial echoed Wald's concern of Nixon administration involvement in the case. It declared "the 'horrors' of the Nixon Administration" as "hardly confined to the White House," and called the Charlotte Three case "one of the 'Justice Department horrors' of [former attorney general John] Mitchell's law-and-order years." Fearing the worst of a Watergate-shrouded Nixon administration, the piece questioned "whether there might have been other little-noted prosecutions in which proper constitutional procedures were conveniently overlooked by the Justice Department in furtherance of a political campaign against dissidents."[86] In February 1975, the Connecticut chapter of the ACLU took up the *New York Times* editorial's invitation for "bar associations and lawyers' groups" to act on these suspicions, calling unsuccessfully for a U.S. House of Representatives "full investigation of the role played by the U.S. Department of Justice."[87]

As the summer of 1975 approached, there seemed ample reason to be hopeful about the fate of the Charlotte Three. The NCPPC activists apparently had done their job. Their pressure on local media had paid dividends in the *Charlotte Observer*'s March 1974 series and the continued scrutiny of the case. Many Charlotteans had taken notice, and the national media had likewise been aroused. Negative stories of North Carolina began to mount, increasing pressure on political leaders to intervene in the case. Finally, despite the extended delays, Ferguson's appeal was pending at Judge Sam Ervin III's court, and the *Charlotte Observer* stories had buoyed hopes that the legal system would finally overturn the Three's convictions. Amid these rising expectations, none of the Three's supporters could see the storm clouds gathering against their cause, and surely none of them saw them gathering over the assumed allied newsroom of the *Charlotte Observer*.

8

"TELLING THE TRUTH"

n May 1975, a legal document on the desk of Judge Sam Ervin III embodied the hopes of the Charlotte Three and their activist supporters. Attorney James Ferguson had filed the December 1974 appeal following a crescendo of new revelations damaging to Charlotte Three prosecutors. Negative local, state, national, and even international pressure had descended on the issue. All of this bode well for the cause. What's more, Ferguson could now turn matters over to the judge. Ervin was regarded as a liberal who would be far more sympathetic than the original trial jurist, Frank Snepp. The fact that Ervin's father, U.S. Senator Sam Ervin Jr., currently enjoyed a mild national cult of personality seemed to only add to the optimism. Senator Ervin's wholesome and homespun demeanor while chairing the televised Watergate committee hearings seemed a welcome contrast to the urbane and hardened witnesses from the Nixon White House.[1] All of the NCPPC's tireless efforts, it seemed, were turning the corner toward victory.

But what the activists did not see coming were the other crusaders who would play their own surprising role in the case. Their crusade was getting to the final heart of the Charlotte Three story in the idealistic newsroom of the *Charlotte Observer.* The late 1960s and early 1970s propelled a generation of young journalists into seeing themselves as critical contributors to a sound democracy. After path-breaking reporting on the Vietnam War and the civil rights movement came the most consequential journalism of the time: the Watergate story, which helped topple a presidential administration (and catapulted *Washington Post* investigative reporters Bob Woodward and Carl Bernstein into public notoriety). "I think Watergate really inspired journalists," recounts former *Observer* reporter Michael Schwartz. "All of a sudden journalism was elevated to almost an heroic kind of occupation where what we did and could do makes a difference. I think it launched almost a whole generation of journalists who really took the job more seriously. There was more of a feeling of weight of duty: 'We have this power and we obviously have the Constitution behind us. What are we going to do with it?'"[2] *Observer* colleague Frye Gaillard recalls "very much operating under the influence of the Watergate story in those times. . . . [Woodward and Bernstein] were deeply committed to telling the truth, and they believed that they served the larger cause of telling the truth."[3]

That energy was reflected even at the university level, where "all of a sudden there was a lot of interest and journalism departments were growing and newspapers were suddenly being inundated with applications," Schwartz enthuses. Not surprisingly, he sprung from his 1972 University of Michigan graduation "kind of fired up."[4] Likewise, *Observer* reporter Mark Ethridge "grew up in an anti-war, pro-civil rights environment, and you felt you had to make a difference. But writing seemed to be the only thing I was good at. But I realized that I could combine making a difference with writing by doing journalism and bringing truth to light." Ethridge would come to see journalism's "watchdog" role as so vital that it functioned as "the fourth branch of government."[5]

The idealism found a healthy home at the *Charlotte Observer*. The paper had already established a reputation as an important voice in the region, especially since the mid-1950s, when the highly respected C. A. "Pete" McKnight took the helm. Before arriving, McKnight had already established himself as a southern, white progressive on race relations. While serving at the city's companion evening newspaper, the *Charlotte News,* he had editorialized in 1950 that segregation could not "as an abstract moral principle . . . be defended by any intellectually or spiritually honest person," and then oversaw a publication monitoring southern compliance with the *Brown v. Board of Education* school decision. A believer in his role as a public advocate for civic and regional improvement, he served as president of the notably liberal Ford Foundation in the early 1960s. When the time came for Charlotte's touted 1963 managed desegregation plan, it was McKnight who was primary author of the Chamber of Commerce resolution. He also used the editorial pages to staunchly defend the *Swann* busing decision.[6]

Now in poor health, McKnight passed the baton to Jim Batten, who immediately began recruiting young talent to reinvigorate the paper's investigative reporting. The tandem who covered the Charlotte Three were part of that new cadre. Schwartz remembers Batten as a "tremendous journalist" who "really believed one of a newspaper's roles was to right wrongs and basically be the watchdog over government."[7] Gaillard remembers the *Observer* at that time as "a *highly* idealistic newspaper. It was full of reporters who had this kind of passionate commitment to telling the truth, and who believed that society is best served by that—sometimes in mysterious ways that we don't even see at the time."[8]

That passion would take Gaillard in particular down a "very painful" road, however. In an effort to gather as much information as possible on the controversial trial, *Observer* editors dispatched four of their best reporters: Ethridge, Schwartz, Gaillard, and metropolitan editor Walker Lundy.[9] Anticipating finding information that would call the convictions further into question, they instead came back with new information on the case—all of it implicating the defendants' guilt. As Judge Ervin deliberated agonizingly slowly and repeatedly delayed what became the Three's last best hope for acquittal, the clock ticked away on the work of those critical four reporters. When May 25 arrived and Ervin still had no decision, activist supporters of the Three feared that across Ervin's desk from the appeal documents lay a startling new *Observer* story: "New Data Implicates the Lazy B Three."[10]

For Frye Gaillard, much more was involved in the "New Data" article than just good newspaper copy. The Reddys' friend and former housemate, Rich Rosen, had been "one of my [Gaillard's] closest friends" during the two's college days at Vanderbilt. When Gaillard came to Charlotte as a journalist, he "spent a lot of time just hanging out" with Rich and his brother, Butch Rosen, at a house they shared with T. J. and Vicki Reddy. After building friendships with many of the activists and others who associated themselves with the Rosen brothers and the Reddy's, Gaillard left for Nashville in mid-1973 to work as the managing editor for *Race Relations Reporter*, a Ford Foundation-funded magazine. He was thus out of town during Ethridge and Schwartz's March 1974 Charlotte Three series exposing Hood and Washington's secret payments. While working for the *Reporter*, Gaillard oversaw two articles on the Three in the magazine. Returning to the Queen City in late 1974, he picked up where he left off in his friendships with the Reddy's and their associates and in his job as an *Observer* journalist. The two roles had previously been largely compatible, but by mid-1975 all that would begin to change.[11]

Now returned to the *Observer* newsroom, Gaillard joined Ethridge and Schwartz in meetings hosted by Walker Lundy. All four reporters agreed that the Charlotte Three prosecution had been politically motivated. The Charlotte Three story had been one of the paper's signature pieces in 1974, but one consuming question remained for Lundy in early 1975: "'Who burned the barn?' That's what Walker Lundy kept saying, 'Okay, but who burned the barn?' . . . and, what we wanted to do was compile and bring to bear every piece of knowledge and evidence we could that touched on that question of guilt or innocence [of the Charlotte Three]. We thought we had invested enough as a newspaper in the story that we owed it to our readers to go forward and answer that last question."[12]

To Gaillard's surprise, the paper's idealism and commitment led him down the dark path of writing a story that inadvertently aided the Three's prosecutors. Despite the dissension and sense of "betrayal" he felt it earned from many of his activist friends, Gaillard now argues that the article "came closest to telling the truth" in a still controversial case. For NCPPC members, the story seemed to doom the Three's chances at the impending appeal decision by Judge Ervin. It would also come to represent the decline of the polarization that had fueled the case's prosecution in the earlier part of the decade.

* * *

The mid-1970s began a thaw in the American polarization of the late 1960s and early 1970s. For conservatives, the Watergate scandal revelations had exposed the ugliness of "law and order" extremism. Congressional committee hearings lay tragically bare the questionable practices of federal law enforcement in pursuing the militants of the 1960s and early 1970s. Senate committee chairman Frank Church led the way, exposing controversial FBI and CIA actions in a cathartic bloodletting of the era's law enforcement excesses in the Church Committee hearings of 1975 and 1976. On the political left, many former activists had now come to find themselves in pursuits far quieter and more introspective than seizing the Columbia University president's office, bombing the University of Wisconsin math building, or declaring war on

"Amerika" at the 1968 Democratic convention. After every president from Eisenhower to Nixon had portrayed Vietnam as a firm line in the sand of powerful American commitments and principles, South Vietnam fell with a shameful whimper in 1975, just two years after U.S. troops withdrew, marking a period already underway of reconsidering the extremes of the Cold War. President Jimmy Carter brought that contentious issue to a more peaceful conclusion for American citizens with his pardon of draft resisters.[13] As the national polarization began to recede, the possibility of perceiving a new kind of moral complexity emerged. On a more personal level, the onset of a series of 1970s recessions forced many to abandon more ambitious pursuits than simply putting food on the family table.

For many Americans, the retreat from that earlier political polarization paved the way for such 1970s escapist pursuits as disco music (blissfully free from the weight of any protest message), pet rocks, and the sexual revolution. For others, the period bred a more sober brand of introspection, such as the expansion of personal therapy, the Human Potential Movement, Transcendental Meditation, and a religious revival marked by both fundamentalist Christianity and alternative sects like the Unification Church and Reverend Jim Jones's People's Temple. Many sought to simply make sense of the dizzying changes of the last fifteen years. This gave way to a more reflective and, hence, more conciliatory national tone.

The 1976 election of President Jimmy Carter symbolized the trend in a number of ways. First, Carter's election on a campaign emphasizing his honesty, integrity, religious commitment, and rural American roots represented the country's desire for reconciliation to a wholesome, pre-Watergate past after the administrations of Nixon and his appointed successor, Gerald Ford. After all, this was a new president who had won the office traveling the country with the promise "I will never lie to you."

But, Carter, as the former governor of Georgia, also represented the South's recent racial reconciliation to a North still groping to understand the racial discord on its own soil. It was no coincidence that 1976 America elected a man who had told his Deep South state at his 1971 gubernatorial inauguration, "I say to you quite frankly that the time for racial discrimination is over."[14] The North and West of the mid-1970s were far more penitent about their own racist excesses, and even looked to the South now as a region that had come through that fire and reemerged stronger for it. If nonsouthern America had once been arrogant enough to see the civil rights movement's purpose as bringing a backward South up to its racially progressive standard, the devastating urban racial riots of the mid- to late 1960s had been a sobering rejoinder. The ugly scenes during Dr. King's 1966 Chicago campaign—including a large rock that struck his skull—had caused the leader to claim that he had "never seen such hostility and hatred anywhere in my life, even in Selma."[15] The decidedly disturbing school busing clashes in many northern and western cities of the early to mid-1970s shook what little remained of many northerners' claims of moral superiority.

Locally, Charlotte had proven an excellent example of that southern phenomenon through its recent experience with the busing crisis. While northern and western cities still struggled mightily with the problem, the Queen City—just as it had done with the desegregation of public accommodations—turned the issue from a crisis to a point of public relations pride. The school riots, racial unrest, and angry school board shouting matches had given way to civic acceptance and determination to make the *Swann* ruling work for the community and its children. In July 1975, Judge James McMillan had finally approved the local school board busing plan, officially closing the *Swann* case and turning school operations completely over to the school board.[16] At the final hearing, the judge who had needed armed guards to protect himself in the early 1970s acknowledged "a deep appreciation to the board members, community leaders, school administrators, teachers and parents who have . . . made possible this court's graduation from *Swann*."[17]

Billing itself as "The City That Made It Work," Charlotte was featured positively in the *New York Times,* the *Washington Post,* and *Newsweek* and on CBS television. Much of this journalism featured contrasts with the tumultuous Boston busing situation.[18] In the fall of 1974, a legendary show of Charlotte "progressivism" bolstered those media reports. Charlotte high school students, concerned by reports of Boston violence against busing, began a letter-writing encouragement campaign to the northern city's students. The correspondence blossomed into student exchange visits, as the once racially maligned South now seemed to have something to teach the North.[19] The success of the Charlotte busing experiment set a pervasive tone of optimism and conciliation across the city that carried into the late 1970s. After the temporary loss of course during the busing crisis, the city was ready to move on and regain its status as a bustling business community too busy to be bothered with any ugly racial problems. Should anyone miss the point, the influential municipal Chamber of Commerce obliged city fathers with its new slogan, "Charlotte—A Good Place to Make Money."[20]

* * *

As Lundy's question about the barn still lingered in the *Observer* newsroom, the reporters' "passionate commitment to telling the truth" prompted Gaillard to inform his office colleagues of rumors he had been hearing about the case since his return to Charlotte in late 1974. Gaillard, traveling in circles of those who knew the Three well, was in a peculiar position to have inside information. Among them, Gaillard recalls, "There were people who said, 'You know you guys ought to be careful before you let T.J. off too lightly *because he burned that barn.*' When I would ask them how they knew, they'd only say, 'Well, we just know.'" These rumblings had begun to erode Gaillard's unquestioning belief in the Charlotte Three's innocence, and served as a catalyst for the four reporters who met about the case.[21]

Rumors also circulated of another journalist's work on the trial. Lawrence Wright was working on a Charlotte Three story for the new progressive political commentary magazine *New Times.* While many other stories had been written by now on the case nationally—and even internationally—Wright's work reportedly had uncovered a shocking new piece of evidence: a previously unknown and unnamed source who claimed to have been a seventh participant in the Lazy B burning.[22] Gaillard, concerned that the *Observer* would be embarrassed by Wright "scooping them in our own backyard," hurriedly went to work with Lundy, Ethridge, and Schwartz.[23]

They began by approaching Dave Washington, who had never been interviewed by the *Charlotte Observer* despite the newspaper's many articles on him and the case. Lawrence Wright had uncovered the alleged seventh participant (whom he called "Brother X") through interviews with Washington, who claimed Brother X was a close friend.[24] Gaillard concedes that one of the reasons that *Observer* writers had never interviewed Washington was "partly because they were afraid to. He was the bad guy in all of our stories," and the reporters reasonably feared personal reprisals from a man with a schizophrenia diagnosis and a record of criminal violence. Lundy and Gaillard did contact Washington, though, and found the fear well-placed. In their series of interviews with Washington, he revealed, "I'd like to kill Ethridge and Shwatz [his butchering of Michael Schwartz's name]" for their unflattering pieces on him and Hood. In a subsequent interview, Washington stiffened at the line of questioning and retrieved his pistol—which lay at his feet for the remainder of the session.[25]

Finding David Washington turned out to be no easy task. The high-profile Lazy B witness had been a fugitive since April 1974. Charged with assault with a deadly weapon over a business dispute, he had escaped police grasp ten days after his hospital release, where he had been treated for gunshot wounds sustained in the crime.[26] Police sources also told the *Observer* correspondents that he was "a prime suspect in five murders." When Ethridge learned on one occasion of the slippery Washington's stay in a hospital, he pursued him for a long-sought interview. "He was always getting into trouble," Ethridge recounts, "and he had been shot and was in the hospital. He was not shot that bad, and I knocked on the door and he was lying there in bed. But he pulled a gun on me and I left. You know, in his mind, people might be coming through, and you just don't want to be anywhere without your piece." Lundy and Gaillard met Washington four times at a location prescribed by Washington— twice at a Charlotte housing project, once at a McDonald's in Rock Hill, South Carolina, and once at a rural tavern in Chester, South Carolina.[27]

Lundy and Gaillard found an uncooperative Washington at their first meeting, however. They had incorrectly forecast that he would be motivated to counter the public incredulity of his Lazy B burning accounts; furthermore, they felt that if he had divulged the name of Brother X to Wright, he would do the same for them. He refused to do so, though, arguing that he could not trust the *Observer* to keep his friend anonymous.[28]

Using Wright's and Washington's sketchy information on Brother X, the four local journalists descended on the streets of Charlotte. They moved among Hood's and Washington's friends and acquaintances—street sources and "thugs" who were a step removed from Grant's and Reddy's circle of political and civil rights activists. Eventually, the newspaper team learned Brother X's street nickname from another friend of Dave Washington. They then took the nickname to police records, found his legal name, and ran it by Washington.

For the first time, Washington confirmed the man's identity. (Hood also later confirmed Brother X's participation.)[29]

Armed with Brother X's real name, Gaillard and Ethridge managed to locate the man's mother, but found themselves in a murky moral quandary. Leveraging their meeting with her to get to Brother X clearly made Gaillard uncomfortable. "It's the making sausage part of journalism," he laments. "You don't want to know. We told her that we didn't know if we could protect his identity in the story or not, but that if we found it out and he didn't talk to us, we certainly couldn't. You know, I don't like that part of the job, but that's what we did."[30]

Whatever the ethics, it worked. Brother X's mother took Gaillard and Ethridge to Boulevard Homes Housing Project, where the startled and en-raged working-class Black man pulled a gun on the two writers. "I thought he was going to hit his mother," Gaillard remembers. Brother X bellowed at the woman: "'What the hell are you bringing these people here for?!' I mean, he just *screamed at her.*" Finally getting inside the door, Gaillard thought to him-self, "'Oh, shit, we found him and this isn't going to work,' because he was so agitated and storming around the room and . . . throwing things around and swearing at his mother." The reporters knew going into the confrontation that, like his friend Dave Washington, Brother X had been "treated for . . . mental problems" that had culminated in "violent behavior." Assuring him that they "only wanted the truth" and that he would remain anonymous, the reporters did finally calm him down to talk. Ethridge remembers him, though, as "not very forthcoming at all. . . . He didn't want to be found. He saw what had hap-pened to the other guys [the Charlotte Three], and he didn't want it to happen to him."[31]

Brother X's version of the burning closely matched Hood's and Washing-ton's, and Gaillard found "his descriptions cogent." "Straight up, I was at the Lazy B," the anonymous participant told them. "Reddy and Parker were there, Grant was not, but he planned the whole thing." Adding to the conflicting sto-ries, Brother X's latter claim contradicted Hood's and Washington's accounts of Grant's presence at the burning, but Brother X asserted that "a general does not go to the front lines." The man said he feared criminal prosecution and personal reprisals, and only agreed to talk to the paper in return for anonym-ity: "Every minute I sit here talking to you, I put my life on the line." At the end of their two-hour interview, he told them, "Man, I know I'm gonna be in jail a week from now because of this. I hope I never see you guys again."[32]

Dave Washington claimed in subsequent interviews with *Observer* reporters that he had given Brother X's name to prosecutors for the first time on the dramatic last day of testimony in the Lazy B Stables trial (when Mecklenburg County district attorney Tom Moore had been frantic to rebut defense testimony that placed Grant in Pennsylvania during the burning, after Judge Snepp—in a private chambers session with Moore—had threatened to dismiss the case at a lunch recess). Washington had not revealed the man's participation before since they were "longtime friends," and he felt responsible for involving Brother X in the crime. "If I really needed Dave [Washington], he would be there," declared Brother X. "The same with me. But I don't know about this shit [Washington's implication of his involvement to reporters]."[33]

Washington and Brother X maintained that District Attorney Moore immediately had police officers pick up Brother X from his workplace for questioning. After an intense and hurried round of interrogation, however, Moore decided not to call him as a witness when he denied any involvement in or knowledge of the burning. (All of this clandestine prosecutorial activity—including ATF agent Bill Walden's retrieval of bank teller witness Laura Booton—may explain why Snepp was forced to hold court in suspension after the lunch break, as he waited impatiently for Moore's tardy return.) When the *Observer* reached Moore for comment on Brother X, he denied ever hearing the man's name, or even knowledge of anyone else's involvement: "Mr. Washington is mistaken." When told of Moore's denial, Washington responded, "He's only keeping his promise [to never disclose the man's identity]."[34]

Also revealed in the *Observer* article were incriminating disclosures by friends of the Charlotte Three. Gaillard, as a friend of Reddy's and friend to many of the NCPPC members and mutual friends, was the link for this side of the story.[35] One rumor circulating was that Charleen Whisnant, Reddy's mentor and editor of the poetry journal *Red Clay Reader*, knew of Reddy's guilt. Gaillard—who knew her—confronted her with the rumor, and "she was pissed, she was really unhappy about being interviewed for this"—a common reaction among sources for the story. She claimed that Reddy had cryptically shown up at her doorstep in the middle of the night, hours after the Lazy B burning had happened. Visibly shaken, it was his first words that were the most mysterious: "Have you ever smelled burning horse flesh?" "He had awareness of the crime that frightened him," she recalled. "What we had on our hands was a terrified person." Whisnant contended that while Reddy did not discuss his own involvement, he gave her the impression that he knew of the burning and who committed it. Although she maintained that she had formed no conclusion about Reddy's possible involvement in the crime, she had responded to Reddy's 1972 request to be a character witness by telling him, "You don't want me to be called to the stand."[36]

Gaillard also phoned others he knew as mutual friends of the Charlotte Three in an effort to confirm these rumors, including a doctor known in the story only as "a prominent Charlotte liberal." Gaillard's simple question of whether the doctor knew anything about Reddy's possible involvement put the source in "a quandary." Torn between a desire to keep the Charlotte Three out of prison and help his friend Gaillard, "he was very testy about it, and he was very mad at me for putting him in that position." This conflict hinged on the doctor's knowledge of Reddy's involvement in the burning, based on a conversation he had had with two friends to whom Reddy had confessed. Charleen Whisnant claimed to be one of those two friends.[37]

The doctor's "quandary" was not unique. The article cited four incriminating sources friendly to the Charlotte Three, and all experienced a similar dilemma. In a second interview, Whisnant backed off her claim that Reddy had opened his late-night conversation by discussing burning horse flesh. She also withdrew her previous assertion that she had been one of the two friends who told the "prominent Charlotte liberal" about Reddy's guilt, and maintained that that statement had only been the product of harassment by reporters "anxious to support your thesis." Lola Moore, a friend of Charles Parker and another source in the story, told the *Observer* that she had overheard Parker admit his participation in the barn burning, but when pressed about her statement's implications, she changed her course: "They [the Charlotte Three] didn't have to be there. No, I don't think they was there. I think they was being framed . . . Dave Washington threw that fire-bomb."[38]

The article's description of Whisnant's and Moore's personal anguish over this predicament was really only the tip of the iceberg, according to Gaillard. He recalls "at least two highly credible sources [claiming to know of the Charlotte Three's involvement] who would not discuss it on the record. . . . So, we couldn't even use them as anonymous sources." After the article's publication Gaillard also recalls that two or three others "called me—because, you know, we were catching hell for it—and said, 'I just want to tell you that your article is right.'" Even those who spoke off the record only represented to Gaillard "a *bunch* of people that'll tell you that T.J. told them he burned the barn."[39]

The curious thing about the 1975 "New Data" article was that no one cited in the article wanted to talk about the case—and they would have been happier if the *Observer* had simply left well enough alone. Washington expressed reticence about involving a friend who had gone previously unscathed by the case. Brother X had deep concerns about his own potential prosecution. Lastly, all the quoted friends of the Charlotte Three feared playing into the prosecution's hands. In addressing the reporters who sought more information from him, the "prominent Charlotte liberal" spoke for his peer sources in telling them, "I will not help you send people to jail for 20 years."[40] The sources' reluctance, though, only added to their credibility for the reporters. Gaillard claims that the difficulty they had in convincing the sources to participate made the information seem more reliable: "If it had been presented to us on a silver platter it would have been less credible to us than it was."[41]

* * *

Gaillard had begun his work on the "New Data" story expecting it to lead to evidence of the Charlotte Three's innocence. His discovery of the reverse did not shift into a belief simply that the Three were guilty, however. Importantly, his confidence that the Three's prosecution was politically motivated remained untrammeled. The new story left him somewhere in between the polarized fringes of the late 1960s and early 1970s. Given the two alternatives of the Three as innocent pawns caught in the clenched fist of "law and order" extremists or as dangerous revolutionaries intent on undermining America, Gaillard believed neither.

Gaillard was as much a product of the times as the doctor, Whisnant, and Moore. For Gaillard, the way he had framed his prior beliefs about Reddy's innocence hindered his ability to reconcile them with the story's incriminating information. Gaillard had thought Reddy innocent because "I thought T. J.

was a victim of persecution, and that sort of shade of gray—that you could be guilty and a victim—hadn't really occurred to me. I just assumed that victims were all innocent. So, for me, it was a little bit of a loss of innocence in my view of the world, of being less black and white . . . than I had thought."[42] Despite his "passionate commitment to telling the truth," the polarization of the early 1970s had restricted his perception of the case. Once he had perceived the Three as "victims," he had automatically fallen to the liberal/leftist side of the ideological war. The "law and order" view of the Three as dangerous revolutionaries was simply untenable. His personal knowledge of the defendants had made that latter view impossible. Anything between the two had been a psychologically uninhabitable no-man's-land. For Gaillard, the story had

> confirmed that things weren't always as simple as they appeared. I *never* saw stories as simply good versus evil after that. As a reporter I never went into a story after the Lazy B case expecting to see a clear difference between right and wrong. . . . I came at every story with caution after that: the world is a complicated place; almost everyone has some good and some bad in them. Some of us who had come out of the [19]60s were fairly radicalized, believing that you couldn't trust anyone older than 30, that good is always on our side. We had to change our perspective.[43]

Mark Ethridge followed a similar trajectory. His reporting in the March 1974 *Observer* series had convinced him that the Charlotte Three had been innocent political targets of federal and state authorities. The 1975 article forced him into a change in judgment similar to Gaillard's. When interviewed, he claimed to have no commitment now on their innocence or guilt. He went on to say, "I suppose that I believe that they did do it *and* they were screwed. It isn't hard to believe that some Black activists during that time—even if they were good guys—would throw some firebombs at a barn." He emphasized a point that became an important foundation for protest among those who could no longer be certain of the Charlotte Three's innocence: "Maybe they did it, but they shouldn't have gone to prison, and they certainly shouldn't have gone for such a long time—it [their sentences] was incredible." "I've come more and more to the conclusion," he recently opined, "this was not just local racist southern cops pursuing some Black activists. It was orchestrated by the White House and feds. At the end of the day, it didn't matter in terms of justice, because [the Three] didn't get it."[44]

Gaillard's and Ethridge's process of understanding the case with more moral complexity preceded the community's, but many others—who had known of these rumors before these white journalists—had already begun to see a "shade of gray" imperceptible in the hysteria of the late 1960s and early 1970s. Gaillard remembers the 1975 "New Data" article as "befuddling to a lot of people" since before it people "fell into one camp or the other: these guys are innocent victims of a police state, or they're Black radical criminals who need to be put away." Marvin Sparrow concedes that "my involvement [in defending the Three] had very little to do with an analysis of whether they were guilty or what the crime was or anything like that. It was just clear that they were on our side in a general sense, and the other side was coming after them and we had to do something about it. But we were on the defensive during that whole period of time, and we were very aware of that."[45]

According to Gaillard, Sparrow was by no means alone in his stance. The entire community, he contends, "almost literally had not given any thought" to the possibility that the truth lay somewhere in between the extremes. While it is unclear whether the 1975 *Observer* article pushed people in that direction, it at least illustrated a gradual shift in the community posture toward the Charlotte Three case. "*I do know*," contends Gaillard, "that there were people who knew T. J. Reddy and incriminating information about the burning who were already wrestling with [the possibility of the coexistence of Reddy's guilt and his persecution]."[46]

* * *

The new middle ground that emerged from the 1975 "New Data" *Observer* article and the Watergate aftermath was far from immediate, however. First came the reaction of the vast majority of Charlotteans, who were shocked to see the Sunday morning front-page headline. Members of the North Carolina Political Prisoners Committee who awaited federal Judge Sam Ervin III's appeal ruling in one week immediately went on the offensive. Nineteen of them gathered on the county courthouse steps to deliver a statement saying the article was based on "unwarranted inferences" from "unnamed, suspect informants." The committee contended that the *Observer*'s publication of the story "borders on the irresponsible and that the use of sensational headlines which are unsupported by the contents of the article is an attempt to try these men in the press."[47]

NCPPC members decried the story as another stage in a continuing conspiracy against the defendants. Butch Rosen maintains that the March 1974 series compelled the *Observer* to feel "like they had to balance the scales by later writing something that went against the defendants." The daily published the 1975 story, then, only to "maintain its pose of objectivity." The NCPPC newsletter that followed the story's publication questioned not just Brother X's veracity but his very existence. The newsletter claimed that "the scenario is obvious. The government had been totally discredited in its attempt to prosecute" the Charlotte Three. While the NCPPC "confidently" awaited Ervin's decision, "admitted agent for the state" David Washington "produced a 'friend' who claimed that Dave was right all along." The newsletter asked whether Lawrence Wright might also be an "agent of the state" and asserted that "numerous people" had complained to the committee and defense attorney James Ferguson of the *Observer*'s "third degree tactics" while seeking information. Activist Kathy Sparrow still contends that federal law enforcement agents produced the story's sources out of fear "that maybe the case wasn't made well enough, and that it should be made again."[48]

Ironically, Frye Gaillard contends that the "New Data" article, which caused such an uproar among NCPPC members, would be written differently today due to a shift in journalistic standards beginning in the late 1970s. According to Gaillard, a contemporary story would not use an anonymous source accusing someone of a crime, since it later became clear that "it's easy to abuse the whole idea of anonymous sources. An unscrupulous reporter could abuse it."[49]

NCPPC members, of course, saw the *Observer* doing just that in the "New Data" story. In retrospect, Gaillard concedes that "the NCPPC was probably right that there was something wrong about . . . using all these anonymous sources, [since] it denied people the right to confront their accusers." Still, he maintains that the 1975 story "came closest to telling the truth about what happened [at the Lazy B burning] than anything else." Ethridge is less conciliatory: "The story pissed off the NCPPC. . . . They felt betrayed. They had felt that we were on their side, that we were believers in the faith, and it turned out we were only believers in the truth—not just a point of view." Gaillard recalls that "one of the things that enraged [NCPPC members] the most" was his own involvement in the story. Since he had close ties to so many of them, they saw it as a "betrayal."[50]

* * *

September 1975 brought the harvest of the NCPPC's worst fears. After a series of lengthy delays over a fourteen-month span, Superior Court judge Sam Ervin III finally ruled against the Charlotte Three defense appeal. One by one, Ervin moved through the questions raised by the original 1974 *Observer* series and methodically dismissed them. The judge declared Lazy B prosecutor District Attorney Thomas Moore's failure to disclose his promise to lift Washington's probation a "harmless error." Ervin also ruled that Moore knew nothing about Hood's and Washington's statements to federal authorities that conflicted with those made to the state; hence, the prosecution made no error in failing to provide them to defense attorneys. Finally, Ervin contended that the "relocation" payments to Hood and Washington were in exchange for testimony in the 1972 Raleigh Two federal trial only. Thus, the prosecution was under no obligation to disclose them in a state trial.[51] Ervin's conclusion on the final point was made despite the fact that federal protection continued after the Raleigh Two trial, and the cash payments were not disbursed until after the Charlotte Three state trial.

This verdict coupled with the 1975 *Observer* story was a crippling blow to NCPPC members, who had thought the defendants' release was imminent. Because Ervin held the appeal for such an extended period of time, the committee inevitably lost the momentum of a distracted community's support. The negative verdict only solidified the public's distancing from the case as it pondered the questions raised in the "New Data" article.

Judge Ervin's ruling distressed the NCPPC not only because it was an unfavorable decision. Ervin's reputation as a liberal judge made him seem the best hope for a judicial system the group saw as increasingly hostile toward African Americans, activists, and social change. After the March 1974 *Observer* series was published and the appeal was handed to Ervin, NCPPC members had allowed their hopes for overturning the Three's convictions to soar. "When the decision *finally* came down," recalls one member, "we were *totally devastated*. It seemed so obvious that an injustice had been done, and if this [notably liberal] judge did not agree, there was little hope that any judge would."[52]

On March 10, 1976, the North Carolina Supreme Court refused to hear defense attorney James Ferguson's appeal of the ruling.[53] Another quick and stunning setback lay just around the corner when Ferguson turned to the federal District Court for the next appeal. Supporters knew that liberal District Court judge James McMillan was the usual arbiter of a case like theirs as it arrived at the federal court on March 31, 1976.[54] McMillan, however, dashed committee hopes for judicial salvation when he surprisingly dismissed himself from considering the appeal in September 1976. The case then went to conservative judge Woodrow Wilson Jones. McMillan gave no public explanation for the move, but privately he cited a recent appearance on a Myers Park Baptist Church panel with T. J. Reddy as a conflict of interest. "It was just such a nonpolitical panel," contends one of the Three's supporters. "I don't remember what they were talking about, but it really had nothing to do with politics—I just didn't understand. Everybody was totally shocked when he did it."[55] Judge Jones fulfilled expectations by denying the appeal in late December 1976.[56]

* * *

In the four years following the "New Data" Observer story, the NCPPC's misfortune in the courtroom paralleled its inability to elicit significant community involvement in the case. NCPPC efforts to generate journalistic interest found much less success in this period. The *Charlotte Observer,* which had played such an important role in community perception of the case, continued to run articles on the Charlotte Three's legal procedures and rulings, but gone were the investigative pieces filling the newspaper between the March 1974 series and the May 1975 "New Data" article. This phenomenon particularly frustrated committee members because of rising attention to the Wilmington Ten case.

Despite that frustration, the NCPPC's cause did prosper by its association in the national consciousness with the Wilmington Ten trial.[57] In startling similarities to the Charlotte Three case, the Wilmington Ten trial featured its own convict witnesses, including one who—like Dave Washington—had psychiatric and criminal records and was allegedly offered financial gain for his testimony. Hall, who testified in return for a promise of leniency on other charges facing him at the time of the Wilmington Ten trial, recanted his trial testimony in an October 1976 sworn statement.[58]

Hall's revelations, substantial as they were, were only the beginning. At an unsuccessful appeal hearing on the Wilmington Ten case in June 1977, the two other key prosecution witnesses joined Hall in recanting *their* trial testimony. Like Hall, they claimed that their testimony had been coached by the prosecution in exchange for promises of money, sentencing leniency on unrelated charges, and jobs.[59] Developments in the Wilmington Ten case intensified national scrutiny on North Carolina as the location for two racially and politically controversial cases.

President Jimmy Carter's intense preoccupation with international human rights served a crucial role in building momentum for a national spotlight on North Carolina's criminal justice system. It gave political activists an entrée with which to challenge alleged domestic judicial injustices such as the Wilmington Ten and Charlotte Three cases. Wilmington Ten defendant and former Charlotte activist Benjamin Chavis wrote Carter an open letter in early March 1977, and noted Carter's recent missive to the Soviet dissident Andrei Sakharov. Carter had written Sakharov of America's "firm commitment to promote respect for human rights. We shall use our good offices to seek the release of prisoners of conscience." Chavis declared himself a "prisoner of conscience" in the United States, and questioned, "How can our government honestly proclaim support for human rights as a matter of foreign policy while allowing domestic violations of human rights to continue under the guise of the administration of an unfair criminal justice system?" Chavis addressed the Wilmington Ten case specifically, but journalists increasingly associated the Charlotte Three case with it—albeit as a lesser known stepchild on the national stage—in portraying the North Carolina judicial system as racistly flawed.[60]

Powerful people joined Chavis's call to reexamine the cases. Just after Carter's inauguration, the *New York Times* featured an "Open Letter to Mr. Carter" from renowned African American author James Baldwin. Writing from France with "a heavy heart" about the Wilmington Ten and Charlotte Three cases, Baldwin called the charges "preposterous," and compared the trials to the Scottsboro case (the highly controversial 1931 Alabama case that convicted eight Black men of raping a white woman). He contended that they were "very small symptoms of the monstrous and continuing wrong" perpetrated on those who demand racial change. Speaking directly to the hope embodied in Carter, Baldwin concluded, "I must add, in honor, that I write to you because I love our country. And you, in my lifetime, are the only President to whom I would have written."[61]

Certain federal officials also began to intervene. U.S. Attorney General Griffin Bell, in a series of conversations with Governor James Hunt, urged him to "give serious consideration to the [Wilmington Ten] pardon request." Representative Charles Rangel of New York wrote Hunt urging his intervention on the Wilmington Ten's behalf. Rangel's colleagues John Conyers and Ronald Dellums (all African Americans) also addressed the matter on the floor of the U.S. House of Representatives.[62]

A publicity push by the human rights organization Amnesty International continued this trend. Having just won the Nobel Peace Prize, it released the names of eighteen alleged American political prisoners in October 1977—a stunning development for a nation that saw itself far above the human rights abuses for which it now stood accused. Of the eighteen cited, two-thirds belonged to the Wilmington Ten and Charlotte Three trials (the latter having been already cited by the group four years earlier)—including all of the Wilmington Ten, Jim Grant, and T. J. Reddy.[63] (Charles Parker had already been paroled in December 1976.)[64] Newspapers across the country printed the news. The *Chicago Sun-Times*'s version of the story also noted the sagging notoriety and support for the Charlotte Three case. It quoted the North Carolina governor's press secretary, who said the governor received "about 20 letters a week" on the Wilmington Ten case, but he asserted, "I don't recall we've ever had a letter on the Charlotte Three." The article concluded that "Interest in the Charlotte Three has waned. They seem to have been superseded as a cause by the Wilmington 10, no doubt in part because they are no longer prisoners [on bail during appeal], at least for the moment."[65]

In January 1978, North Carolina governor James Hunt finally intervened on behalf of the Wilmington Ten. He reduced the sentences of the defendants, which led to all ten being paroled by December 1979.[66] Reflecting the national tone of reconciliation, Hunt asserted in a television address to North Carolinians, "It is time for us all now to turn away from the bitterness and rancor of the past. Because bitterness and anger and distrust of each other can tear us apart as a state." In an effort to rid the state of the troublesome issue, Hunt described his move as a compromise decision between those who asked for a full pardon and those content to leave the Wilmington Ten in prison.[67]

Despite Hunt's action, controversy over the two trials did not disappear. Eight of the Wilmington Ten would soon be released, but Grant and Reddy—who remained free during appeals—and Ben Chavis still had lengthy sentences hanging over them. Furthermore, supporters still sought pardons for all of the original defendants.

Despite these otherwise encouraging events, NCCPC members found it quite challenging to maintain support for the Charlotte Three after the publication of the 1975 "New Data" story. NCPPC member Kathy Sparrow compares their efforts to "climbing a mountain"; Butch Rosen remembers the committee's struggle as "Sisyphus rolling his boulder uphill." Former *Observer* reporter Mark Ethridge claims that the issue had become "unimportant" to the city's business community (which had played such a crucial role in pacifying civil rights activists in order to avoid controversy) since "the level of protest over this thing was not anywhere near the civil rights protests [of the 1960s]. There were not mobs in the streets over this."[68] The city's progressiveness—absent the threat of significant negative publicity—clearly had its limits.

As protests became decreasingly effective, the Charlotte Three's legal battle hit a dead end. In October 1978, the U.S. Supreme Court declined to hear their appeal, and the defendants' supporters now had only one recourse: action by the governor. Defense attorney James Ferguson had in fact filed an official petition for pardon the previous December, but the governor's office remained quiet on the issue.[69]

* * *

The Supreme Court's appeal denial also meant that Grant and Reddy—out on bail since June 1976—had to return to prison. The two men had been quite industrious during their appeal release. Grant spent the time as a community organizer in Raleigh for the Southern Coalition on Prisons and Jails, the North Carolina-Virginia Commission for Racial Justice, and the state branch of Chavis's and Angela Davis's organization, the National Alliance Against Racist and Political Repression. Reddy completed a master's degree in education at UNC Charlotte, taught in the university's Black Studies Department, served as a field coordinator with the Charlotte-Mecklenburg Youth Council, and counseled and taught at a local community college offender aid program. Reddy's last job was as a western field representative for the North Carolina Cultural Arts Coalition, a nonprofit organization promoting African American artists.[70] In a disheartening twist, Charles Parker (paroled in December 1976) had returned to jail in April 1978 on a fifteen-month sentence for shoplifting a pair of pliers, thus violating his probation terms.[71]

The *Charlotte Observer* and the Raleigh daily the *News and Observer* each ran reflective interviews with Grant and Reddy in the last month before their return to prison. Their views echoed the shift away from the polarization of the early 1970s. Grant saw the national transformation from the outside looking in, insisting, "I haven't changed my views. I still think it will take a complete change in the political and economic system in this country if Black people are to ever be free." He lamented the loss of the 1960s public fervor for marching and demonstrating, saying, "We must . . . understand that we should go back to the streets, because when people are in the streets the man knows that there's a real possibility his system will be destroyed."[72]

While the national transformation away from activism had left Grant an anachronism in his own times, Reddy claimed that "times have changed, and I've stayed abreast of them." In the newspapers' interviews, Reddy indicated his growing concern that social change advocacy can sometimes produce unexpected results: "I don't fear direct action, but a lot of times it turns more people off than it helps, and it doesn't change the system." Reddy now saw his current work with Charlotte's Afro American Cultural Center and his promotion of Black artists through the North Carolina Cultural Arts Coalition as the most effective way for him to advocate change. "I think . . . that many people are more receptive to lessons taught through a performing situation," he asserted.[73]

Other marches and demonstrations continued to push Governor Hunt for a pardon, as frustrations turned to speculative accusations that Hunt deliberately delayed since he was said to be considering his own political future. Rumors, in fact, circulated that Hunt was already planning a 1984 run for the U.S. Senate (which did later materialize). Hunt legal advisor Jack Cozort told the press that the governor had gathered all the information he needed to decide on the Charlotte Three case, and would do so "in the very near future."[74]

As the governor's definition of "the very near future" grew increasingly enigmatic, Charlotte Three supporters continued protests and pressure tactics, picking up important organizational support along the way in April through June 1978. St. Peter's Episcopal Church in Charlotte hosted an April "Freedom Fair" for the Three and the Wilmington Ten, sponsored by the NCPPC. Arts and crafts were exhibited and sold as a fundraiser.[75] In May, the North Carolina Council of Churches, the all-Black General Baptist State Convention, and the Mecklenburg County Democratic Party urged the governor to commute the Charlotte Three's sentences.[76] Governor Hunt's May commencement address at UNC Charlotte brought further protests from students and faculty. After unsuccessful NCPPC requests to cancel Hunt's invitation, the committee ensured that placards, banners, and distributed armbands demanding freedom for the Charlotte Three and Wilmington Ten were displayed. In late June, Charlotte's "Spirit Square" center for the arts began a month-long exhibition of Reddy's paintings.[77]

While the NCPPC continued to assert the Three's innocence, Charlotte's leadership had begun redefining the issue from that of guilt or innocence to that of moving on from a needlessly troublesome—and sometimes embarrassing—public issue. By 1978, the "New Data" story had changed the landscape of the issue. On the media front, the *Charlotte Observer* began to focus less on possible government excesses than on the superfluousness of sending the two defendants back to prison. A week after their 1978 reincarceration, the newspaper featured an editorial contending, "Neither the trial nor our investigation has made us certain of their guilt *or* innocence. Guilt or innocence is no longer the only question, however."[78] The piece focused on the men's accomplishments while on bond release, asking, "What is the point in returning them to prison? If the purpose of prison is to turn criminals into productive human beings, then further imprisonment clearly isn't necessary." It noted the calmer national climate and struck a placatory posture toward "law and order" conservatives: "Perhaps the long sentences handed down years ago may have constituted a warning against violence. But times have changed. Today the Charlotte Three present no danger to North Carolina." The *Observer's* evolving stance on the case reflected the increasing impulse for reconciliation, urging the governor to "heal an old wound by freeing them."[79]

A November 1978 Charlotte City Council resolution and subsequent *Observer* editorial also avoided the question of the Charlotte Three's guilt by discussing the changed times that made their imprisonment no longer necessary. In early November, the City Council passed a resolution urging the governor to review the case and "provide whatever relief you deem appropriate through commutation of their terms of imprisonment." The resolution sidestepped the defendants' guilt or innocence, claiming, "Of central importance to us is the question of whether the public interest is served by further imprisonment. We do think the public interest can be served by tempering the arm of justice with the hand of mercy." Striking a conciliatory tone enabled by hindsight, the statement concluded, "The turmoil and social upheaval evident in the country during the era can never be eradicated or forgotten. . . . But we can build on the lessons that that era of our history has taught us all."[80] Similarly, an *Observer* editorial applauding the resolution three days later claimed that the Charlotte Three sentences "seem due less to their crime than to their being Black civil rights activists at a time when much of white society feared a violent racial revolution."[81]

An October 1978 *Observer* editorial provided Frye Gaillard the opportunity to reflect on the case in a public forum. He recounted a 1977 phone call from "a concerned liberal minister from Connecticut" who contemplated involving his congregation on the Charlotte Three's behalf. When the minister questioned Gaillard on rumors of "genuine doubt about their innocence," Gaillard tried unsuccessfully to convince the man that "he was missing the issue. The question in 1977 was not who set fire to the Lazy B Stables here during the racial upheavals of a decade ago. The issue was the incarceration of three men who, whatever they did or didn't do in the past, were demonstrably capable of leading decent lives." The minister, discouraged by the moral ambiguity of the case, informed Gaillard that his congregation would be better advised to involve itself elsewhere, "where the issues were more clearcut."[82]

Gaillard's editorial used the encounter to contemplate public reaction to the Charlotte Three. The cleric, "like almost everyone else in the case since the beginning, saw the issue so completely in political terms that the basic human concerns were overlooked." Snepp sentenced the defendants, he contended, "precisely in proportion to their political militance," but the judge was not alone in seeing the case only in political terms. Gaillard contended that Charlotte Three supporters "fell into the same trap." He recounted "a heated discussion" during a trial recess. He had argued with Charlotte Three backers over "whether it was wise—knowing Snepp's volatile temperament—for shaggy-haired supporters to rally en masse at the courthouse, especially dressed in such uncourtly attire as T-shirts and jeans." Gaillard linked their stance to the real possibility of higher sentences: "But the rallies continued because, as the supporters said, there were political points to be made." Maintaining that, six years later, "the points have been made," Gaillard insisted, "It is senseless to dwell on Snepp's excesses—or even on the question of guilt or innocence," since "prison has done its job" of rehabilitation. He asserted that the governor, by pardoning the Charlotte Three, "has the opportunity to define the issue just that simply. If he does, he'll be the first in the sad history of the case to move from the realm of politics to the realm of basic human compassion."[83]

* * *

On July 20, 1979, the long wait ended. One and a half years after James Ferguson submitted the formal petition for pardon and the North Carolina governor started giving numerous indications that his decision was impending, Governor James Hunt intervened in the Charlotte Three case. As in his Wilmington Ten decision a year and a half earlier, Hunt avoided the more controversial move to commute or pardon the Charlotte Three. The governor simply reduced the men's sentences—from twenty-five to eleven years for Grant, and from twenty to ten years for Reddy—making them immediately eligible for parole. Grant and Reddy were both released within two weeks. "These defendants have served a substantial time in prison for the crime," Hunt told the press. "On the basis of their records and the progress they have made toward rehabilitation I have concluded that justice would best be served" by the reduction.[84]

Defending his decision to do no more than reduction, Hunt contended that there was "no justification" for overturning the convictions. "The trial court found—correctly, in my judgement—that the deliberate burning of the stables in disregard of the lives of the horses trapped inside was a serious crime, deserving substantial punishment." Hunt also saw "no evidence that the [relocation] payments [of $4,000 each] were made in exchange for testimony at this trial." While Hunt had felt the sentences overly harsh since they were first issued, he claimed "the press of other business" had prevented him from acting sooner.[85]

Charlotte Three supporters reacted with relief but little enthusiasm. "We're glad the governor finally took some action, but it's not the action we wanted," stated defense attorney James Ferguson, who had hoped for a full pardon. A weary T. J. Reddy was also "expecting a pardon."[86]

Despite the disappointment over the governor's refusal to pardon the Three, though, the important historical question here is not why the governor didn't pardon them—it is why he took action at all. It had been eleven years since the fire, seven years since the conviction, and one and a half years since the defense petitioned for a pardon. After so much time, so much tumult and protest, and so much negative press attention, what motivated the governor to act in 1979? One NCPPC member, while citing the pressure of Amnesty International, surmises that "in the end . . . he [Hunt] just got tired. We kept bugging him. [Attorney] Jim Ferguson kept calling him, writing him, meeting with him, and many of us on the committee did so too."[87]

The prior governors, though, had shown no evidence of tiring before July 1979, and Hunt seemed no different. Public pressure and media attention had been going on for years, but it was not until the late 1970s that the Charlotte Three's release seemed somehow less dangerous. In other words, only when keeping the Charlotte Three imprisoned became less important did a governor become weary enough of the pressure to take action. As Mark Ethridge says, "[U]ltimately, it was very clear that these guys were not a threat. If they ever had been a threat, they were no longer so."[88] They were no longer seen as such because of the changed social mood. Gaillard contends that the governors "put it [intervention in the case] off until the climate changed enough. I don't think governors wanted to be perceived as soft on Black radicals, but when somehow the issue was defined in a different way I think it became easier to do that." Gaillard asserts that the governor was able to see the case less politically in the late 1970s, and without the politics surrounding it, there was no driving force to keep the men in prison.[89]

The North Carolina Political Prisoners Committee had, of course, taken a different tack during their years of activism on the case. Members had felt it was to the prosecution's advantage to avoid the political implications of the case, and the committee's efforts had consistently framed the case in political terms. This raises the question as to whether the NCPPC unwittingly worked against its own goal of freeing the Charlotte Three. "It was an irony in this case," asserts Gaillard, "that the more noise [NCPPC members] made in defense of [the Charlotte Three], the more it got the back up from the prosecutor and the judge."[90]

At the same time, the NCPPC played a crucial role in keeping attention focused on the case, and if it heightened tensions around the case, it certainly did no more than the governmental forces arrayed against the defendants. Gaillard emphasizes, "I'm not saying that I think that the North Carolina Political Prisoners Committee should have just *shut up*. Because, I don't believe that. For one thing, I'm not sure the *Observer* would have paid much attention to this without them, and for another, people might have just locked those guys up and thrown away the key."[91] Hence, given the activist background of committee members, the evidence of the single-minded governmental pursuit of militant Black leaders, and the polarization of the early 1970s, the NCPPC response to the trial was quite understandable. Without a committee at all, it is doubtful that the Charlotte Three would have had an early release—even if the release was delayed by the political tensions. In all likelihood, the case and its defendants simply would have been forgotten.

As the final days before the Charlotte Three's release had counted down, then, the case had undergone a transformation in the public mind. The NCPPC had labored mightily to draw attention to the plight of the Three, particularly targeting the media. That strategy, of course, paid off handsomely in early 1974 in the *Charlotte Observer* series. It would be a great irony of the case, however, that the NCPPC's consistent pressure that successfully kept their cause afloat also spurred reporters to push one last big story on the case in the spring of 1975. Hence, that pressure inadvertently spawned the damaging "New Data" story. When the Three finally left their North Carolina prison cells, it would no longer be as perceived political prisoners, but as now harmless convicts who had paid for their crimes. The deescalation of the political polarization that had characterized the early part of the decade may have opened the door for the liberal *Observer* newsroom to more actively consider their potential guilt. It also, though, lifted the political veil that had always covered the case. Once that was done, the Three no longer seemed so dangerous, and their sentences certainly seemed unjustified.

The Charlotte Three case, however, had never been just about the guilt or innocence of three men who may have burned a barn full of horses. When it did become that simple in 1979, the men were released from prison. Up until the last few years of the 1970s, the case was not about what the defendants had done. It was about what they *might do.* The judge and prosecution understood that the defendants might not have committed a crime more heinous than burning fifteen horses, but it was their public duty to stop the Three before they had a chance to do so. During sentencing, Snepp himself had revealingly told them, "You burned 15 horses in that stable. What you would do to human beings, God only knows."[92]

9

AND THEN THERE
WERE NONE

The victory celebration for the Charlotte Three's release brought approximately fifty people to Charlotte's Freedom Park Community Center in August 1979. Jim Grant told friends and supporters that their release was "a people's victory, not our victory." Thanking all those who had worked for the cause, Grant assured them, "If it were not for the petitions, telegrams and letters, we wouldn't be standing here now." The odds had been so great, he recalled, that "[m]any times I never thought we'd reach this point." Reddy was more measured in his remarks, seeing the lack of a full pardon as an incomplete success. "Even though we didn't win," he contended, "we did not lose either, and we're here."[1]

Longtime Charlotte activist and NCPPC member Marvin Sparrow, however, was not there. He had left town over a year before. Attending law school in Atlanta, his role in the Three's cause since then had been a smaller, quieter, and decidedly human one. Every other Sunday afternoon, Sparrow climbed into his car and drove to the nearby federal prison to see inmate Jim Grant. "Jim liked to have me visit," remembers Sparrow, "because I was the only one who knew all these political groups. And he was always right on top of it. [Grant would say to me,] 'Well, I see that the RSVP has split from the whatever. . . .' And I at least knew that that was going on." Before Marvin Sparrow left Charlotte, though, his dream of "a society where people had equal opportunity, where there was a quality of power among people" had preceded him out of town.[2]

The prosecution of the Charlotte Three had proven an extremely successful tactic for suppressing activism. The Three's conviction ensured the removal

GOING TO HELL TO GET THE DEVIL

of three troublesome insurgents from the streets of Charlotte for a prolonged period of time. The isolation of one of the "top militants in North Carolina"— Jim Grant—was a particular achievement on that scale. Clearly, that view was fueled by the polarization of the period.

It must be said, however, that circumstantial evidence pointing toward guilt of the Three also contributed to the demise of public support for the activists' cause. When pressed, some NCPPC members admit avoiding the issue of the Three's guilt or innocence. "To tell you the truth," concedes Kathy Sparrow, "I don't know if they did it or they didn't. I think they are honorable people, and I believe them. I suppose that the only way I'd know for sure is if they sat down and told me directly whether or not they did it." Marvin Sparrow admits, "I never asked anybody. I tried to figure it out. I know that there were a lot of serious questions about it, and legally it's a very shaky thing to prove. On the other hand, there were people that came forward and said, 'Yeah, they did it.'" One issue, though, still lingers in his mind: "I'll tell you, the thing that bothers me more than anything . . . is Clarence Harrison, who walked in one day and said, 'I plead guilty,' and is never heard from again. You know, you just think a guy doesn't come in and plead guilty unless he did something. And, so, I'll say that I wouldn't be convinced that they didn't do it. I'm not convinced that they did it. I'm convinced that it wasn't proven that they did it."[3]

On this score, the "New Data" story was a big blow. The imprisonment of the Three itself was one successful tactic in ending support for their cause. Many moderate Charlotteans—Black and white—had qualms merely about rallying to three men who were accused felons in an unsavory crime. The taint of now being a convicted criminal would be enough to discourage many other potential supporters. The *Observer*'s presentation of more incriminating evidence in 1975 clearly weakened the cause.

Beyond the question of the Three's culpability in the barn burning, the advisability of some of the Three's actions can still be called into question. One wonders if civil rights activists in an earlier time would have formed friendships and alliances with two men (Hood and Washington) who continued to be charged with violent felonies in the late 1960s. Further, the Afro American Unity Organization doubtless bred little "unity" by having a shootout with other African Americans at the Black-owned Chicken 'n Ribs restaurant in 1969. Likewise, the needlessly incendiary car chase and shooting involving two white teenage couples surely undermined support in both the city's white and Black communities for the cause of Black Power. More importantly, in light of activists' objections to law enforcement's obvious surveillance, use of informants and provocateurs, and even—by the words of a federal judge— "harassment," some of the agitators' actions now appear naive. Given their own observations on alleged police misconduct, surely these hardened Black Power veterans could deduce that law agents eagerly awaited the opportunity to arrest them on whatever charges they could. If they were so committed to the cause, shouldn't they pick a better battle to risk imprisonment on than a verbal confrontation at a traffic light, leading to a car chase with white teens?

As Marvin Sparrow, who avows uncertainty over the Three's guilt, says, "If [the Three] burned the stables because they didn't get the right to ride, that not only seems wrong to me, it seems like a very foolish kind of thing to do. There are many more injustices that are more important to deal with than whether you get to go ride at a stable. Now, I'm not a Black person, and I didn't want to go ride any horses. And I'm just saying that . . . I can see how an experience with discrimination would make a person angry enough that they would go do something. . . . But I don't think it was a smart thing to do."[4]

Furthermore, if Charlotte's Black Power and New Left activists were going to be successful, they needed to overcome another formidable opponent: the traditional American aversion to economic redistribution. As the city's grassroots activists veered toward economic solutions to the plight of the city's Black population, they found the same resistance among civic and business leadership that countless activists found in myriad other American cities in the late 1960s and early 1970s.

One lesson of the civil rights movement years was that activists had great difficulty when their opponents were not only determined but wily and organized. The truth is that despite Americans' laudatory celebration of the civil rights movement's towering achievements with limited resources, social change movements are far more difficult to win than is apparent in America's cursory annual Black History Months. Albany, Georgia, police chief Laurie Pritchett, who had studied carefully the civil rights tactics of the Southern Christian Leadership Conference and the Student Nonviolent Coordinating Committee, proved a shrewd and substantial opponent against the early 1960s civil rights efforts of activists for much of a decade. Mayor Richard Daley had been the consummate politician in Chicago long before Martin Luther King arrived in 1965 to launch his ambitious campaign for racial and economic change. He would engineer one of King's most apparent failures. It should be no surprise, then, that the late 1960s' and early 1970s' critical combination of the potent series of federal crime bills, Nixon's mobilization of an organized intelligence campaign, and the collusion of federal law enforcement with their southern state and local counterparts proved crippling for the long-fought African American freedom struggle.

Given these difficult odds, a more careful, disciplined, and savvy approach was necessary than was delivered by too many of Charlotte's young advocates for social change. We might acknowledge activists' right to pursue their cause in any way they deem fit, but embracing street criminals and flirting with violence was sure to draw many detractors at a time when rallying public support and avoiding law enforcement crackdowns was critical. As Grant conceded to the *Charlotte Observer* during a post-release interview, violence had seemed a justifiable tactic before his imprisonment, "But I don't feel that way today. In the '60s, people felt violence would bring about social change, and some changes did come during those times. But violence also brought down the strength of the government on those who favored social change. It's become unacceptable to the masses of people. It's not a viable tactic in the context of today."[5]

Perhaps the most effective component of the Charlotte Three prosecution, however, had nothing to do directly with the incarceration of Reddy, Grant, and Parker. As a result of the trial and conviction, the Three's supporters became embroiled in a cause that had little direct bearing on their original goals for reforming Charlotte. Community organizers who had previously targeted the improvement of the city's impoverished and downtrodden became slide show educators for the middle class, cocktail party hosts, and bail fundraisers—a far cry from improving the life of the poor and African Americans. Marvin Sparrow was

> very bitter for a long time that so much energy was going into the fact that these three people were in prison, and the Wilmington Ten were in prison, and that we were spending so much time, you know, putting together a slide show and going out and talking to people, and that there were a hun-

dred other things that I'd rather be talking about changing in America than whether these people get out of prison. . . . [But,] I don't think there was any choice. It wasn't like we could say, "Oh, forget them. They're in prison." But, I think our energy was very much diverted from what our goals were at the time. But, that's just the nature of struggle.[6]

Hence, law enforcement had taken not only the Charlotte Three away from their cause of social change, but the countless activists who rallied to them.

By the time the Three were released, and those activists might have returned to their original cause of "building another world," contends Marvin Sparrow, exhaustion and disillusionment had long since set in. "In a lot of ways," Sparrow recalls, "I think we just sort of said, 'Screw it'" by the mid-1970s. At the 1974 downfall of their sworn enemy Richard Nixon, Sparrow remembers nothing but apathy. "[B]y the time Nixon resigned—which was sort of like a moment of victory—all of us were saying, 'Who cares?'" Contemplating what their absorption in the Charlotte Three cause did to their activism, Sparrow turns pensive. "I might have been able to walk away from that case, if I had been more convinced that they really had done it, and had seen less that it was a concentrated plan of trying to suppress this activity." In the end, though, he contends, "the power structure did exactly what they intended to do—tie people up for a long time and put a lot of pressure on them."[7]

Attorney Jim Ferguson, who spent his career at the nexus of civil rights activism and the courtroom, likewise sagely reflected in 2008 on "how grassroots and community activism intersect and interact with legal activism. It's often a hard balance to make. My own view is that they should go hand in hand because sometimes in order to get a successful legal outcome, you need to create a certain climate in the community. . . . And courts, though they like to say they're nonpolitical, react to what's going on in the community. . . . The danger in it is that going through the legal process is slow, and you don't get into a legal case and get it resolved in a few weeks. It takes years, and sometimes there's nothing that can kill a movement more than a legal case."[8]

* * *

Other factors certainly figured in the demise of activism in the 1970s: national exhaustion over rapid 1960s social change, the erosion of public goodwill as some activists veered into more leftist and violent agendas, the nationwide conflation of nonviolent demonstrations with urban riots by many of Richard Nixon's "silent majority," and the diversion of African American energies from grassroots protests into the long-sought political opportunities made available by the 1965 Voting Rights Act. Just as certain, however, was law enforcement's vital part of that puzzle.

Among those impacted by the repercussions of the Charlotte Three case were the city's indigent African American population. The work to improve racial and economic justice in the Queen City still lies largely undone. Today, as in virtually every other American city, the issues of economic devastation in Charlotte's Black community are even more troublesome than they were in the 1970s. Certainly some African Americans have become notable successes. Harvey Gantt, a successful architect, became the city's first Black mayor in 1983 (and was followed nonconsecutively by three others). But few could convince poor and working-class Black Charlotteans that their lot is not worse than when T. J. Reddy, Charles Parker, and Jim Grant took to the streets in the late 1960s and early 1970s.

During the 1980s, the War on Crime shifted into the War on Drugs under the eager hand of conservative President Ronald Reagan, who oversaw the highest growth in the income gap between rich and poor since 1929. Charlotte rated particularly grimly, arriving dead last among the nation's fifty largest cities in economic mobility (i.e., the likelihood that working-class citizens' children could climb into the upper class) in a 2014 government report. With that widening class disparity has come the growth of national prison populations, from 96 for every 100,000 Americans in 1973 to a phenomenal 1,000 per 100,000 in 2008. Reagan's presidency would fulfill the conservative reaction to crime that had begun in the late 1960s.[9]

Now that grassroots activism on race and economic issues had been substantially curtailed, the poor themselves would be the primary casualties in this "war." The poverty percentage of state prison inmates significantly increased after Reagan's presidency and the War on Drugs. In 1986, 31 percent of state prison inmates had no pre-arrest full-time employment. That number had grown substantially to 45 percent by 1991, meaning the percentage of state prisoners who were poor had grown from less than one-third to almost half in just five years.[10] In 2010, approximately half of prison inmates were illiterate, and 80 percent were regarded by their trial judges as indigent. Furthermore, African Americans went to prison at four times the rate of whites in 1960. They were shipped off at seven times the number in 2000.[11]

And while the 1980s brought an escalation of decidedly expensive prison building to accommodate the sharply rising numbers of the incarcerated, there was a clear reduction in public funding to address poverty. The federal minimum wage remained static from 1981 to 1989, and thus those dependent on it fell significantly behind in real family income. In 1976, 46 percent of African American workers aged 20–24 held blue-collar jobs (a traditional refuge for the poorly educated seeking to support families on a decent wage in America). Only 20 percent of Blacks remained in those ranks by 1984. Young Black families earned just 60 percent of their white counterparts' income in 1973, but dropped precipitously to 46 percent by 1986. Similarly, those young Black families saw their real earnings plummet by half between 1973 and 1986.[12]

Despite the loss of grassroots activist momentum in the early 1970s, not everyone had given up. Immediately after his release from prison in 1979, Jim Grant sat on his cousin's porch and told the *Observer* that "there is no question that the whole labor and economic area will be the next great movement in this part of the country. People are being squeezed. The major corporations are all setting up operations in the Sunbelt because there are no unions. I think that conditions will impel people to act, to combat the repression that is still going on. People down here are going to have to continue to push for change. If they don't, history will roll back on top of them." Of course, that "next great movement" has yet to arrive, the Sunbelt still functions as a great magnet for industries hungry for nonunion, low-wage labor, and there is no indication that history will stop rolling on top of the poor in the foreseeable future.[13]

* * *

Sparrow, who went on to work as a criminal defense attorney for troubled youth, ironically worked in the same system that once drained the life out of his activism for "building another world." As he says, though, a person committed to social change doesn't always get to choose where his work will lie. Sparrow argues that today's American courts "are probably just as bad as they were when we started. In fact, they were probably better in the '60s and early

'70s. . . . The courts are probably the most unfair aspect of our country. They're the place where power is really exercised." For an activist who had sought three decades ago to bring about a "society where people had equal opportunity, where there was a quality of power among people," then, perhaps there is no better place to be.[14]

Shortly after his release from prison, Charles Parker got a construction job and faded into a now welcome obscurity. Jim Grant continued his practice of moving fluidly from job to job throughout North Carolina and the Southeast. All of those jobs, of course, remained where his heart was: in community organizing the poor and disenfranchised. His tireless commitment to the cause garnered him the North Carolina ACLU's 2015 Frank Porter Graham Award for his "longstanding and significant contributions to the fight for individual freedom and civil liberties." "I'm just a person, a soldier, out here trying to get something done," he claimed at the time. "That's always what it's been. It's always been about the struggle. It's never been about me." Rather than derailing his activism, the Charlotte Three case "made him more committed" according to friend and Charlotte Three attorney Jim Ferguson: "The Charlotte Three experience demonstrated to him that none of us are immune from being affected by the injustices and wrongs that society sometimes visits upon people." After over a half-century of activism, Grant passed away in 2021, honored by many—including the Reverent William Barber II, co-chair of the National Poor People's Campaign, who remembered, "You know if Jim Grant is coming, you can count on him. He's not going to run. He'll stick with you. . . . He would go in places and stand beside people when other people and even other organizations wouldn't."[15]

As for T. J. Reddy, he established himself in Charlotte as a local artist and art shop owner before his premature death from cancer in 2019. His work was displayed numerous times in and around the Charlotte area in those intervening years. One such early exhibition of his paintings took place in February 1991 at Charlotte's First Union Gallery. For an artist who focused heavily on the disenfranchised, it was perhaps ironic that the gallery was housed in First Union Bank, one of the principal economic titans in the city's meteoric Sunbelt rise. The works, said a review, were cast in "bright, luminescent colors," but the subject matter was considerably darker. Reddy's artistic depiction of "bag ladies, drunkards, the homeless, and others whose daily existence lies on the fringes of society" stood as a rejoinder to the surrounding opulence of the high-rise banking institution. "With expressions of disillusionment, ragged figures of all ages huddle over trash cans and wander through littered urban streets," observed reviewer Bryan Bayles. The content clearly struck Bayles, who noted that Reddy's "agenda to expose cultural indifference to the plight of the destitute places faith in art's suggestive powers. Indeed, it is this faith in art's ability to communicate diverse cultural experiences and to pose challenging questions that must serve as the primary stimulus for art concerned with social change. . . . Seducing us aesthetically and then confronting us ideologically, Reddy offers a notable contribution to the ongoing critical dialogue of how to respond to society's outcasts."[16]

Reddy, who had increasingly painted since his release from prison, still imagined himself first and foremost as a poet. "I always see myself as a poet, even if I'm painting," he maintained. That stance compelled one art critic to describe his paintings as "poetry painted on the surfaces of panel and paper."[17]

At the 1991 First Union exhibition, then, it was not unusual to see him include one of his poems. It hung, untitled, on the wall amid his visual pieces. The first line forms a question that still hangs over his home city. Just as the poem did not offer a clear solution to the query, so the answer outside the art gallery lies just as mysteriously unanswered: "What will become of them, the dispossessed?"[18]

CHRONOLOGY

1957 Dr. Reginald Hawkins helps lead the effort to desegregate Charlotte schools following the 1954 *Brown v. Board of Education* decision.

1960 Charlotte students participate in sit-ins at local eateries.

1963 Dr. Hawkins leads protests to force Charlotte leaders to desegregate hospitals, hotels, restaurants, and movie theaters; the Charlotte Chamber of Commerce responds by appearing at local restaurants in an integrated fashion as a show of support, leading to positive national publicity.

1965 Bombing of four prominent Black leaders' homes (Hawkins, African American city councilman Fred Alexander, NAACP chapter president Kelly Alexander, and civil rights attorney Julius Chambers); the case is never solved.

1967 Charlotte is awarded a Model Cities grant, leading to conflict between white civic and African American leaders over how to use the funding.

1968 Major "War on Crime" legislation passes (Omnibus Crime Control and Safe Streets Act); North Carolina governor race features an unsuccessful campaign by Reginald Hawkins and a victorious one by Bob Scott (whose campaign employed Nixonesque "silent majority" and "law and order" rhetoric).

April 1968 Martin Luther King Jr. is assassinated on the eve of coming to North Carolina in support of Hawkins's gubernatorial campaign.

May 1968 Poor People's Campaign makes a stop in Charlotte on its way to Washington, D.C.

August 1968 Jim Grant and T. J. Reddy are questioned by the Charlotte Police Intelligence Division for leafletting against the Vietnam War draft.

September 1968 Lazy B Stables burn.

December 1968 Jim Grant is fired from the federally funded Charlotte Area Fund poverty program amid white leaders' complaints of the group's activism; prominent Black Power leader Stokely Carmichael speaks at the University of North Carolina at Charlotte.

May 1969 Law enforcement raids AAUO headquarters, seizing firearms; hippie house case against Marvin and Kathy Sparrow on charges of contributing to the delinquency of a minor (convicted, but later overturned on appeal).

June 1969 Newly created Black Solidarity Committee (whose members included Hawkins, T. J. Reddy and civil rights attorney Julius Chambers) calls for resignation of Charlotte police chief due to his alleged "brutal" treatment of Black Charlotteans.

August 1969 AAUO members are arrested in two incidents (the first involving a heated car chase with white teens; the second involving a gunfight where members were injured and arrested); Dave Washington is given a twenty- to twenty-five-year suspended sentence for armed robbery.

November 1969 Al Hood is given a thirty-day sentence for assault on a police officer.

May 1970   Al Hood and Dave Washington are arrested for carrying guns and dynamite into the riot area of Oxford, North Carolina (Hood and Washington will later turn witnesses against Jim Grant and Ben Chavis, claiming the latter instigated them to break the law).

September 1970   Al Hood and Dave Washington fail to appear at federal trial for charges related to the Oxford riot, fleeing to Canada.

February 1971   Dave Washington is sentenced to a psychiatric hospital for his September 1970 bond-jumping charges (and released two months later). Al Hood is arrested for armed robbery.

March 1971   Hood signs a sworn statement implicating Jim Grant and Ben Chavis for aiding his prior bond-jumping and escape to Canada.

July 1971   Al Hood and Dave Washington sign sworn statements against the Charlotte Three and Ben Chavis, implicating the former in the 1968 Lazy B Stables burning and the latter (together with Charlotte Three defendant Jim Grant) in the 1970 Oxford violence. This begins Hood's and Washington's federal protective custody up to the Charlotte Three trial.

January 1972   The Charlotte Three are indicted for the 1968 Lazy B Stables burning.

April 1972   Ben Chavis is acquitted and Jim Grant found guilty at the Raleigh Two trial (involving Jim Grant and Ben Chavis) over charges stemming from the violence in Oxford, North Carolina, in 1970.

July 1972   The Charlotte Three trial; the North Carolina Political Prisoners Committee forms.

August 1972   Federal agents deliver payment to Hood and Washington for their cooperation in the Charlotte Three and Raleigh Two trials.

August 1972 Al Hood is indicted (one week after receiving his federal cash payment) for his alleged role in the murder of a heroin pusher.

March 1973 T. J. Reddy and Charles Parker are released from prison on bail.

August 1973 Amnesty International declares Jim Grant a political prisoner.

January 1974 T. J. Reddy and Charles Parker return to prison (following the North Carolina Court of Appeals' denial of their appeal).

March 1974 The *Charlotte Observer* publishes a series of investigative articles raising questions about the Charlotte Three case, including the heretofore secret cash payments to Hood and Washington.

July 1974 North Carolina governor James Holshouser declines to pardon Charlotte Three.

December 1974 Superior Court judge Sam Ervin III holds Charlotte Three appeal hearing.

May 1975 *Charlotte Observer* publishes article "New Data Implicates Lazy B Three."

September 1975 Judge Sam Ervin III denies Charlotte Three appeal.

March 1976 North Carolina Supreme Court declines to hear Charlotte Three appeal.

June 1976 Jim Grant and T. J. Reddy are released from prison awaiting the result of their appeal.

December 1976 Charles Parker released from prison upon concluding his sentence.

January 1978 North Carolina governor James Hunt reduces Wilmington Ten sentences.

October 1978   U.S. Supreme Court declines to hear Charlotte Three appeal, which leads to Grant and Reddy returning to prison.

July 1979   North Carolina Governor James Hunt reduces sentences for remaining Charlotte Three inmates, Reddy and Grant.

NOTES

Introduction

1. The weakening of Black rights in the legal system in the late nineteenth century was bolstered by a series of regrettable Supreme Court decisions that doomed the new hopes of legal justice raised by the constitutional amendments of the First Reconstruction (numbers 13, 14, and 15), culminating with the now infamous 1896 *Plessy v. Ferguson* decision, which claimed that "separate but equal" accommodations did not violate a citizen's equal rights. For more, see Charles A. Lofgren's *The Plessy Case: A Legal-Historical Interpretation* (New York: Oxford Univ. Press, 1987); Thomas J. Davis, "Race, Identity, and the Law: Plessy v. Ferguson (1896)," in *Race on Trial: Law and Justice in American History*, ed. Annette Gordon-Reed (New York: Oxford Univ. Press, 2002); Philip Dray, *At the Hands of Persons Unknown: The Lynching of Black America* (New York: Random House, 2002), 109–122; and Williamjames Hull Hoffer, *Plessy v. Ferguson: Race and Inequality in Jim Crow America* (Lawrence: Univ. Press of Kansas, 2012).

2. Nixon's veto of the Voting Rights Act renewal was overridden by Congress in 1970. Rick Perlstein, *Nixonland: The Rise of a President and the Fracturing of America* (New York: Scribner, 2008), 506–509; William Chafe, *The Unfinished Journey: America Since World War II* (New York: Oxford Univ. Press, 1995), 284–286.

3. While the perception by many white southern law officers and civilians may have persisted that federal law officers were the enemies of the decades-long southern white supremacy, the reputation—in the view of many civil rights veterans—was not well earned. FBI agents, in particular, were notorious for their policy of refusing to intervene during lawless violence exacted on peaceful activists. See Kenneth O'Reilly, *"Racial Matters": The FBI's Secret File on Black America, 1960–1972* (New York: Free Press, 1989), and David Garrow, *The FBI and Martin Luther King, Jr.: From "Solo" to Memphis* (New York: Norton, 1981).

4. Kenneth O'Reilly asserts that "the deference" of Nixon officials "who certainly did share [FBI Director J. Edgar Hoover's] conservative values" made possible Hoover's now infamous and legally questionable "private war against Black people." (O'Reilly, *"Racial Matters,"* 225, 258.) Likewise, David Garrow contends that the FBI, with its "paranoid style," was hardly "a renegade institution secretly operating outside . . . American values, but a virtually representative bureau-

cracy" of the national mainstream (Garrow, *The FBI and Martin Luther King, Jr.*, 208–213). The literature on this subject is wide. Among the notables: Athan Theoharis, *The FBI and American Democracy: A Brief Critical History* (Lawrence: Univ. of Kansas Press, 2004); Dan T. Carter, *The Politics of Rage: George Wallace, the Origins of the New Conservatism, and the Transformation of American Politics* (New York: Simon and Schuster, 1995); Allen J. Matusow, *The Unraveling of America: A History of Liberalism in the 1960s* (New York: Harper and Row, 1984), part III; Kim McQuaid, *The Anxious Years: America in the Vietnam-Watergate Era* (New York: Basic Books, 1989), 49–51, 129–166; David Cunningham, *There's Something Happening Here: The New Left, the Klan, and FBI Counterintelligence* (Berkeley: Univ. of California Press, 2004); Bryan Burrough, *Days of Rage: America's Radical Underground, the FBI, and the Forgotten Age of Revolutionary Violence* (New York: Penguin, 2016); and Seth Rosenfeld, *Subversives: The FBI's War on Student Radicals, and Reagan's Rise to Power* (New York: Farrar, Straus, and Giroux, 2012).

5. Janette Greenwood explored the historic roots of those race relations in her study of turn-of-the-century Charlotte, *Bittersweet Legacy: The Black and White "Better Classes" in Charlotte, 1850–1915* (Chapel Hill: Univ. of North Carolina Press, 1994). Greenwood finds a delicate and fluid relationship between the growing business and professional classes of both the white and Black communities—the self-named "better classes"—that created a window of interracial cooperation and accommodation before it closed by 1900.

6. Frye Gaillard, *The Dream Long Deferred* (Chapel Hill: Univ. of North Carolina Press, 1988); See also Davison Douglas, *Reading, Writing, and Race: The Desegregation of the Charlotte Schools* (Chapel Hill: Univ. of North Carolina Press, 1995). Other sources on Charlotte's navigation through the busing crisis and into the 1970s include Bernard Schwartz, *Swann's Way: The School Busing Case and the Supreme Court* (New York: Oxford Univ. Press, 1986), and, more recently, Matthew D. Lassiter's *The Silent Majority: Suburban Politics in the Sunbelt South* (Princeton, N.J.: Princeton Univ. Press, 2006) and Stephen Samuel Smith, *Boom for Whom? Education, Desegregation, and Development in Charlotte* (Albany: State Univ. of New York Press, 2004).

1. Business Leadership and Desegregation in 1960s Charlotte

1. Roy Covington, "Moore Lauds General Tire at Plant Dedication," *Charlotte Observer*, 29 November 1967, 1C; Emery Wister, "Moore Hails 'New South' of Greater Opportunities," *Charlotte News*, 28 November 1967, 1A.

2. Covington, "Moore Lauds"; Wister, "Moore Hails." Moore's selected quote comes from Cash's brief and vaguely hopeful conclusion to the otherwise pessimistic *The Mind of the South*. See W. J. Cash, *The Mind of the South* (London: Thames and Hudson, 1971), 429. For more on Cash's connections to Charlotte (as a journalist briefly with the *Charlotte Observer*, then more prominently with the *Charlotte News*), see Bruce Clayton, *W. J. Cash: A Life* (Baton Rouge: Louisiana State Univ. Press, 1991).

3. William Chafe's vital study of North Carolina's self-cultivated "progressive mystique" and its racial ironies, *Civilities and Civil Rights: Greensboro, North Carolina, and the Black Struggle for Freedom* (New York: Oxford Univ. Press, 1981), set the foundation for future inquiries into the state's racial history. More recently, Robert R. Korstad and James L. Leloudis's *To Right These*

Wrongs: The North Carolina Fund and the Battle to End Poverty and Inequality in 1960s America (Chapel Hill: Univ. of North Carolina Press, 2010) examines how Governor Terry Sanford's pursuit of Ford Foundation dollars to create the North Carolina Fund (which served as a model for future programs of the War on Poverty) further added to the state's reputation. The Queen City's local poverty agency, the Charlotte Area Fund, in fact, was one of the Fund's beneficiaries. Sanford's racial views were also comparatively enlightened among his southern gubernatorial peers. As he took office, a friend claimed the new governor felt "deep down" that racial tension "was going to have to be settled if . . . we were to grow as a state." Sanford, in fact, took the politically risky step of enrolling his two children in an integrated school in 1961 (see Korstad and Leloudis, 36–46). Another milestone of North Carolina racial progressivism was allowing its flagship public university in Chapel Hill to become the South's first to desegregate in 1951 (see Korstad and Leloudis, 74–75).

4. "Mind of the New South," *Charlotte News*, 29 November 1967, 10A. Two weeks prior, the *Charlotte News* had run a lengthy review of Joseph L. Morrison's *W. J. Cash: Southern Prophet* and reprinted two Cash editorials from his days as a *News* staff editorial writer.

5. Thomas W. Hanchett, *Sorting Out the New South City: Race, Class, and Urban Development in Charlotte, 1875-1975* (Chapel Hill: Univ. of North Carolina Press, 1998), 14–37, 90–95, 184–200, 224–227; David Goldfield, "A Place to Come To," in *Charlotte, North Carolina: The Global Evolution of a New South City*, ed. William Graves and Heather A. Smith (Athens: Univ. of Georgia Press, 2010), 10–16; Damaria Leach, "Progress Under Pressure: Changes in Charlotte Race Relations, 1955–1965" (Master's thesis, University of North Carolina at Chapel Hill, 1976), 3–11; Peter Applebome, *Dixie Rising: How the South Is Shaping American Values, Politics, and Culture* (New York: Harcourt Brace, 1997), 156–163.

6. Leach, "Progress Under Pressure," 3–11. See Thomas Hanchett's *Sorting Out the New South City* for a full and fascinating discussion of how Charlotte's business leaders had dominated city politics throughout the city's history.

7. "Guess Who's Boss of Our Town," *Charlotte Observer*, 12 February 1960, 2B.

8. James C. Cobb, "The Sunbelt South: Industrialization in Regional, National, and International Perspective," in *Searching for the Sunbelt: Historical Perspectives on a Region*, ed. Raymond A. Mohl (Athens: Univ. of Georgia Press, 1993), 25–31; David R. Goldfield, *Promised Land: The South Since 1945* (Wheeling, Ill.: Harlan Davidson, 1987), 1–20.

9. The "Sunbelt" concept has been considerably critiqued by historians. The debates include how to define the Sunbelt region (for example, does one include Oregon, Mississippi?), how to differentiate the considerable regional self-promotion from legitimate demographic facts, and (perhaps most particularly) the troubling and abiding poverty in some areas (for example, the rural Deep South) amid the apparent dynamic economic growth of the broader region one celebrates. For perhaps the best examination of these dilemmas, see Raymond A. Mohl, ed., *Searching for the Sunbelt: Historical Perspectives on a Region* (Athens: Univ. of Georgia Press, 1993). See also Michelle Nickerson and Darren Dochuk, eds., *Sunbelt Rising: The Politics of Space, Place, and Region* (Philadelphia: Univ. of Pennsylvania Press, 2014); Numan Bartley, *The New South, 1945–1980: The Story of the South's Modernization* (Baton Rouge: Louisiana State Press, 1995), 417–454; and Goldfield, *Promised Land*, 122–161, 196–219. For two good multifaceted looks at the issue, see

NOTES TO PAGE 12

the edited collections David C. Perry and Alfred J. Watkins, eds., *The Rise of the Sunbelt Cities* (Beverly Hills: Sage Publications, 1977), and Randall M. Miller and George E. Pozzetta, *Shades of the Sunbelt: Essays on Ethnicity, Race, and the Urban South* (New York: Greenwood, 1988). James Cobb devotes some time to the issues surrounding the Sunbelt (especially in chapter 7) in his *The South and America Since World War II* (New York: Oxford Univ. Press, 2011). For a look back at the origins of the "Sunbelt" concept, see the important works by Kevin Phillips, *The Emerging Republican Majority* (New Rochelle, N.Y.: Arlington House, 1969) (which first coined the term), and Kirkpatrick Sale, *Power Shift: The Rise of the Southern Rim and Its Challenge to the Eastern Establishment* (New York: Random House, 1975) (which used the term "southern rim" to describe the same Sunbelt phenomenon).

10. Kevin Kruse, *White Flight: Atlanta and the Making of Modern Conservatism* (Princeton, N.J.: Princeton Univ. Press, 2005), 149.

11. The quote comes from Kruse, *White Flight*, 200. During Atlanta's school desegregation drive, influential mayor William Hartsfield had already distributed to the city's prominent businessmen copies of a study highlighting Little Rock's millions of dollars of lost business following their 1957 tumultuous school desegregation crisis. It was Hartsfield who also coined the slogan "City Too Busy to Hate" when Atlanta peacefully desegregated its public golf courses in December 1958. The motto gained further attention when it was promoted in the 1960 "Forward Atlanta" Chamber of Commerce campaign promoting the city to businesses looking to expand or relocate operations. Irene Holliman, "From Crackertown to Model City? Urban Renewal and Community Building in Atlanta, 1963–1966," *Journal of Urban History* 35 (2009): 383. For more on Atlanta and civil rights, see Kruse's *White Flight*, 146–150. Matthew D. Lassiter makes many explicit comparisons between Charlotte and Atlanta in his *Silent Majority*, noting the class dimensions of white suburbanites' responses to school desegregation and busing. As Lassiter states succinctly, "The politics of racial moderation in postwar Atlanta always sought peace and progress, never justice and equality, through the conscious replication and then the triumphant enhancement of national patterns of metropolitan development and spatial segregation" (115–116). See also Ronald Bayor, *Race and the Shaping of Twentieth-Century Atlanta* (Chapel Hill: Univ. of North Carolina Press, 2000). Jason Sokol's *There Goes My Everything: White Southerners in the Age of Civil Rights, 1945–1975* (New York: Knopf, 2006) also includes illuminating sections on civil rights issues in Atlanta. Tomiko Brown-Nagin's *Courage to Dissent: Atlanta and the Long History of the Civil Rights Movement* (New York: Oxford Univ. Press, 2011) layers Atlanta's civil rights story further by examining the debates within the local African American community and between local and national civil rights leaders as to how to pursue legal change. Karen Ferguson's *Black Politics in New Deal Atlanta* (Chapel Hill: Univ. of North Carolina Press, 2002) traces the development of an educated African American elite, to whom moderate whites made limited racial and economic concessions (as a way to stave off larger racial reforms), to the beginning of the twentieth century. It should also be noted that even the careful management of Atlanta's racial affairs did not forestall some decidedly ugly racial incidents: an unsettlingly bloody 1906 race riot, the 1913 lynching of Leo Frank, the prestigious Peachtree Street becoming the national headquarters for the Ku Klux Klan in the 1920s and 1930s, and hosting some of the South's more notable segregationist political figures (including Lester Maddox and Eugene and Herman Tal-

madge). Nashville also provided a model for the same type of paternalistic racial moderation—something residents of the Tennessee city called "The Nashville Way." For further explorations on that, see Benjamin Houston's *The Nashville Way: Racial Etiquette and the Struggle for Social Justice in a Southern City* (Athens: Univ. of Georgia Press, 2012) and David Halberstam's *The Children* (New York: Random House, 1998).

12. Numan Bartley's *The New South, 1945–1980: The Story of the South's Modernization* (Baton Rouge: Louisiana State Univ. Press, 1995) succinctly places that "revolt's" origin at February 1, 1960 (see especially pages 298–305). Another important outcome of the college sit-in movement was the formation within the year of the Student Nonviolent Coordinating Committee (SNCC), which remained a powerful force in the broader civil rights movement. For more on SNCC, see Clayborne Carson's *In Struggle: SNCC and the Black Awakening of the 1960s* (Cambridge, Mass.: Harvard Univ. Press, 1981). Other works include Halberstam, *The Children*; John Lewis with Michael D'Orso, *Walking with the Wind: A Memoir of the Movement* (New York: Simon and Schuster, 1998); Emily Stoper, *The Student Nonviolent Coordinating Committee: The Growth of Radicalism in a Civil Rights Organization* (Brooklyn, N.Y.: Carlson Publishing, 1989); Wesley C. Hogan's *Many Minds, One Heart: SNCC's Dream for a New America* (Chapel Hill: Univ. of North Carolina Press, 2007); and Constance Curry, *Deep in Our Hearts: Nine White Women in the Freedom Movement* (Athens: Univ. of Georgia Press, 2000). While not centering their stories on SNCC necessarily, two very important books on the civil rights movement in Mississippi spend a great deal of time on the organization's crucial work in that state (and thus capture the vital nature and spirit of SNCC): John Dittmer, *Local People: The Struggle for Civil Rights in Mississippi* (Urbana: Univ. of Illinois Press, 1994), and Charles M. Payne, *I've Got the Light of Freedom: The Organizing Tradition and the Mississippi Freedom Struggle* (Berkeley: Univ. of California Press, 1995). SNCC's achievements may also, of course, be found within innumerable studies of the larger movement.

13. Roy Covington, "Negroes' Protests Close Local Diners," *Charlotte Observer*, 10 February 1960, Charlotte Desegregation—History Clipping File, Charlotte-Mecklenburg Public Library (hereafter referred to as CMPL); Dick Rigby, "Pastors to Join Students in Renewed Demonstrations," *Charlotte News*, 23 June 1960, Charlotte Desegregation—History Clipping File, CMPL; Roy Covington, "Students Seek Aid of Negro Adults," *Charlotte Observer*, Charlotte Desegregation—History Clipping File, CMPL; J. Charles Jones, interview, New South Voices, University of North Carolina-Charlotte, J. Murrey Atkins Library, May 18, 2005, http://newsouthvoices.uncc.edu/interview/bbj00025 (accessed 30 June 2017); Martin Oppenheimer, *The Sit-In Movement* (Brooklyn, N.Y.: Carlson Publishing, 1989), 117–124; Leach, "Progress Under Pressure," 114.

14. The students renewed their protests by first picketing two prominent downtown department stores' restaurants (Belk's and Ivey's). The July 1960 agreement had involved only the desegregation of Belk's and Ivey's less formal lunch counters. The students had hoped that the two restaurants and other public accommodations would soon follow the lunch counters. These hopes proved fruitless, however, and they tried the less confrontational route of taking their grievance to Ivey's management. When this move brought no change, the students took their frustration to the streets with picketing. They did so in front of Belk's and Ivey's as well as several other segregated restaurants, hotels, and motels. Oppenheimer, *The Sit-In Movement*, 123; Leach, "Progress Under Pressure," 118–120.

15. Marianne Bumgarner-Davis, "Rending the Veil: Desegregation in Charlotte, 1954–1975" (Ph.D. diss., University of North Carolina at Chapel Hill, 1995), 158–161; Leach, "Progress Under Pressure," 167–169.

16. Bumgarner-Davis, "Rending the Veil," 167–170; Leach, "Progress Under Pressure," 168–169.

17. Paul Jablow, "He's Called Many Things, But Not 'Fool,'" *Charlotte Observer*, 10 March 1968, Reginald Hawkins Clipping File, CMPL; Leach, "Progress Under Pressure," 123–145; Reginald Hawkins, interview by Melinda Desmarais, 11 June 2001, Tega Cay, South Carolina, J. Murrey Atkins Library, University of North Carolina at Charlotte, http://newsouthvoices.uncc.edu/interview/ohha0077 (accessed 1 July 2015).

18. Reginald Hawkins, interview by Melinda Desmarais, 11 June 2001, Tega Cay, South Carolina, J. Murrey Atkins Library, University of North Carolina at Charlotte, http://newsouthvoices.uncc.edu/interview/ohha0077 (accessed 1 July 2015).

19. Stanford R. Brookshire, Untitled Public Statement, Stanford Brookshire Papers, Special Collections, J. Murrey Atkins Library, University of North Carolina at Charlotte, box 6, folder 4 (hereafter referred to as SRBP); Reginald Hawkins, interview by Melinda Desmarais, 11 June 2001, Tega Cay, South Carolina, J. Murrey Atkins Library, University of North Carolina at Charlotte, http://newsouthvoices.uncc.edu/interview/ohha0077 (accessed 1 July 2015); Jerry Shinn, "Unidentified Man Tears Signs of Negro Pickets at Hospital," *Charlotte Observer*, 4 March 1962, Reginald A. Hawkins Papers, Special Collections, J. Murrey Atkins Library, University of North Carolina at Charlotte (hereafter referred to as RAHP); "Brookshire Says He Regrets Pickets' Use of 'Coercion,'" *Charlotte Observer*, 4 March 1962, RAHP; Paul Jablow, "He's Called Many Things, But Not 'Fool'"; Leach, "Progress Under Pressure," 93, 127–154. For a fuller study of Hawkins's drive to desegregate Charlotte's hospitals, see Michael B. Richardson, "'Not Gradually . . . But Now': Reginald Hawkins, Black Leadership, and Desegregation in Charlotte, North Carolina," *North Carolina Historical Review* 82 (July 2005): 347–379.

20. *New Yorker* magazine based their survey of the nation's best trade areas on a variety of factors, including total retail sales, department store sales, and average family income. "Better Credit Rating Given to Charlotte," *Charlotte Observer*, 21 March 1963, 1B; "County Joins City, Has AA Credit Rating," *Charlotte Observer*, 26 March 1963, 1B; Harry Snook, "Charlotte Ranked 34th in U.S. Trade," *Charlotte Observer*, 20 March 1963, 18A; Harry Snook, "19 Shows Brought City $3.2 Million," *Charlotte Observer*, 7 March 1963, 1C; John DeMott, "Local C of C Wins 1st Place," *Charlotte Observer*, 2 April 1963, 1B; Leach, "Progress Under Pressure," 167–172.

21. Bumgarner-Davis, "Rending the Veil," 86–87.

22. Ibid., 87–88. As Thomas Hanchett aptly notes, the Mecklenburg Declaration of Independence is today regarded as having little reputable historical evidence (see Hanchett, *Sorting Out the New South City*, 15).

23. L. M. Wright, "Charlotte Has Built Its Integration Road," *Charlotte Observer*, 14 July 1963, 1A.

24. Ibid. For more on the 1963 Birmingham civil rights campaign, see Glenn Eskew's insightfully nuanced account, *But for Birmingham: The Local and National Movements in the Civil Rights Struggle* (Chapel Hill: Univ. of North Carolina Press, 1997), as well as J. Mills Thornton, *Dividing*

Lines: Municipal Politics and the Struggle for Civil Rights in Montgomery, Birmingham, and Selma (Tuscaloosa: Univ. of Alabama Press, 2006); Adam Fairclough, *To Redeem the Soul of America: The Southern Christian Leadership Conference and Martin Luther King, Jr.* (Athens: Univ. of Georgia Press, 1987), 111–139; Taylor Branch, *Parting the Waters: America in the King Years, 1954–1963* (New York: Touchstone, 1988), 673–802; David R. Goldfield, *Black, White, and Southern: Race Relations and Southern Culture, 1940 to the Present* (Baton Rouge: Louisiana State Univ. Press, 1990), 134–141; David Garrow, *Bearing the Cross: Martin Luther King, Jr., and the Southern Christian Leadership Conference* (New York: Morrow, 1986), 231–273. Jonathan Bass's *Blessed Are the Peacemakers: Martin Luther King, Jr., Eight White Religious Leaders, and the "Letter from Birmingham Jail"* (Baton Rouge: Louisiana State Univ. Press, 2001) provides an in-depth examination of Dr. King's important epistle during the campaign. Andrew Manis's *A Fire You Can't Put Out: The Civil Rights Life of Birmingham's Reverend Fred Shuttlesworth* (Tuscaloosa: Univ. of Alabama Press, 1999) covers the courageous local leader of the Birmingham freedom movement.

25. Ron Thompson, "The Charlotte Image: Carolina Boom Town," *Winston-Salem Journal and Sentinel,* 11 August 1963, 1D, SRBP, box 6, folder 23.

26. "How Charlotte, N.C., Desegregated Quietly," *Washington Daily News,* 25 July 1963, SRBP, box 6, folder 23; Stanford R. Brookshire, "It's Time to Solve the Race Problem," *New York Herald Tribune,* 16 June 1963, SRBP, box 6, folder 23; Leach, "Progress Under Pressure," 184.

27. Leach, "Progress Under Pressure," 185–186.

28. Reginald A. Hawkins, interview by Melinda Desmarais, New South Voices, 11 June 2001, http://newsouthvoices.uncc.edu/interview/ohha0077 (accessed 18 May 2017).

29. Gaillard, *The Dream Long Deferred,* 35–36; Leach, "Progress Under Pressure," 29–34; Reginald A. Hawkins, interview by Melinda Desmarais, New South Voices, 11 June 2001, http://newsouthvoices.uncc.edu/interview/ohha0077 (accessed 18 May 2017). Disturbingly, the bombing was the second endured by Chambers within the year. The first occurred outside a speech Chambers delivered for the NAACP in New Bern, North Carolina, the prior January. With the pressure of the governor seeking to defend the state's moderate reputation and FBI assistance, authorities identified three men who had driven a car fitting witnesses' description, had purchased dynamite three weeks earlier, and had boasted that day in town that "there were enough damn Klansmen to keep Negroes in Craven County in their place." Two of the suspects made a full confession. The local prosecutor, however, claimed unspecified "legal technicalities" weakening the case, and he accepted a plea deal that included no jail time and a promise to pay for the dynamited automobile. For more on this and Chambers's legacy in general, see Richard Rosen and Joseph Mosnier, *Julius Chambers: A Life in the Legal Struggle for Civil Rights* (Chapel Hill: Univ. of North Carolina Press, 2016), 78–81.

30. "'Raise High the Roof Beam,'" *Charlotte Observer,* 2 December 1965, 2C (reprinted from the *Boston Globe* by the *Observer*).

31. Ibid.; Stanford R. Brookshire, "Statement—Community Meeting—Ovens Auditorium," 28 November 1965, SRBP, box 6, folder 4; Wilkins as quoted in Bumgarner-Davis, "Rending the Veil," 210. Hawkins did attend the rally but refused to speak "because it was a farce.... [T]hey put up a show, mainly a face to lure business. You know Charlotte's a good town: good schools, you know—good race relations.... which was a lie and dehumanizing to me." Reginald A. Hawkins,

interview by Melinda Desmarais, New South Voices, 11 June 2001, http://newsouthvoices.uncc
.edu/interview/ohha0077 (accessed 18 May 2017).

32. Doug Smith, "Negro Home Bomb Case Is Unsolved," *Charlotte News,* 22 November 1968,
11A; Leach, "Progress Under Pressure," 34; Reginald A. Hawkins, interview by Melinda Desmarais, New South Voices, 11 June 2001, http://newsouthvoices.uncc.edu/interview/ohha0077 (accessed 18 May 2017).

33. Leach, "Progress Under Pressure," 30.

34. Eric Foner, *Reconstruction: America's Unfinished Revolution, 1863–1877* (New York:
Harper and Row, 1988), 425.

35. Michal R. Belknap, *Federal Law and Southern Order: Racial Violence and Constitutional
Conflict in the Post-*Brown *South* (Athens: Univ. of Georgia Press, 1995), 18. For an extended dis-
cussion on the federal government's reluctance to intervene on behalf of Black southerners while
simultaneously throwing its weight behind southern officials' racially repressive measures, see
Mary Frances Berry, *Black Resistance, White Law: A History of Constitutional Racism in America*
(New York: Penguin Press, 1994). For a revealing examination of the conflation of criminality and
African Americans in a national context, see Khalil Gibran Muhammad's *The Condemnation of
Blackness: Race, Crime, and the Making of Modern Urban America* (Cambridge, Mass.: Harvard
Univ. Press, 2010).

36. David Oshinsky, *"Worse Than Slavery": Parchman Farm and the Ordeal of Jim Crow Justice* (New York: Free Press, 1996), 29–48; Randall Kennedy, *Race, Crime and the Law* (New York:
Pantheon, 1997).

37. For an extensive discussion of how vagrancy laws, enticement statutes, and other new
postbellum southern laws created a frequent system of involuntary servitude that hovered tragically close to slavery, see Douglas A. Blackmon, *Slavery by Another Name: The Re-Enslavement
of Black Americans from the Civil War to World War II* (New York: Doubleday, 2008), and William Cohen's earlier work, "Negro Involuntary Servitude in the South, 1865–1940: A Preliminary
Analysis," *Journal of Southern History* 42 (February 1976): 31–60. See also David Oshinsky's account of the Mississippi justice system's inhuman treatment of Black prisoners (including the
wide use of convict leasing) in his *"Worse Than Slavery"* as well as Edward L. Ayers, *Vengeance
and Justice: Crime and Punishment in the 19th-Century American South* (New York: Oxford Univ.
Press, 1984), especially chapter 6.

38. Bill Chaze, "Hawkins Aiming at Roots of Riots," *Charlotte News,* 12 March 1968, 3A; "Riot
Issue Bobs Up in N.C. Campaign," *Charlotte News,* 15 April 1968, 3A; James Ross, "Hawkins: 'In
This to Win,'" *Greensboro Daily News,* 18 January 1968, Reginald Hawkins Clipping File, CMPL.
The nomenclature surrounding what was commonly named "riots" in the 1960s and 1970s has
become contested ground in recent historiography. Most prominently, Elizabeth Hinton, a noted
historian of the intersection of race and criminal justice in the 1960s and beyond, has promoted
the term "rebellion" to describe the phenomena of these explosive events, which seemed particularly epidemic in the mid-1960s to early 1970s. Hinton contends that "rebellion" better con-
notes that these incidents "did not represent a wave of criminality, but a sustained insurgency"
in which "tens of thousands of Black Americans who participated in this collective violence were
rebelling not just against police brutality. They were rebelling against a broader system that had

entrenched unequal conditions and anti-Black violence over generations" (Elizabeth Hinton, *America on Fire: The Untold History of Police Violence and Black Rebellion Since the 1960s* [New York: Liveright, 2021], 6–7). While Hinton makes many cogent points about the nature and naming of these events, this author will use the more familiar term "riot" or "uprising" until the historical field seems more settled and understood by the reading audience. This seems especially appropriate as this book will not have the proper space to engage in the wider discussion in which Hinton's book (and other recent sources) have so aptly raised these questions. As to the timing of the nation's awareness and concern about these urban "riots," certainly the nation had experienced other race riots prior to Watts (including a quite recent example in Harlem in 1964), but Watts became the event that caused the country to stand up and take notice. On the 1964 Harlem uprising, see Michael Flamm's excellent *In the Heat of the Summer: The New York Riots of 1964 and the War on Crime* (Philadelphia: Univ. of Pennsylvania Press, 2017).

39. As quoted in Bumgarner-Davis, "Rending the Veil," 145.

40. Bill Chaze, "The Governor's Campaign: Personalities, Not Issues," *Charlotte News*, 30 April 1968, 1A.

41. See especially James C. Cobb, *The Selling of the South: The Southern Crusade for Industrial Development, 1936–1980* (Baton Rouge: Louisiana State Univ. Press, 1982), chapter 10.

42. The Poor People's Campaign united protestors of all ethnic backgrounds in Washington, D.C., during the summer of 1968 to pressure the federal government for further commitment to end American poverty. King's April 1968 assassination, of course, meant that the effort was forced to proceed without him. Largely regarded as a failure by contemporary observers and subsequent historical accounts, the Southern Christian Leadership Conference (founded in 1957 with King as chairman) bravely soldiered on under his successor, the Reverend Ralph Abernathy. The campaign's difficulties were due to a variety of factors, including the loss of King's charisma, torrential rains that turned the encampment into a sea of mud, rising public resentment against 1960s calls for social change, media distracted by a presidential election, and even FBI activities seeking its demise. For more on Dr. King's general shift into politics and economic policy, see Michael K. Honey, *Going Down Jericho Road: The Memphis Strike, Martin Luther King's Last Campaign* (New York: Norton, 2008), and his more recent *To the Promised Land: Martin Luther King and the Fight for Economic Justice* (New York: Norton, 2018); Garrow, *Bearing the Cross*, 527–624; Manning Marable, *Race, Reform, and Rebellion: The Second Reconstruction in Black America, 1945–1990* (Jackson: Univ. Press of Mississippi, 1991), 101–105; Fairclough, *To Redeem the Soul of America*, 333–383. Gerald McKnight offers a full-length treatment of the Poor People's Campaign, highlighting the FBI's role against it, in *The Last Crusade: Martin Luther King, Jr., the FBI, and the Poor People's Campaign* (Boulder, Colo.: Westview Press, 1998).

43. James Ross, "Martin Luther King Plans Aid to Hawkins in Race," *Greensboro Daily News*, 27 March 1968, Reginald Hawkins Clipping File, CMPL; James Ross, "Hawkins Expects Negro Vote," *Greensboro Daily News*, 28 March 1968, Reginald Hawkins Clipping File, CMPL.

44. Bill Chaze, "600 Walk Quietly in King Memorial," *Charlotte News*, 8 April 1968, 1A.

45. "Lazy B Stables Barn Burns," *Charlotte News*, 25 September 1968, Thomas James Reddy Papers, University of North Carolina at Charlotte Special Collections (hereafter referred to as TJRP), 3:1.

2. "Outside Agitators" and the Struggle for Power

1. Tom Seslar, "Marchers Ask City's Help," *Charlotte News,* 30 April 1968, 16A; Tom Seslar, "Mayor Against Bringing March Through Charlotte," *Charlotte News,* 3 May 1968, 1C.

2. James Chaney, an African American, was on the Congress on Racial Equality staff, working in tandem with white activists Schwerner and Goodman (working for the Student Nonviolent Coordinating Committee, or SNCC). As a local African American Mississippian, he could not justly be considered an outsider. Many Mississippi whites, however, neatly fit Chaney into the scenario by portraying him as naively misled (since his ethnicity caused whites to depict him stereotypically as intellectually inferior, and hence easily duped by the clever white northern outsiders).

3. These views, of course, tapped heavily into historic American fears that communism was an inherently alien culture whose agents eagerly sought entry. And, just as most Americans had long seen communism as a misguided philosophy that could only be introduced by "un-American" foreign immigrants, so white southerners believed that only a misguided northerner would seek to change a racial system that had seemed to serve the Caucasian so well for a century. Indeed, many white southerners perceived those who questioned the racial status quo as actually undermining the country's social stability to make way for hidden communist infiltrators. Scholars have engaged in a debate in recent years over the efficacy of southern white supremacists' tagging civil rights reformers as communists in order to suppress them. George Lewis's *The White South and the Red Menace: Segregationist Anti-Communism and Massive Resistance, 1945-1968* (Gainesville: Univ. Press of Florida, 2004) and Jeff Woods's *Black Struggle, Red Scare: Segregation and Anti-Communism in the South* (Baton Rouge: Louisiana State Univ. Press, 2004) both argue for its effectiveness. In *Cold War Civil Rights: Race and the Image of American Democracy* (Princeton, N.J.: Princeton Univ. Press, 2011), Mary Dudziak reminds readers that the Cold War impetus to impress third-world peoples with America's altruism may have provided occasional valuable checks on allowing southern injustices to run amok (lest communists use headlines about American racism to court these peoples coming into their own at end of the age of colonialism). On the outside agitator concept's roots in earlier twentieth-century anxieties over communism, see Frank Donner, *The Age of Surveillance: The Aims and Methods of America's Political Intelligence System* (New York: Vintage Books, 1980), 11-20.

4. For more on Charlotte's history of welcoming corporate "outsiders," see Goldfield, "A Place to Come To," 10-23; Hanchett, *Sorting Out the New South City,* 25-26.

5. Kay Reimler, "Poor Folks' Band Greensboro-Bound," *Charlotte News,* 15 May 1968, 1A; Tom Seslar, "Marchers Ask City's Help," *Charlotte News,* 30 April 1968, 16A; Tom Seslar, "Mayor Against Bringing March Through Charlotte," *Charlotte News,* 3 May 1968, 1C.

6. Reimler, "Poor Folks"; Kay Reimler, "Poor People's Marchers Arrive in City For Night," *Charlotte News,* 14 May 1968, 1A.

7. The emerging literature on the Black Power movement has become one of the most vibrant in twentieth-century studies. Peniel Joseph has written a number of important treatises on the subject, most especially his important overview, *Waiting 'Til the Midnight Hour: A Narrative History of Black Power in America* (New York: Owl Books, 2006), and his more recent work on one

of the movement's most pivotal figures: *Stokely: A Life* (New York: Basic Civitas, 2014). Joshua Bloom and Waldo Martin made a significant contribution with their *Black Against Empire: The History and Politics of the Black Panther Party.* (Oakland: Univ. of California Press, 2014). See also Leonard Moore, *The Defeat of Black Power: Civil Rights and the National Black Political Convention of 1972* (Baton Rouge: Louisiana State Univ. Press, 2018); William L. Van Deburg, *New Day in Babylon: The Black Power Movement and American Culture, 1965–1975* (Chicago: Univ. of Chicago Press, 1992); John T. McCartney, *Black Power Ideologies: An Essay in African-American Political Thought* (Philadelphia: Temple Univ. Press, 1992), 1–14, 111–132; Jeffrey Ogbar, *Black Power: Radical Politics and African American Identity* (Baltimore, Md.: Johns Hopkins Univ. Press, 2004); and Simon Wendt, *The Spirit and the Shotgun: Armed Resistance and the Struggle for Civil Rights* (Gainesville: Univ. Press of Florida, 2007). For more specific studies, see Lance Hill's incisive study of an important Black Power organization in *The Deacons for Defense: Armed Resistance and the Civil Rights Movement* (Chapel Hill: Univ. of North Carolina Press, 2004); an examination of Black Power leader and artist Amiri Braka in Komozi Woodard's *A Nation Within a Nation: Amiri Braka (LeRoi Jones) and Black Power Politics* (Chapel Hill: Univ. of North Carolina Press, 1999); Matthew Countryman, *Up South: Civil Rights and Black Power in Philadelphia* (Philadelphia: Univ. of Pennsylvania Press, 2006), and Devin Fergus's analysis of Black Power's dialectical interaction with North Carolina liberalism in *Liberalism, Black Power, and the Making of American Politics, 1965–1980* (Athens: Univ. of Georgia Press, 2009). Recent works on the Black Panther Party include Judson L. Jeffries's examination of its cofounder, *Huey P. Newton: The Radical Theorist* (Jackson: Univ. Press of Mississippi, 2002), Charles E. Jones, ed., *The Black Panther Party (Reconsidered)* (Baltimore, Md.: Black Classic Press, 1998), Jama Lazerow and Yohuru Williams, eds., *In Search of the Black Panther Party: New Perspectives on a Revolutionary Movement* (Durham, N.C.: Duke Univ. Press, 2006), Yohuru Williams, *Black Politics/White Power: Civil Rights, Black Power, and the Black Panthers in New Haven* (Malden, Mass.: Blackwell Publishing, 2008), and Judson Jeffries, ed., *Comrades: A Local History of the Black Panther Party* (Bloomington: Indiana Univ. Press, 2007). For the early underpinnings of the broader movement, see Timothy Tyson's *Radio Free Dixie: Robert F. Williams and the Roots of Black Power* (Chapel Hill: Univ. of North Carolina Press, 1999). For recent biographies of an inspirational figure for the Black Power movement, see Les Payne and Tamara Payne, *The Dead Are Arising: The Life of Malcom X* (New York: Liveright, 2020), and Manning Marable's *Malcom X: A Life of Reinvention* (New York: Penguin, 2011).

8. Notable studies of the New Left movement include Kirkpatrick Sale's early study of the prominent organization of the movement, *SDS* (New York: Random House, 1973), as well as David Barber, *A Hard Rain Fell: SDS and Why It Failed* (Jackson: Univ. Press of Mississippi, 2010), Terry H. Anderson, *The Movement and the Sixties: Protest in America from Greensboro to Wounded Knee* (New York: Oxford Univ. Press, 1995), Wini Breines, *Community and Organization in the New Left, 1962–1968: The Great Refusal* (New Brunswick, N.J.: Rutgers Univ. Press, 1989), James Miller, *"Democracy Is in the Streets": From Port Huron to the Siege of Chicago* (New York: Touchstone, 1987), Maurice Isserman, *If I Had a Hammer . . . The Death of the Old Left and the Birth of the New Left* (New York: Basic Books, 1987). Other works include Van Gosse, *Rethinking the New Left: An Interpretive History* (New York: Palgrave Macmillan, 2005), and Re-

becca Klatch, *A Generation Divided: The New Left, the New Right, and the 1960s* (Berkeley: Univ. of California Press, 1999). Dan Berger's *Outlaws of America: The Weather Underground and the Politics of Solidarity* (Oakland, Calif.: AK Press, 2005) examines the radical organization that spun off from Students for a Democratic Society. Jeremy Varon's *Bringing the War Home: The Weather Underground, the Red Army Faction, and Revolutionary Violence in the Sixties and Seventies* (Berkeley: Univ. of California Press, 2004) includes a focus on the violent New Left splinter group, Weather Underground. For a focused look at the antiwar movement (which occupied considerable attention among New Left activists), see Tom Wells, *The War Within: America's Battle Over Vietnam* (New York: Owl Books, 1994). For a retrospective collection on the importance of the Free Speech Movement and leader Mario Savio, see Robert Cohen and Reginald E. Zelnik, eds., *The Free Speech Movement: Reflections on Berkeley in the 1960s* (Berkeley: Univ. of California Press, 2002). Burrough's *Days of Rage* follows the more radical violence of several leftist groups into the 1970s (including the Weatherman, the Symbionese Liberation Army, the Black Liberation Army, and the FALN).

9. Marable, *Race, Reform, and Rebellion,* 92–99.

10. T. J. Reddy, "Black Cultural Group Gets Home, 'A Beginning,'" *Charlotte Observer,* 8 March 1970, 23A; Edward Cody, "Self Calls for Black History in Schools," *Charlotte Observer,* 5 September 1968, 13C. The Black Culture Association began in the summer of 1968 with the goal of advancing Black culture and history. After receiving a grant of $15,000 from the National Episcopal Church in late 1969, it expanded its goals into advocating for local policy and community change, hoping to create "a new image in the Black community collectively and individually" and to "respectively present our Black problems to established authority."

11. Bill Noblitt, "All-Black Political Group Runs Five for Council," *Charlotte News,* 24 March 1969, 1B; John Goodwin, "Kerry Appointed to School Board," *Charlotte News,* 10 April 1968, 6A; Devid Gelsanliter, "Negro Community Becomes Key to Mayoral Election," *Charlotte Observer,* 29 April 1969, Charlotte Elections—1969 Clipping File, Carolina Room, Charlotte-Mecklenburg Public Library.

12. Stan Brennan, "Model-Cities Grant Will Take on Slums," *Charlotte Observer,* 17 November 1967, 1A; "Slum Has Grim Statistics," *Charlotte Observer,* 17 November 1967, 1A; Ray Holt, "5 Carolina Cities Disappointed Over U.S. Grant Rebuff," *Charlotte Observer,* 17 November 1967, 32A.

13. Bill Noblitt, "Poor Ask Voice in Model City," *Charlotte News,* 8 December 1967, 1C.

14. Ibid.

15. Bill Noblitt, "Protestors Jeopardize Model Program—Mayor," *Charlotte News,* 19 December 1967, 1B; Bill Noblitt, "Rejection of Old Order Behind Model City Fuss," *Charlotte News,* 27 December 1967, 1B.

16. Bill Noblitt, "Model Cities Council Grows," *Charlotte News,* 15 December 1967, 1C; Bill Noblitt, "Residents Okay Solution on Model City Delegates," *Charlotte News,* 29 December 1967, 1B.

17. Kay Reimler, "Merger: A White Scheme?" *Charlotte News,* 22 May 1968, 1B; Hanchett, *Sorting Out the New South City,* 250–252.

18. Marvin Sparrow, interview by author, 9 June 1998, Durham, North Carolina.

19. For more on Saul Alinsky (who actually treated the New Left with some suspicion largely due to his perception of the movement's strong allegiance to ideology over practicality), see San-

ford D. Horwitt's biography, *Let Them Call Me Rebel: Saul Alinsky—His Life and Legacy* (New York: Knopf, 1989); Neil Betten and William E. Hershey, "Conflict Approach to Community Organizing: Saul Alinsky and the CIO," in *The Roots of Community Organizing, 1917–1939* (Philadelphia: Temple Univ. Press, 1990); Donald C. Reitzes and Dietrich C. Reitzes, *The Alinsky Legacy: Alive and Kicking* (Greenwich, Conn.: JAI Press, 1987); and Aaron Schutz and Mike Miller, eds., *People Power: The Community Organizing Tradition of Saul Alinsky* (Nashville: Vanderbilt Univ. Press, 2015). See also Alinksy's famous handbooks to educate community activists: *Reveille for Radicals* (Chicago: Univ. of Chicago Press, 1946) and *Rules for Radicals: A Practical Primer for Realistic Radicals* (New York: Vintage Books, 1971).

20. Marvin Sparrow interview.

21. Ibid.; Nick Taylor, "Hippies Lose in Court This Time," *Charlotte News*, 8 May 1969, 1B.

22. Marvin Sparrow interview.

23. Butch and Shirley Rosen, interview by author, 31 March 1994, Charlotte, North Carolina; Bill Noblitt, "Young People Form Coalition," *Charlotte News*, 17 January 1969, 1B.

24. Ibid.

25. Ibid.

26. The bill outlawed discriminatory sales and rental of housing in the country. Robert Dallek, *Flawed Giant: Lyndon Johnson and His Times, 1961–1973* (New York: Oxford Univ. Press, 1998), 517–518; Bartley, *The New South*, 361–362; Garrow, *Bearing the Cross*, 599–601; Fairclough, *To Redeem the Soul of America*, 382. See also the more recent study of housing discrimination in the twentieth century, Stephen Grant Meyer, *As Long as They Don't Move Next Door: Segregation and Racial Conflict in American Neighborhoods* (Lanham, Md.: Rowman and Littlefield, 2000).

27. Holliman's "From Crackertown to Model City?," 369–386, is an especially good look at how urban renewal played out in another business-oriented southern city like Charlotte. N.D.B. Connolly provides another excellent case study of the tragic flaws of urban renewal in Miami in *A World More Concrete: Real Estate and the Remaking of Jim Crow South Florida* (Chicago: Univ. of Chicago Press, 2014). Like Charlotte's civic leaders, Florida's pivotal governor of the late 1950s, Leroy Collins, sought to protect his state from ugly publicized racial violence, and saw urban renewal as a way to signal governmental concern and investment in the lot of the urban Black poor. See also Eric Avila and Mark Rose, "Race, Culture, Politics and Urban Renewal," *Journal of Urban History* 35 (2009): 335–347; Andrew Highsmith, "Demolition Means Progress: Urban Renewal, Local Politics, and State-Sanctioned Ghetto Formation in Flint, Michigan," *Journal of Urban History* 35 (2009): 348–368; Guian McKee, "'I've Never Dealt with a Government Agency Before': Philadelphia's Somerset Knitting Mills Project, the Local State, and the Missed Opportunities of Urban Renewal," *Journal of Urban History* 35 (2009): 387–409; Thomas J. Sugrue, *The Origins of the Urban Crisis: Race and Inequality in Postwar Detroit* (Princeton, N.J.: Princeton Univ. Press, 1996); Bayor, *Race and the Shaping of Twentieth-Century Atlanta*; Colin Gordon, *Mapping Decline: St. Louis and the Fate of the American City* (Philadelphia: Univ. of Pennsylvania Press, 2008); Thomas O'Connor, *Building a New Boston: Politics and Urban Renewal, 1950–1970* (Boston: Northeastern Univ. Press, 1993); Arnold R. Hirsch, *Making the Second Ghetto: Race and Housing in Chicago, 1940–1960* (Cambridge: Cambridge Univ. Press, 1983).

28. "Urban Renewal in Charlotte: The First Five Years," 6, SRBP, box 2, folder 13.

29. Hanchett, *Sorting Out the New South City,* 249–251.

30. Stan R. Brookshire, "What Community Improvement Means to Our City," 25 March 1966, Community Improvement Meeting speech, SRBP, box 2, folder 6.

31. "A Better Charlotte Starts in Your Own Back Yard," SRBP, box 2, folder 6.

32. Hanchett, *Sorting Out the New South City,* 249–251; "Urban Renewal in Charlotte: The First Five Years," 8–9; "Charlotte Area Fund Proposal to the North Carolina Fund," 30 January 1964, 12–22, North Carolina Fund Records, UNCC, box 11.

33. Leach, "Progress Under Pressure," 208–214; Hanchett, *Sorting Out the New South City,* 249–251. For more on the Federal Housing Administration's role in building segregated neighborhoods, see George Lipsitz, "The Possessive Investment in Whiteness: Racialized Social Democracy and the 'White' Problem in American Studies," *American Quarterly* 47 (September 1995): 372–375.

34. The Earle Village Homes had in fact been a response to an Urban Renewal Administration threat to cut off funding. Charlotte authorities had zealously demolished so many Black homes at the city core with federal funding that they had run afoul even of federal housing officials' noted leniency. The Charlotte Redevelopment Authority thus hurriedly created the new Earle Village public housing units, which were still far fewer in number than the bulldozed Black residences, but enough to keep the city in federal officials' good graces. Hanchett, *Sorting Out the New South City,* 250–251; Leach, "Progress Under Pressure," 210–213.

35. Pete Kohler, "'We're Building Our Watts,'" *Charlotte Observer,* 30 October 1966, 1C, Kelly Alexander, Sr. Papers, Special Collections, University of North Carolina at Charlotte (hereafter referred to as KASP), box 28, folder 4.

36. These urban riots or rebellions remain contested ground for current historians as well. In *America on Fire,* Elizabeth Hinton has a different set of numbers for these rebellions (the term she prefers): 17 in 1966, 75 in 1967, and 504 in 1968.

37. Stewart Spencer, "A Visit to Earle Village," *Charlotte News,* 13 October 1967, 18A; "Earle Village Being Filled," *Charlotte News,* 3 October 1967, 3A; "Opening Delayed at Earle Center," *Charlotte News,* 20 October 1967, 4A; "Artist Critical of Earle Village," *Charlotte News,* 12 April 1969, 16B.

38. The law firm also included the white attorney Adam Stein, whose addition made it the first integrated law firm in North Carolina. Rosen and Mosnier, *Julius Chambers,* 134.

39. "Repression in North Carolina: The Lazy B Stables Case," published by the North Carolina Political Prisoners Committee, TJRP, OF 2:8, 13; Gaillard interview, 15 March 1994; Charleen Whisnant and Robert Waters Grey, eds., *Eleven Charlotte Poets* (Charlotte, N.C.: Red Clay Publishers, 1971); Benjamin Chavis, interview by Bridgette Sanders, 2 July 2005, Charlotte, North Carolina, J. Murrey Atkins Library, University of North Carolina at Charlotte, http://newsouth voices.uncc.edu/interview/uach0006 (accessed 21 July 2016).

40. David Gelsanliter, "Army Recruiting Stirs Protests," *Charlotte Observer,* 1C.

41. Bob Rosenblatt, "Anti-Draft Workers Forced to Leave," *Charlotte Observer,* 10 August 1968, 1C.

42. William Cockerham, "Views on Black Activist Clash," *Hartford Courant,* 18 November 1972, 14, TJRP, box 4, folder 1; "Repression in North Carolina," TJRP, OF 2:8, 13.

43. "Black Men Search for Their Identity," *Carolina Journal* (UNCC student newspaper), 20 March 1969, 2; Mark Ethridge, Michael Schwartz, and Paul Clancy, "2 Lazy B Witnesses Got $4,000 Each," *Charlotte Observer*, 24 March 1974, 1A; FBI Letterhead Memorandum (hereafter referred to as LHM), 27 August 1969, 3, FBI File on the Black Panther Party, North Carolina (Wilmington, Del.: Scholarly Resources, 1986) (hereafter referred to as NCBPP); Benjamin Chavis, interview by Bridgette Sanders, 2 July 2005, Charlotte, North Carolina, J. Murrey Atkins Library, University of North Carolina at Charlotte, http://newsouthvoices.uncc.edu/interview/uach0006 (accessed 21 July 2016); Humphrey Cummings, interview by Bridgette Sanders, 14 December 2004, Charlotte, North Carolina, J. Murrey Atkins Library, University of North Carolina at Charlotte, http://newsouthvoices.uncc.edu/interview/uacu0007 (accessed 21 July 2016).

44. While the September 1968 student boycott did not produce the hoped-for Black studies classes, the city's school superintendent did distribute a series of materials to teachers and school librarians intended to heighten school personnel's awareness of African American history. Kay Reimler, "Negro Students Fail in Boycott," *Charlotte News*, 4 September 1968, 1B; Kate Simpson, "Black Culturalists Receive $15,000," *Charlotte News*, 8 December 1968, 8B. "Rally Sponsored by The Black Cultural Association: City of Charlotte Inter-Office Communication," September 13, 1968, box 4, folder 2, SRBP; J. C. Goodman, "Rally Sponsored by The Black Cultural Association: City of Charlotte Inter-Office Communication," September 20, 1968, SRBP, box 4, folder 2. Many thanks to Michael Ervin for pointing me to some new materials emerging on the BCA, as well as his master's thesis, "'Public Order Is Even More Important Than the Rights of Negroes': Race and Recreation in Charlotte, North Carolina, 1927–1973" (Master's thesis, University of North Carolina at Charlotte, 2015).

45. Bob Rosenblatt, "Go Downtown, Get Gym,' Fuller Tells Young Negroes," *Charlotte Observer*, April 12, 1968; James Grossman, "Park Board: It's Our Policy; Black Association: Change It," *Charlotte Observer*, September 18, 1968;

46. J. C. Goodman, "Rally Sponsored by The Black Cultural Association: City of Charlotte Inter-Office Communication," September 20, 1968, SRBP, box 4, folder 2; Pat Alford, "Negro Complaints Say Police Threw Them Out of Station," *Charlotte Observer*, 28 September 1968; "Rally Sponsored by The Black Cultural Association: City of Charlotte Inter-Office Communication," September 13, 1968, SRBP, box 4, folder 2; James Grossman, "Park Board: It's Our Policy; Black Association: Change It," *Charlotte Observer*, September 18, 1968.

47. Tom Seslar, "Negroes Told War 'Plot' by Whites," *Charlotte News*, 7 December 1968, 1B; "Anti-Negro Plot Talk Is Nonsense," *Charlotte Observer*, 11 December 1968, 2B; Betty Jo Hamrick, interview by author, 19 July 1993, Charlotte, North Carolina; Benjamin Chavis, interview by Bridgette Sanders and Lois Stickel, 7 February 2005, J. Murrey Atkins Library, University of North Carolina at Charlotte, http://nsv.uncc.edu/interview/uach0006 (accessed 1 July 2015).

48.Tom Seslar, "Negroes Told War 'Plot' by Whites," *Charlotte News*, 7 December 1968, 1B; "Anti-Negro Plot Talk Is Nonsense," *Charlotte Observer*, 11 December 1968, 2B.

49. Korstad and Leloudis, *To Right These Wrongs*, 283–285. Ample coverage of Fuller and his participation in programs of the North Carolina Fund may be found in the wider pages of Korstad and Leloudis and in Fergus, *Liberalism, Black Power, and the Making of American Politics*.

50. Kay Reimler, "CAF Unit to Vote on Use of Activist," *Charlotte News*, 27 December 1967,

1B; "Annual Report of the North Carolina Fund, 1967–68: The Charlotte Area Fund," 2, North Carolina Fund Records, Special Collections, University of North Carolina at Charlotte Library, box 11 (hereafter referred to as NCFR).

51. Kay Reimler, "Area Fund 'Communication Gap' Hit," *Charlotte News*, 17 January 1968, 1B. See also "Minutes of December 19, 1996 Meeting of the Board of Directors of the Charlotte Area Fund," KASP, box 28, folder 17, and County Board of Commissioners Chairman John Campbell to Charles M. Lowe, Chairman, Board of Directors, Charlotte Area Fund, 29 December 1966, KASP, box 28, folder 17.

52. Ed Kelton, "Youth Workers March; Will Get Checks Today," *Charlotte Observer*, 19 July 1968, 14A. The CAF's Summer Youth Program itself became the target of protest marches in July 1968 when it was late in issuing paychecks to its teen employees.

53. Kay Reimler, "John Zuidema Expected to Resign as CAF Chief," *Charlotte News*, 17 September 1968, 1B; Kay Reimler, "Negro Students Fail in Boycott," *Charlotte News*, 4 September 1968, 1B; Bill Chaze, "CAF: Boycotter Acting on His Own," *Charlotte News*, 5 September 1968, 1B; Tom Seslar, "Republicans Call Drive 'Tribute,'" *Charlotte News*, 22 February 1968, 1C.

54. Tom Seslar, "Area Fund Kept in Public Spotlight," *Charlotte News*, 25 February 1969, 87C; "Zuidema Confirms His Plan to Resign as CAF Director," *Charlotte News*, 18 September 1968.

55. Kay Reimler, "Campbell Quits, Predicts 'Trouble' for CAF, City: County Commissioner Criticizes Two Grants," *Charlotte News*, 28 September 1968, 1A; Tom Seslar, "CAF Could Have Set Off Rioting—Campbell," *Charlotte News*, 30 October 1968, 1B.

56. Kay Reimler, "Campbell Hits CAF Model City Role," *Charlotte News*, 22 December 1967, 7A.

57. "Report of the Reorganization Committee of the Charlotte Area Fund," 17 October 1968, 34–40, SRBP, box 1, folder 17; Tom Seslar, "CAF Revamp Plan Asks Tighter Rein Over Staff," *Charlotte News*, 16 October 1968, 1B.

58. Jack Claiborne, "I'm Not Attacking Welfare Here, Noble Coleman Says," *Charlotte Observer*, 21 July 1968, 1C.

59. Tom Seslar, "Commission Less Hostile as CAF Fires 'Agitators,'" *Charlotte News*, 19 October 1968, 1B.

60. Tom Seslar, "Washington Office Fires Anti-Draft VISTA Man," *Charlotte News*, 11 December 1968, 1B; "CAF Worker Supervision Is 'Lagging,'" *Charlotte News*, 11 December 1968, 1B. Person claimed to know about Grant doing "draft counseling" but not about his leafletting. Grant contended that Person "knew about everything I was doing even though I never discussed it with him. Several Area Fund workers talked to him about it, and he made inquiries of others. He always was given straight answers because I always have had an open-door policy. I've never tried to hide anything." Greta de Jong's *You Can't Eat Freedom: Southerners and Social Justice After the Civil Rights Movement* (Chapel Hill: Univ. of North Carolina Press, 2016) illuminates how the War on Poverty's Community Action Program provision to actively involve the impoverished recipients in how funds were used threatened the traditional southern white power structure, who were previously used to controlling poverty funding to maintain the racial and economic caste system.

3. Let Justice Roll Down like Waters: From a War on Poverty to a War on Crime

1. Bill Noblitt, "Angry Charlotte Blasts U.S. for Racial Charge," *Charlotte News*, 22 September 1967, 1A; "Clark, Ervin Clash on Rights in South," *Charlotte News*, 22 September 1967, 4A. The reasons for cross burnings at the homes of the mayor and mayor pro tem were apparently never fully explored. Brookshire refused to discuss the alleged cross burning at his home, claiming doing so might encourage additional incidents. Whittington claimed the reason for the cross burning at his residence remained a "mystery." As slow to move on racial change as Brookshire and Whittington might have seemed to activists, the muted support they were seen to provide might have been reason enough to activate local white supremacists.

2. Ibid. Ingersoll also claimed that one of the crimes listed by Clark was just ten days old and under investigation, and that a few of the crimes were never reported to police.

3. Max Frankel, "President Signs Broad Crime Bill, with Objections," *New York Times*, 20 June 1968, 1; Jack Newfield, "Does the Country Deserve Ramsey Clark in '72?" *New York*, 20 July 1970, 37–43; Jonathan Simon, *Governing Through Crime: How the War on Crime Transformed American Democracy and Created a Culture of Fear* (New York: Oxford Univ. Press, 2007), 77–94. Simon calls the bill the "foundational piece of legislation for the war on crime," and notes that President Johnson understood the rise in the crime rate as a threat to the Democratic Party's post-New Deal coalition. Clark, recalling his days as attorney general, later opined, "A lot of this [federal law enforcement] surveillance gets silly; at one point there were agents from six different agencies following Rap Brown. His mother used to invite them all in for breakfast when they were waiting outside." On the FBI specifically, Clark lamented that it "likes to do a lot of bugging. . . . The Bureau wanted me to bug the fellows planning the demonstrations at the 1968 Democratic convention, but I said no. . . . I remember in August of 1967, when Spiro Agnew was governor of Maryland, he said that he had evidence that the same people started the riots in Newark and Detroit. So I called him up, and he didn't have any evidence. . . . It was the same with [Chicago] Mayor [Richard] Daley. He said that people were coming to Chicago in 1968 to assassinate the candidates. There was no evidence of that. It was just rumors in police circles, stuff from informants. But a lot of police informants are mentally unbalanced people. The rumor mill among law enforcement agencies is immense." Clark's liberal views in a growingly conservative and reactive time made him a dark horse darling of liberals—so much so that his name was being suggested for a 1972 presidential run. For more on the legislation, see also Michael W. Flamm's *Law and Order: Street Crime, Civil Unrest, and the Crisis of Liberalism in the 1960s* (New York: Columbia Univ. Press, 2005), chapters 7 and 8; Elizabeth Hinton, *From the War on Poverty to the War on Crime: The Making of Mass Incarceration in America* (Cambridge, Mass.: Harvard Univ. Press, 2016), especially chapter 4.

4. Flamm, *Law and Order*, 170–172.

5. "Clark, Ervin Clash," *Charlotte News*.

6. That specific poll was taken from February 1 to February 6, 1968, and was published on February 28, 1968. *The Gallup Poll: Public Opinion, 1935–1971*, vol. 3, *1959–1971* (New York: Random House, 1972), 2107. Other polls on the question in 1967–1970 may be found in the same

volume on pages 2090, 2128, 2151, 2158, 2180, 2228, 2248–2249, 2252–2253, and 2258–2259. For a very good review of the impact of "law and order" on politics and American social trends, see Flamm, *Law and Order*. Flamm argues that "law and order" became a powerful and visceral issue to catalyze conservatives' momentum going into the 1970s and beyond: "What ultimately gave law and order such potency, then, was precisely its amorphous quality, its ability to represent different concerns to different people at different moments. . . . Law and order identified a clear cast of violent villains (protesters, rioters, and criminals), explained the causes for their actions (above all the doctrine of civil disobedience and the paternalism of the welfare state), and implied a ready response (limited government, moral leadership, and judicial firmness)" (4). For Flamm's examination of the beginnings of the nation's turn to the themes of law and order and the War on Crime, see his *In the Heat of the Summer*.

7. 29 May 1968 Gallup poll in *The Gallup Poll: Public Opinion, 1935–1971*, vol. 3, *1959–1971*, 2128. Between 2 May and 7 May 1968, Gallup pollsters asked "residents of large cities" the following question: "As you may know, the mayor of a large city has ordered the police to shoot on sight anyone found looting stores during race riots. How do you feel about this—do you think this is the best way to deal with this problem, or do you think there is a better way?" 47 percent responded that "shooting is the best way," 49 percent contended "there's a better way," and 4 percent claimed no opinion. In an indication of the desperation felt by many Americans, 36 percent of those polled (35 percent of whites and 48 percent of Blacks) in June 1968 agreed that the United States was a "sick society" (3 July 1968 Gallup poll in *The Gallup Poll: Public Opinion, 1935–1971*, vol. 3, *1959–1971*, 2138).

8. "Riots No. 1 Issue, Legislators Say," *Charlotte News*, 25 April 1968, 8B.

9. "Militant Blacks, Students 'Threat,'" *Charlotte News*, 18 May 1968, 1A. Founded officially in 1963 by African American college students in Ohio, the Revolutionary Action Movement (RAM) advocated a program of Black nationalism and armed struggle fused with Marxist analysis. The Nation of Islam's origins remain murkier, but are generally seen to be the 1930 temple in Detroit by a still rather mysterious figure, W. D. Fard. Its numbers grew notably in the post-World War II era, especially with the emergence of its most newsworthy minister, Malcolm X. Despite Malcolm's departure from the sect and his assassination shortly thereafter, the sect continued to raise alarms in the halls of white authority. See Ogbar, *Black Power*, chapter 3; and Joseph, *Waiting 'Til the Midnight Hour*, 55–63.

10. Robert Goldstein, *Political Repression in Modern America: From 1870 to the Present* (Boston, Mass.: G. K. Hall, 1978), 439.

11. After its passage, the North Carolina Welfare Commission's Clifton Craig affirmed his intention to enforce the law in the Tar Heel state. "Rioters Can Lose Welfare Payments," *Charlotte News*, 29 May 1968, 6A.

12. Goldstein, *Political Repression in Modern America*, 441.

13. Ibid., 441–442.

14. Robert Morgan, North Carolina Attorney General, Raleigh, to Members of the Governor's Committee on Law and Order, 27 August 1969, Robert Scott Papers (hereafter referred to as RSP), North Carolina State Archives (hereafter referred to as NCA), box 32.

15. "Moore Declines Call for Special Session," *Charlotte News*, 18 April 1968, 3A. A 1964 riot

in Harlem might more accurately be seen as the true forerunner of the coming epidemic of urban riots in the late 1960s. The event aroused enough concern—especially as riots soon followed in St. Louis, Rochester, New York, and Philadelphia—that President Johnson considered holding a conference on law enforcement in August of that year to reassure the public. Ultimately his advisers warned that doing so would only add gravitas to Republican presidential nominee Barry Goldwater's campaign theme that the country was spinning dangerously into social disorder. But Watts proved to be far more tragically destructive, bringing the issue front and center to national attention. For more, see Michel Flamm's *Law and Order*, chapter 2, and his *In the Heat of the Summer*; Joseph, *Waiting 'Til the Midnight Hour*, 110-117; and Hinton, *From the War on Poverty to the War on Crime*, chapter 2. For a fuller consideration of these urban uprisings or riots that follows them to the present era, see Hinton, *America on Fire*.

16. "Stickley Lashes Rights Bill Okay," 11 April 1968, 3A.

17. "I'd Maintain Law, Order—Rep. Gardner," *Charlotte News*, 12 April 1968, 4A; "Riot Issue Bobs Up in N.C. Campaign," *Charlotte News*, 15 April 1968, 3A; Korstad and Leloudis, *To Right These Wrongs*, chapter 6.

18. Most observers—including the *Charlotte Observer*—understood Scott's remarks on Black Power as references to two particular recent campus events in the state. UNC Chapel Hill had recently taken some heat for hiring Black Power advocate Howard Fuller (who would later raise Charlotteans' eyebrows when the CAF brought him in for training). UNC Greensboro had also been the site of a forum on Black Power. Scott went on to cite the recent rioting in Winston-Salem as a "classic example" of "the most irrational and ugly expression of lawlessness" ("Scott Takes Militant Stand Against Disrespect of Law," *Charlotte Observer*, 16 November 1967, 9A).

19. "Kick Out Student Boycotters—Scott," *Charlotte News*, 17 May 1968, 5A.

20. Lieutenant Governor Robert W. Scott, speech delivered to the Raleigh Jaycees, Raleigh, North Carolina, 6 August 1968, RSP, NCA, box 303. Nixon's use of the "silent majority" theme has been well covered in biographies. Perlstein, *Nixonland*, especially chapters 13, 20, and 21, is a fairly recent example. Matthew Lassiter looks at the "silent majority" voters to which Nixon appeals from the ground up in *The Silent Majority: Suburban Politics in the Sunbelt South*.

21. "OEO Says Bob Scott's Charges Unsupported," *Charlotte News*, 1 October 1968, 3A.

22. Once in office, Scott took on regional recognition for his "law and order" stance by serving as chairman of the Southern Governors' Conference Committee on Law Enforcement, Justice and Public Safety ("Scott Will Head Law Enforcement," *Charlotte News*, 15 December 1969, 11A).

23. After future U.S. senator Jesse Helms decried the UNC speakers, whom he alleged included "avowed Communists, leftwingers, [and] ultra-liberals in a solid phalanx," in one of his television editorials, Morgan tired of UNC administrators' "arrogance" in refusing to "heed the public outcry" over the taxpayers' university system breeding such civil unrest. Another Helms editorial had highlighted an Ohio law banning communist speakers, which then became a model for North Carolina's law. William Link, "William Friday and the North Carolina Speaker Ban Crisis, 1963-1968," *North Carolina Historical Review* 72 (April 1995): 198-206. See also William J. Billingsley's book-length treatment of the speaker ban controversy: *Communists on Campus: Race, Politics, and the Public University in Sixties North Carolina* (Athens: Univ. of Georgia Press, 1999).

24. Bill Chaze, "Speaker Ban Still 'Serves Purpose,'" *Charlotte News*, 22 February 1968, 1C; Korstad and Leloudis, *To Right These Wrongs*, 39–43.

25. Emery Wister, "Crime Top Problem, Chamber Told," *Charlotte News*, 15 December 1967, 2A.

26. Crime statistics for 1967 revealed an alarming across-the-board increase, including a jump in every "crime index offense" but two. Ernie Stallworth, "Murder Rate Jumped 45% Here During '67," *Charlotte News*, 22 January 1968, 7B.

27. Ernie Stallworth, "Local Crime Shows 36 Per Cent Increase," *Charlotte News*, 27 March 1968, 5A.

28. Tom Seslar, "Forget the 'Forgotten,' Negro Leader Says," *Charlotte News*, 2 October 1968, 12A.

29. Faye Setzer, "Vote Board Assailed by Hawkins," *Charlotte News*, 24 May 1968, 1A; Tom Bradbury, "Hawkins Case Dismissed," *Charlotte News*, 24 May 1968, 1A; Steven Golob, "Hawkins Cleared by Judge," *Charlotte Observer*, 25 May 1968, 1A.

30. Marjorie Marsh, "Exchange Sharp in Dental Hearing," *Charlotte News*, 8 February 1968, 1B.

31. Beginning in 1971, Hawkins filed a series of unsuccessful appeals, culminating in the U.S. Supreme Court's refusal to hear the case. Following the case's conclusion at the U.S. Supreme Court, a spokesperson for the Dental Society claimed that race might have played a role in the case, "but not in the way claimed. If anything, the deck was stacked in their [Hawkins's] favor solely by consequence of which they were allowed extraordinary latitude" (Bumgarner-Davis, "Rending the Veil," 104–106).

32. Marilyn Mayes, "2 Warrants Sworn Out Against Ex-CAF Aide," *Charlotte News*, 17 December 1968, 3B; Doug Smith, "Ex-CAF Worker Gets Suspended Sentences," *Charlotte News*, 10 February 1969, 2A.

33. Joe Flanders, "Ex-CAF Employee Charged," *Charlotte News*, 30 October 1968, 1B.

34. Marilyn Mayes, "2 Warrants Sworn Out Against Ex-CAF Aide," *Charlotte News*, 17 December 1968, 3B; Doug Smith, "Ex-CAF Worker Gets Suspended Sentences," *Charlotte News*, 10 February 1969, 2A.

35. "Chapter of ACLU Slated Here," *Charlotte News*, 2 May 1968, 18C.

36. Marvin Sparrow interview.

37. Nick Taylor, "Hip Attorney Helps Hippies," *Charlotte News*, 8 April 1969, 1B.

38. Taylor, "Hip Attorney."

39. Nick Taylor, "Officers Violated Rights in 'Hippie' Case—Judge," *Charlotte News*, 5 March 1969, 1B; Marvin Sparrow interview; "Panel to Rule on Hippies," *Charlotte News*, 18 July 1969.

40. Vivian Monts, "Morgan Says Vagrancy Law Legal if Properly Enforced," *Charlotte News*, 14 August 1969, 1B; "Panel to Rule on Hippies," *Charlotte News*, 18 July 1969, 2A.

41. Vivian Monts, "'Vagrants' Are Spice of Literature," *Charlotte News*, 12 August 1969, 1B.

42. Bob Fitzpatrick, "Federal Court Holds N.C. Vagrancy Laws Invalid," *Charlotte News*, 15 November 1969, 16B.

43. Gaillard, *The Dream Long Deferred*, 39–42; Schwartz, *Swann's Way*, 3–13. See also Douglas, *Reading, Writing, and Race*, and more recently, Lassiter's *The Silent Majority*, and Smith's *Boom for Whom?*

44. Nick Taylor, "Officers Violated Rights in 'Hippie' Case—Judge," *Charlotte News*, 5 March 1969, 1B; Marvin Sparrow interview.

45. "'Hippie Cop' Returns," *Charlotte Observer*, 7 March 1969, 20A.

46. Nick Taylor, "Sentence Greeted with Clenched-Fist Salute," *Charlotte News*, 30 May 1969, 2C; Marvin Sparrow interview.

47. Ibid.

48. Dr. W. A. Jarrell, Sparrow's neighbor, unamused at residing next to a hippie house, was equally disenchanted with the judge's denial of his complaint. Arbuckle even sentenced Jarrell to a day in jail after the plaintiff muttered a critique of the justice rendered during the proceedings: "Well, the phantoms have struck again." Vivian Monts, "'Hippies' Win Acquittal, Accuser Ordered to Jail," *Charlotte News*, 18 November 1969, 1B.

49. Joe Flanders, "Sen. Evans' 'Hippie' Measure Sidetracked," *Charlotte News*, 10 June 1969, 3B.

50. FBI LHM, Charlotte FBI Field Office to FBI Director, "Marvin Ray Sparrow: Security Matter—Southern Student Organizing Committee," 17 February 1969, 8–9, Marvin Sparrow FBI File (Freedom of Information Act Request), owned by Marvin Sparrow (hereafter referred to as Sparrow FBI File).

51. FBI LHM, Charlotte FBI Office to FBI Director, "Marvin Sparrow—Subversive Matter," 31 October 1974, Sparrow FBI File; telegram by messenger, FBI Director to the President, Vice President, U.S. Secret Service and Attorney General, 15 October 1971, in FBI LHM, "Marvin Sparrow—Security Matter—New Left," 9 September 1971, Sparrow FBI File; FBI LHM from Charlotte FBI Office to U.S. Secret Service, 17 February 1969, Sparrow FBI File; FBI Airtel, Charlotte FBI Office to FBI Director, "Demonstration Protesting Appearance of General William C. Westmoreland at Charlotte, NC, 12/9/69," 10 December 1969, Sparrow FBI File.

52. FBI LHM, Charlotte FBI Field Office to FBI Director, "Charlotte Report, 9/9/71 on Marvin Ray Sparrow," 15 December 1971, Sparrow FBI file. An explanation on the use of the FBI's "Administrative Index" may be found in Donner, *The Age of Surveillance*, 166–167.

53. FBI LHM, Charlotte FBI Field Office, "Marvin Ray Sparrow," 12 November 1975, Sparrow FBI file.

54. "Black History Demand Backed by Committee," *Charlotte News*, 6 September 1968, 6A.

55. Vivian Monts, "100 Blacks Want Chief's Resignation," *Charlotte News*, 19 June 1969, 1B.

56. On an additional BSC demand, Chief Goodman did take action: allowing "integrated [police patrol] cars" with Black and white officers riding together. Doug Smith, "Blacks Plan to Protest Police Brutality Findings," *Charlotte News*, 7 July 1969, 7B; Doug Smith, "Police Dept. Meets One 'Demand' of Black Group," *Charlotte News*, 8 July 1969, 5B.

57. Vivian Monts, "Blacks to Discuss Alleged Brutality," *Charlotte News*, 27 August 1969, 2A.

58. Rita Simpson, "Church Aid Asked in Black Problems," *Charlotte News*, 10 September 1969, 5A.

59. Eldridge Cleaver's personna as a convict, of course, was further enhanced by the publication of his celebrated book, *Soul on Ice* (New York: Dell, 1968), as was Jackson's by the publication of his prison correspondence in *Soledad Brother: The Prison Letters of George Jackson* (New York:

Coward, McCann, 1970). For more on their influence, see Dan Berger's *Captive Nation: Black Prison Organizing in the Civil Rights Era* (Chapel Hill: Univ. of North Carolina Press, 2014) and Eric Cummins's *The Rise and Fall of California's Radical Prison Movement* (Stanford, Calif.: Stanford Univ. Press, 1994).

60. "Petition for Pardon in the Matter of Thomas James Reddy, James Earl Grant, Jr. and Charles Parker" (hereafter referred to as "Petition for Pardon"), 10, 30 December 1977, TJRP; "Repression in North Carolina," TJRP, OF 2:8.

61. Bradley Martin, "Disabled Veteran Convicted in Robbery, Gets Probation," *Charlotte Observer*, 7 August 1969, 22A; Ethridge, Schwartz, and Clancy, "2 Lazy B Witnesses Got $4,000 Each"; William Walden, Special Investigator of Alcohol, Tobacco, and Firearms Agency in Raleigh, North Carolina, to Chief Special Investigator of Charlotte Police Department, 28 June 1971 (hereafter referred to as Walden memorandum to Charlotte Chief Special Investigator), 4, enclosed in "Petition for Pardon," TJRP, 1:1.

62. Ethridge, Schwartz, and Clancy, "2 Lazy B Witnesses Got $4,000 Each."

63. James E. Ferguson and Adam Stein, Charlotte, to Governor James B. Hunt, 30 December 1977, 11, enclosed in "Petition for Pardon," TJRP, 1:1. The Vietnam War experience rendered long-lasting impacts of disillusionment not only on many Black veterans. Kathleen Belew's *Bring the War Home: The White Power Movement and Paramilitary America* (Cambridge, Mass.: Harvard Univ. Press, 2018) documents how a critical segment of white veterans directed their alienation inwardly on America and its government.

64. "Man Sought in Holdup Arrested," *Charlotte News*, 15 February 1969, TJRP, 3:1; Joe Flanders, "Trial Goes to Jury Today: Armed Robbery Case," *Charlotte News*, 5 August 1969, 1B; Bradley Martin, "Holdup Witness Says Policemen Beat Him," *Charlotte Observer*, 6 August 1969, 7A.

65. Flanders, "Trial Goes to Jury Today," 5 August 1969.

66. Bryson also addressed Washington's work for "a Black Muslim newspaper": "I would quit writing these hate letters too. They're not doing you any good." Joe Flanders, "Man's Confession Ends Holdup Trial: Sentence Suspended," *Charlotte News*, 6 August 1969, 1C; Martin, "Disabled Veteran Convicted in Robbery."

67. A newspaper account noted a detective who stood across the street from the police station with a camera during the demonstration. Tom Bradbury, "Official Supports Protest Handling," *Charlotte News*, 22 March 1969, 1B.

68. ACLU attorney George Daly acted as Hood's attorney in the case. "Kick Nets Student 30 Days in Jail," *Charlotte News*, 19 November 1969, 2A.

69. Frye Gaillard, interview by author, 15 March 1994, Charlotte, North Carolina.

70. See Bloom and Martin, *Black Against Empire*, for an important examination of an organization that became increasingly at ease ignoring the socially stigmatized line between the Black criminal and Black activist. As they write, "The times did not make the Black Panther Party, but the specific practices of the Black Panthers became influential precisely because of the political context. Without the success of the insurgent civil rights movement, and without its limitations, the Black Power ferment from which the Black Panther Party emerged would not have existed. Without widespread exclusion of Black people from political representation, good jobs, government employment, quality education, and the middle class, most Black people would have

opposed the Panthers' politics. Without the Vietnam War draft and the crisis of legitimacy in the Democratic Party, few non-Black allies would have mobilized resistance to state repression of the Party" (13). Black Panther Party cofounder Huey Newton in fact defined two types of political prisoners: first, those who were imprisoned due to their activism. These prisoners "recognize that to be a 'legitimate capitalist' is to exploit the oppressed and ... perpetuate a social order where the privileges of some are based on the poverty and powerlessness of others." But Newton blurred the traditional line by characterizing inmates arrested on traditional common crimes also as political prisoners. These latter inmates were "illegitimate capitalists" who were "the unemployables, the Blacks, Browns and poor whites who have no choice, no real method of partaking of the good things in life except by ripping off the system. They have no political consciousness, but their attack upon the property system, motivated as it is by ... capitalism, is in a sense political" (Donald Fredrick Tibbs, "Black Power and Prison Power: The Prisoner Union Movement in North Carolina, 1967–1979" [Ph.D. diss., Arizona State University, 2014], 79–80). The linkage of Black activism and incarceration is a vibrant new area of study. See also Hinton, *From the War on Poverty to the War on Crime*; Berger, *Captive Nation*; Heather Ann Thompson, *Blood in the Water: The Attica Prison Uprising of 1971 and Its Legacy* (New York: Pantheon, 2016).

71. Butch and Shirley Rosen interview.

72. Joseph, *Waiting 'Til the Midnight Hour*, 221–236; Carson, *In Struggle*, 278–290; Chafe, *The Unfinished Journey*, 408–409. On the US organization, see Scot Brown, *Fighting for US: Maulana Korenga, the US Organization, and Black Cultural Nationalism* (New York: New York Univ. Press, 2005). For the most important new study of the Black Panther Party, see Bloom and Martin, *Black Against Empire*.

73. FBI Airtel, "Demonstration Protesting Appearance of General William C. Westmoreland at Charlotte, NC, 12/9/69," 10 December 1969, Sparrow FBI File.

74. Civil Intelligence Bulletin, North Carolina SBI, 6 February 1970, NCA, RSP, box 176, SBI Reports folder; Julia Gunn, "A Good Place to Make Money": Business, Labor and Civil Rights in Twentieth-Century Charlotte" (Ph.D. diss., University of Pennsylvania, 2014), 145–153.

75. "Mountain Top to Valley March," SCLC memorandum, 4 April 1969, Golden Frinks, North Carolina Field Secretary, NCA, RSP, box 118, Human Relations-4 folder; U.S. Military Daily Intelligence Summary Number 9108, 18 April 1969, NCA, RSP, box 118, Human Relations-4 folder; Michael Myerson, *Nothing Could Be Finer* (New York: International Publishers, 1978), 39.

76. Vanessa Gallman, "The Charlotte 3: Where Are They Now?," *Charlotte Observer*, 11 July 1976, 1C. The story of Hyde County's school protests is fully recounted in David S. Cecelski, *Along Freedom Road: Hyde County, North Carolina, and the Fate of Black Schools in the South* (Chapel Hill: Univ. of North Carolina Press, 1994).

77. State Highway Patrol S.I.R. on Cleveland County, City of Shelby, 17 September 1970, NCA, RSP, box 185, DMV-HP Reports-2 folder; C. Max Bryan, SBI Intra-Bureau Correspondence, to SBI Director, 24 November 1971, NCA, RSP, box 451, SBI Reports folder.

78. FBI LHM, 23 January 1969, NCBPP; Kay Reimler, "Carmichael Gives Message— Violence," *Charlotte News*, 10 December 1968, 4A; "Blacks Form UNC-C Union," *Charlotte News*, 24 February 1969, 16B; Bill Noblitt, "All-Black Political Group Runs Five for Council," *Charlotte News*, 24 March 1969, 1B.

79. Ronald Caldwell, interview by Lois Stickel, 31 May 2005, Asheville, North Carolina, J. Murrey Atkins Library, University of North Carolina at Charlotte, http://newsouthvoices.uncc .edu/interview/uaca0005 (accessed 21 July 2016)

80. FBI LHM, 23 January 1969, NCBPP; FBI Airtel, From San Francisco Division to FBI Director, 16 December 1968, NCBPP.

81. "1,000 Blacks Raise Complaints," *Charlotte Observer*, 30 June 1969, 8B; Paul Clancy, "Suit to Shut Off All U.S. Funds Prepared," *Charlotte Observer*, 30 June 1969, 1B; Marsha Canfield, "Negro Rally to Discuss City Action," *Charlotte Observer*, 24 June 1969, 1C; FBI Teletype, 19 May 1969, Charlotte Office to FBI Director, NCBPP; FBI LHM, 23 August 1969, Charlotte Office, NCBPP; FBI LHM, 25 August 1969, Charlotte Office, NCBPP; FBI LHM, 24 July 1969, Charlotte office, NCBPP; FBI Teletype, 12 July 1969, Charlotte office to FBI Director, NCBPP.

82. Pat Stith, "Evictions with Tension," *Charlotte News*, 31 July 1969, 1B.

83. BCA members asserted that surveillance included such tactics as taking photographs of visitors to the house and writing down visitors' car license tag numbers. J. C. Goodman, Charlotte Chief of Police, memorandum to Mayor Stan R. Brookshire, 13 September 1968, SRBP, 4:2; J. C. Goodman, Charlotte Chief of Police, memorandum to Mayor Stan R. Brookshire, 20 September 1968, SRBP, 4:2.

84. FBI Teletype, Charlotte FBI office to FBI Director, 19 May 1969, NCBPP, reel 1.

85. FBI Airtel, Charlotte FBI Office to FBI Photographic Unit, 28 May 1969, NCBPP; FBI Airtel, Charlotte FBI Office to FBI Director, 29 May 1969, NCBPP; FBI Airtel, Charlotte FBI Office to FBI Photographic Section and FBI Laboratory, 27 June 1969, NCBPP.

86. FBI LHM, 24 July 1969, 6–7, NCBPP; FBI Charlotte Office Report, 23 May 1969, Bureau File #105-165706-8, 2, NCBPP; LHM, 24 July 1969, 5, NCBPP; FBI LHM, 24 July 1969, NCBPP, 8; FBI Charlotte Office Report, 23 May 1969, Bureau File #105-165706-8, 8, NCBPP; FBI LHM, 23 December 1969, 2, NCBPP.

87. As quoted in Lennox Hinds, *Illusions of Justice: Human Rights Violations in the United States* (Iowa City: University of Iowa School of Social Work, 1978), 263.

88. FBI memo, G. C. Moore to W. C. Sullivan, 29 February 1968, 3, quoted in Select Committee to Study Governmental Operations with Respect to Intelligence Activities, *Final Report, volume III: Supplementary Detailed Staff Reports on Intelligence Activities and the Rights of Americans*, United States Senate, 23 April 1976, 220; "FBI Philadelphia Office to FBI Director," 30 August 1967, quoted in Ward Churchill and Jim Vander Wall, *Agents of Repression: The FBI's Secret Wars Against the Black Panther Party and the American Indian Movement* (Boston: South End Press, 1988), 45–46. That pattern of harassment and selective enforcement of the law by federal, state, and local law officers was repeated against activists in myriad other locales across America in the late 1960s and early 1970s. The FBI had over 2,000 agents investigating the New Left movement in 1969, as well as one thousand undercover informants. In the early 1970s, state authorities sentenced John Sinclair, a leader of Michigan's White Panther Party (a group espousing a cultural assault on mainstream America through alternative lifestyles and music) to nine and a half years in jail for smoking marijuana. Black militant Lee Otis from Texas Southern University received a thirty-year sentence for giving a marijuana cigarette to an undercover agent. Both were overturned on appeal. A Cincinnati judge sentenced a nineteen-year-old to thirty days in the work-

house or one day on a pig farm for disorderly conduct and calling a policeman a "pig." After renting a house behind the office of the Jackson, Mississippi, underground newspaper *Kudzu* to maintain a twenty-four-hour surveillance, local police arrested one staff member for throwing a cigarette butt in the gutter and eight others for marijuana possession after an armed search of the premises. (The charge was later dismissed for lack of evidence.) Goldstein, *Political Repression in Modern America*, 514–518; Anderson, *The Movement and the Sixties*, 274; James Kirkpatrick Davis, *Assault on the Left: The FBI and the Sixties Antiwar Movement* (Westport, Conn.: Praeger, 1997), 139–142; Rosenfeld, *Subversives*.

89. FBI memo, G. C. Moore to W. C. Sullivan, 29 February 1968, 3, quoted in Select Committee to Study Governmental Operations with Respect to Intelligence Activities, *Final Report, volume III: Supplementary Detailed Staff Reports on Intelligence Activities and the Rights of Americans*, United States Senate, 23 April 1976, 220; "FBI Philadelphia Office to FBI Director," 30 August 1967, quoted in Churchill and Vander Wall, *Agents of Repression*, 45–46. See also Bloom and Martin, *Black Against Empire*, especially chapter 8.

90. The Panthers had good reason for suspicion. The FBI carried on a very aggressive surveillance campaign against them, including an ongoing phone tap and extensive informant infiltration of the organization. FBI LHM, 23 January 1969, NCBPP; FBI Charlotte Office Report, 23 May 1969, Bureau File #105-165706-8, NCBPP; FBI LHM, 25 August 1969, 1, NCBPP; Kate Coleman and Paul Avery, "The Party's Over: How Huey Newton Created a Street Gang at the Center of the Black Panther Party," *New Times*, 10 July 1978, 25–28.

91. FBI LHM, 3 November 1969, 73–103, NCBPP; FBI LHM, 29 October 1969, 1–3, NCBPP.

92. FBI LHM, 29 October 1969, 3, NCBPP.

93. FBI LHM, Charlotte office, "Black Panther Party—Raids, Racial Matters—Seditious Conspiracy," 23 December 1969, NCBPP; Doug Smith, "Guns Seized, Two Jailed After Raid on Panthers," *Charlotte News*, 28 May 1969, 1C; Bradley Martin, "U.S. Agents Raid Black Panthers," *Charlotte Observer*, 28 May 1969, 1D; FBI Airtel, Charlotte FBI office to FBI Director, 29 May 1969, NCBPP.

94. FBI Director to Assistant Attorney General, Internal Security Division, RE: Black Panther Party, Charlotte, North Carolina, Racial Matters, 4 June 1969, NCBPP; FBI Airtel, Charlotte Office to FBI Director, "RE: Black Panther Party," 10 June 1969, NCBPP; FBI Director to Assistant Attorney General, "RE: Black Panther Party, Charlotte, North Carolina," 16 June 1969, NCBPP.

95. FBI Report, Charlotte Office, "Racial Matters: Black Panther Party," 23 May 1969, NCBPP.

96. FBI LHM, 29 October 1969, NCBPP, 1–2; Henry Woodhead, "Gun Battle with Panthers Leaves at Least 2 Injured," *Charlotte News*, 16 August 1969, 1B; Warren King, "2 Men Charged After Shoot-Out," *Charlotte Observer*, 17 August 1969, 1D.

97. Joe Flanders, "10 Arrested After Chase, Shooting," *Charlotte News*, 4 August 1969, 1B; Thomas Belden, "Panthers Charged in Shooting," *Charlotte Observer*, 4 August 1969, 1B; FBI LHM, "Black Panther Party—Violence, Racial Matters: Violent Acts, Charlotte, North Carolina," 5 January 1970, NCBPP.

98. Vivian Monts, "Law Used Against Whites Convicts Two Blacks Here," *Charlotte News*, 22 November 1969, 1B; Vivian Monts, "2 Blacks Deny They Had Guns," *Charlotte News*, 21 November 1969, 1C.

99. Vivian Monts, "Law Used Against Whites Convicts Two Blacks Here," *Charlotte News,* 22 November 1969, 1B; Vivian Monts, "2 Blacks Deny They Had Guns," *Charlotte News,* 21 November 1969, 1C.

4. Blood Revolution in a Tobacco Town: Racial Turmoil in Oxford, North Carolina

1. "Mrs. Elisabeth Chavis, Civil Rights Activist, Community Leader," *Henderson Dispatch,* 17 August 1995, 4A, Chavis Clipping File, Richard B. Thornton Library, Oxford, North Carolina; Hugh Currin, Mayor of Oxford, North Carolina, interview by author, 12 May 1998, Oxford, North Carolina.

2. Judge Daniel F. Finch, interview by author, 13 May 1998, Oxford, North Carolina.

3. George Wright, interview by author, 13 May 1998, Oxford, North Carolina; Timothy Tyson, "Burning for Freedom: Oxford, North Carolina and the Black Struggle for Equality" (Master's thesis, Duke University, 1990), 102; Timothy Tyson, *Blood Done Sign My Name* (New York: Crown, 2004), 197–98.

4. Tyson, "Burning for Freedom," 28, 48–49; Tyson, *Blood Done Sign My Name,* 11–15; "Racially Tense Oxford Calm as Mayor Continues Curfew," *Durham Morning Herald,* 28 May 1970, 13C; *City Directory: Oxford, North Carolina* (Livonia, Mich.: R. L. Polk, 1997), 6 (statistics drawn from Granville County-Oxford Chamber of Commerce materials).

5. Ralph A. Hunt Sr., interview by author, 9 June 1998, Durham, North Carolina; Wright interview.

6. Hunt interview.

7. Wright interview.

8. Ibid.

9. Nathan E. White, interview with author, 9 June 1998, Oxford, North Carolina.

10. Ibid. Mr. White proved a valuable interview subject, but frequently used unspoken gestures and allowed his voice to trail off when he felt his meaning was already understood by the interviewer. Hence, many bracketed remarks are necessary to understandably convert his thoughts into the printed word.

11. Hunt interview; Colin Warren-Hicks, "Longtime Local Politico, Former State Sen. Ralph Hunt Sr. Has Passed Away," *Herald Sun* (Durham, North Carolina), 16 May 2017, https://www.heraldsun.com/news/local/counties/durham-county/article150825952.html (accessed 19 June 2019).

12. Hunt interview; Charles Craven, "Oxford Father, Son Bound Over in Death," *News and Observer* (Raleigh, N.C.), 14 May 1970, 1. Henry Marrow was first taken to a nearby Oxford hospital, but medical personnel there declared his gunshot wounds too extensive to be treated there. Hence, Marrow's dying body was taken by ambulance into Durham.

13. Jim Grant, "Rebellion in Oxford," *Southern Patriot* 28 (June 1970): 1.

14. Ibid.; Charles Craven, "Lack of Justice Said Main Oxford Grievance," *News and Observer* (Raleigh, N.C.), 15 May 1970, 3.

15. Jim Grant, "Rebellion in Oxford," *Southern Patriot* 28 (June 1970): 1.

16. President Nixon had announced the ground troop invasion of Cambodia in a presidential address on April 30, 1970.

17. Wells, *The War Within*, 422–426.

18. "May Day," *Newsweek*, 11 May 1970, 32–33.

19. "The Rebellion of the Campus," *Newsweek*, 18 May 1970, 31.

20. Wells, *The War Within*, 425–426; Anderson, *The Movement and the Sixties*, 351; Goldstein, *Political Repression in Modern America*, 431. For more on the ferment of protest and radicalism that shook the country in the late 1960s and 1970s, see also Burrough, *Days of Rage*; Varon, *Bringing the War Home*; Clara Bingham, *Witness to the Revolution: Radicals, Resisters, Vets, Hippies, and the Year America Lost Its Mind and Found Its Soul* (New York: Random House, 2016); and Berger, *Outlaws of America*; Perlstein, *Nixonland*, chapter 23.

21. Wells, *The War Within*, 426; Anderson, *The Movement and the Sixties*, 351; "The Sudden Rising of the Hardhats," *Time*, 25 May 1970, 20–21.

22. O'Reilly, "*Racial Matters*," 331–332; Bloom and Martin, *Black Against Empire*, chapter 10; "Jackson: Kent State II," *Time*, 25 May 1970, 22; "The South: Dark Day in Jackson," *Newsweek*, 25 May 1970, 35–36.

23. The grand jury did claim that the lack of evidence necessary to produce indictments stemmed from the Black Panthers' refusal to testify in the case. "The grand jury is forced to conclude," the report maintained, "that [the Panthers] are more interested in the issue of police persecution than they are in obtaining justice. Perhaps revolutionary groups do not want the legal system to work." For their part, the Panthers harbored suspicions and resentment grounded in the legacy of white authorities' lack of commitment to fully pursue justice in such incidents. "Black Panthers: Questions Remain," *Time*, 25 May 1970, 26; "Black Panthers: Slap on the Wrist," *Newsweek*, 25 May 1970, 41.

24. "A Senseless Waste," *Newsweek*, 25 May 1970, 36, 41; "Augusta: Race Riot No.1," *Time*, 25 May 1970, 22. For more on the continuing spate of Black uprisings responding to law enforcement aggression in the 1970s, see Hinton, *America on Fire*.

25. Craven, "Oxford Father"; Timothy Tyson provides an extensive account of the shooting and its immediate aftermath in chapter 6 of *Blood Done Sign My Name*.

26. Tyson, "Burning for Freedom," 32–33, 43–46, 79; Tyson, *Blood Done Sign My Name*, chapter 3; Currin interview; Tom Ragland, former city manager for Oxford, North Carolina, interview by author, 12 May 1998, Oxford, North Carolina; Wright interview.

27. Granville County Court Records, cases #69-CR-1238, #69-CR-1239, #70-CR-425, #70-CR-1532; Nathan White interview; Ragland interview; Tyson, "Burning for Freedom," 82–84; Rod Cockshutt, "Oxford—A Quiet Town Becomes a Battleground," *News and Observer* (Raleigh, N.C.), 28 May 1970, 1.

28. Granville County Court Records, cases #69-CR-1238, #69-CR-1239, #70-CR-425, #70-CR-1532; Ragland interview; Tyson, "Burning for Freedom," 82–84; Cockshutt, "Oxford—A Quiet Town Becomes a Battleground," 1.

29. Craven, "Oxford Father."

30. Grant, "Rebellion in Oxford," *Southern Patriot*.

31. Ibid. Hugh Currin, mayor at the time, recalls a rumor he heard that Klansmen had come from Dawes County to protect the Teel home (Hugh Currin, Mayor of Oxford, North Carolina, interview by author, 12 May 1998, Oxford, North Carolina).

32. Ragland interview; Wright interview.

33. The Granville County location on Interstate 85 was not the only KKK sign in North Carolina to arouse citizens' concern. Clearly, the state could not escape some contradictions to its progressive image, as a number of such KKK signs signaled the Klan's presence across North Carolina. Robert Levy of Augusta, Georgia, and Mrs. James Chimento of Fort Bragg, North Carolina, wrote the governor in 1970 of a KKK sign on Interstate 95 near Dunn, North Carolina—a city just thirty-six miles south of Raleigh (and seventy-six south of Oxford). Chimento told the governor in the same year that, while she was white, she was nonetheless "appalled" and "offended." Mickey Terry alerted the governor to another on U.S. Highway 301 in eastern North Carolina in July 1970. R. R. Vancil wrote of an "inflammatory" KKK sign on Highway 70 west of Smithfield, North Carolina, in January 1972. Ragland interview; Myerson, *Nothing Could Be Finer*, 11; Jean Dember, Copiague, New York, to Governor James Holshouser, Raleigh, North Carolina, 22 August 1973, Governor James Holshouser Papers, box 117, Ku Klux Klan folder, NCA; Mrs. Earl Spellman, Unionville, Pennsylvania, to Governor Robert Scott, Raleigh, North Carolina, 6 February 1971, RSP, box 356, Ku Klux Klan folder; Robert Levy, Augusta, Georgia, to Governor Robert Scott, 25 August 1970, RSP, box 216, Ku Klux Klan folder; Mrs. James Chimento, Fort Bragg, North Carolina, to Governor Robert Scott, 25 August 1970, RSP, box 216, Ku Klux Klan folder; Mickey Terry, Greenville, North Carolina, to Governor Robert Scott, 3 July 1970, RSP, box 216, Ku Klux Klan folder; R. R. Vancil, Vandemere, North Carolina, to Governor Robert Scott, Raleigh, North Carolina, 13 January 1972, RSP, box 500, Ku Klux Klan folder.

34. The other rally occurred five miles south of Creedmoor, in Granville County. Major Edwin C. Guy, Director, Enforcement Division, North Carolina Highway Patrol, memorandum to Governor Dan K. Moore, Raleigh, North Carolina, 4 April 1967, Governor Dan K. Moore Papers, box 373.21, Highway Patrol Reports—1967 folder, NCA; Major Edwin C. Guy, Director, Enforcement Division, North Carolina Highway Patrol, memorandum to Governor Dan K. Moore, Raleigh, North Carolina, 22 May 1967, Governor Dan K. Moore Papers, box 373.21, Highway Patrol Reports—1967 folder, NCA.

35. White also remembers talk of a broader community role that the KKK played in Granville County: "Years ago, when I was real young, and you done something to your sister, done something to your mama, they [KKK] used to ride out and say, 'Come over here. I want to see you.' And, they carried him out there and whooped his ass. He didn't go threatening [a woman and hitting] the sauce anymore. I'll tell you something else they did. Somebody's always going home and beating on their wife and beating on the children, going off two or three days, and they're sitting there with nothing to eat and he's coming in and beating them. They'll [KKK] ride out there one day and say, 'You know, you've got a nice family, you're doing this and doing that. You're mistreating them.' They'll turn around and take one of them big wide belts and you'll never hear of him beating and abusing people" (Nathan White interview). While such stories of the KKK as a kind of moral watchdog are unsubstantiated, they are also common in areas where Klan strength is strong as a partial rationalization for its presence.

36. Korstad and Leloudis, *To Right These Wrongs*, 314. See also David Cunningham's larger study of the Klan in North Carolina, *Klansville, U.S.A.: The Rise and Fall of the Civil Rights-Era Ku Klux Klan* (New York: Oxford Univ. Press, 2013).

37. Craven, "Oxford Father," 1; Charles Craven, "Lack of Justice Said Main Oxford Grievance," *News and Observer* (Raleigh, N.C.), 15 May 1970, 3.

38. Currin interview.

39. Wright interview.

40. Grant, "Rebellion in Oxford"; Craven, "Oxford Father"; "Three Charlotteans Arrested in Oxford," *Charlotte Observer*, 16 May 1970, TRJP, 3:1.

41. Civil Intelligence Bulletin, North Carolina State Bureau of Investigation, 14 May 1970, NCA, RSP, box 176, SBI Reports folder; Myerson, *Nothing Could Be Finer*, 44; Civil Intelligence Bulletin, SBI, 13 May 1970, NCA, RSP, box 176, SBI Reports folder; SBI Intelligence Section memorandum to SBI Director Charles Dunn, "Projection of Civil Intelligence Trouble Spots Throughout the State for the Months of May and June 1970, File No. CI-102, 15 May 1970, NCA, RSP, box 176, SBI Reports folder. The Civil Intelligence Bulletin for Grant and Goins's appearance at the rally as speakers actually garbles Goins's and Grant's last names, calling Grant "Jim Graham" and Goins "Joe Barnes." Phonetic misspellings of subjects' names at such large rallies, of course, are not uncommon. Placed in context with the rest of the document, however, as well as other secondary sources that confirm that the two were there, were working with Chavis, and were playing a leadership role, it is clear to whom the Civil Intelligence Bulletin is referring.

42. Grant, "Rebellion in Oxford."

43. "Three Charlotteans Arrested in Oxford," *Charlotte News*, 16 May 1970, TJRP, 3:1; "Three Charlotteans Arrested in Racially Troubled Oxford," *Charlotte Observer*, 16 May 1970, 2B; "3 Arrested on Firearms Charges," *News and Observer* (Raleigh, N.C.), 16 May 1970, 3

44. "Three Charlotteans Arrested," *Charlotte Observer*, 16 May 1970; "Repression in North Carolina," TJRP, OF 2:8, 4.

45. Finch interview; Ragland interview. Ragland further recalled that prior to the arrest, "S.T. Wooten Company was doing some road work on I-85. A report had come out three or four days previous to that that someone had broken into their storage facility and stolen some dynamite. It didn't take no wizard to figure out what that was about."

46. North Carolina Bureau of Investigation intra-bureau correspondence, Intelligence Section to the Director, 15 May 1970, File No. CI-102, NCA, RSP, box 176, SBI Reports folder. The Bureau's reference to the arrestees as Black clearly implies that that makes them even more subversively suspicious. In a November 1970 report on civic unrest in Henderson, North Carolina, the SBI highlights the arrival of "several out-of-state cars in town occupied by Negroes *with Afro hair cuts.*" If being Black increased your propensity for subversion, being Black with an "Afro hair cut" took you one step closer to extremism (Civil Intelligence Bulletin, 4 November 1970, NCA, RSP, box 185, DMV-Highway Patrol Reports folder, my italics).

47. Currin interview; Ragland interview.

48. Ragland interview.

49. "Charlotteans' Bond Reduced," *Charlotte Observer*, 19 May 1970, TJRP, 3:1; "Repression in North Carolina," TJRP, OF 2:8, 3.

50. Ethridge, Schwartz, and Clancy. "2 Lazy B Witnesses Got $4,000 Each," 1A.

51. Jim Lewis, "Scott Sends Patrolmen to Oxford," *News and Observer* (Raleigh, N.C.), 27 May 1970, 1; "Most Destructive Fire in History of City Leaves $1 Million Loss," *Oxford Public Ledger,* 29 May 1970, 1; Ragland interview.

52. Colonel Edwin C. Guy, North Carolina Highway Patrol, to David P. Murray, Special Assistant to the Governor, Raleigh, North Carolina, North Carolina Highway Patrol memorandum, "Report from Captain J.T. Jenkins Regarding Patrol Assistance in Oxford, North Carolina, Monday, 25 May," 28 May 1970, NCA, RSP, box 270, Oxford folder; Rod Cockshutt, "Oxford—A Quiet Town Becomes a Battleground," *News and Observer* (Raleigh, N.C.), 28 May 1970, 1.

53. Cockshutt, "Oxford—A Quiet Town Becomes a Battleground"; Rod Waldorf, "Oxford Marchers Rally Here," *News and Observer* (Raleigh, N.C.), 25 May 1970, 30; "Oxford Youth Plan March to Raleigh," *News and Observer* (Raleigh, N.C.), 22 May 1970, 3; Tyson, "Burning for Freedom," 199–206; Tyson, *Blood Done Sign My Name,* chapter 7.

54. Craven, "Lack of Justice."

55. Ibid.

56. Ibid.

57. "Black Grievances and Demands," 17 May 1970, NCA, RSP, box 270, Oxford Demonstrations folder; "City Board Grants Demands of Blacks," *Oxford Public Ledger,* 22 May 1970, 1.

58. The stated goals included: the promotion of nondiscriminatory hiring in government and business positions, improved funding for recreational facilities for Black residents, more training and a mandatory high school diploma for police officers, the promotion of one of the three Black police officers to lieutenant rank, a federal investigation into the county judicial system, street improvements, and the enforcement of residential zoning codes in the town's Black neighborhoods. "County Board Reopens Door of Mary Potter," *Oxford Public Ledger,* 22 May 1970, 1.

59. Wright interview; Tyson, "Burning for Freedom," 199–206.

60. Wright interview; Tyson, "Burning for Freedom," 199–206.

61. "Courtroom Glimpses," *Oxford Public Ledger,* 31 July 1970, 1; Tyson, "Burning for Freedom," 181–183; Tyson, *Blood Done Sign My Name,* 127.

62. "'You Don't Ever Put Your Idealism Aside,'" *Business Journal,* 17 December 1990, James Ferguson Clipping File, Carolina Room, Charlotte-Mecklenburg Public Library; "Ferguson a Worthy Honoree," 12 March 1991, James Ferguson Clipping File, Carolina Room, Charlotte-Mecklenburg Public Library; Hunt interview; James Ferguson, interview by Rudy Acree, 3 March 1992, Charlotte, North Carolina, Southern Historical Collection, Louis Round Wilson Library, http://dc .lib.unc.edu/cdm/ref/collection/sohp/id/12595 (accessed 12 October 2017); Rosen and Mosnier, *Julius Chambers,* 126–131.

63. Granville County Courthouse Records, Case #70-CR-1847; Granville County Courthouse Records, Case #70-CR-1849; Tyson, "Burning for Freedom," 181–194; Tyson, *Blood Done Sign My Name,* chapter 10.

64. Ross Scott, "Teel's Half-Brother Says He Held Gun," *Durham Morning Herald,* 1 August 1970, 1A; Tyson, "Burning for Freedom," 182–185.

65. While Hunt had no direct evidence that several men standing and watching against the

wall were Klansmen, he had been told this by people he deemed reliable sources. Hunt interview; "Freed by Jury, Father and Son Returned to Jail After Judge Makes New Charges," *Oxford Public Ledger*, 4 August 1970, 1; Ross Scott, "Teels Acquitted of Murder; Court Issues Bench Warrants," *Durham Morning Herald*, 3 August 1970, 1A.

66. Granville County Court Records, Robert Gerald Teel, Case #70-CR-3232; Granville County Court Records, Robert Larry Teel, Case #70-CR-3233; Granville County Court Records, Grand Jury, 10 February 1971; "Freed by Jury, Father and Son Returned to Jail After Judge Makes New Charges," 1; Ross Scott, "Teels Acquitted of Murder; Court Issues Bench Warrants," *Durham Morning Herald*, 3 August 1970, 1A.

67. In his post-1970 years, the elder Teel continued to compile a lengthy rap sheet of violent offenses. Two encounters for drunken driving ended with him beating the arresting officers unconscious. For more on the latter years of Teel, see chapter 12 of Tim Tyson's excellent account of the Oxford riot and its aftermath in *Blood Done Sign My Name*.

5. Strange Bedfellows: Al Hood, Dave Washington, and the War on Crime

1. William Walden, interview with author, 24 February 1999, Morganton, North Carolina.
2. Ibid.
3. Ibid.
4. Marvin Sparrow interview.
5. Civil Intelligence Bulletin, 30 October 1970, NCA, RSP, box 185, DMV-Highway Patrol Reports folder; Civil Intelligence Bulletin, Chronological Listing of Events, 2 December 1970, NCA, RSP, box 531, DMV-Highway Patrol Reports folder; Special Incident Report, 27 April 1971, NCA, RSP, box 332, Reports-3 folder; Myerson, *Nothing Could Be Finer*, 43, 57–65, 76.
6. When the Kerner Commission made its final report to President Johnson in March 1968, the president dubbed it a "good report by good men of good will," but he apparently was frustrated by the report's call for further "massive" funding to inner-city programs. "They always print that we don't do enough," Johnson asserted. "They don't print what we do." In terms of creating Johnson administration policy, that essentially would be the end of the report. As an historical document, the Kerner Commission report remains much remembered for its insight and candor about the state of the nation and the rocky racial road that lay ahead. William O'Neill, *Coming Apart: An Informal History of America in the 1960s* (New York: Times Books, 1971), 177, 180; Samuel Walker, *Popular Justice: A History of American Criminal Justice* (New York: Oxford Univ. Press, 1980), 222–227; *Report of the National Advisory Commission on Civil Disorders* (New York: E. P. Dutton, 1968), 1. For an insightful review of the tragic influence and impact of the 1964 Harlem uprising, see Flamm, *In the Heat of the Summer*.
7. As quoted in Gary T. Marx, "Civil Disorder and the Agents of Social Control," *Journal of Social Issues* 26 (1970): 20.
8. As quoted ibid., 35.
9. Richard Harris, *The Fear of Crime* (New York: Praeger, 1969), 22–23; Walker, *Popular Justice*, 229–231.

10. Ibid., 38, 44.

11. Ibid., 31–33.

12. Ibid., 21–24. For more on the expansive impact of the LEAA, see Hinton, *From the War on Poverty to the War on Crime*, especially chapter 4.

13. As quoted in James O. Finckenauer, "Crime as a National Political Issue, 1964–1976: From Law and Order to Domestic Tranquility," *Crime and Delinquency* 24 (January 1978): 17–18.

14. James D. Calder, "Presidents and Crime Control: Kennedy, Johnson and Nixon and the Influences of Ideology," *Presidential Studies Quarterly* 12 (1982): 574–589; Gerald M. Caplan, "Reflections on the Nationalization of Crime, 1964–1968," *Law and the Social Order* (1973): 583–635; Goldstein, *Political Repression in Modern America*, 492. For an excellent examination of the 1964 Harlem riot and its political implications, particularly on the year's presidential campaign, see Flamm, *In the Heat of the Summer*.

15. Caplan, "Reflections on the Nationalization of Crime," 609–610; Walker, *Popular Justice*, 232–236. For a less sanguine view of the Johnson administration's role in contributing to the War on Crime, see Hinton, *From the War on Poverty to the War on Crime*.

16. O'Reilly, "*Racial Matters*," 266.

17. Milton Viorst, "Attorney General Mitchell's Philosophy," *New York Times Magazine*, 10 August 1969, 10. During his first term, Nixon also increased funding thirteen-fold for the Law Enforcement Assistance Administration (an agency created under the 1968 Omnibus Crime Control and Safe Streets Act to provide federal grants for local and state law enforcement improvements). When the president supported and then signed a particularly harsh anticrime bill for the District of Columbia (which included preventive detention, no-knock warrants, and life imprisonment for three felony convictions), North Carolina senator Sam Ervin worried that it was a "blueprint for a police state." Robert Perkinson, *Texas Tough: The Rise of America's Prison Empire* (New York: Metropolitan Books, 2010), 298. For a fuller description of the impact the Law Enforcement Assistance Administration, see Hinton, *From the War on Poverty to the War on Crime*, especially chapter 4.

18. O'Reilly, "*Racial Matters*," 258.

19. Stanley Kutler, *The Wars of Watergate: The Last Crisis of Richard Nixon* (New York: Norton, 1990), 104–105.

20. "Operational Restraints on Intelligence Collection," Statement of Information, Hearings Before the Committee on the Judicary, House of Representatives, Ninety-Third Congress, Book VII, Part 1, White House Surveillance Activities and Campaign Activities, 438–442; "Special Report, Interagency Committee Intelligence (Ad Hoc)," Statement of Information, Hearings Before the Committee on the Judicary, House of Representatives, Ninety-Third Congress, Book VII, Part 1, White House Surveillance Activities and Campaign Activities, 384–431; J. Anthony Lukas, *Nightmare: The Underside of the Nixon Years* (New York: Penguin, 1988), 30–31.

21. Kutler, *The Wars of Watergate*, 99–101.

22. J. Anthony Lukas, *Nightmare: The Underside of the Nixon Years* (New York: Penguin, 1988), 35–36. For further information on evidence that the Nixon administration implemented other Huston Plan initiatives, see pages 36–39.

23. Richard E. Morgan, *Domestic Intelligence: Monitoring Dissent in America* (Austin: Univ. of

Texas Press, 1980), 37–87; Goldstein, *Political Repression in Modern America*, 444–504; Burrough, *Days of Rage*, especially chapters 5–7, 10, and 16; Rosenfeld, *Subversives*.

24. Lukas, *Nightmare*, 32–39. For more on the rise of domestic intelligence on militants in the late 1960s and 1970s, see O'Reilly, *"Racial Matters,"* and Donner, *The Age of Surveillance*.

25. Lukas, *Nightmare*, 214–215; Donner, *The Age of Surveillance*, 76; Tom Wicker, *One of Us: Richard Nixon and the American Dream* (New York: Random House, 1991), 485–490; Wells, *The War Within*, 469. "You talk of wearing flags in lapels—this guy would have sewn a flag on his back if they'd let him," a Justice Department colleague told the *Washington Post* in 1973 (Patricia Sullivan, "Robert Mardian; Attorney Caught Up in Watergate Scandal," *Washington Post*, July 21, 2006, https://www.washingtonpost.com/politics/robert-mardian-attorney-caught-up-in-watergate-scandal/2012/05/31/gJQARJ6vFV_story.html [accessed 19 July 2016]). For more on Mardian, see Lukas, *Nightmare*, chapter 8. Nixon contended that he later rescinded his approval of the Huston Plan when FBI Director J. Edgar Hoover voiced objections. Nevertheless, some of its recommendations clearly went into effect.

26. Walden interview, 24 February 1999.

27. Ibid.

28. Ibid.

29. Ethridge, Schwartz, and Clancy, "2 Lazy B Witnesses Got $4,000 Each," 1A; "Charlotteans' Bond Reduced," *Charlotte Observer*, 19 May 1970, TJRP, 3:1; "Repression in North Carolina," TJRP, OF 2:8, 3.

30. Walden memorandum to Charlotte Chief Special Investigator, 28 June 1971, 1.

31. Ethridge, Schwartz, and Clancy, "2 Lazy B Witnesses Got $4,000 Each"; Walden memorandum to Charlotte Chief Special Investigator, 28 June 1971, 2.

32. Ethridge, Schwartz, and Clancy, "2 Lazy B Witnesses Got $4,000"; "Tear Gas Flushes Man From Attic," *Charlotte News*, 28 December 1970, 2A.

33. Ethridge, Schwartz, and Clancy, "2 Lazy B Witnesses Got $4,000 Each."

34. Walden memorandum to Charlotte Chief Special Investigator, 28 June 1971, 4.

35. Ethridge, Schwartz, Clancy, "2 Lazy B Witnesses Got $4,000 Each."

36. Walden interview, 24 February 1999.

37. Walden memorandum to Charlotte Chief Special Investigator, 28 June 1971, 1.

38. Ibid.; Ethridge, Schwartz, and Clancy, "2 Lazy B Witnesses Got $4,000 Each"; Myerson, *Nothing Could Be Finer*, 39.

39. Walden memorandum to Charlotte Chief Special Investigator, 28 June 1971, 2.

40. Ibid.

41. Ethridge, Schwartz, and Clancy, "2 Lazy B Witnesses Got $4,000 Each."

42. Charlotte Police Intelligence Officer Joseph Europa claimed that he had not charged Washington with any of the five murders because Washington's status as a suspect in each of them "is not supported by enough evidence for indictment." Walden memorandum to Charlotte Chief Special Investigator, 28 June 1971. Ethridge, Schwartz and Clancy, "2 Lazy B Witnesses Got $4,000 Each." William Chafe's *The Unfinished Journey* has good background on the federal government's extreme methods in suppressing this leftist threat to national security. See particularly pages 412–419. See also Burrough, *Days of Rage*; Theoharis, *The FBI and American Democracy*.

43. ATF Special Investigator Stanley Noel to Assistant Chief, Enforcement Branch, ATF, Southeast Regional Office, "Request for Authorization of Expenditure of Funds for Purchase of Evidence," 17 September 1971, Exhibit 8, "Petition for Pardon," 30 December 1977, TJRP.

44. Walden memorandum to Charlotte Chief Special Investigator, 28 June 1970, 2; Ethridge, Schwartz, and Clancy, "2 Lazy B Witnesses Got $4,000 Each."

45. Ibid.

46. Washington also contended this group firebombed Norman's Meat Market in Charlotte (which housed the local 1968 presidential campaign headquarters for Governor George Wallace) later that year. This latter accusation never emerged as an indictment. Walden memorandum to Charlotte Chief Special Investigator, 28 June 1971, 3; "Government Testimony: Black Militant Blamed for Fires," *Charlotte Observer*, 25 April 1972, 1C.

47. Walden memorandum to the Charlotte Chief Special Investigator, 28 June 1971, 3–4.

48. Walden interview, 24 February 1999. This was not the first occasion in those polarized times that Walden had handled potential witnesses who reluctantly provided information but were terrified of possible reprisals. Many witnesses felt caught in the middle of these explosive cases, and desperately desired a way out of the fractiousness attached to the investigations of such controversial advocates for racial justice. During his investigation of racial unrest in Wilmington that produced the Wilmington Ten trial in 1972, "I had to go to witnesses in the middle of the night sometimes—for instance, some of the local Black business people in the Wilmington area. These people didn't have wide support even in their own communities. They were scared to death [about what could happen to them if they were seen talking to law enforcement]." In another instance in Wilmington, "I interviewed a priest one time who made an I.D. and signed a sworn statement for me implicating someone. When he got in the courtroom he lied up and down. It turned out his bishop had told him not to get involved. He [the priest witness] passed me on the way out of the court all red-faced. He knew that I knew that he'd just lied on the stand. But I understood."

49. Walden memorandum to Charlotte Chief Special Investigator, 28 June 1971, 4.

50. Brief for Amicus Curiae, Appeal to the United States Court of Appeals for the Fourth Circuit, No. 77–1480, Barry Nakel, Associate Professor of Law, University of North Carolina at Chapel Hill, Chapel Hill, North Carolina to William K. Slate, Clerk, United States Court of Appeals, Richmond, Virginia, *Thomas James Reddy et al. v. David L. Jones et al.*, 5 May 1977, Law Office of James Ferguson, Charlotte, North Carolina.

51. Brief for Amicus Curiae, U.S. Court of Appeals For the Fourth Circuit, 25 May 1977, 3; Defendants Appellants' Brief, *State of North Carolina v. James Earl Grant et al.*, North Carolina Court of Appeals, Fall Session 1973.

52. "Petition for Pardon," TJRP, 5–6.

53. Frank Donner, *Protectors of Privilege: Red Squads and Police Repression in Urban America* (Berkeley: Univ. of California Press, 1990), 76–79. See also Morgan, *Domestic Intelligence*, 83–87.

54. Kathy Sparrow interview, 21 March 1994.

55. Butch and Shirley Rosen interview.

56. Marvin Sparrow interview.

57. Walden interview, 24 February 1999.

58. Ethridge, Schwartz, and Clancy, "2 Lazy B Witnesses Got $4,000 Each." Whether "United Soul" was merely Hood and Washington's imaginative fiction to play to authorities' paranoia of the Three as part of larger, more organized conspiracy remains a matter of dispute. In either case, the name likely derived from the "US" Black Power organization based in the Los Angeles area. For more on the latter group, see Brown, *Fighting for US*.

59. Brief for Amicus Curiae, U.S. Court of Appeals for the Fourth Circuit, 5; "Petition for Pardon," TJRP, 5–6.

60. Mark Ethridge, interview by author, 21 March 1994, Charlotte, North Carolina.

61. Mark Ethridge and Michael Schwartz, "The Months of Bargaining Behind Lazy B Testimony," *Charlotte Observer*, 29 December 1974, 1A.

62. Brief for Amicus Curiae, 25 May 1977, 4–5; Walden interview, 24 February 1999.

63. "Months of Bargaining"; William Walden, phone interview with author, 5 June 1999, Morganton, North Carolina.

64. "Petition for Pardon," TJRP, 4–5; "Repression in North Carolina," TJRP, OF 2:8, 4.

65. Ethridge, Schwartz, and Clancy, "2 Lazy B Witnesses Got $4,000 Each."

66. "Months of Bargaining."

67. Mark Ethridge, interview by author, 18 March 1994, Charlotte, North Carolina.

68. "Government Testimony: Black Militant Blamed"; Nancy Bentson, "Militants Ask for Mistrial," *Charlotte Observer*, 26 April 1972, 1C.

69. A fourth trial (which occurred in June 1973) charged Chavis and two associates (Donald Nixon and Mollie Hicks) with telling police a false story about a 1971 accidental shooting. Nixon had first reported to police that the shooting victim, Black student activist Clifton Wright, had been killed by a white man. Nixon later confessed that Wright had inadvertently killed himself as he played with a shotgun. Authorities then charged Chavis and Hicks (to whom Nixon claimed he had revealed the truth) with aiding Nixon to tell the false story. Although state prosecutors convicted Hicks in the trial, the defense successfully moved for a mistrial for Chavis's alleged crime. Jim Hefner, "State's Two Key Witnesses Tell of Coverup," *Wilmington Morning Star*, 21 June 1973, 1B; "Justice Dept. Probe Sought in Killing of Clifton Wright," *Wilmington Morning Star*, 28 March 1971, 1A; "Local Officials Take Exception to Request," *Wilmington Morning Star*, 28 March 1971, 1A; "Williamson Refutes CRC Charges," *Wilmington Morning Star*, 28 March 1971, 1A; "Murder in Wilmington," *Southern Patriot* 29 (April 1971): 6; Jim Hefner, "Charges Dismissed Against Chavis," *Wilmington Morning Star*, 23 June 1973, 17.

70. Two marshals did remain seated directly behind Grant and Chavis throughout the trial, however. Gary Pearce, "Witness Accuses 2 Activists: Tells of Oxford Slaying Offer," *News and Observer* (Raleigh, N.C.), 21 April 1972; Gary Pearce, "Charges Dismissed Against Witnesses," *News and Observer* (Raleigh, N.C.), 19 April 1972, 5.

71. "Government Testimony: Black Militant Blamed"; Nancy Bentson, "Militants Ask for Mistrial," *Charlotte Observer*, 26 April 1972, 1C.

72. "Government Testimony: Black Militant Blamed."

73. Ibid.; Kathy Sparrow interview, 21 March 1994.

74. Gary Pearce, "Witness Admits Lie," *News and Observer* (Raleigh, N.C.), 25 April 1972.

75. Pearce, "Witness Accuses 2 Activists."

76. Gary Pearce, "Witness Cites Bomb Threat," *News and Observer* (Raleigh, N.C.), 22 April 1972, 30.

77. "Government Testimony: Black Militant Blamed"; Pearce, "Witness Admits Lie," 5.

78. "Government Testimony: Black Militant Blamed"; Kathy Sparrow interview, 21 March 1994.

79. Gary Pearce, "Chavis Defense Calls No Witnesses," *News and Observer* (Raleigh, N.C.), 26 April 1972, 38.

80. Pearce, "Witness Accuses 2 Activists: Tells of Oxford Slaying Offer," *News and Observer* (Raleigh, N.C.), 21 April 1972, 1.

81. Gary Pearce, "Witness Cites Bomb Threat," *News and Observer* (Raleigh, N.C.), 22 April 1972, 30.

82. Pearce, "Witness Accuses 2 Activists: Tells of Oxford Slaying Offer," 1.

83. Gary Pearce, "Charges Dismissed Against Witnesses," 5; Nancy Bentson, "Charlotte Activist Gets 10 Years in Conspiracy: Jury Frees Chavis, Convicts Grant," *Charlotte Observer,* 27 April 1972, 1C.

84. Bentson, "Militants Ask for Mistrial," 26 April 1972.

85. The defense also moved unsuccessfully for a mistrial on the grounds that Washington's statements implicating Ferguson "may have had a negative effect on the jury." Pearce, "Chavis Defense Calls No Witnesses," 38.

86. Gary Pearce, "Chavis Acquitted; Grant Convicted," *News and Observer* (Raleigh, N.C.), 27 April 1972, 62.

87. Nancy Bentson, "Charlotte Activist Gets 10 Years in Conspiracy: Jury Frees Chavis, Convicts Grant," *Charlotte Observer,* 27 Apr 1972, 1C.

88. Pearce, "Chavis Acquitted; Grant Convicted," 62.

89. Bentson, "Charlotte Activist Gets 10 Years in Conspiracy."

90. Ibid.

91. Pearce, "Chavis Acquitted; Grant Convicted"; Bentson, "Charlotte Activist Gets 10 Years in Conspiracy."

92. Pam Jones, "Chavis Trial Is Called Smoke Screen," *News and Observer* (Raleigh, N.C.), 28 April 1972, 46; Bill Chaze, "McBryde Is Out as SBI Director," *Charlotte News,* 20 November 1968, 4A.

93. Pearce, "Chavis Acquitted; Grant Convicted."

94. "Chavis Indicted in Wilmington," *News and Observer* (Raleigh, N.C.), 26 April 1972, 16.

95. Pearce, "Chavis Acquitted; Grant Convicted."

96. Bentson, "Charlotte Activist Gets 10 Years in Conspiracy."

97. "The Price of Militancy: Ten Years in North Carolina," *Southern Patriot* 30 (May 1972): 4.

98. White also appeared at a Charlotte march in protest of the taking of "political prisoners" later that week. The march highlighted the indictees in the Wilmington trial that would include the recently acquitted Chavis, and the indictees—including Grant—for burning the Lazy B Stables in Charlotte. The leaflet distributed for the march described these activists as "being guilty" of "standing up against white racist oppression" and "being Black." Jones, "Chavis Trial Is Called

NOTES TO PAGES 116–121

Smoke Screen," 46; "Militants' Supporters Plan Charlotte March," *Charlotte Observer,* 28 April 1972, 2B.

6. Convicting the Wizard, the Poet, and Little Charlie: The Charlotte Three Trial

1. Gaillard, *The Dream Long Deferred,* 82–83; Douglas, *Reading, Writing, and Race,* 242.

2. Gaillard, *The Dream Long Deferred,* 35–36, 82–83.

3. "'You Don't Ever Put Your Idealism Aside,'" Business Journal, 17 December 1990, James Ferguson Clipping File, Carolina Room, Charlotte-Mecklenburg Public Library.

4. Douglas, *Reading, Writing, and Race,* 176–177.

5. Gaillard, *The Dream Long Deferred,* 82–83; Douglas, *Reading, Writing, and Race,* 176–177.

6. Gaillard, *The Dream Long Deferred;* Douglas, *Reading, Writing, and Race;* Goldfield, *Black, White, and Southern,* 132–134, 258–259; Lassiter, *Silent Majority;* Reverend Eugene Owens, interview by author, 9 December 1992, Charlotte, North Carolina.

7. Anonymous source #2, interview by author, 14 April 1994, Charlotte, North Carolina.

8. Ian F. Haney López, *Racism on Trial: The Chicano Fight for Justice* (Cambridge, Mass.: Belknap, 2003), 92–93.

9. Donner, *The Age of Surveillance,* 355–356. The alleged abuse of grand juries to expand the secretive powers of prosecutors is ironic, as the original purpose of grand juries was to restrict the overreach of aggressive prosecutors by forcing them to present their cases objectively to average citizens, who would comprise the grand juries. (See Marvin Frankel and Gary Naftalis, *The Grand Jury: An Institution on Trial* (New York: Hill and Wang, 1977), 6–13; Andrew Leipold, "Why Grand Juries Do Not and Cannot Protect the Accused," *Cornell Law Review* 80 (January 1995): 280–288. Critics complain that grand juries are given troublingly wide latitude; for example, the U.S. Supreme Court ruled in the 1974 case United States v. Calandra that grand juries are allowed to consider otherwise inadmissible evidence (which was illegally obtained) when issuing indictments. Further, the subject of a grand jury investigation (except in rare cases on a state level) has no right to testify before the body unless subpoenaed, no right to force it to hear witnesses sympathetic to the defense, and no right to be present when witnesses testify against him or her (Frankel and Naftalis, *The Grand Jury,* 25–31).

10. Marvin Sparrow interview.

11. Douglas, *Reading, Writing, and Race,* 40–41, 172–185. At the time of the trial, Judge Snepp's son was fully engaged across the world in another decidedly divisive issue for the country, as he functioned as the CIA's chief analyst of North Vietnamese strategy in Saigon. In a fascinating 2015 email exchange with the Charlotte Observer (prompted by a new article about Grant's ongoing lifelong activism), the younger Snepp recounted that when he "later learned of the sentence I was outraged" and claimed to have "long been haunted by this case and my father's handling of it." Jim Morrill, "Frank Snepp 'Haunted' by His Father's Ruling in Charlotte 3 Case," *Charlotte Observer,* last modified February 27, 2015, https://www.charlotteobserver.com/news/politics-government/campaign-tracker-blog/article11361542.html#storylink=cpy; Glenn Hatstedt, *Spies, Wiretaps, and Secret Operations: An Encyclopedia of American Espionage* (Santa Barbara, Calif.: ABC-CLIO, 2011), 711–712.

NOTES TO PAGES 121–124

12. Douglas, *Reading, Writing, and Race,* 40–41, 172–185.

13. Ellison Clary, "No Politics for Snepp: Judge to Seek New Term," *Charlotte News,* 3 May 1973, A1, Charlotte-Mecklenburg Public Library, Carolina Room, Frank Snepp and Family Clipping File (hereafter referred to as Snepp File); Kay Reimler, "Snepp: Judge Responsible for Rights," *Charlotte News,* 9 November 1968, 1B; Gary L. Wright, "The Gavel Falls on Career of a Legend," *Charlotte Observer,* 12 August 1989, Snepp File.

14. Ellison Clary, "No Politics for Snepp: Judge to Seek New Term," *Charlotte News,* 3 May 1973, A1, Snepp File); Reimler, "Snepp: Judge Responsible for Rights," 1B; Wright, "The Gavel Falls on Career of a Legend."

15. Nick Taylor, "Criminals Play 'Game' with Rights Snepp Tells Civitan," *Charlotte News,* 18 October 1968, 1B; Wright, "The Gavel Falls on Career of a Legend." The Supreme Court under Chief Justice Earl Warren (who oversaw the court from 1953–1969) came under increasing conservative criticism for expanding the rights of criminal defendants. Key were four decisions: *Mapp v. Ohio* (1961) (which foreclosed using evidence during trial obtained through an unreasonable search), *Gideon v. Wainwright* (1963) (which gave poor defendants the right to state-paid attorneys), *Escobedo v. Illinois* (1964) (which declared that a suspect has the right to consult with an attorney as soon as police are targeting her or him for a crime), and *Miranda v. Arizona* (1966) (which guaranteed a suspect's right to be warned of her or his rights at the time of her or his arrest). So important were these rulings that they were dubbed the "due process revolution." Conservatives complained that they allowed guilty criminals to be freed on mere "technicalities."

16. Barbara Brawley, "Mrs. Frank Snepp Likes to Serve in Background," *Charlotte Observer,* Snepp File.

17. Morrill, "Frank Snepp 'Haunted.'"

18. Howard Maniloff, "Jury Selection Is Ruled Fair in Burning Indictment," *Charlotte Observer,* 7 July 1972, 2C.

19. Howard Maniloff, "Lazy B Stables: Defense to See Evidence in Burning," *Charlotte Observer,* 8 July 1972, 1C; Maniloff, "Jury Selection Is Ruled Fair." Ferguson did not fare as well on another objection: that drawing jury members from voter registration lists "systematically and arbitrarily" excluded African Americans. Presiding Judge Frank Snepp denied the motion, which had been based on figures showing only 14 percent of the county's registered voters were Black, although 21 percent of the county were African Americans.

20. Nancy Brachey, "One Pleads Guilty as Lazy B Trial Opens," *Charlotte Observer,* 11 July 1972, 1C; "Repression in North Carolina," TJRP, OF 2:8, 6; Lawrence Wright, "The Lazy B 3 in Black and White," *New Times,* 27 June 1975, 59.

21. Ellison Clary, "Judge Won't Drop Charges in Fire," *Charlotte News,* 10 July 1972, 1B.

22. "Repression in North Carolina," TJRP, OF 2:8, 5.

23. Clary, "Judge Won't Drop Charges in Fire."

24. Ibid.

25. Tommy Denton, "Ruling Delayed on Picket Ban," *Charlotte News,* 11 July 1972, 1B.

26. Nancy Brachey, "One Pleads Guilty as Lazy B Trial Opens," *Charlotte Observer,* 11 July 1972, 1C; Clary, "Judge Won't Drop Charges."

27. Denton, "Ruling Delayed on Picket Ban"; "Repression in North Carolina," TJRP, OF 2:8, 6.

28. Denton, "Ruling Delayed on Picket Ban."

29. Nancy Brachey, "Sobbing Witness Recalls Fire That Killed Her Horse," *Charlotte Observer,* 12 July 1972, 1B.

30. Ibid.

31. Ellison Clary, "Witness in Burning Trial: Men Had Firebombs, Rifles," *Charlotte News,* 12 July 1972, 2B; "Repression in North Carolina," TJRP, OF 2:8, 6–7.

32. Clary, "Witness in Burning Trial"; "Repression in North Carolina," TJRP, OF 2:8, 7.

33. Clary, "Witness in Burning Trial"; Betty Jo Hamrick (Myers Park Baptist Church Deacon), interview by author, 19 July 1993, Charlotte, North Carolina.

34. "Repression in North Carolina," TJRP, OF 2:8, 7.

35. Clary, "Witness in Burning Trial"; "Repression in North Carolina," TJRP, OF 2:8, 7; Ethridge, Schwartz, and Clancy, "2 Lazy B Witnesses Got $4,000 Each."

36. "Nancy Brachey, "Stables Fire Called Revenge for Grudge," *Charlotte Observer,* 13 July 1972, 1B; Clary, "Witness in Burning Trial"; "Repression in North Carolina," TJRP, OF 2:8, 7.

37. Clary, "Witness in Burning Trial"; "Repression in North Carolina," TJRP, OF 2:8, 7.

38. Brachey, "Stables Fire Called Revenge for Grudge"; "Repression in North Carolina," TJRP, OF 2:8, 7; Clary, "Witness in Burning Trial"; Wright, "The Lazy B 3 in Black and White," 60.

39. "Repression in North Carolina," TJRP, OF 2:8, 7–8.

40. Brief for Appellants, U.S. Court of Appeals for the Fourth Circuit, Appeal from the U.S. District Court for the Western District of North Carolina, 24 May 1977, 52.

41. Ibid., 54–56; "Repression in North Carolina," TJRP, OF 2:8, 7–8.

42. Brief for Amicus Curiae, 10.

43. "Repression in North Carolina," TJRP, OF 2:8, 10–11.

44. Butch and Shirley Rosen interview; "Repression in North Carolina," TJRP, OF 2:8, 10 11.

45. "Repression in North Carolina," TJRP, OF 2:8, 10–11.

46. Ellison Clary, "Doors Are Bolted for Final Remarks," *Charlotte News,* 14 July 1972, 1B; "Repression in North Carolina," TJRP, OF 2:8, 11.

47. Anonymous source #2, interview.

48. William Walden interview, 24 February 1999; Wright, "The Lazy B 3 in Black and White," 57.

49. Ellison Clary, "Witness Testifies: Grant Elsewhere at Time of Fire," *Charlotte News,* 13 July 1972, 1B; "Repression in North Carolina," TJRP, OF 2:8, 11.

50. Butch and Shirley Rosen interview.

51. "Lazy B Jury Was Fair," *Charlotte Observer,* 27 July 1972, 14A.

52. Walden interview, 24 February 1999.

53. "Political Burglary against Jim Grant," *Southern Patriot* 31 (June 1973): 8.

54. Kathy Sparrow interview, 21 March 1994; Butch and Shirley Rosen interview; "Repression in North Carolina," TJRP, OF 2:8, 11.

55. Anonymous source #3, phone interview by author, 15 May 1994, Charlotte, North Carolina.

56. Butch and Shirley Rosen interview.

57. Butch Rosen goes further, attacking the state's witness as well: "Give me a break. It was four years earlier, and she remembers this guy in an army jacket one day?" He and his wife, Shirley, contend that defense attorneys later discovered that the witness's husband or boyfriend had

gotten into trouble with the police. "They had her," he surmises, and her testimony was a way to buy the police off of him. Butch and Shirley Rosen interview; Anonymous source #2 interview; "Repression in North Carolina," TJRP, OF 2:8, 11.

58. Nancy Brachey, "Lazy B Frame-Up Charged," *Charlotte Observer*, 15 July 1972, 1C; "Repression in North Carolina," TJRP, OF 2:8, 12.

59. "Repression in North Carolina," TJRP, OF 2:8, 12.

60. Nancy Brachey, "3 Men Sentenced in Lazy B Burning," *Charlotte Observer*, 16 July 1972, 1A; "Repression in North Carolina," TJRP, OF 2:8, 12.

61. Butch and Shirley Rosen interview.

62. Brachey, "3 Men Sentenced in Lazy B Burning"; "Repression in North Carolina," TJRP, OF 2:8, 12.

63. Butch and Shirley Rosen interview; Brachey, "3 Men Sentenced in Lazy B Burning."

64. Nancy Brachey, "4th Defendant in Stables Fire Fined," *Charlotte Observer*, 18 July 1972, 1B; Ellison Clary, "Suspended Term Given in Burning," *Charlotte News*, 17 July 1972, 1B.

65. Clary, "Suspended Term Given"; "Repression in North Carolina," TJRP, OF 2:8, 12; Brachey, "4th Defendant in Stables Fire Fined."

66. Ibid.

67. Brief for Appellants, 24 July 1977, 52.

68. Brief for Amicus Curiae, 10.

69. "Repression in North Carolina," TJRP, OF 2:8, 12.

70. Ethridge, Schwartz, and Clancy, "2 Lazy B Witnesses Got $4,000 Each"; "Repression in North Carolina," TJRP, OF 2:8, 12; Brachey, "3 Men Sentenced in Lazy B Burning."

71. Butch and Shirley Rosen interview.

72. Kathy Sparrow interview, 21 March 1994; Butch and Shirley Rosen interview.

73. Butch and Shirley Rosen interview.

74. Brachey, "3 Men Sentenced in Lazy B Burning"; "Repression in North Carolina," TJRP, OF 2:8, 12. Nat Turner, the leader of the infamous 1831 Virginia slave revolt, was the archetype for a dangerously deluded Black man who might lead other Blacks (whom whites viewed as simplistically susceptible to powerful, demagogic leaders) nefariously astray.

75. Ethridge interview, 21 March 1994; Ethridge, Schwartz, and Clancy, "2 Lazy B Witnesses Got $4,000 Each."

76. "Repression in North Carolina," TJRP, OF 2:8, 12; Brachey, "3 Men Sentenced in Lazy B Burning."

77. Clary, "Jury Deliberates Fate of 3 in Stables Fire."

78. Butch and Shirley Rosen interview.

79. Mark Ethridge and Michael Schwartz, "The Months of Bargaining behind Lazy B Testimony," *Charlotte Observer*, 29 December 1974, 1A; "Request for Authorization of Expenditure of Funds for Purchase of Evidence," Stanley Noel, Special Investigator, to Assistant Chief, Enforcement Branch, ATF, Southeast Regional Office, 21 July 1972, Exhibit 2, in "Petition for Pardon," TJRP.

80. Ethridge and Schwartz, "Months of Bargaining."

81. Mark Ethridge and Michael Schwartz, "Warrant Was Out on Lazy B Figure," *Charlotte*

Observer, 21 April 1974, 1A; "Request for Authorization of Expenditure of Funds," Stanley Noel, 21 July 1972, Exhibit 2, "Petition for Pardon," TJRP; Ethridge, Schwartz, and Clancy, "2 Lazy B Witnesses Got $4,000 Each"; "Agent Says He Knew State Wanted Witness," *Charlotte Observer,* 27 April 1974, 4B.

82. Butch and Shirley Rosen interview.

7. The North Carolina Political Prisoners Committee

1. Marvin Sparrow, letter in my possession, February 27, 2023; Kathy Sparrow interview, March 16, 2023. Marvin Sparrow remembers the number of people receiving the NCCPC newsletter as 125.

2. Butch and Shirley Rosen interview; North Carolina Political Prisoners Committee Press Release, 24 July 1972, TJRP, 1:2.

3. Butch and Shirley Rosen interview.

4. Ibid.; "Lazy B Bail Cut Asked," *Charlotte Observer,* 29 July 1972, 1C; North Carolina Political Prisoners Committee News Release: "North Carolina Political Prisoners Committee Is Formed—Unreasonable Bails Are Appealed," 15 August 1972, TJRP, 1:2; "Repression in North Carolina," TJRP, OF 2:8, 14.

5. O'Reilly, *"Racial Matters,"* 264–269.

6. Two days after Harrison's sentencing, a woman identifying herself only as "a member of the Black militants" phoned in a bomb threat on the Superior Court courthouse to "protest the sentencing in the burning of the Lazy B Riding Stables." Police evacuated, closed, and searched the building for the day. Mecklenburg County Manager Glenn Blaisdell told the press of rumored bomb threats during the Charlotte Three trial, and claimed that some of the trial's spectators had been overheard discussing "painting" the courthouse. He believed "painting" was the code word that Hood and Washington testified to mean "burning." The day after the bomb threat, the courthouse tightened security, leaving open only three doors guarded by deputies, who searched packages and bags. Following three additional bomb threats in the late summer and early fall of 1972, the county held an October seminar on court security. In the heightened tension, Snepp thought a deputy sheriff's recommendations—which included a bulletproof bench and a judge's emergency buzzer system—contained "good procedures and suggestions." North Carolina Political Prisoners Committee Press Release, 24 July 1972, TJRP, 1:2; Ellison Clary, "Courthouse Is Evacuated After Bomb Threat," *Charlotte News,* 19 July 1972, 1B; Nancy Brachey, "Courthouse Closed by Bomb Threat," *Charlotte Observer,* 20 July 1972, 1C; Ellison Clary, "Officers, Judges Confer About Trial Disruptions: Court's Security Is Topic," *Charlotte News,* 17 October 1972, 1B.

7. "The Sentences in the Stable Fire," *Charlotte Observer,* 18 July 1972, 14A.

8. "Reddy 'Trial' Was Tragic," *Charlotte Observer,* 21 July 1972, 18A.

9. "Lazy B Jury Was Fair," *Charlotte Observer,* 27 July 1972, 14A. The claim that providing education for African Americans actually leads to an increase in crime (based on the racist presumption that an education will only amplify mischievous behavior among Blacks, who inherently lack proper moral inhibitions) was promoted by some white social scientists in the late nineteenth century. See Muhammad, *The Condemnation of Blackness,* chapter 3.

10. William Pinson, interview by author, 20 November 1992, Charlotte, North Carolina; Reverend Carlyle Marney, Asheville, North Carolina, letter to William Pinson, Charlotte, North Carolina, 12 January 1973, in the possession of William Pinson, Charlotte, North Carolina.

11. "False Charges in 'Lazy B' Case?" *Charlotte Observer,* 9 December 1974, 14A; Wheeler interview; Vivian Ross, "50 Help Out on Legal Fees," *Charlotte Observer,* 31 March 1973, 1B.

12. Wheeler interview.

13. Ethridge interview, 18 March 1994. Edward Gargan, "Raymond M. Wheeler Dies; Documented Hunger of Poor," *New York Times,* 20 January 1982, http://www.nytimes.com/1982/02/20/obituaries/raymond-m-wheeler-dies-documented-hunger-of-poor.html. The Southern Regional Council had a long and distinguished history as a moderate, mostly white, southern civil rights organization. Wheeler himself devoted over three decades championing the cause of the southern poor and African Americans through congressional testimony, documentary films, and books. His work is sometimes credited as one of the motivations for the federal food stamp program. A January 1975 *Charlotte Observer* political cartoon implies the defendants' education renders them far more credible witnesses than Hood and Washington. Displaying silhouettes of the Three (with individual labels reading "poet," "poverty worker," and "chemistry teacher") and Hood and Washington (with individual labels reading "auto thief with long criminal record" and "armed robber and murder suspect"), it asks, "Can you guess which of these two groups, according to the government, are credible witnesses who should be highly paid for their testimony and which are menaces to society who should be jailed?" An October 1978 *Observer* cartoon shows a row of jail cells with "T.J. Reddy, Poet" affixed to one and uses a Dostoevsky quote ("The degree of civilization in a society can be judged by entering its prisons") to suggest the needlessness of his imprisonment.

14. A definitive scholarly overview of this subject has yet to be written, and the list of potential political prisoner cases in the late 1960s and early 1970s United States is virtually impossible to catalog completely. An admittedly partial list would surely have to include those cited in the text as well as George Jackson, the New Haven prosecution of Black Panthers Bobby Seale and Erika Huggins, the Huey Newton murder trial, Cleveland Sellers's Orangeburg trial, LeRoi Jones's Newark riot case, and the antiwar cases of the Fort Hood Three and the Harrisburg Seven (the latter two can be located in Wells, *The War Within,* 99–100, 535–537). Jack Nelson and Ronald J. Ostrow look further at the famous Berrigan brothers in *The FBI and the Berrigans* (New York: Coward, McCann and Geoghegan, 1972), the Milwaukee 14, the D.C. Nine, and the Chicago 15. Larry A. Williamson examines the Catonsville Nine case in "Crime as Rhetoric: The Trial of the Catonsville Nine," in *Popular Trials: Rhetoric, Mass Media, and the Law,* ed. Robert Hariman (Tuscaloosa: Univ. of Alabama Press, 1990). James W. Ely Jr. provides a good look at the Chicago Eight conspiracy trial (which then became the "Chicago Seven" when Black Panther Bobby Seale's indictment was severed from the others shortly after the trial began) in "The Chicago Conspiracy Case," in *American Political Trials,* rev. ed., ed. Michal R. Belknap (Westport, Conn.: Praeger, 1994); David Farber's *Chicago '68* (Chicago: Univ. of Chicago Press, 1988) surveys the Chicago Democratic convention as a whole; there are numerous other works, including Jason Epstein, *The Great Conspiracy Trial: An Essay on Law, Liberty and the Constitution* (New York: Random House, 1970), and Paul Bass and Douglas W. Rae, *Murder in the Model City: The Black*

Panthers, Yale, and the Redemption of a Killer (New York: Basic Books, 2006). Peter Zimroth covers New York's Panther Twenty-One trial in his *Perversions of Justice: The Prosecution and Acquittal of the Panther 21* (New York: Viking, 1974). Williams, *Black Politics/White Power*, includes a look at the Seale and Huggins trial there. Bass and Rae cover the New Haven Nine case in *Murder in the Model City*. For an excellent overview of the Wounded Knee trials, see John William Sayer, *Ghost Dancing the Law: The Wounded Knee Trials* (Cambridge, Mass.: Harvard Univ. Press, 1997). For more on Chicano activist prosecutions, see López, *Racism on Trial*, and Edward J. Escobar, "The Dialectics of Repression: The Los Angeles Police Department and the Chicano Movement, 1968–1971," *Journal of American History* 79 (March 1993): 1483–1514. Marable's *Race, Reform, and Rebellion*, 126–132, also provides a brief overview of the political prisoner phenomenon among African American activists. Eric Cummins's *The Rise and Fall of California's Radical Prison Movement* offers a critical look at liberals' support of such political prisoners, while also examining George Jackson, among others, as does Dan Berger's more recent *Captive Nation*. Bryan Burrough takes a somewhat less sanguine view of radicals and their sometimes violent means in *Days of Rage*.

15. Wiley McKellar, "Violence Trial Defendants All Given Prison Sentences," *Wilmington Morning Star*, 19 October 1972, 2A; "Ben Chavis Gets 34 Years for Conviction in Rioting," *Charlotte News*, 18 October 1972, 1A.

16. Kathy Sparrow interview, 21 March 1994; Marvin Sparrow interview.

17. Marvin Sparrow interview.

18. Kathy Sparrow interview, 21 March 1994; Marvin Sparrow interview.

19. Marvin Sparrow interview.

20. Ibid.

21. Gaillard interview, 15 March 1994; Kathy Sparrow interview, 21 March 1994; Anonymous source #3 interview.

22. Gaillard interview, 15 March 1994.

23. Kathy Sparrow interview, 21 March 1994. Angela Davis had been fired from UCLA because of her communist beliefs in 1969 and then charged with participation in a Black Panther shootout with police in 1970. Davis went underground rather than surrender to arrest, and set off a national manhunt when she was declared one of the FBI's Ten Most Wanted. She was eventually jailed and then freed in 1972 amid a significant media spotlight. Joseph, *Waiting 'Til the Midnight Hour*, 271–275; Marable, *Race, Reform, and Rebellion*, 128. Ron Aldredge and Bob Boyd, "Chavis, 10 Others Go On Trial Today in Arson, Assault," *Charlotte Observer*, 11 September 1972, 4C; "Ben Chavis Gets 34 Years for Conviction in Rioting," *Charlotte News*, 18 October 1978, 1A; Neil A. Lewis, "Seasoned by Civil Rights Struggle: Benjamin Franklin Chavis, Jr.," *New York Times*, 11 April 1993, 20.

24. Hanchett, *Sorting Out the New South City*, 255–256; Randy Peninger, "The Emergence of Black Political Power in Charlotte, North Carolina: The City Council Tenure of Frederick Douglas Alexander, 1965–1974" (Master's thesis, University of North Carolina at Charlotte, 1989), 106–111; Reverend J. B. Humphrey, First Baptist Church, West Pastor, interview by author, 4 November 1992, Charlotte, North Carolina.

25. North Carolina Political Prisoners Committee News Release, "North Carolina Political

Prisoners Committee Is Formed—Unreasonable Bails Are Appealed," 15 August 1972, TJRP, 1:2; Ethridge interview, 18 March 1994.

26. Gaillard interview, 15 March 1994.

27. William Cockerham, "Dixie Fire Frameup, Says Ex-City Man Serving 25 Years," *Hartford Courant*, 16 November 1972, 1, TJRP, 3:2; William Cockerham, "Sentence Called Outrageous," *Hartford Courant*, 17 November 1972, TJRP, 4:1, 1; William Cockerham, "Views on Black Activist Clash," TJRP, 3:2.

28. Cockerham, "Dixie Fire Frameup," TJRP, 3:2; Cockerham, "Sentence Called Outrageous," TJRP, 4:1, 1; Cockerham, "Views on Black Activist Clash," TJRP, 3:2; "Repression in North Carolina," TJRP, OF 2:8; North Carolina Political Prisoners Committee Press Release, 24 July 1972, TJRP, 1:2; North Carolina Political Prisoners Committee News Release, "Black Activists Sentenced in North Carolina," 1 August 1972, TJRP, 1:2; North Carolina Political Prisoners Committee News Release, "North Carolina Political Prisoners Committee Is Formed—Unreasonable Bails Are Appealed," 15 August 1972, TJRP, 1:2; Butch and Shirley Rosen interview.

29. Cockerham, "Dixie Fire Frameup," TJRP, 3:2; Cockerham, "Sentence Called Outrageous," TJRP, 4:1; Cockerham, "Views on Black Activist Clash," TJRP, 3:2.

30. Given their swollen numbers, North Carolina Klan members proudly referred to their state as "Klansville USA." Cunningham, *Klansville, USA*, 3–7.

31. Don O. Noel, Jr., "Where Is Justice in N.C. Courts? James Grant Is 'Guilty' of Black Activism," *Charlotte Observer*, 12 January 1973, 17A.

32. David Kaiser, Hartford, Connecticut, letter to Governor James Holshouser, Raleigh, North Carolina, 25 December 1973, TJRP, 2:3; Grace Kitty, Warehouse Point, Connecticut, letter to Governor-elect James Holshouser, Raleigh, North Carolina, 4 December 1972, TJRP, 2:3.

33. Cockerham, "Views on Black Activist Clash," TJRP, 3:2

34. Governor Meskill, Connecticut, letter to Governor Holshouser, Raleigh, North Carolina, 25 January 1974, TJRP, 2:3.

35. Frye Gaillard, "Sponsors of Angela Davis Concerned Over Impact," *Charlotte Observer*, 8 December 1972, 1B.

36. Frye Gaillard, "Angela Davis Addresses Rally by Telephone," *Charlotte Observer*, 9 December 1972, 1C; Frye Gaillard, "Angela Davis Finally Arrives," *Charlotte Observer*, 10 December 1972, 5C; Tommy Denton, "Rally Hears Angela Davis Through Phone Hookup," *Charlotte News*, 9 December 1972, TJRP, 3:2.

37. U.S. Representative John Conyers, Washington, D.C., letter to Pamela Owens of the North Carolina Political Prisoners Committee, Charlotte, North Carolina, 7 June 1973, TJRP, 1:2.

38. U.S. Senator Lowell Weicker, Washington, D.C., letter to North Carolina Political Prisoners Committee, Charlotte, North Carolina, 14 June 1973, TJRP, 1:2.

39. Dean Duncan, "Heroin Pusher Shot Dead; Police Charge Three Men: One Is Lazy B Witness," *Charlotte Observer*, 31 August 1972, 1C; Pete Stoddard, "A Dangerous Game: Slain Pusher Ranked No. 1," *Charlotte News*, 31 August 1972, 1A, TJRP, 3:2; "2 Men Surrender in Pusher's Death," *Charlotte Observer*, 9 September 1972, 2D; Nancy Brachey, "Three to Face Grand Jury in Oaklawn Man's Murder," 27 September 1972, 2C; Cockerham, "Dixie Fire Frameup," TJRP, 3:2.

40. Dean Duncan, "Arson Witness Held on Drug Charge," *Charlotte Observer*, 22 November 1972, 3C; "Possession Warrant Out for Witness," *Charlotte Observer*, 19 December 1972, 1B; "'Pot' Suspect Awaiting Trial Nabbed Again on Same Charge," *Charlotte Observer*, 20 December 1972, 2B.

41. Wright, "The Lazy B 3 in Black and White," 59.

42. Ellison Clary, "Fund Drive May Free 2 Activists," *Charlotte News*, 15 March 1973, 1B; Ellison Clary, "$75,000 Posted, Activists Free," *Charlotte News*, 16 March 1973, 9A; Nellie Dixon, "Lazy B Fire Defendants Describe Jail Ordeal," *Charlotte Observer*, 27 March 1973, 2B.

43. "Free on Bond—2 of the Charlotte 3," *North Carolina Political Prisoners Committee Newsletter*, vol. 1, no. 7, TJRP, 4:3; Mark Ethridge and Michael Schwartz, "Jail Doors Close on 2 as Friends, Kin Weep," *Charlotte Observer*, 30 January 1974, 1B.

44. Dixon, "Lazy B Fire Defendants Describe Jail Ordeal"; Vivian Ross, "50 Help Out on Legal Fees," *Charlotte Observer*, 31 March 1973, 1B; J.A.C. Dunn, "Poet-Playwright-Artist, and Under $50,000 Bond," *Winston-Salem Journal and Sentinel*, 3 June 1973, TJRP, 3:2; *North Carolina Political Prisoners Committee Newsletter*, vol. 1, no. 8, TJRP, 4:3.

45. "'Charlotte 3' Appeal Made to N.C. Court," *Charlotte News*, 22 August 1973, 6C; "Convictions Blamed on Politics: 'Hostility' Is Cited in Lazy B Appeal," *Charlotte Observer*, 22 August 1973, 1C. For more on Amnesty International's initial involvement in the Charlotte Three case (and subsequently in the Wilmington Ten case), see Kenneth Robert Janken, *The Wilmington Ten: Violence, Injustice, and the Rise of Black Politics in the 1970s* (Chapel Hill: Univ. of North Carolina Press, 2015), 125–127.

46. The court further declared that the trial record provided no evidence of any hostility toward the defendants from Snepp, and that Snepp had done nothing wrong in jury selection. "Convictions Blamed on Politics," *Charlotte Observer*, 22 August 1973, 1C.

47. Ethridge and Schwartz, "Jail Doors Close on 2 as Friends, Kin Weep"; "An Injustice? Lazy B Case Needs Inquiry," *Charlotte Observer*, 23 January 1974, 10A.

48. Ibid.

49. "Gov. Holshouser and the Lazy B," *Charlotte Observer*, 18 February 1974, 20A.

50. Kutler, *The Wars of Watergate*, 464–465; Rick Perlstein, *The Invisible Bridge: The Fall of Nixon and the Rise of Reagan* (New York: Simon and Schuster, 2014), chapters 8–13.

51. "Lazy B: Still a Topic of Concern," *Charlotte Observer*, 21 February 1974, 14A.

52. "Lazy B Terms Are Outrageous," *Charlotte Observer*, 10 February 1974, 2B.

53. Colman McCarthy, "North Carolina Justice," *Washington Post*, 5 March 1974, TJRP, 3:3.

54. Gaillard interview, 15 March 1994; Butch and Shirley Rosen interview; Kathy Sparrow interview, 21 March 1994.

55. Michael Schwartz, phone interview by author, 18 March 2021, Atlanta, Georgia.

56. Mark Ethridge, phone interview by author, 20 July 2021, Charlotte, North Carolina.

57. Butch and Shirley Rosen interview.

58. Schwartz interview.

59. Ethridge interview, 18 March 1994; Michael Schwartz and Mark Ethridge, "Key Lazy B Accounts Have Nine Conflicts," *Charlotte Observer*, 25 March 1974, 1A; "Statement of Purchase of Evidence," Submitted by U.S. Department of the Treasury Special Investigator Stanley Noel to

NOTES TO PAGES 151-154

Assistant Chief, Enforcement Branch, Southeast Region, 22 August 1972, enclosed in "Petition for Pardon," 30 December 1977, TJRP, 1:1; U.S. Marshal Seibert Lechman, Western District of North Carolina, memorandum to Charles Eastman, Acting Chief, Witness Support Unit, United States Marshals Service, 18 July 1972, enclosed in "Petition for Pardon," 30 December 1977, TJRP, 1:1; Ethridge and Schwartz, "The Months of Bargaining."

60. Ethridge interview, 18 March 1994; Schwartz and Ethridge, "Key Lazy B Accounts Have Nine Conflicts"; "Statement of Purchase of Evidence," Submitted by U.S. Department of the Treasury Special Investigator Stanley Noel to Assistant Chief, Enforcement Branch, Southeast Region, 22 August 1972, enclosed in "Petition for Pardon," 30 December 1977, TJRP, 1:1; U.S. Marshal Seibert Lechman, Western District of North Carolina, memorandum to Charles Eastman, Acting Chief, Witness Support Unit, United States Marshals Service, 18 July 1972, enclosed in "Petition for Pardon," 30 December 1977, TJRP, 1:1; Ethridge and Schwartz, "The Months of Bargaining."

61. Ethridge, Schwartz, and Clancy, "2 Lazy B Witnesses Got $4,000 Each"; Ethridge and Schwartz, "Warrant Was Out on Lazy B Figure"; "Agent Says He Knew State Wanted Witness."

62. Schwartz and Ethridge, "Key Lazy B Accounts Have Nine Conflicts."

63. Mardian's other pursued cases included the Harrisburg Seven, the Camden Twenty-Eight, the Seattle Seven, and the VVAW Eight. For more on Mardian, see Lukas, *Nightmare*, chapter 8.

64. Anthony Ripley, "Federal Grand Jury Indicts 7 Nixon Aides on Charges of Conspiracy on Watergate," *New York Times*, 2 March 1974, 1; "Sketches of the Seven Nixon Aides Indicted by the Watergate Grand Jury: Robert Charles Mardian," *New York Times*, 2 March 1974, 16; Ethridge, Schwartz, and Clancy, "2 Lazy B Witnesses Got $4,000 Each"; Donner, *The Age of Surveillance*, 355.

65. "'Charlotte 3' Appeal Made to N.C. Court," *Charlotte News*, 22 August 1973, 6C; "Convictions Blamed on Politics: 'Hostility' Is Cited in Lazy B Appeal," *Charlotte Observer*, 22 August 1973, 1C.

66. Walden interview, 24 February 1999; Walden interview, 5 June 1999.

67. Moore chose not to comment on Hood's sixteen-month-old marijuana charges and nineteen-month-old murder charge that still had no trial date. Ethridge, Schwartz, and Clancy, "2 Lazy B Witnesses Got $4,000 Each."

68. "Lazy B Testimony Wasn't Bought, Treasury Man Says," *Charlotte Observer*, 31 March 1974, 1A; Ethridge and Schwartz, "Warrant Was Out on Lazy B Figure."

69. "Lazy B Testimony Wasn't Bought, Treasury Man Says"; Mark Ethridge and Michael Schwartz, "Lazy B Investigators Urging New Trials and Site in Case," *Charlotte Observer*, 10 April 1974, 1A.

70. Butch and Shirley Rosen interview.

71. Gaillard interview, 15 March 1994.

72. Ethridge interview, 18 March 1994.

73. Ibid.

74. The *Charlotte Observer* articles in this period: Michael Schwartz and Mark Ethridge, "Lazy B Defense Puts Off Retrial Decision," *Charlotte Observer*, 27 March 1974, 1B; Mark Ethridge and Michael Schwartz, "Parole Unit Takes Look at Lazy B," *Charlotte Observer*, 28 March 1974, 1B, TJRP, 2:8; "Lazy B Testimony Wasn't Bought, Treasury Man Says," *Charlotte Observer*, 31 March

1974, 1A; Ethridge and Schwartz, "Lazy B Investigators Urging New Trials and Site in Case"; "Lazy B Witness Shot in Argument," *Charlotte Observer*, 19 April 1974, 1A; Mark Ethridge and Michael Schwartz, "Ex-Official Denies Asking Payments," *Charlotte Observer*, 20 April 1974, 1A; Ethridge and Schwartz, "Warrant Was Out on Lazy B Figure"; Mark Ethridge and Michael Schwartz, "Message Missed: City Police Lose Lazy B Witness," *Charlotte Observer*, 27 April 1974, 1A; "Agent Says He Knew State Wanted Witness."

75. See Appendix 1 for the political cartoon. "The Lazy B: New Facts Call for Review," *Charlotte Observer*, 26 March 1974, 16A; "Lazy B Stables" (political cartoon), *Charlotte Observer*, 26 March 1974, 17A.

76. Ethridge interview, 18 March 1994; Butch and Shirley Rosen interview; Anonymous source #2 interview.

77. "Carolina Panel Weighs Stable Fire Convictions," *New York Times*, 1 April 1974, 16; George W. Goodman, "Today's Court System: A Distillation of Justice?" *Hartford Times*, 16 June 1974, TJRP, 3:3.

78. Michael Schwartz and Mark Ethridge, "Lazy B Defense Puts Off Retrial Decision," *Charlotte Observer*, 27 March 1974, 1B; Mark Ethridge and Michael Schwartz, "Parole Unit Takes Look at Lazy B," *Charlotte Observer*, 28 March 1974, 1B, TJRP, 3:3; Michael Schwartz and Mark Ethridge, "Overturn Lazy B Verdicts—Lawyer," *Charlotte Observer*, 12 July 1974, 1A; William Cockerham, "Pardon Ruled Out for Ex-City Man," *Hartford Courant*, 19 July 1974, 9, TJRP, 3:3.

79. Harriet Doar, "A Conversation with Poet-Artist T.J. Reddy," *Charlotte Observer*, 8 September 1974, 6B; Joe DePriest, "Poet-Prisoner Writes for 'Survival,'" *Shelby Daily Star* (Shelby, N.C.), 31 August 1974, 7B, TJRP, 3:3; S. C. Beinhorn, "Poetry Tool to Get Three Men Out," *Middletown Press* (Middletown, Conn.), 27 August 1974, TJRP, 3:3; J.A.C. Dunn, "Poet in Prison: 'I Am History,' Says T.J. Reddy," *Winston-Salem Journal and Sentinel*, 15 September 1974, C4, TJRP, 3:3; T. J. Reddy, "Spirit Breaking Trying Time," in *Less Than a Score, But a Point* (New York: Vintage Books, 1974), 52–53; Mordecia Strickland, "He Painted in Prison, Even Without Paint, and Kept Doing 'The Work': Now See His Retrospective," *Charlotte Observer*, 26 July 2017, https://www.charlotteobserver.com/entertainment/arts-culture/article163685833.html (accessed 17 June 2019).

80. Michael Schwartz and Mark Ethridge, "Witness in Lazy B Wanted $50,000," *Charlotte Observer*, 11 December 1974, 1A; Mark Ethridge and Michael Schwartz, "Lazy B Deal Not Disclosed—Prosecutors," *Charlotte Observer*, 12 December 1974, 1A.

81. Colman McCarthy, "Is Justice for Sale?" *Washington Post*, 7 December 1974, TJRP, 3:3.

82. Tom Wicker, "Law and Vengeance," *New York Times*, 27 December 1974, 31; Tom Wicker, "Well-Groomed Get Different Justice," *News and Observer* (Raleigh, N.C.), 11 January 1975, 4 (reprinted from *New York Times*). Wicker's quote on Attica comes from Tom Wicker, *A Time to Die* (New York: Quadrangle, 1975), 309. For an excellent historical account of the uprising and its aftermath, see Thompson, *Blood in the Water*.

83. "Aid to Witnesses by U.S. Disclosed: Cash Paid for Testimony in Blacks' Trial for Arson," *New York Times*, 15 December 1974, 33.

84. "False Charges in 'Lazy B' Case?" *Charlotte Observer*, 9 December 1974, 14A; Wheeler interview.

85. See Gaillard, *The Dream Long Deferred,* chapters 9 and 10; or, the more recent account by Matthew Lassiter in his *The Silent Majority.*

86. "Who Was Subversive?" *New York Times,* 1 January 1975, 16.

87. William Cockerham, "CCLU Urges House Unit Review of Grant Case," *Hartford Courant,* 7 February 1975, TJRP, 3:3.

8. "Telling the Truth"

1. On the career of Senator Sam Ervin, see Karl Campbell's *Senator Sam Ervin, Last of the Founding Fathers* (Chapel Hill: Univ. of North Carolina Press, 2007).

2. Schwartz interview.

3. Gaillard interview, 12 May 1994.

4. Schwartz interview.

5. Ethridge interview, 20 July 2021.

6. One should not mistake McKnight, however, for a radical. The Chamber of Commerce's 1963 managed desegregation plan was often his preferred brand of racial progressivism. The fuller text of his 1950 editorial, which claimed segregation could not be defended—bold in the 1950 South for a white newspaperman—included his caution that white supremacy should best be "worn down, bit by bit." Four years before the landmark *Brown* decision, he fretted that the federal government might move faster on racial change than the South could handle. Robin Brabham, "Colbert Augustus (Pete) McKnight," NCPedia, 1991, https://www.ncpedia.org/biography /mcknight-colbert-augustus (accessed 21 July 2020); Gunn, "A Good Place to Make Money," 73–74; Jack Claiborne, *Charlotte Observer: Its Time and Place, 1869-1986* (Chapel Hill: Univ. of North Carolina Press, 1986), 273–276.

7. Schwartz interview; Ethridge interview, 20 July 2021.

8. Gaillard interview, 15 March 1994; Claiborne, *Charlotte Observer,* chapter 10.

9. Mark Ethridge, Michael Schwartz, Frye Gaillard, and Walker Lundy, "New Data Implicates Lazy B Three: Unnamed Man Admits Involvement," *Charlotte Observer,* 25 May 1975, 1A.

10. Ethridge, Schwartz, Gaillard, and Lundy, "New Data Implicates Lazy B Three."

11. Gaillard interview, 12 May 1994; "Payoffs Revealed in Activist Case," *Race Relations Reporter,* 29 April 1974, 3–4. The *Observer's* Ethridge and Schwartz adapted stories for the *Race Relations Reporter.* The *Reporter* also ran an article in July 1973 (vol. 4, no. 14).

12. Gaillard interview, 15 March 1994; Wright, "The Lazy B 3 in Black and White," 59.

13. The Church Committee was formally called the Senate Select Committee on Intelligence Activities. A similar committee took shape in the House of Representatives in the same period under Representative Otis Pike. Alienated former CIA agents also exposed abuses in two memoirs (Philip Agee's *Inside the Company: CIA Diary* [New York: Stonehill, 1975] and John Stockwell's *In Search of Enemies: A CIA Story* [New York: Norton, 1978]). See O'Reilly, "*Racial Matters,*" 348–353; Garrow, *The FBI and Martin Luther King, Jr.,* 9–10; Loch Johnson, *A Season of Inquiry: The Senate Intelligence Investigation* (Lexington: Univ. Press of Kentucky, 1985); Kathryn S. Olmsted, *Challenging the Secret Government: The Post-Watergate Investigations of the CIA and FBI* (Chapel Hill: Univ. of North Carolina Press, 1996); Thomas Borstelmann, *The 1970s: A New*

Global History from Civil Rights to Economic Inequality (Princeton, N.J.: Princeton Univ. Press, 2012), chapter 1. On amnesty for Vietnam War draft evaders, see Frank Kusch, *All American Boys: Draft Dodgers in Canada from the Vietnam War* (Westport, Conn.: Praeger, 2001), 121–129.

14. "Jimmy Carter's Gubernatorial Inaugural Address, 1971," in *Major Problems in the History of the American South*, vol. 2, *The New South*, ed. Paul D. Escott and David R. Goldfield (Lexington, Mass.: D.C. Heath, 1990), 612; Numan V. Bartley, *The Creation of Modern Georgia* (Athens: Univ. of Georgia Press, 1990), 231–232.

15. Even a Chicago police officer agreed with King's negative assessment of the city when an August 1966 civil rights march faced a white mob of four thousand to eight thousand: "This night has to rate as one of the worst in our history. The outrageous cop-fighting we experienced here was about the most vicious I've ever seen in nearly thirty years of service." Alan B. Anderson and George W. Pickering, *Confronting the Color Line: The Broken Promise of the Civil Rights Movement in Chicago* (Athens: Univ. of Georgia Press, 1986), 228–231. See also James Ralph Jr., *Northern Protest: Martin Luther King, Jr., Chicago, and the Civil Rights Movement* (Cambridge, Mass.: Harvard Univ. Press, 1993).

16. Douglas, *Reading, Writing, and Race*, 242.

17. Gaillard, *The Dream Long Deferred*, 149–52.

18. Douglas, *Reading, Writing, and Race*, 251.

19. Gaillard, *The Dream Long Deferred*, 161–166.

20. Applebome, *Dixie Rising*, 154.

21. Gaillard interview, 15 March 1994; Gaillard interview, 12 May 1994.

22. "Die Zeugen der Anklage waren Verbrecher," *Das Thema*, 9 March 1974, TJRP, 3:3; "Zu Gast in Kassel: Robert Grant, Biologe Aus den USA," *Hessische Allgemeine*, 6 January 1976, TJRP, 4:2.

23. Gaillard interview, 15 March 1994. The young Lawrence Wright has gone on to a distinguished journalistic career, capped by a 2007 Pulitzer Prize for his book exploring the rise of Osama bin Laden, *The Looming Tower*.

24. The alleged seventh Lazy B burning participant would only talk to Wright and the *Observer* reporters on the condition that he remained anonymous. Wright thus named him "Brother X," and the *Observer* simply used a variety of terms.

25. Gaillard interview, 15 March 1994.

26. "Lazy B Witness Shot in Argument"; Mark Ethridge and Michael Schwartz, "City Police Lose Lazy B Witness: Message Missed," *Charlotte Observer*, 27 April 1974, 1A.

27. Gaillard interview, 15 March 1994; Ethridge interview, 20 July 2021.

28. Gaillard interview, 15 March 1994.

29. Ethridge, Schwartz, Gaillard, and Lundy, "New Data Implicates Lazy B Three"; Gaillard interview, 15 March 1994.

30. Gaillard interview, 15 March 1994.

31. Ethridge interview, 18 March 1994; Gaillard interview, 15 March 1994; Gaillard interview, 12 May 1994.

32. Ethridge, Schwartz, Gaillard, and Lundy, "New Data Implicates Lazy B Three."

33. Ibid.; Walden interview, 24 February 1999.

34. Ethridge, Schwartz, Gaillard, and Lundy, "New Data Implicates Lazy B Three"; Wright, "The Lazy B 3 in Black and White," 57; Walden interview, 24 February 1999.

35. Gaillard interview, 15 March 1994.

36. Ethridge, Schwartz, Gaillard, and Lundy, "New Data Implicates Lazy B Three"; Gaillard interview, 15 March 1994.

37. Ethridge, Schwartz, Gaillard, and Lundy, "New Data Implicates Lazy B Three"; Gaillard interview, 15 March 1994.

38. Ibid.

39. Gaillard interview, 15 March 1994; Gaillard interview, 12 May 1994. An anonymous source told this author, in fact, that she knew that Reddy had participated in the barn burning. She declined to give specifics about how she knew or allow this author to use her name, but insisted she knew with certainty. (Anonymous source #1, interview by author, 14 March 1994, Charlotte, North Carolina.)

40. Ethridge, Schwartz, Gaillard, and Lundy, "New Data Implicates Lazy B Three."

41. Gaillard interview, 15 March 1994; Ethridge interview, 18 March 1994.

42. Gaillard interview, 15 March 1994.

43. Gaillard interview, 12 May 1994.

44. Ethridge interview, 18 March 1994; Ethridge interview, 20 July 2021.

45. Gaillard interview, 15 March 1994; Marvin Sparrow interview.

46. Gaillard interview, 15 March 1994.

47. "Group Raps Lazy B Article in Observer," Charlotte Observer, 27 May 1975, 1B; Ethridge, Schwartz, Gaillard, and Lundy, "New Data Implicates Lazy B Three."

48. Butch and Shirley Rosen interview; "New Evidence," North Carolina Political Prisoners Committee Newsletter, July/August 1975, TJRP, 4:3; Kathy Sparrow interview, 21 March 1994.

49. Gaillard interview, 12 May 1994.

50. Ethridge interview, 18 March 1994; Gaillard interview, 15 March 1994.

51. Mark Ethridge and Michael Schwartz, "Conviction of Lazy B 3 Upheld; Appeal Planned," Charlotte Observer, 24 September 1975, 1A.

52. Anonymous source #2 interview.

53. Petition for Writ of Habeas Corpus in the U.S. District Court for the Western District of North Carolina, Charlotte Division, 31 March 1976, TJRP, 1:1.

54. Petition for Writ of Habeas Corpus, 31 March 1976.

55. "Judge McMillan Removes Himself from 'Lazy B' Case," Charlotte Post, 23 September 1976, 3; Anonymous source #2 interview.

56. Michael Schwartz, "2 Ordered Back to Jail in Stable Fire," Charlotte Observer, 30 December 1976, 1D.

57. Kathy Sparrow interview, 21 March 1994.

58. "Chavis Cites Federal Involvement: Defense Says Al Hall Lied," Charlotte Post, 14 October 1976, 1. For a full treatment of the subject, see Janken, The Wilmington Ten.

59. "North Carolina Black Leaders Rage Over Treatment of Wilmington 10," Charlotte Post, 16 June 1977, 1; Vernon E. Jordan Jr., "Justice Denied Wilmington 10," Charlotte Post, 22 September 1977, 2.

60. "Rev. Chavis' Letter," *Carolina Journal*, 19 April 1977, 7; Michael Miner, "U.S. 'Prisoners of Conscience,'" *Chicago Sun-Times*, 23 October 1977, TJRP, 4:2.

61. James Baldwin, "An Open Letter to Mr. Carter," *New York Times*, 23 January 1977, IV, 17.

62. "Pardons For Wilmington '10' Close?" *Charlotte Post*, 18 August 1977, 1; Baldwin, "An Open Letter."

63. Wayne King, "North Carolina's Leaders Worried by Blemishes on the State's Image," *New York Times*, 22 February 1978, A1.

64. Gallman, "The Charlotte 3: Where Are They Now?"

65. Miner, "U.S. 'Prisoners of Conscience'"; "Amnesty Group Is Investigating the Cases of 18 U.S. Prisoners," *New York Times*, 7 November 1977, 19.

66. Jeri Harvey, "Governor Jim Hunt's Decision 'Disappoints' Black Community: Governor's Action Was Not Surprising to Most," *Charlotte Post*, 26 January 1978, 1; Hoyle H. Martin Sr., "Does Justice Elude the '10'?" *Charlotte Post*, 26 January 1978, 2; "Pardons for Wilmington '10' Close?" *Charlotte Post*, 18 August 1977, 1.

67. Ibid.

68. Kathy Sparrow interview, 21 March 1994; Butch and Shirley Rosen interview; Ethridge interview, 21 March 1994.

69. Milton Jordan, "Charlotte 3 Lose in Highest Court: Final Appeal Denied," *Charlotte Observer*, 6 October 1978, 1C; "Petition for Pardon," 30 December 1977, TJRP.

70. Milton Jordan, "2 Lazy B Activists Have New Tactics, Old Goals," *Charlotte Observer*, 24 September 1978, 1D; "2 of the Charlotte Three Look Ahead and Behind," *News and Observer* (Raleigh, N.C.), 25 September 1978, 22.

71. Gallman, "The Charlotte 3: Where Are They Now?"; Bob Drogin, "Charlotte 3's Reddy and Grant Return to Prison Cells Today," *Charlotte Observer*, 17 October 1978, 1B.

72. Milton Jordan, "2 Lazy B Activists Have New Tactics, Old Goals," *Charlotte Observer*, 24 September 1978, 1D; "2 of the Charlotte 3 Look Ahead and Behind," *News and Observer* (Raleigh, N.C.), 25 September 1978, 22.

73. Ibid.

74. Beverly Mills, "Hunt Is Using Charlotte 3 for Own Gain, Minister Says," *News and Observer* (Raleigh, N.C.), 25 March 1979, 23; Jack Betts, "The Wilmington 10: A Look Back," *Charlotte Observer*, 17 April 1993, 15A; Eileen Hanson, "Week of Marching Culminated with Demonstration at State Capitol," *Charlotte Post*, 29 March 1979, 1.

75. Eileen Hanson, "Freedom Fair to Benefit Wilmington 10, Charlotte 3," *Charlotte Post*, 19 April 1979, 1; "Freedom Fair," *Charlotte Observer*, 20 April 1979, 3C.

76. "Baptists Urge Convicts' Freedom," *News and Observer* (Raleigh, N.C.), 10 May 1979, 18; "N.C. Church Group Backs Charlotte Three," *Charlotte News*, 2 May 1979; "Commutation Urged," *Charlotte Observer*, 23 May 1979, 4D.

77. Eileen Hanson, "Spirit Square Will Feature an Exhibit of T.J. Reddy's Paintings," *Charlotte Post*, 28 June 1979, 1.

78. "Charlotte Three: Why Imprison Them Now?" *Charlotte Observer*, 26 October 1978, 18A. Italics are the editorialist's.

79. Ibid. The *Observer* also ran a political cartoon on the case two days after Grant and Reddy's re-imprisonment.

80. Henry Scott, "City Council Makes Plea for Charlotte 3: Resolution Asks Hunt to Shorten Sentences," *Charlotte Observer,* 7 November 1978, 1A.

81. "Council Right on Charlotte 3," *Charlotte Observer,* 9 November 1978, 26A.

82. Frye Gaillard, "Charlotte Three: The Real Issue," *Charlotte Observer,* 27 October 1978, 16A.

83. Ibid.

84. Parker had already been paroled again from his April 1978 larceny conviction. Marion A. Ellis and Vanessa Gallman, "Charlotte 3 Sentences Reduced," *Charlotte Observer,* 21 July 1979, 1A; A. L. May, "Hunt Reduces Jail Sentences for Charlotte 3," *Charlotte Observer,* 21 July 1979, 1; Howard Covington, "Governor Says Grant, Reddy Terms Harsh," *Charlotte Observer,* 27 July 1979, 1B.

85. Ibid.

86. Ellis and Gallman, "Charlotte 3 Sentences Reduced"; May, "Hunt Reduces Jail Sentences for Charlotte 3"; Carolyn Sanford, "Hunt's '3' Action Gets Mixed Reviews," *Charlotte News,* 21 July 1979, 8A.

87. Anonymous source #3 interview.

88. Ethridge interview, 21 March 1994.

89. Gaillard interview, 15 March 1994.

90. Ibid.

91. Ibid.

92. Brachey, "3 Men Sentenced in Lazy B Burning."

9. And Then There Were None

1. Robert Conn, "Grant, Reddy Say Thanks to Supporters," *Charlotte Observer,* 20 August 1979, 1C.

2. Marvin Sparrow interview. Grant was in a federal prison in Atlanta serving time for his Raleigh Two conviction.

3. Kathy Sparrow interview, 21 March 1994; Marvin Sparrow interview.

4. Marvin Sparrow interview.

5. Frye Gaillard, "A New Story Starts as Charlotte Three Come Back to Life," *Charlotte Observer,* 29 July 1979, 1A.

6. Marvin Sparrow interview.

7. Ibid.

8. James Ferguson, interviewed by Willie Griffin, 16 May 2008, interview number U-0424 from the Southern Oral History Program Collection (#4007).

9. The economic mobility study was produced by the National Bureau of Economic Research based on research by Harvard University, the University of California, Berkeley, and the U.S. Treasury Department. It examined the probability that children whose parents were in the bottom 20 percent of income could reach the top 20 percent of the national income distribution (Gavin Off, "Charlotte's Poor Struggle to Move Up," *Charlotte Observer,* January 24, 2014, www. charlotteobserver.com/news/state/article209019939.html). Jeffrey Reiman, *The Rich Get Richer and the Poor Get Prison: Ideology, Class, and Criminal Justice* (Boston: Allyn and Bacon, 1998),

29–30, 134–135; Steven R. Donziger, ed. *The Real War on Crime: The Report of the National Criminal Justice Commission* (New York: Harper Perennial, 1996), 115. Michelle Alexander's *The New Jim Crow: Mass Incarceration in the Age of Colorblindness* (New York: New Press, 2010) documents the extraordinary growth of federal funding for the War on Drugs during and immediately after the Reagan administration. Antidrug funding from 1981 to 1991 increased from $86 million for the Drug Enforcement Agency to over $1 billion, and antidrug funding for the FBI grew from $38 million to $181 million in the same period (Alexander, *The New Jim Crow*, 49). The percentage of Americans in prison has only continued to escalate since the 1990s. The American Civil Liberties Union reports that in 2014 there were 909 Americans in jail or prison per 100,000 in the population (American Civil Liberties Union, "The Prison Crisis," https://www.aclu.org/prison-crisis [accessed 18 October 2016]). Other recent works include Hinton, *From the War on Poverty to the War on Crime*; Flamm, *Law and Order*.

10. Reiman, *The Rich Get Richer and the Poor Get Prison*, 134–135. The poverty statistics for the incarcerated have continued tragically apace in the twenty-first century. According to a 2015 Prison Policy Initiative report (based on Bureau of Justice Statistics data), the median annual income for incarcerated people ages 27–42 prior to incarceration was $19,185, while the median annual income for nonincarcerated people ages 27–42 was $32,505 (Prison Policy Initiative, "Prisons of Poverty: Uncovering the Pre-Incarceration Incomes of the Imprisoned," 9 July 2015, Prison Policy Initiative, https://www.prisonpolicy.org/reports/income.html [accessed 15 June 2020]).

11. Perkinson, *Texas Tough*, 2–3.

12. Lipsitz, "The Possessive Investment in Whiteness," 380–381; Center on Budget and Policy Priorites, "Falling Behind: A Report on How Blacks Have Fared Under the Reagan Policies" (Washington, D.C.: Center on Budget and Policy Priorities, 1984); reprint, *Journal of Black Studies* 17 (December 1986): 148–171; Joe Feagin, "Slavery Unwilling to Die: The Background of Black Oppression in the 1980s," *Journal of Black Studies* 17 (December 1986): 173–200. De Jong's *You Can't Eat Freedom* documents how the coterminous modernization of southern agriculture undermined Black southerners' farm labor job opportunities, leading to the significant outmigration of the Black population in many of the communities that had just ostensibly gained political power.

13. Gaillard, "A New Story Starts as Charlotte Three Come Back to Life." For more on the long struggle of the southern working class in the post-1960s, see Timothy Minchin's *Fighting Against the Odds: A History of Southern Labor since World War II* (Gainesville: Univ. Press of Florida, 2006) and *Don't Sleep with Stevens! The J. P. Stevens Campaign and the Struggle to Organize the South, 1963–1980* (Gainesville: Univ. Press of Florida, 2005).

14. Marvin Sparrow interview. Harvard law professor William Stuntz notes that, beginning in the 1960s, African Americans had the double misfortune of experiencing the growth of crime victimization and rising discrimination by police against Black suspects. Ironically, this growing phenomena coincided with the expansion of civic rights outside the court system. William J. Stuntz, *The Collapse of American Criminal Justice* (Cambridge, Mass.: Belknap, 2011), 1–8.

15. Butch and Shirley Rosen interview; Marvin Sparrow interview; Reverend Leon White, former director of the North Carolina-Virginia Commission for Racial Justice, United Church of Christ, interview by author, 15 June 1998, New Bern, North Carolina; Gaillard, "A New Story

Starts as Charlotte Three Come Back to Life"; Jim Morill, "Jim Grant to Be Honored as a Voice for the Voiceless," *Charlotte Observer* online, last modified February 27, 2015, https://www.charlotteobserver.com/news/local/article11252756.html#storylink=cpy; "Meet the 2015 Frank Porter Graham Award Recipients," ACLU North Carolina, last modified January 8, 2015, https://www.acluofnorthcarolina.org/en/news/meet-2015-frank-porter-graham-awards-recipients, February 27, 2015; Martha Quillin, "Jim Grant Is Remembered for Decades of NC Civil Rights Advocacy and Labor Organizing," Raleigh News and Observer, 10 December 2021, www.newsobserver.com/news/local/article256460851.html (accessed 17 March 2023).

16. Bryan Bayles, "T.J. Reddy, First Union Gallery [art exhibition review]," *New Art Examiner,* February 1991, TJRP, 4:5; Bruce Henderson, "TJ Reddy, Artist and Poet Once Jailed as Part of the 'Charlotte Three,' Dies at 73," *Charlotte Observer,* https://www.charlotteobserver.com/living/article229384139.html#storylink=cpy.

17. "Poetraits," *The Leader,* 31 August 1990, 19, TJRP, 4:5.

18. Bayles, "T.J. Reddy, First Union Gallery [art exhibition review]," TJRP, 4:5.

BIBLIOGRAPHY

Primary Sources

GOVERNMENT DOCUMENTS

Brief for Amicus Curiae, Appeal to the United States Court of Appeals for the Fourth Circuit, No. 77–1480, Barry Nakel, Associate Professor of Law, University of North Carolina at Chapel Hill, Chapel Hill, North Carolina, to William K. Slate, Clerk, United States Court of Appeals, Richmond, Virginia, *Thomas James Reddy et al. v. David L. Jones et al.*, 5 May 1977, Law Office of James Ferguson, Charlotte, North Carolina.

"Operational Restraints on Intelligence Collection." Statement of Information, Hearings Before the Committee on the Judiciary, House of Representatives, Ninety-Third Congress, Book VII, Part 1, White House Surveillance Activities and Campaign Activities, 438–442.

Report of the National Advisory Commission on Civil Disorders. New York: E. P. Dutton, 1968.

Select Committee to Study Governmental Operations with Respect to Intelligence Activities. *Final Report, volume III: Supplementary Detailed Staff Reports on Intelligence Activities and the Rights of Americans.* Washington, D.C.: United States Senate, 23 April 1976.

"Special Report, Interagency Committee Intelligence (Ad Hoc)." Statement of Information, Hearings Before the Committee on the Judiciary, House of Representatives, Ninety-Third Congress, Book VII, Part 1, White House Surveillance Activities and Campaign Activities, 384–431.

MANUSCRIPTS

Charlotte-Mecklenburg Public Library, Carolina Room, Charlotte, North Carolina
    Charlotte Desegregation—History Clipping File
    Charlotte Elections—1969 Clipping File
    James Ferguson Clipping File
    Reginald Hawkins Clipping File
    Frank Snepp and Family Clipping File
    Ron Leeper Clipping File
North Carolina State Archives (NCA), Raleigh, North Carolina
    Governor James Holshouser Papers
    Governor Dan K. Moore Papers
    Governor Robert Scott Papers (RSP)
Marvin Sparrow File, Federal Bureau of Investigation, Freedom of Information Act
    Request, owned by Marvin Sparrow
Special Collections, J. Murrey Atkins Library, University of North Carolina at Charlotte
    Kelly Alexander, Sr. Papers (KASP)
    Stanford R. Brookshire Papers (SRBP)
    Charlotte Area Fund Records
    Thomas James Reddy Papers (TJRP)
    Reginald A. Hawkins Papers (RAHP)
Richard B. Thornton Public Library, North Carolina Room, Oxford, North Carolina
    Chavis Family Vertical File
    Granville County School Integration Vertical File

NEWSPAPERS AND PERIODICALS

Carolina Journal (University of North Carolina at Charlotte student newspaper), 1968–
    1979.
The Carolinian (Raleigh, North Carolina), 1947.
Charlotte News, 1960–79.
Charlotte Observer, 1959–1994.
Charlotte Post, 1973–1992.
Durham Morning Herald, 1970.
News and Observer (Raleigh, North Carolina), 1970–1979.
New Times, 1975.
New York Times, 1965–1993.
Newsweek, 1970.

Oxford Public Ledger, 1970–1971.
Southern Patriot, 1970–75.
Time, 1970.

INTERVIEWS

Anonymous source #1. Interview by author, 14 March 1994, Charlotte, North Carolina.

Anonymous Source #2. Interview by author, 14 April 1994, Charlotte, North Carolina.

Anonymous Source #3. Phone interview by author, 15 May 1994, Charlotte, North Carolina.

Chavis, Benjamin. Interview by Bridgette Sanders and Lois Stickel, 7 February 2005, Charlotte, North Carolina. J. Murrey Atkins Library, University of North Carolina at Charlotte, http://nsv.uncc.edu/interview/uach0006 (accessed 1 July 2015).

Clark, Ramsey. Interview by Harri Baker, 3 June 1969, Falls Church, Virginia. Oral History Collection, Lyndon Baines Johnson Library. http://www.lbjlibrary.net/assets /documents/archives/oral_histories/clark_r/clark-r5.pdf (accessed 14 June 2010).

Currin, Hugh, Mayor of Oxford, North Carolina. Interview by author, 12 May 1998, Oxford, North Carolina.

Dae, Dorothy. Interview by Bridgette Sanders and Lois Stickel, 11 October 2004, Charlotte, North Carolina. J. Murrey Atkins Library, University of North Carolina at Charlotte. http://newsouthvoices.uncc.edu/interview/uada0009 (accessed 30 July 2015).

Ethridge, Mark. Interview by author, 18 March 1994, Charlotte, North Carolina.

———. Phone interview by author, 21 March 1994, Charlotte, North Carolina.

———. Phone interview by author, 20 July 2021, Charlotte, North Carolina.

Ferguson, James. Interview by Rudy Acree, 3 March 1992, Charlotte, North Carolina. Southern Historical Collection, Louis Round Wilson Library. http://dc.lib.unc. edu/cdm/ref/collection/sohp/id/12595 (accessed 12 October 2017).

Ferguson, James. Interview by Willie Griffin, 16 May 2008. SOHP, Southern Historical Collection, UNC Chapel Hill.

Finch, Judge Daniel F. Interview by author, 13 May 1998, Oxford, North Carolina.

Gaillard, Frye. Interview by author, 15 March 1994, Charlotte, North Carolina.

Gaillard, Frye. Phone interview by author, 12 May 1994, Charlotte, North Carolina.

Hamrick, Betty Jo, Myers Park Baptist Church Deacon. Interview by author, 19 July 1993, Charlotte, North Carolina.

Hawkins, Reginald. Interview by Melinda Desmarais, 11 June 2001, Tega Cay, South Carolina. J. Murrey Atkins Library, University of North Carolina at Charlotte. http://newsouthvoices.uncc.edu/interview/ohha0077 (accessed 1 July 2015).

Humphrey, Reverend J. B., First Baptist Church, West pastor. Interview by author, 4 November 1992, Charlotte, North Carolina.

Hunt, Ralph A., Sr. Interview by author, 9 June 1998, Durham, North Carolina.

Jones, J. Charles. Interview. New South Voices. May 18, 2005. http://newsouthvoices. uncc.edu/interview/bbj00025 (accessed 30 June 2017).

Owens, Reverend Eugene, former Myers Park Baptist Church senior pastor. Interview by author, 9 December 1992, Charlotte, North Carolina.

Pendergrass, Reverend Preston, Antioch Baptist Church pastor. Interview by author, 2 December 1992, Charlotte, North Carolina.

Pinson, William. Interview by author, 20 November 1992, Charlotte, North Carolina.

Ragland, Tom, former city manager for Oxford, North Carolina. Interview by author, 12 May 1998, Oxford, North Carolina.

Riddick, Reverend Leon C., former Mount Carmel Baptist Church pastor. Interview by author, 11 January 1993, Charlotte, North Carolina.

Rosen, Butch and Shirley. Interview by author, 31 March 1994, Charlotte, North Carolina.

Schwartz, Michael. Phone interview by author, 18 March 2021, Atlanta, Georgia.

Sparrow, Kathy. Interview by author, 21 March 1994, Charlotte, North Carolina.

———. Phone interview by author, 16 March 2023, Charlotte, North Carolina.

Sparrow, Marvin. Interview by author, 9 June 1998, Durham, North Carolina.

Walden, William, former Bureau of Alcohol, Tobacco, and Firearms special agent. Interview by author, 24 February 1999, Morganton, North Carolina.

———, former Bureau of Alcohol, Tobacco, and Firearms special agent. Phone interview by author, 5 June 1999.

Wheeler, Julie. Interview by author, 14 March 1994, Charlotte, North Carolina.

White, Reverend Leon, former director of the North Carolina-Virginia Commission for Racial Justice, United Church of Christ. Interview by author, 15 June 1998, New Bern, North Carolina.

White, Nathan E., former assistant police chief of Oxford, North Carolina. Interview by author, 9 June 1998, Oxford, North Carolina.

Wright, George. Interview by author, 13 May 1998, Oxford, North Carolina.

OTHER PRIMARY SOURCES

City Directory: Oxford, North Carolina. Livonia, Mich.: R. L. Polk, 1997.

Federal Bureau of Investigation file on the Black Panther Party, North Carolina. Microfilm collection, 2 reels. Wilmington, Del.: Scholarly Resources, 1986.

The Gallup Poll: Public Opinion, 1935–1971, vol. 3: *1959–1971.* New York: Random House, 1972.

Granville County Courthouse Records, Oxford, North Carolina.

Hays Collection. Richard B. Thornton Public Library, North Carolina Room, Oxford, North Carolina.

Marney, Reverend Carlyle, Asheville, North Carolina. Letter to William Pinson, Charlotte, North Carolina, 12 January 1973. In the possession of William Pinson, Charlotte, North Carolina.

Reddy, T. J. *Less Than a Score, But a Point.* New York: Vintage Books, 1974.

Secondary Sources

Agee, Philip. *Inside the Company: CIA Diary.* New York: Stonehill, 1975.

Alexander, Michelle. *The New Jim Crow: Mass Incarceration in the Age of Colorblindness.* New York: New Press, 2010.

Alinsky, Saul. *Reveille for Radicals.* Chicago: Univ. of Chicago Press, 1946.

———. *Rules for Radicals: A Practical Primer for Realistic Radicals.* New York: Vintage Books, 1971.

Anderson, Alan B., and George W. Pickering, *Confronting the Color Line: The Broken Promise of the Civil Rights Movement in Chicago.* Athens: Univ. of Georgia Press, 1986.

Anderson, Martin. *The Federal Bulldozer: A Critical Analysis of Urban Renewal, 1948–1962.* Cambridge, Mass.: Massachusetts Institute of Technology Press, 1964.

Anderson, Terry. *The Movement and the Sixties: Protest in America from Greensboro to Wounded Knee.* New York: Oxford Univ. Press, 1995.

Applebome, Peter. *Dixie Rising: How the South Is Shaping American Values, Politics, and Culture.* New York: Harcourt and Brace, 1997.

Ashmore, Susan Youngblood. *Carry It On: The War on Poverty and the Civil Rights Movement in Alabama, 1964–1972.* Athens: Univ. of Georgia Press, 2008.

Avila, Eric, and Mark Rose. "Race, Culture, Politics and Urban Renewal." *Journal of Urban History* 35 (2009): 335–347.

Ayers, Edward L. *The Promise of the New South: Life After Reconstruction.* New York: Oxford Univ. Press, 1992.

———. *Vengeance and Justice: Crime and Punishment in the 19th-Century American South.* New York: Oxford Univ. Press, 1984.

Badger, Tony. "Southerners Who Refused to Sign the Southern Manifesto." *Historical Journal* 42 (June 1999): 517–534.

Bacciocca, Edward. *The New Left in America: Reform to Revolution, 1956 to 1970.* Stanford, Calif.: Hoover Institution, 1974.

Barber, David. *A Hard Rain Fell: SDS and Why It Failed.* Jackson: Univ. Press of Mississippi, 2010.

Bartley, Numan V. *The Creation of Modern Georgia.* Athens: Univ. of Georgia Press, 1990.

———. *The New South, 1945–1980: The Story of the South's Modernization.* Baton Rouge: Louisiana State Univ. Press, 1995.

———. *The Rise of Massive Resistance: Race and Politics in the South During the 1950s.* Baton Rouge: Louisiana State Univ. Press, 1969.

Bass, Jonathan. *Blessed Are the Peacemakers: Martin Luther King, Jr., Eight White Religious Leaders, and the "Letter from Birmingham Jail."* Baton Rouge: Louisiana State Univ. Press, 2001.

Bass, Paul, and Douglas W. Rae. *Murder in the Model City: The Black Panthers, Yale, and the Redemption of a Killer.* New York: Basic Books, 2006.

Bayor, Ronald. *Race and the Shaping of Twentieth-Century Atlanta.* Chapel Hill: Univ. of North Carolina Press, 2000.

Beifuss, Joan Turner. *At the River I Stand: Memphis, the 1968 Strike, and Martin Luther King.* Memphis, Tenn.: B and W Books, 1985.

Belew, Kathleen. *Bring the War Home: The White Power Movement and Paramilitary America.* Cambridge, Mass.: Harvard Univ. Press, 2018.

Belknap, Michal R. *Federal Law and Southern Order: Racial Violence and Constitutional Conflict in the Post-Brown South.* Athens: Univ. of Georgia Press, 1995.

Berger, Dan. *Captive Nation: Black Prison Organizing in the Civil Rights Era.* Chapel Hill: Univ. of North Carolina Press, 2014.

———. *Outlaws of America: The Weather Underground and the Politics of Solidarity.* Oakland, Calif.: AK Press, 2005.

Berry, Mary Frances. *Black Resistance, White Law: A History of Constitutional Racism in America.* New York: Penguin Press, 1994.

Betten, Neil, and William E. Hershey. "Conflict Approach to Community Organizing: Saul Alinsky and the CIO." In *The Roots of Community Organizing, 1917–1939.* Philadelphia: Temple Univ. Press, 1990.

Billingsley, William J. *Communists on Campus: Race, Politics, and the Public University in Sixties North Carolina.* Athens: Univ. of Georgia Press, 1999.

Bingham, Clara. *Witness to the Revolution: Radicals, Resisters, Vets, Hippies, and the Year America Lost Its Mind and Found Its Soul.* New York: Random House, 2016.

Blackmon, Douglas A. *Slavery by Another Name: The Re-Enslavement of Black Americans from the Civil War to World War II.* New York: Doubleday, 2008.

Bloom, Joshua, and Waldo Martin. *Black Against Empire: The History and Politics of the Black Panther Party.* Oakland: Univ. of California Press, 2014.

Borstelmann, Thomas. *The 1970s: A New Global History from Civil Rights to Economic Inequality*. Princeton, N.J.: Princeton Univ. Press, 2012.

Branch, Taylor. *Parting the Waters: America in the King Years, 1954–1963*. New York: Touchstone, 1988.

Breines, Wini. *Community and Organization in the New Left, 1962–1968: The Great Refusal*. New Brunswick, N.J.: Rutgers Univ. Press, 1989.

Brown, Scot. *Fighting for US: Maulana Korenga, the US Organization, and Black Cultural Nationalism*. New York: New York Univ. Press, 2005.

Brown-Nagin, Tomiko. *Courage to Dissent: Atlanta and the Long History of the Civil Rights Movement*. New York: Oxford Univ. Press, 2011.

Bumgarner-Davis, Marianne. "Rending the Veil: Desegregation in Charlotte, 1954–1975." Ph.D. diss., University of North Carolina at Chapel Hill, 1995.

Burrough, Bryan. *Days of Rage: America's Radical Underground, the FBI, and the Forgotten Age of Revolutionary Violence*. New York: Penguin, 2016.

Calder, James D. "Presidents and Crime Control: Kennedy, Johnson and Nixon and the Influences of Ideology." *Presidential Studies Quarterly* 12 (1982): 574–589.

Camp, Jordan T. *Incarcerating the Crisis: Freedom Struggles and the Rise of the Neoliberal State*. Berkeley: Univ. of California Press, 2016.

Campbell, Karl. *Senator Sam Ervin, Last of the Founding Fathers*. Chapel Hill: Univ. of North Carolina Press, 2007.

Caplan, Gerald M. "Criminology, Criminal Justice, and the War on Crime." *Criminology* 14 (May 1976): 3–16.

———. "Reflections on the Nationalization of Crime, 1964–1968." *Law and the Social Order* (1973): 583–635.

Carson, Clayborne. *In Struggle: SNCC and the Black Awakening of the 1960s*. Cambridge, Mass.: Harvard Univ. Press, 1981.

Carter, Dan T. *The Politics of Rage: George Wallace, the Origins of the New Conservatism, and the Transformation of American Politics*. New York: Simon and Schuster, 1995.

Cash, W. J. *The Mind of the South*. London: Thames and Hudson, 1971.

Cecelski, David S. *Along Freedom Road: Hyde County, North Carolina, and the Fate of Black Schools in the South*. Chapel Hill: Univ. of North Carolina Press, 1994.

Center on Budget and Policy Priorities. "Falling Behind: A Report on How Blacks Have Fared Under the Reagan Policies." Washington, D.C.: Center on Budget and Policy Priorities, 1984; reprint, *Journal of Black Studies* 17 (December 1986): 148–171.

Chafe, William. *Civilities and Civil Rights: Greensboro, North Carolina, and the Black Struggle for Freedom*. New York: Oxford Univ. Press, 1981.

———. "The End of One Struggle, the Beginning of Another." In *The Civil Rights Movement in America*, ed. Charles Eagles. Jackson: Univ. Press of Mississippi, 1986.

———. *The Unfinished Journey: America Since World War II.* New York: Oxford Univ. Press, 1995.

Churchill, Ward, and Jim Vander Wall. *Agents of Repression: The FBI's Secret Wars Against the Black Panther Party and the American Indian Movement.* Boston: South End Press, 1988.

Claiborne, Jack. *The Charlotte Observer: Its Time and Place, 1869–1986.* Chapel Hill: Univ. of North Carolina Press, 1986.

Clayton, Bruce. *W. J. Cash: A Life.* Baton Rouge: Louisiana State Univ. Press, 1991.

Cleaver, Eldridge. *Soul on Ice.* New York: Dell, 1968.

Cobb, James C. *The Selling of the South: The Southern Crusade for Industrial Development, 1936–1980.* Baton Rouge: Louisiana State Univ. Press, 1982.

———. *The South and America Since World War II.* New York: Oxford Univ. Press, 2011.

———. "The Sunbelt South: Industrialization in Regional, National, and International Perspective." In *Searching for the Sunbelt: Historical Perspectives on a Region,* edited by Raymond A. Mohl, 25–31. Athens: Univ. of Georgia Press, 1993.

Cohen, Robert, and Reginald E. Zelnik, eds. *The Free Speech Movement: Reflections on Berkeley in the 1960s.* Berkeley: Univ. of California Press, 2002.

Cohen, William. "Negro Involuntary Servitude in the South, 1865–1940: A Preliminary Analysis." *Journal of Southern History* 42 (February 1976): 31–60.

Coleman, Kate, and Paul Avery. "The Party's Over: How Huey Newton Created a Street Gang at the Center of the Black Panther Party." *New Times,* 10 July 1978.

Collier, Peter, and David Horowitz. *Destructive Generation: Second Thoughts About the 60s.* New York: Touchstone, 1990.

Cone, James H. *Martin and Malcolm and America: A Dream or a Nightmare.* Maryknoll, N.Y.: Orbis, 1991.

Connolly, N.D.B. *A World More Concrete: Real Estate and the Remaking of Jim Crow South Florida.* Chicago: Univ. of Chicago Press, 2014.

Countryman, Matthew. *Up South: Civil Rights and Black Power in Philadelphia.* Philadelphia: Univ. of Pennsylvania Press, 2006.

Crow, Jeffrey J., Paul D. Escott, and Flora Hatley. *A History of African Americans in North Carolina.* Raleigh, N.C.: Division of Archives and History, North Carolina Department of Cultural Resources, 1992.

Cummins, Eric. *The Rise and Fall of California's Radical Prison Movement.* Stanford, Calif.: Stanford Univ. Press, 1994.

Cunningham, David. *Klansville, U.S.A.: The Rise and Fall of the Civil Rights-Era Ku Klux Klan.* New York: Oxford Univ. Press, 2013.

———. *There's Something Happening Here: The New Left, the Klan, and FBI Counterintelligence.* Berkeley: Univ. of California Press, 2004.

Curry, Constance. *Deep in Our Hearts: Nine White Women in the Freedom Movement.* Athens: Univ. of Georgia Press, 2000.

———. *Silver Rights.* Chapel Hill, N.C.: Algonquin Books, 1995.

Dallek, Robert. *Flawed Giant: Lyndon Johnson and His Times, 1961–1973.* New York: Oxford Univ. Press, 1998.

Davis, James Kirkpatrick. *Assault on the Left: The FBI and the Sixties Antiwar Movement.* Westport, Conn.: Praeger, 1997.

Davis, Thomas J. "Race, Identity, and the Law: Plessy v. Ferguson (1896)." In *Race on Trial: Law and Justice in American History,* edited by Annette Gordon-Reed. New York: Oxford Univ. Press, 2002.

de Jong, Greta. *You Can't Eat Freedom: Southerners and Social Justice After the Civil Rights Movement.* Chapel Hill: Univ. of North Carolina Press, 2016.

Dittmer, John. *Local People: The Struggle for Civil Rights in Mississippi.* Urbana: Univ. of Illinois Press, 1994.

Donner, Frank. *The Age of Surveillance: The Aims and Methods of America's Political Intelligence System.* New York: Vintage Books, 1980.

———. *Protectors of Privilege: Red Squads and Police Repression in Urban America.* Berkeley: Univ. of California Press, 1990.

Donziger, Steven R., ed. *The Real War on Crime: The Report of the National Criminal Justice Commission.* New York: Harper Perennial, 1996.

Douglas, Davison M. *Reading, Writing, and Race: The Desegregation of the Charlotte Schools.* Chapel Hill: Univ. of North Carolina Press, 1995.

Dray, Philip. *At the Hands of Persons Unknown: The Lynching of Black America.* New York: Random House, 2002.

Dudziak, Mary. *Cold War Civil Rights: Race and the Image of American Democracy.* Princeton, N.J.: Princeton Univ. Press, 2011.

Eagles, Charles, ed. *The Civil Rights Movement in America.* Jackson: Univ. Press of Mississippi, 1986.

Ely, James W. "The Chicago Conspiracy Case." In *American Political Trials,* rev. ed., edited by Michal R. Belknap. Westport, Conn.: Praeger, 1994.

Epstein, Jason. *The Great Conspiracy Trial: An Essay on Law, Liberty and the Constitution.* New York: Random House, 1970.

Ervin, Michael Worth. "'Public Order Is Even More Important Than the Rights of Negroes': Race and Recreation in Charlotte, North Carolina, 1927–1973." Master's thesis, University of North Carolina at Charlotte, 2015.

Escott, Paul D., and David R. Goldfield, eds. *Major Problems in the History of the American South.* Vol. 2: *The New South.* Lexington, Mass.: D.C. Heath, 1990.

Eskew, Glenn. *But for Birmingham: The Local and National Movements in the Civil Rights Struggle.* Chapel Hill: Univ. of North Carolina Press, 1997.

Escobar, Edward J. "The Dialectics of Repression: The Los Angeles Police Department and the Chicano Movement, 1968–1971." *Journal of American History* 79 (March 1993): 1483–1514.

Fairclough, Adam. *To Redeem the Soul of America: The Southern Christian Leadership Conference and Martin Luther King, Jr.* Athens: Univ. of Georgia Press, 1987.

Farber, David. *The Age of Great Dreams: America in the 1960s.* New York: Hill and Wang, 1994.

Farber, David. *Chicago '68.* Chicago: Univ. of Chicago Press, 1988.

Feagin, Joe. "Slavery Unwilling to Die: The Background of Black Oppression in the 1980s." *Journal of Black Studies* 17 (December 1986): 173–200.

Fergus, Devin. *Liberalism, Black Power, and the Making of American Politics, 1965–1980.* Athens: Univ. of Georgia Press, 2009.

Ferguson, Karen. *Black Politics in New Deal Atlanta.* Chapel Hill: Univ. of North Carolina Press, 2002.

Finckenauer, James O. "Crime as a National Political Issue, 1964–1976: From Law and Order to Domestic Tranquility." *Crime and Delinquency* 24 (January 1978): 13–27.

Flamm, Michael W. *In the Heat of the Summer: The New York Riots of 1964 and the War on Crime.* Philadelphia: Univ. of Pennsylvania Press, 2017.

———. *Law and Order: Street Crime, Civil Unrest, and the Crisis of Liberalism in the 1960s.* New York: Columbia Univ. Press, 2005.

Foner, Eric. *Reconstruction: America's Unfinished Revolution, 1863–1877.* New York: Harper and Row, 1988.

Frankel, Marvin, and Gary Naftalis. *The Grand Jury: An Institution on Trial.* New York: Hill and Wang, 1977.

Gaillard, Frye. *The Dream Long Deferred.* Chapel Hill: Univ. of North Carolina Press, 1988.

Garrow, David. *Bearing the Cross: Martin Luther King, Jr., and the Southern Christian Leadership Conference.* New York: Morrow, 1986.

———. *The FBI and Martin Luther King, Jr.: From "Solo" to Memphis.* New York: Norton, 1981.

Gelfand, Mark. *A Nation of Cities: The Federal Government and Urban America, 1933–1968.* New York: Oxford Univ. Press, 1975.

Goldfield, David. *Black, White, and Southern: Race Relations and Southern Culture, 1940 to the Present.* Baton Rouge: Louisiana State Univ. Press, 1990.

———. "A Place to Come To." In *Charlotte, North Carolina: The Global Evolution of a New South City,* edited by William Graves and Heather A. Smith, 10–23. Athens: Univ. of Georgia Press, 2010.

———. *Promised Land: The South Since 1945.* Wheeling, Ill.: Harlan Davidson, 1987.

———. *Region, Race, and Cities: Interpreting the Urban South.* Baton Rouge: Louisiana State Univ. Press, 1997.

Goldstein, Robert Justin. *Political Repression in Modern America: From 1870 to the Present.* Boston: G. K. Hall, 1978.

Gordon, Colin. *Mapping Decline: St. Louis and the Fate of the American City.* Philadelphia: Univ. of Pennsylvania Press, 2008.

Gordon-Reed, Annette, ed. *Race on Trial: Law and Justice in American History.* New York: Oxford Univ. Press, 2002.

Gosse, Van. *Rethinking the New Left: An Interpretive History.* New York: Palgrave Macmillan, 2005.

Graves, William, and Heather A. Smith, eds. *Charlotte, North Carolina: The Global Evolution of a New South City.* Athens: Univ. of Georgia Press, 2010.

Greenberg, Jack. *Crusaders in the Courts: How a Dedicated Band of Lawyers Fought for the Civil Rights Revolution.* New York: Basic Books, 1994.

Greenwood, Janette Thomas. *Bittersweet Legacy: The Black and White "Better Classes" in Charlotte, 1850–1910.* Chapel Hill: Univ. of North Carolina Press, 1994.

Gunn, Julia. "'A Good Place to Make Money': Business, Labor and Civil Rights in Twentieth-Century Charlotte." Ph.D. diss., University of Pennsylvania, 2014.

Haines, Herbert H. *Black Radicals and the Civil Rights Mainstream, 1954–1970.* Knoxville: Univ. of Tennessee Press, 1988.

Halberstam, David. *The Children.* New York: Random House, 1998.

Hanchett, Thomas. "Salad-Bowl Suburbs: A History of Charlotte's East Side and South Boulevard Immigrant Corridors." In *Charlotte, North Carolina: The Global Evolution of a New South City,* edited by William Graves and Heather A. Smith, 247–262. Athens: Univ. of Georgia Press, 2010.

———. *Sorting Out the New South City: Race, Class, and Urban Development in Charlotte, 1875–1975.* Chapel Hill: Univ. of North Carolina Press, 1998.

Harris, Richard. *The Fear of Crime.* New York: Praeger, 1969.

Hatstedt, Glenn. *Spies, Wiretaps, and Secret Operations: An Encyclopedia of American Espionage.* Santa Barbara, Calif.: ABC-CLIO, 2011.

Highsmith, Andrew, "Demolition Means Progress: Urban Renewal, Local Politics, and State-Sanctioned Ghetto Formation in Flint, Michigan." *Journal of Urban History* 35 (2009): 348–368.

Hill, Lance. *The Deacons for Defense: Armed Resistance and the Civil Rights Movement.* Chapel Hill: Univ. of North Carolina Press, 2004.

Hinds, Lennox. *Illusions of Justice: Human Rights Violations in the United States.* Iowa City: University of Iowa School of Social Work, 1978.

Hinton, Elizabeth. *America on Fire: The Untold History of Police Violence and Black Rebellion Since the 1960s.* New York: Liveright, 2021.

———. *From the War on Poverty to the War on Crime: The Making of Mass Incarceration in America.* Cambridge, Mass.: Harvard Univ. Press, 2016.

Hirsch, Arnold R. *Making the Second Ghetto: Race and Housing in Chicago, 1940–1960.* Cambridge: Cambridge Univ. Press, 1983.

Hoff, Joan. *Nixon Reconsidered.* New York: Basic Books, 1994.

Hoffer, Williamjames Hull. *Plessy v. Ferguson: Race and Inequality in Jim Crow America.* Lawrence: Univ. Press of Kansas, 2012.

Hogan, Wesley C. *Many Minds, One Heart: SNCC's Dream for a New America.* Chapel Hill: Univ. of North Carolina Press, 2007.

Holliman, Irene. "From Crackertown to Model City? Urban Renewal and Community Building in Atlanta, 1963–1966." *Journal of Urban History* 35 (2009): 383.

Honey, Michael. *Going Down Jericho Road: The Memphis Strike, Martin Luther King's Last Campaign.* New York: Norton, 2008.

———. *Southern Labor and Black Civil Rights: Organizing Memphis Workers.* Urbana: Univ. of Illinois Press, 1993.

———. *To the Promised Land: Martin Luther King and the Fight for Economic Justice.* New York: Norton, 2018.

Horwitt, Sanford D. *Let Them Call Me Rebel: Saul Alinsky—His Life and Legacy.* New York: Knopf, 1989.

Houston, Benjamin. *The Nashville Way: Racial Etiquette and the Struggle for Social Justice in a Southern City.* Athens: Univ. of Georgia Press, 2012.

Isserman, Maurice. *If I Had a Hammer . . . The Death of the Old Left and the Birth of the New Left.* New York: Basic Books, 1987.

Jackson, George. *Soledad Brother: The Prison Letters of George Jackson.* New York: Coward, McCann, 1970.

Jackson, Kenneth. *Crabgrass Frontier: The Suburbanization of the United States.* New York: Oxford Univ. Press, 1985.

Janken, Kenneth Robert. *The Wilmington Ten: Violence, Injustice, and the Rise of Black Politics in the 1970s.* Chapel Hill: Univ. of North Carolina Press, 2015.

Jeffries, Judson, ed. *Comrades: A Local History of the Black Panther Party.* Bloomington: Indiana Univ. Press, 2007.

———. *Huey P. Newton: The Radical Theorist.* Jackson: Univ. Press of Mississippi, 2002.

Johnson, Loch. *A Season of Inquiry: The Senate Intelligence Investigation.* Lexington: Univ. Press of Kentucky, 1985.

Jones, Charles E., ed. *The Black Panther Party (Reconsidered).* Baltimore, Md.: Black Classic Press, 1998.

Joseph, Peniel E. *Stokely: A Life.* New York: Basic Civitas, 2014.

———. *Waiting 'Til the Midnight Hour: A Narrative History of Black Power in America.* New York: Owl Books, 2006.

Kelley, Robin D. G. *Race Rebels: Culture, Politics, and the Black Working Class.* New York: Free Press, 1994.

Kennedy, Randall. *Race, Crime and the Law.* New York: Pantheon, 1997.

King, Martin Luther, Jr. *Stride Toward Freedom: The Montgomery Story.* New York: Harper, 1958.

———. *Where Do We Go from Here: Chaos or Community?* New York: Harper and Row, 1967.

Kinney, Joy Marie. "The Gradual Integration of Schools in Granville County, North Carolina." December 1987. Richard B. Thornton Library, North Carolina Room, Oxford, North Carolina.

Klatch, Rebecca. *A Generation Divided: The New Left, the New Right, and the 1960s.* Berkeley: Univ. of California Press, 1999.

Korstad, Robert R., and James L. Leloudis. *To Right These Wrongs: The North Carolina Fund and the Battle to End Poverty and Inequality in 1960s America.* Chapel Hill: Univ. of North Carolina Press, 2010.

Kruse, Kevin M. *White Flight: Atlanta and the Making of Modern Conservatism.* Princeton, N.J.: Princeton Univ. Press, 2005.

Kusch, Frank. *All American Boys: Draft Dodgers in Canada from the Vietnam War.* Westport, Conn.: Praeger, 2001.

Kutler, Stanley. *The Wars of Watergate: The Last Crisis of Richard Nixon.* New York: Norton, 1990.

Lasch, Christopher. *The Culture of Narcissism: American Life in an Age of Diminishing Expectations.* New York: Warner, 1979.

Lassiter, Matthew D. "Searching for Respect: From 'New South' to 'World Class' at the Crossroads of the Carolinas." In *Charlotte, North Carolina: The Global Evolution of a New South City,* edited by William Graves and Heather A. Smith, 24–49. Athens: Univ. of Georgia Press, 2010.

Lassiter, Matthew D. *The Silent Majority: Suburban Politics in the Sunbelt South.* Princeton, N.J.: Princeton Univ. Press, 2006.

Lawson, Steven F. *In Pursuit of Power: Southern Blacks and Electoral Politics, 1965–1982.* New York: Columbia Univ. Press, 1985.

———. *Running for Freedom: Civil Rights and Black Politics in America Since 1941*. New York: McGraw Hill, 1997.

Lazerow, Jama, and Yohuru Williams, eds. *In Search of the Black Panther Party: New Perspectives on a Revolutionary Movement*. Durham, N.C.: Duke Univ. Press, 2006.

Leach, Damaria. "Progress Under Pressure: Changes in Charlotte Race Relations, 1955–1965." Master's thesis, University of North Carolina at Chapel Hill, 1976.

Lee, Chana Kai. *For Freedom's Sake: The Life of Fannie Lou Hamer*. Urbana: Univ. of Illinois Press, 1999.

Leipold, Andrew. "Why Grand Juries Do Not and Cannot Protect the Accused." *Cornell Law Review* 80 (January 1995): 260–324.

Lewis, George. *The White South and the Red Menace: Segregationist Anti-Communism and Massive Resistance, 1945–1968*. Gainesville: Univ. Press of Florida, 2004.

Lewis, John, with Michael D'Orso. *Walking with the Wind: A Memoir of the Movement*. New York: Simon and Schuster, 1998.

Link, William. "William Friday and the North Carolina Speaker Ban Crisis, 1963–1968." *North Carolina Historical Review* 72 (April 1995): 198–206.

Lipsitz, George. "The Possessive Investment in Whiteness: Racialized Social Democracy and the 'White' Problem in American Studies." *American Quarterly* 47 (September 1995): 369–387.

Lofgren, Charles A. *The Plessy Case: A Legal-Historical Interpretation*. New York: Oxford Univ. Press, 1987.

López, Ian F. Haney. *Racism on Trial: The Chicano Fight for Justice*. Cambridge, Mass.: Belknap, 2003.

Lukas, J. Anthony. *Nightmare: The Underside of the Nixon Years*. New York: Penguin, 1988.

Malcolm X. *The Autobiography of Malcolm as told to Alex Haley*. New York: Ballantine, 1965.

Manis, Andrew. *A Fire You Can't Put Out: The Civil Rights Life of Birmingham's Reverend Fred Shuttlesworth*. Tuscaloosa: Univ of Alabama Press, 1999.

Marable, Manning. *Malcolm X: A Life of Reinvention*. New York: Penguin, 2011.

———. *Race, Reform, and Rebellion: The Second Reconstruction in Black America, 1945–1990*. Jackson: Univ. Press of Mississippi, 1991.

Marsh, Charles. *God's Long Summer: Stories of Faith and Civil Rights*. Princeton, N.J.: Princeton Univ. Press, 1997.

Marx, Gary T. "Civil Disorder and the Agents of Social Control." *Journal of Social Issues* 26 (1970): 19–57.

Matusow, Allen J. *The Unraveling of America: A History of Liberalism in the 1960s*. New York: Harper and Row, 1984.

McCall, Nathan. *Makes Me Wanna Holler: A Young Black Man in America.* New York: Random House, 1994.

McCartney, John T. *Black Power Ideologies: An Essay in African-American Political Thought.* Philadelphia: Temple Univ. Press, 1992.

McKee, Guian. "'I've Never Dealt with a Government Agency Before': Philadelphia's Somerset Knitting Mills Project, the Local State, and the Missed Opportunities of Urban Renewal." *Journal of Urban History* 35 (2009): 387–409.

McKnight, Gerald. *The Last Crusade: Martin Luther King, Jr., the FBI, and the Poor People's Campaign.* Boulder, Colo.: Westview Press, 1998.

McMillan, John, and Paul Buhle, eds. *The New Left Revisited.* Philadelphia: Temple Univ. Press, 2002.

McQuaid, Kim. *The Anxious Years: America in the Vietnam-Watergate Era.* New York: Basic Books, 1989.

Meier, August, and Elliot Rudwick. *CORE: A Study in the Civil Rights Movement, 1942–1968.* New York: Oxford Univ. Press, 1973.

Meyer, Stephen Grant. *As Long as They Don't Move Next Door: Segregation and Racial Conflict in American Neighborhoods.* Lanham, Md.: Rowman and Littlefield, 2000.

Miller, James. *"Democracy Is in the Streets": From Port Huron to the Siege of Chicago.* New York: Touchstone, 1987.

Miller, Randall M., and George E. Pozzetta. *Shades of the Sunbelt: Essays on Ethnicity, Race, and the Urban South.* New York: Greenwood, 1988.

Minchin, Timothy. *Don't Sleep with Stevens! The J. P. Stevens Campaign and the Struggle to Organize the South, 1963–1980.* Gainesville: Univ. Press of Florida, 2005.

———. *Fighting Against the Odds: A History of Southern Labor since World War II.* Gainesville: Univ. Press of Florida, 2006.

Mohl, Raymond A., ed. *Searching for the Sunbelt: Historical Perspectives on a Region.* Athens: Univ. of Georgia Press, 1993.

Moody, Anne. *Coming of Age in Mississippi.* New York: Dell, 1968.

Moore, Leonard. *The Defeat of Black Power: Civil Rights and the National Black Political Convention of 1972.* Baton Rouge: Louisiana State Univ. Press, 2018.

Morgan, Richard E. *Domestic Intelligence: Monitoring Dissent in America.* Austin: Univ. of Texas Press, 1980.

Morris, Aldon D. *The Origins of the Civil Rights Movement: Black Communities Organizing for Change.* New York: Free Press, 1984.

Muhammad, Khalil Gibran. *The Condemnation of Blackness: Race, Crime, and the Making of Modern Urban America.* Cambridge, Mass.: Harvard Univ. Press, 2010.

Myerson, Michael. *Nothing Could Be Finer.* New York: International Publishers, 1978.

Nelson, Jack, and Ronald J. Ostrow. *The FBI and the Berrigans*. New York: Coward, McCann and Geoghegan, 1972.

Nickerson, Michelle, and Darren Dochuk, eds. *Sunbelt Rising: The Politics of Space, Place, and Region*. Philadelphia: Univ. of Pennsylvania Press, 2014.

Norrell, Robert J. *Reaping the Whirlwind: The Civil Rights Movement in Tuskegee*. New York: Knopf, 1985.

Ogbar, Jeffrey. *Black Power: Radical Politics and African American Identity*. Baltimore, Md.: Johns Hopkins Univ. Press, 2004.

O'Connor, Thomas. *Building a New Boston: Politics and Urban Renewal, 1950–1970*. Boston: Northeastern Univ. Press, 1993.

O'Neill, William. *Coming Apart: An Informal History of America in the 1960s*. New York: Times Books, 1971.

Olmstead, Kathryn S. *Challenging the Secret Government: The Post-Watergate Investigations of the CIA and FBI*. Chapel Hill: Univ. of North Carolina Press, 1996.

Oppenheimer, Martin. *The Sit-In Movement*. Brooklyn, N.Y.: Carlson Publishing, 1989.

O'Reilly, Kenneth. *"Racial Matters": The FBI's Secret File on Black America, 1960–1972*. New York: Free Press, 1989.

Oshinsky, David. *"Worse Than Slavery": Parchman Farm and the Ordeal of Jim Crow Justice*. New York: Free Press, 1996.

Patterson, James T. *Grand Expectations: The United States, 1945–1974*. New York: Oxford Univ. Press, 1996.

Payne, Charles M. *I've Got the Light of Freedom: The Organizing Tradition and the Mississippi Freedom Struggle*. Berkeley: Univ. of California Press, 1995.

Payne, Les, and Tamara Payne. *The Dead Are Arising: The Life of Malcom X*. New York: Liveright, 2020.

Peltason, J. W. *Fifty-Eight Lonely Men: Southern Federal Judges and School Desegregation*. New York: Harcourt, Brace and World, 1961.

Peninger, Randy. "The Emergence of Black Political Power in Charlotte, North Carolina: The City Council Tenure of Frederick Douglas Alexander, 1965–1974." Master's thesis, University of North Carolina at Charlotte, 1989.

Perkinson, Robert. *Texas Tough: The Rise of America's Prison Empire*. New York: Metropolitan Books, 2010.

Perlstein, Rick. *The Invisible Bridge: The Fall of Nixon and the Rise of Reagan*. New York: Simon and Schuster, 2014.

———. *Nixonland: The Rise of a President and the Fracturing of America*. New York: Scribner, 2008.

Perry, Bruce. *Malcolm: The Life of a Man Who Changed Black America*. New York: Station Hill, 1991.

Perry, David C., and Alfred J. Watkins, eds., *The Rise of the Sunbelt Cities*. Beverly Hills: Sage Publications, 1977.

Phillips, Kevin. *The Emerging Republican Majority*. New Rochelle, N.Y.: Arlington House, 1969.

Piven, Frances Fox, and Richard Cloward. *Poor People's Movements: Why They Succeed, How They Fail*. New York: Pantheon, 1977.

Pratt, Robert A. *The Color of Their Skin: Education and Race in Richmond, Virginia, 1954–1989*. Charlottesville: Univ. Press of Virginia, 1992.

Ralph, James, Jr. *Northern Protest: Martin Luther King, Jr., Chicago, and the Civil Rights Movement*. Cambridge, Mass.: Harvard Univ. Press, 1993.

Reiman, Jeffrey. *The Rich Get Richer and the Poor Get Prison: Ideology, Class, and Criminal Justice*. Boston: Allyn and Bacon, 1998.

Reitzes, Donald C., and Dietrich C. Reitzes. *The Alinsky Legacy: Alive and Kicking*. Greenwich, Conn.: JAI Press, 1987.

Richardson, Michael B. "'Not Gradually . . . But Now': Reginald Hawkins, Black Leadership, and Desegregation in Charlotte, North Carolina." *North Carolina Historical Review* 82 (July 2005): 347–379.

Robinson, Armstead L., and Patricia Sullivan, eds. *New Directions in Civil Rights Studies*. Charlottesville: University of Virginia, 1991.

Rosen, Richard A., and Joseph Mosnier. *Julius Chambers: A Life in the Legal Struggle for Civil Rights*. Chapel Hill: Univ. of North Carolina Press, 2016.

Rosenfeld, Seth. *Subversives: The FBI's War on Student Radicals, and Reagan's Rise to Power*. New York: Farrar, Straus and Giroux, 2012.

Sale, Kirkpatrick. *Power Shift: The Rise of the Southern Rim and Its Challenge to the Eastern Establishment*. New York: Random House, 1975.

———. *SDS*. New York: Random House, 1973.

Sayer, John William. *Ghost Dancing the Law: The Wounded Knee Trials*. Cambridge, Mass.: Harvard Univ. Press, 1997.

Schaller, Michael, and George Rising. *The Republican Ascendancy: American Politics, 1968–2001*. Wheeling, Ill.: Harlan Davidson, 2002.

Schutz, Aaron, and Mike Miller, eds. *People Power: The Community Organizing Tradition of Saul Alinsky*. Nashville: Vanderbilt Univ. Press, 2015.

Schwartz, Bernard. *Swann's Way: The School Busing Case and the Supreme Court*. New York: Oxford Univ. Press, 1986.

Sellers, Cleveland. *The River of No Return: The Autobiography of a Black Militant and the Life and Death of SNCC*. Jackson: Univ. Press of Mississippi, 1990.

Silberman, Charles E. *Criminal Violence, Criminal Justice*. New York: Random House, 1978.

Simon, Jonathan. *Governing Through Crime: How the War on Crime Transformed American Democracy and Created a Culture of Fear*. New York: Oxford Univ. Press, 2007.

Sitkoff, Harvard. *The Struggle for Black Equality, 1954–1980*. New York: Hill and Wang, 1981.

Smith, Albert C. "'Southern Violence' Reconsidered: Arson as Protest in Black-Belt Georgia, 1865–1910." *Journal of Southern History* 51 (November 1985): 527–564.

Smith, Stephen Samuel. *Boom for Whom? Education, Desegregation, and Development in Charlotte*. Albany: State Univ. of New York Press, 2004.

Sokol, Jason. *There Goes My Everything: White Southerners in the Age of Civil Rights, 1945–1975*. New York: Knopf, 2006.

Stockwell, John. *In Search of Enemies: A CIA Story*. New York: Norton, 1978.

Stoper, Emily. *The Student Nonviolent Coordinating Committee: The Growth of Radicalism in a Civil Rights Organization*. Brooklyn, N.Y.: Carlson Publications, 1989.

Stuntz, William J. *The Collapse of American Criminal Justice*. Cambridge, Mass.: Belknap, 2011.

Sugrue, Thomas J. *The Origins of the Urban Crisis: Race and Inequality in Postwar Detroit*. Princeton, N.J.: Princeton Univ. Press, 1996.

Theoharis, Athan. *The FBI and American Democracy: A Brief Critical History*. Lawrence: Univ. of Kansas Press, 2004.

———. *Spying on Americans: Political Surveillance from Hoover to the Huston Plan*. Philadelphia: Temple Univ. Press, 1978.

Thompson, Heather Ann. *Blood in the Water: The Attica Prison Uprising of 1971 and Its Legacy*. New York: Pantheon, 2016.

Thornton, J. Mills. *Dividing Lines: Municipal Politics and the Struggle for Civil Rights in Montgomery, Birmingham, and Selma*. Tuscaloosa: Univ. of Alabama Press, 2006.

Tibbs, Donald Fredrick. "Black Power and Prison Power: The Prisoner Union Movement in North Carolina, 1967–1979." Ph.D. diss., Arizona State University, 2014.

Ture, Kwame, and Charles V. Hamilton. *Black Power: The Politics of Liberation in America*. New York: Vintage, 1992.

Tyson, Timothy. *Blood Done Sign My Name*. New York: Crown, 2004.

———. *Radio Free Dixie: Robert F. Williams and the Roots of Black Power*. Chapel Hill: Univ. of North Carolina Press, 1999.

———. "Burning for Freedom: Oxford, North Carolina and the Black Struggle for Equality." Master's thesis, Duke University, 1990. Richard B. Thornton Library, North Carolina Room, Oxford, North Carolina.

Van Deburg, William L. *New Day in Babylon: The Black Power Movement and American Culture, 1965–1975*. Chicago: Univ. of Chicago Press, 1992.

Varon, Jeremy. *Bringing the War Home: The Weather Underground, the Red Army Faction, and Revolutionary Violence in the Sixties and Seventies.* Berkeley: Univ. of California Press, 2004.

Viorst, Milton. "Attorney General Mitchell's Philosophy." *New York Times Magazine,* 10 August 1969, 10ff.

———. *Fire in the Streets: America in the 1960s.* New York: Touchstone, 1981.

Walker, Anders. *The Ghost of Jim Crow: How Southern Moderates Used* Brown v. Board of Education *to Stall Civil Rights.* New York: Oxford Univ. Press, 2009.

Walker, Samuel. *Popular Justice: A History of American Criminal Justice.* New York: Oxford Univ. Press, 1980.

———. "Reexamining the President's Crime Commission: The Challenge of Crime in a Free Society after Ten Years." *Crime and Delinquency* 24 (January 1978): 1–12.

Wells, Tom. *The War Within: America's Battle Over Vietnam.* New York: Owl Books, 1994.

Wendt, Simon. *The Spirit and the Shotgun: Armed Resistance and the Struggle for Civil Rights.* Gainesville: Univ. Press of Florida, 2007.

Wheaton, Elizabeth. *Codename Greenkil: The 1979 Greensboro Killings.* Athens: Univ. of Georgia Press, 1987.

Whisnant, Charleen, and Robert Waters Grey, eds. *Eleven Charlotte Poets.* Charlotte, N.C.: Red Clay Publishers, 1971.

Wicker, Tom. *One of Us: Richard Nixon and the American Dream.* New York: Random House, 1991.

———. *A Time to Die.* New York: Quadrangle, 1975.

Wilhoit, Francis. *The Politics of Massive Resistance.* New York: Braziller, 1973.

Williams, Yohuru. *Black Politics/White Power: Civil Rights, Black Power, and the Black Panthers in New Haven.* Malden, Mass.: Blackwell Publishing, 2008.

Williamson, Larry A. "Crime as Rhetoric: The Trial of the Catonsville Nine." In *Popular Trials: Rhetoric, Mass Media, and the Law,* edited by Robert Hariman. Tuscaloosa: Univ. of Alabama Press, 1990.

Woodard, Komozi. *A Nation Within a Nation: Amiri Braka (LeRoi Jones) and Black Power Politics.* Chapel Hill: Univ. of North Carolina Press, 1999.

Woods, Jeff. *Black Struggle, Red Scare: Segregation and Anti-Communism in the South.* Baton Rouge: Louisiana State Univ. Press, 2004.

Woodward, C. Vann. *Origins of the New South, 1877–1913.* Baton Rouge: Louisiana State Univ. Press, 1971.

Zimroth, Peter. *Perversions of Justice: The Prosecution and Acquittal of the Panther 21.* New York: Viking, 1974.

INDEX

INDEX

Keddie, Wells, 127, 128
Kennedy, Cordell, 69
Kennedy, Robert F., 13, 98, 100, 117
Kent State University, 77–79
Kerner Commission (National Advisory Commission on Civil Disorders), 95–96
Kerry, Rev. Colemon, 29, 31
King, Martin Luther, Jr., 7, 12, 22, 25–26, 35, 52, 61, 117, 190
Ku Klux Klan, 53, 68, 82–83, 88, 91, 137, 145

Lake, I. Beverly, 52
Lanning, Jim, 117
"law and order" as a political issue, 46, 47–48, 138, 151–158, 159, 171–172, 181; in North Carolina politics, 49–52, 121–122
law enforcement and troubled history with African Americans, 20–21
Law Enforcement Assistance Administration, 97
Leake, Rev. George, 29, 53
Long, David (U.S. attorney), 103, 107, 135, 153
Lundy, Walker, 162–163, 166–167
lynching, 20, 53, 76–77, 124, 149

Malcolm X, 40, 61, 125
Mallory v. United States, 97
Mapp v. Ohio, 96
Mardian, Robert, 99–100, 139, 149, 152, 158
Marrow, Henry, 87, 88, 104, 134; murder of, 76, 80–82; murder trial of, 90–92
Marrow, Willie Mae, 76
McCarthy, Colman, 150, 157
McClellan, John, 97
McKnight, C. A. "Pete," 144, 161–162
McMillan, James, 8, 57–58; role in Swann v. Charlotte-Mecklenburg County Board of Education, 116–118, 121
Medlin, Bill, 2, 125, 126
Miller, Robert, 128
Mintz, Judge Rudolph, 58–59
Miranda v. Arizona, 96–97, 121

Mitchell, John, 98–99, 150, 152, 159
Model Cities Program, 29, 30–31, 43
Moore, Dan (governor), 9–10, 19, 49
Moore, Lola, 170
Moore, Tom (Charlotte district attorney), 103–104, 105–106, 108, 128, 130, 132, 134, 135
Morgan, Robert (NC state senator), 52, 56

Nation of Islam, 48, 61
National Association for the Advancement of Colored People (NAACP), 18, 19, 37, 52, 73, 84, 90, 116, 120, 121
National Security Agency, 99
New Left, 3, 8, 27, 28, 29, 48, 67, 137; in Charlotte, 32–34, 71, 138, 189
New York Times, 144, 155, 157, 158, 159, 165, 177–178
Nixon, Richard, 28, 46, 59, 164, 191; administration's "law and order" policies, 4, 5, 46, 50, 78, 97, 98–100, 119–120, 138, 154, 159; "Southern Strategy," 4–5; "Silent Majority" theme, 50–51, 192; administration's aggressive pursuit of activists, 98–100, 119–120, 138–139, 153–154, 159, 190; and Watergate scandal, 138, 149, 152, 153, 159, 160, 163
Noel, Stanley, 108, 109, 134–135
North Carolina Highway Patrol, 83, 84, 86, 88, 90, 101, 105
North Carolina Political Prisoners Committee (NCPPC), 150–151, 176, 181; formation of, 136–138; early challenge of gaining public support, 140–143; strategy of using North Carolina's progressive image as leverage, 144–146; and 1975 "New Data" Charlotte Observer story, 174–176, 179; role in getting Charlotte Three released, 184–185

Oakley, Roger, 91–92
Oatman, Charles, 80
Office of Economic Opportunity (OEO), 29, 42, 52

280

State Bureau of Investigation, NC, 19, 52,
64–65; surveillance of activists, 51–52,
64–65, 66, 84–85, 86
Stein, Adam, 90–91, 117
Stickley, John, 48
Students for a Democratic Society (SDS),
32, 48
Sunbelt, 11; and Charlotte, 5–6, 7–8, 11–12,
16–17, 22, 36, 44, 193, 194
Swann v. Charlotte-Mecklenburg County
Board of Education, 7, 18, 23, 29, 39, 57, 116,
121, 124, 161; Charlotte resolves busing unrest, 159, 165–166. See also school busing

Teel, Larry, 104–105, 107, 112, 117; and murder
of Henry Marrow, 76–77, 80–81, 82, 91
Teel, Robert, 83, 104–105, 107, 112, 117; and
murder of Henry Marrow, 76–77, 82; criminal charges prior to Marrow murder, 80–82;
on trial for Marrow murder, 90–92
Tenth Street Community Center, 38, 41,
125
Till, Emmett, 25
Tyson, Rev. Vernon, 80

"United Soul" (alleged conspiratorial Black
Power organization), 108, 110, 112, 125, 128,
133
University of North Carolina at Chapel Hill,
10, 50, 52, 144–145
University of North Carolina at Charlotte,
39, 41, 73, 105, 123, 147, 179, 181; and Black
Student Union, 28, 39, 41, 65–66
Urban Redevelopment Commission,
36–37
urban renewal, 13, 28, 35–38
urban riots/uprisings, 7, 8, 21, 22, 31, 37–38,
42, 47–48, 49–51, 60, 78, 79–80, 82, 95–96,
114, 164–165, 192; and Charlotte, 60, 117; in
Oxford, NC, 83–90, 104; in Wilmington,
NC, 114, 141

US (Los Angeles–based Black Power organization), 64
U.S. v. Wade, 97

vagrancy law, 56–57
Vietnam War, 22, 46, 160, 164; activism
against, 39, 41, 48, 50, 59, 65, 66, 77–79, 100,
128; David Washington's participation in,
62–63, 110, 111
Volunteers in Service to America (VISTA), 2,
32, 38, 40, 43–44, 64, 113
Voting Rights Act, 4, 53, 70, 192

Wald, George, 140, 158
Walden, William, 3, 100–101, 114, 141, 152–153;
background of, 93–94; negotiations with Al
Hood and Dave Washington to deliver testimony, 101–105, 107–109; during Charlotte
Three trial, 128–129, 169
War on Crime, 94–100. See also crime, as a
political issue
War on Drugs, 192–193
War on Poverty, 2–3, 8, 29, 30, 32, 44, 46, 48,
49, 50, 51, 61, 192–193
Washington, David, 3, 123, 139, 157, 170, 188;
involvement in Black Power movement,
62–63; and 1969 armed robbery trial, 62–63;
and Oxford, NC, racial disturbances, 85–86,
88, 101; deal made with law enforcement,
92, 94–95, 101–113, 151, 153–154, 162, 175;
flees to Canada, 101; and Raleigh Two trial,
110–113; and Charlotte Three trial, 125–127,
128, 129, 131–132, 133, 124–135, 152, 169; post–
Charlotte Three trial legal trouble, 147, 167;
and 1975 Charlotte Observer "New Data"
story, 166–169, 171, 174
Washington Post, 150, 157, 160, 165
Watergate scandal. See Nixon, Richard
Weatherman organization, 103
Welfare Rights Organization, 42, 43, 54
Westmoreland, William, 59